COMPONENT-BASED DEVELOPMENT FOR ENTERPRISE SYSTEMS

APPLYING THE SELECT PERSPECTIVE™

Managing Object Technology Series

Charles F. Bowman
Series Editor

and

President
SoftWright Solutions
Suffern, New York

Additional Volumes in Preparation

COMPONENT-BASED DEVELOPMENT FOR ENTERPRISE SYSTEMS

APPLYING THE SELECT PERSPECTIVE™

Paul Allen
and
Stuart Frost

CAMBRIDGE
UNIVERSITY PRESS

SIGS
BOOKS

PUBLISHED BY THE PRESS SYNDICATE OF THE UNIVERSITY OF CAMBRIDGE
The Pitt Building, Trumpington Street, Cambridge, United Kingdom

CAMBRIDGE UNIVERSITY PRESS
The Edinburgh Building, Cambridge CB2 2RU, UK   www.cup.cam.ac.uk
40 West 20th Street, New York, NY 10011-4211, USA   www.cup.org
10 Stamford Road, Oakleigh, Melbourne 3166, Australia
Ruiz de Alarcón 13, 28014 Madrid, Spain

Published in association with SIG Books and Multimedia

First published 1998
Reprinted 1999

Design and compostion by Kevin Callahan
Cover design by Yin Moy

Printed in the United States of America

Typeset in ITC Officina Sans and ITC Officina Serif

A catalog record for this book is available from the British Library

Library of Congress Cataloging in Publication Data is available

ISBN 0 521 64999 4 paperback

To my mother, Gwendoline, and late father, Eric.

—*Paul Allen*

To my children, Rebecca, Laura, Owen, and Alistair.

—*Stuart Frost*

About the Authors

● ● ● ● ● ● ● ● ● ● ● ● ● ● ● ● ●

PAUL ALLEN is Vice President of Methods at SELECT Software Tools, where he leads development of The SELECT Perspective. He specializes in working with organizations to develop strategies for transitioning to and implementing component-based development. Allen is an active member of both the OMG (Object Management Group) and the Dynamic Systems Development Consortium (DSDM).

Prior to joining SELECT in 1995, Allen was senior methods advisor to a major telecommunications company migrating to object technology and consultant manager with Yourdon Inc., where he advised on enterprise software development projects around the globe. With over 20 years of software industry experience, Allen has worked in a variety of other project roles ranging from programming to a spell of five years as a project manager for a life insurance company. Allen is also an experienced teacher, respected author, and popular speaker worldwide at leading industry conferences.

STUART FROST is founder, chairman, and chief executive officer of SELECT Software Tools, a worldwide supplier of software development tools. Frost founded SELECT in 1988 at the age of 26 and is clearly the driving force behind the company's development. Through his leadership, SELECT has become a recognized leader in component modeling and management.

Frost's key strengths lie in his ability to assimilate the mass of information the industry produces and forecast future industry trends. For example, it was Frost who set his company on the course of supporting James Rumbaugh's Object Modeling Technique (OMT) combined with Jacobson's Use Case technique. This combination has since proven to be the dominant OO modeling approach and the basis for the Unified Modeling Language (UML). Frost is a respected authority on model-driven component-based development and has published a variety of articles on the subject.

Foreword

• • • • • • • • • • • • • • • • •

During the past 20 years, there have been a series of breathtaking technological developments in the computer field, including the advent of the PC and the Internet. As we move into the latter part of the 1990s, one of the most important technologies—from the perspective of productivity, quality, and rapid development of distributed systems—is turning out to be the technology of component-based development. Whether they're implemented in Java or ActiveX or involve such standards as Microsoft's DCOM or the Object Management Group's CORBA, the software industry is gradually forming a consensus that components provide the kind of plug-and-play building blocks that we need for developing today's large, complex systems.

At the same time, the software engineering field has gone through several generations of methods and techniques for developing such systems. The 1970s are often referred to as the decade of structured programming and structured methods; similarly, the 1980s were often described as the decade of data modeling methods and techniques. And much of the 1990s have been focused on methods and techniques to support prototyping, iterative development, and a variety of rapid application development (RAD) techniques. In Paul Allen and Stuart Frost's Component-Based Development for Enterprise Systems, we see an excellent example of the convergence of technology and methods into an approach known as The SELECT Perspective.

The Perspective approach emphasizes a number of concepts that have often been advocated as stand-alone strategies, without being integrated into an overall methodology. Thus, software reuse and software quality are part of Perspective, as is the integration of legacy software components into the development process. There is a considerable emphasis on designing and building a sensible architecture for today's systems (indeed, Allen and Frost refer to the Perspective approach as rapid architected application development (RAAD) rather than simple RAD). And the Perspective approach is based on the object-oriented modeling notation known as UML (Unified Modeling Language) developed recently by Messrs. Booch, Rumbaugh, and Jacobson.

There is a considerable amount of detail behind the Perspective approach, and a busy developer or project manager might resist the investment of time required to read the book from cover to cover. However, the material has been carefully organized into clusters of chapters that can be read in a stand-alone fashion. If you're primarily interested in issues of architecture, you can focus on chapter 2. If you care more about software processes (including reuse, iterative development, etc.), you can concentrate on chapters 11-14. And if you're interested in such techniques as use case modeling, state modeling, or object-oriented class modeling, you should read chapters 3-10. Although none of this represents a panacea for the difficulties and complexities of building today's large-scale software systems, Perspective is a commonsense, pragmatic, eminently readable approach. As the authors point out, software development continues to get harder with each passing year; with their advice and guidance, the project team can significantly increase its chances of success.

—Ed Yourdon
New York, 1997

Preface

● ● ● ● ● ● ● ● ● ● ● ● ● ● ● ●

The SELECT Perspective was first created in 1994–1995 in response to demand from SELECT's customers for an approach to software development that allowed them to build well-architected applications quickly. Since then, many hundreds of software projects have been successfully completed using this approach. In the software industry, however, nothing stands still for very long, and it became clear to us that it was time to update and expand on the information provided to our customers.

Our story begins three years ago.

This book takes the original ideas and concepts behind The SELECT Perspective and adds a great deal more detail, based on our experiences in applying the approach on many projects around the world. In addition, the work has been updated to include such topical issues as component-based development and the Unified Modeling Language (UML).

This book distills our experiences.

The Need for The SELECT Perspective

Over the last decade, the pace of change in the business world has accelerated considerably. At the same time, businesses of all kinds have become more and more dependent on Information Technology (IT). This combination of events has greatly increased the pressure on software development organizations. Thus, although some progress has been made in speeding up the software development process, the gap between business demand and

Software development gets harder.

the ability of software developers to meet this demand has widened. During the next few years this problem is set to get even worse as resources become tied up on Year 2000 and European Monetary Union projects. It is therefore imperative that software developers make effective moves now in order to increase productivity and reduce waste by improving their ability to understand and meet the demands of the businesses they work for.

This book is designed to help.

The SELECT Perspective has been designed to specifically meet the needs of software developers in a rapidly changing and demanding business environment. It goes well beyond the notational guidelines of UML to provide a software development process, a component-based architecture and management guidelines. The end result is a comprehensive, yet very flexible, approach to software development.

A Brief History of The SELECT Perspective

Use cases and OMT form our starting point.

SELECT Software Tools first entered the market of object-oriented (OO) modeling tools in 1993. At that time, there were several OO notations competing for market leadership. These included Rumbaugh's Object Modeling Technique (OMT), Coad-Yourdon, and Shlaer-Mellor. More by luck than judgment, SELECT decided to concentrate on OMT. This proved to be an excellent choice, as OMT rapidly became the dominant OO notation. At about the same time, Jacobson's book on use cases was published. Initially, many saw Jacobson's notation as an alternative to OMT, but we at SELECT quickly realized that the two approaches were in fact complementary. Thus, use cases and OMT were combined to create the first version of the SELECT Perspective in 1994–1995. This also proved to be a good decision, given the recent moves by the Object Management Group (OMG) to create a standard for object modeling. The leading candidate to become the standard notation, UML, is fundamentally a combination of use cases and OMT.

Successful application of use cases...

As can be seen from the following, use cases are at the heart of the SELECT Perspective:

• They provide a bridge between business processes and components.
• They form the basis of dividing an application into incremental deliveries.
• They tie a service-based architecture to object-based components.

The end result of applying use cases in this way is a holistic approach to software development, which enables complex business applications to be built quickly, while at the same time ensuring that the software architecture is fundamentally sound and scalable. The Gartner Group refer to this kind of software development as rapid architected application development or RAAD.

...requires a holistic approach.

The Move to Components

We regard components as having evolved from objects as opposed to being a new technology. In fact, if you trace the history of the market acceptance of objects, it becomes clear that, in many ways, components represent a new way of presenting objects to the market. Objects were first marketed as a means of achieving reuse. Unfortunately, very few organizations were able to realize significant benefits from object-based reuse programs. The class libraries used were at too low a level of granularity and the necessary standards were not in place so as to make widespread reuse practical.

Components have evolved from objects.

In the next wave of object marketing, companies such as SELECT and Forté realized that objects could be used as a means of speeding up the software development life-cycle, using the inherent traceability of objects to allow for iterative development. Given the pressures on IT organizations to improve time to market and responsiveness to business requirements, this approach proved rather more successful and object orientation began to appeal to many more organizations. Most people buying into OO today can still be regarded as early adopters, however.

Components reflect the move from early adoption...

In order to help OO move into the mainstream, the concepts have now been represented to the market in the guise of component-based development. Given that most of the software industry has now adopted this paradigm, it seems that it is now poised to go mainstream.

...to mainstream development.

Most vendors of tools and applications have now made a commitment to the component-based paradigm. In addition, Microsoft and the OMG have put in place many of the necessary standards to make components a practical reality. Let's now take a look at each major area in turn to see how the software development industry is being driven towards components:

The software industry is being driven toward components.

Development tools

The first tool vendors to latch onto the move to components were those selling modeling tools, such as SELECT. Next, with the move by Microsoft to assist component-based development by creating their own repository, the market for repositories was given a boost. Vendors such as Softlab and Unisys seem best placed to exploit this opportunity. Other tool vendors are

Without good tools components remain a theoretical promise.

now starting to catch up and we can expect to see component-oriented process management and testing tools shortly. Clearly this is a major step forward, as without tools it would be impossible to effectively develop software using the new approach.

Infrastructure

Fast-maturing
infrastructure

By infrastructure we mean middleware, TP monitors and databases. In each of these areas, there are clear signs that the component paradigm is gaining ground.

...middleware

In the middleware arena, both CORBA and DCOM are now approaching an adequate level of maturity. The OMG, Microsoft, IBM, Iona, and BEA are playing critical roles in making this a reality.

...TP monitors

The related area of TP monitors is also being slowly integrated into the component paradigm, with Microsoft, BEA, and IBM all working in this area.

...databases

Object databases have not been able to gain any significant level of market penetration. However, moves by Informix and, perhaps more significantly, Oracle to embrace the component paradigm with their recent releases will mean that this new way of developing software will become a standard part of any database development.

...provides industrial strength

All of these moves are significant, as without the availability of necessary component-based infrastructure it would be almost impossible to build a sizable application.

Programming Languages

"Components" are now familiar to many programmers.

Given the widespread popularity of Visual Basic, many programmers have become familiar with the component paradigm. Indeed, the first viable market for components was created around DLLs and OLE Controls for use with Visual Basic. This market didn't really progress beyond GUI controls and the like, however.

Java opens up truly component-based development.

Several object-oriented languages such as C++ and Forté can, of course, be used to build components. A major step forward occurred with the introduction of Java, however, which in our view is the first truly component-oriented language. To program properly in Java, you simply have to think in terms of components. Given the current hype surrounding this new language, it is clear that this will be a major driver towards components as it gains maturity.

Packaged Applications

Most packaged applications today have relatively closed, proprietary archi-   The closed world of
tectures based on two-tier client–server principles. It is therefore very diffi- software packages...
cult for application developers to access data held in these packages. As
businesses become more reliant on these packages for their major lines of
business and more vital corporate data is held in them, however, it is clear
that this situation is no longer tenable—applications built to support additional business processes simply must have access to the corporate data.

Recognizing this, all of the major package vendors are taking steps to   ...is opening up to
open up access to their applications suites. Without exception, all of them   component technol-
are turning to a component-based interface. They may not have yet redevel-   ogy.
oped their internal architectures, but it is clear that in most cases this is simply a matter of time.

A Component-Based Approach

In our view, this represents the final, compelling reason for the software   The SELECT
industry to move to a component-based paradigm. Thus it seems clear that   Perspective has
in the near future most software applications will be assembled from a set of evolved to a compo-
components rather than being constructed from scratch. Given this trend   nent-based
toward components, any software development approach that does not   approach.
embrace components at all levels is destined to be very short lived. Thus, we
decided to comprehensively update The SELECT Perspective to incorporate
a component-based architecture and to include the latest developments in
UML. In addition, we decided to split the development process in order to
take advantage of a supplier–consumer model of software development,
where component suppliers create components for reuse by component consumers as they build complete applications.

The Purpose of This Book

This book is intended for anyone who wants to learn about practical tech-   This book is for
niques and guidelines for component-based development in a business-ori-   software profession-
ented enterprise setting. Most obviously this includes anyone who has a   als responsible for
background in software development; for example, systems architects and   meeting business
analysts, systems designers, software developers, software project leaders,   needs.
and software trainers and educators.

...also domain experts who provide the business knowledge...

...and business managers responsible for overall planning.

The book can be speed-read.

Business users or domain experts form a small but important part of our potential audience. Our view is that any system will only be as good as the quality of the domain knowledge that goes into developing it. Chapters 3 and 4, which cover business processes and use cases, respectively, are particularly relevant for this group.

Business managers who do not have a software background but who need to understand the place of software projects with respect to their business plans and objectives, should also benefit from this book. In particular, chapters 11 to 14 cover process issues, which are helpful in understanding the overall management aspects of component-based development.

All of these groups, particularly domain experts and managers, may wish to gain a quick overview of the overall approach. We have therefore provided margin summaries for the speed reader.

Structure of This Book

Here are the five parts...

This book is divided into five basic parts:

1. overview of The SELECT Perspective (chapter 1),
2. service-based architecture (chapter 2),
3. modeling techniques (chapters 3 to 10),
4. software process (chapters 11 to 14),
5. case study (chapter 15).

The core techniques follow a consistent pattern...

The modeling techniques chapters are constructed in terms of the following sections:

1. introduction,
2. principles and concepts,
3. notation,
4. techniques library,
5. practical guidelines,
6. summary.

The techniques are modularized...

Each technique in the library is described in about a page of text with an accompanying example. The practical guidelines come in the form of useful hints, tips, and measures that represent a synthesis of our experiences in applying The SELECT Perspective.

Modeling techniques are of little value unless the reader understands where to apply them in the context of the software process. In chapter 11 we provide an overview of the main process concepts. In chapters 12 and 13 the reader is shown where each technique, described in chapters 3 to 10, fits into the software process. We also show where other techniques outside the immediate scope of this book, such as prototyping and quality planning, fit in and provide salient references for more detailed information. Chapter 14 covers the key topic of how team roles are used to support the software process.

...and referenced from the process guide.

Where to Next?

One of the great frustrations about writing is that once a book is published it's pretty well fixed. Nothing in software or in business stays still for long. We keep learning and refining our ideas and we would like to pass these ideas on to our readers. Our intention is therefore to use the SELECT web site (www.selectst.com) both as a vehicle for publicizing new developments in The SELECT Perspective and also as a channel for responding to ideas and questions that our audience will undoubtedly have.

Use www.selectst.com as a forum.

Acknowledgments

· · · · · · · · · · · · · · · · · · ·

We are indebted to many individuals. Many people have contributed in many ways, both direct and indirect, to this book. To try to list everyone who has influenced us in one way or another is an impossible task. Nevertheless our special gratitude goes to the following people:

- First and foremost to our wives and children for enduring our distraction for the best part of 2 years.
- To those we have attempted to teach, whose questions and insights have proved that learning is very much a two-way process.
- To those who have helped shaped many of the ideas in this book "in anger" on live projects; in particular to Ally Gill, David Grafton, David Bryson, Mike Horne, and Andy Wilson.
- To William Favero and Colin Bright for their insightful reviews.
- To Viv Everest for her help and advice on business process modeling.
- To the editorial staff at SIGS Publications, particularly Peter Arnold, and to the anonymous reviewers who provided numerous valuable comments.
- And last but by no means least, to all at SELECT who have helped provide both stimulus and sounding board for our own thinking. We particularly thank Jennifer Clapham, who did such a sterling job of

administrative work; Simon Birch, David Piper, Sabah Merad, Andy Mutton, Ian Pedder, Tim Nelms, and Dave Norris for their detailed comments; Steve Eyre and Steve Ash for their help with case-study examples; Hedley Apperly for his help with database issues; Glenna Colson for such a thorough review of the case study; Mark O'Hare for his technical inspiration; and Stewart Hayden for his insights on business process modeling.

Contents

• • • • • • • • • • • • • • • • •

CHAPTER 1

• • • • • • • • • • • • • • • • • • • •

Overview

1.1 Introduction

The SELECT Perspective is a component-based approach for developing enterprise systems. An enterprise system is one that meets the needs of a large business with complex business processes. A fundamental characteristic of such systems is that they need to be delivered rapidly in tight time frame while facilitating reuse through component technology. Note that throughout this book "The SELECT Perspective" is shortened to "Perspective" for brevity.

This book distills the lessons we have learned applying and refining Perspective on practical projects. It reflects the clear need for a fresh, pragmatic approach that can serve as the foundation for a new generation of analysis and design tools. The reader will find little in this book in terms of philosophizing about object-oriented concepts. The emphasis is on practical guidance and examples are used throughout for illustration. In this chapter we track the driving forces behind the more recent development of Perspective before outlining the major themes of the approach.

This book describes an approach for the development of enterprise systems.

Perspective is not a theoretical methodology.

1.2 What Is Perspective?

Perspective is a collection of industry best-practice modeling techniques that are applied and adapted using process templates within an architectural framework across a wide range of developments in a component-based setting.

Perspective is a
unique approach...

We believe that this is the first time the techniques, architecture and process have been brought together in a coherent approach that can be used by the developers of enterprise systems.

1.2.1 The Beginnings of Perspective

...that arose out of
a need for
streamlined software
development.

In the early 1990s, several commentators were suggesting approaches to software development devoid of analysis and design phases. This was accompanied by an upsurge in trends such as Rapid Application Development (RAD) using 4GLs (fourth-generation languages) and other graphical user interface (GUI) based development tools. At the same time others were suggesting that the available methodologies were *not comprehensive enough* to accurately model systems and sought to make them ever more complex. Neither of these arguments was convincing to the mainstream of software development: above all there was a clear need for a pragmatic method.

The emphasis is on
usefulness.

The first generation of Perspective (Frost, 1995) was therefore built around the modeling techniques that practitioners had found most *useful*. These were object modeling and state modeling (Rumbaugh, 1991), use cases, and object-interaction diagrams (Jacobson et al., 1992). The models worked best when emancipated from the bureaucracy of waterfall life cycles and allowed to evolve from feasibility to implementation. So we introduced a streamlined iterative process, driven by use cases to provide early user value in the form of evolving software increments. Ease of maintenance and scalability were key criteria. Therefore the techniques were employed within the context of a three-tier layered architecture, which partitioned the models according to user interface, business, and data storage layers. Further division of the business layer into local and corporate layers provided the potential to separate out reusable business logic.

1.2.2 The Evolution of Perspective

Progress in software
development is
evolutionary rather
than revolutionary.

Since those early days we have gleaned an immense amount of experience in applying Perspective in a variety of contexts. With the emergence of any new technology there is always a tendency to throw out the previous generation of techniques under the illusion that the new technology represents some panacea for all ills. This happened in the early 1990s, as many analysts threw out their structured models with the emergence of object-oriented methods. It seems to be happening again today: With the emergence of component technology there is a tendency to dismiss objects as passé. Evolving Perspective has not been like throwing out one set of notations and replacing it with another, then relabeling it under some new marketing hype! The best techniques have been adapted, customized, and blended for a variety of large-scale organizations. What we have tried to do in this book is to share with the reader a snapshot of that knowledge base. Many of the techniques presented are in fact probably familiar to the reader, often it's the way they are applied that is subtly different.

The Unified Modeling Language (UML, 1997) has emerged as the notational standard for object-oriented modeling. By effectively ending the so-called "methods wars" this initiative can only serve to hasten the rapid industry-wide adoption of object-oriented methods. At the same time we wanted to avoid introducing notation for the sake of it and retain a practical focus. We have therefore standardized on a streamlined set of notations that employ UML in a pragmatic fashion.

> There is an increasing need to standardize on modeling notations.

Despite the media hype software development grows no easier! The big issues include:

> Software development is getting harder!

- how to support increasingly adaptive businesses,
- how to capitalize on the rapid advances in component technology,
- how to deal with legacy systems,
- how to plan and build for reuse,
- how to better tackle quality issues,
- how to retain a pragmatic focus in the face of increasing complexity.

In the next sections we'll take a look at the main drivers of change and how have we sought to meet them.

1.3 Drivers of Change

1.3.1 Adaptive Businesses

Developments in distributed object-oriented technology and the Internet are having a significant effect on the ways in which businesses are adapting themselves to meet today's challenges. Most businesses today are undergoing a period of rapid change, driven by trends such as business process improvement and downsizing. The Internet doesn't **only** present new technical challenges it also raises new business opportunities, such as the virtual corporation. The organization is becoming flatter, with a high degree of empowerment, particularly at the business unit level.

> Businesses are growing evermore adaptive.

In the past the order of the day has been to reorganize the technology each time a business changes. This is no longer acceptable. An effective

> Business process modeling is now integrated into Perspective.

method must facilitate software solutions that adapt as the business adapts, that are as technically neutral as possible. A process-based view of the business, as opposed to an organizational view, is imperative in addressing this situation. Perspective now includes business process models[1], which address this process-based view and give a secure business foundation from which to develop component-based solutions. This in fact echoes one of the earliest themes of Perspective: Solutions must be traceable back to originating business requirements.

Reuse of business components is a key to producing software that adapts as the business adapts. Although reuse of GUI and database-interaction components is increasingly prevalent, the vision of system assembly from tried and tested business components has been very slow to appear. One of the most successful examples of the reuse of software components occurs in the Visual Basic environment, which provides a framework for development. To establish reuse for enterprise business systems there is an argument that analogous common frameworks must be established that reflect the semantics of the business.

The Perspective architecture has been enhanced so that organizations can add or change services (see section 1.3.5) without having to reprogram them. In particular *business* services provide for black-box reuse of business functionality, regardless of implementation. Business-oriented component modeling techniques have been introduced and existing techniques upgraded to focus on capturing the business services. In addition business-oriented component modeling provides means of capturing the generic business models that are so important for white-box reuse in the style of frameworks.

Reuse of business-oriented components is a major challenge.

Business-oriented component modeling is now integrated into Perspective.

1.3.2 Component Technology

1.3.2.1 What Are Components?

> A component is an executable unit of code that provides physical black-box encapsulation of related services. Its services can only be accessed through a consistent, published interface that includes an interaction standard. A component must be capable of being connected to other components (through a communications interface) to form a larger group.

---

[1]Note that business requirements may be captured in a number of ways, other than business process models, including business requirement definition documents, which express the business requirements as a set of textual propositions.

Encapsulation is one of the major principles of object orientation (OO). However, encapsulation of objects is often imperfect because implementation dependencies are often exposed through OO programming language interfaces. Technology such as CORBA (Common Object Request Broker Architecture) IDL (Interface Definition Language) can help to resolve this issue by providing clean separation between clients and implementations in terms of component *interfaces*, which are separate from implementations providing isolation of changes.

Components realize encapsulation.

Example component technologies include ActiveX (machine-dependent binary) and Java (machine-independent byte-compiled code). We can configure whole families of such components to meet our needs, plugging new components in, replacing old components based on a published interface without knowledge of their internal details.

Components provide "plug and play" capability.

Components range from user-interface icons and controls, like menu bars and hypertext navigators, to complete software products, like word processors. Although it is objects that form the underlying fabric of software solutions it is components that provide the effective granularity of reuse through consistent published interfaces that encapsulate the implementation. In fact this makes components a particularly powerful type of object.

Components provide effective granularity.

1.3.2.2 Toward the Component Marketplace

One of the main enabling technologies for component reuse is the standardization of the middleware, as shown in Figure 1.1. Models such as DCOM (Distributed Component Object Model) from Microsoft and CORBA from the Object Management Group (OMG) describe how objects communicate among each other. They do this in technically neutral fashion discarding language, address space, and operating-system boundaries. To enable interoperability among components, two language-neutral industry standards have correspondingly emerged: Microsoft's vtable and OMG's IDL. These standards are applied to interfaces of components.

Standards for distributed-object technology are stabilizing.

The stabilization of distributed-object standards and the emergent component technologies move us beyond the world of client-server into a world where the network **is** a living system that evolves in harmony with business needs. This is a world of heterogeneous technology, in which components can be "moved around" at execution time and deployed in a way that optimizes the technology in order to deliver the most business benefit. The Internet applies this concept globally: It is based on a world network that more and more is taking on the appearance of one gigantic computer. In combination these technologies open up the possibility of a *component marketplace* based on the consumer–supplier concept first defined by Brad Cox (1986), who likened software

Software development is on the threshold of significant change.

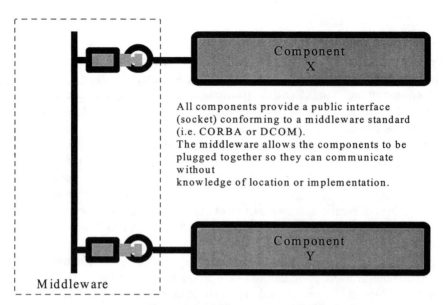

All components provide a public interface (socket) conforming to a middleware standard (i.e. CORBA or DCOM).
The middleware allows the components to be plugged together so they can communicate without
knowledge of location or implementation.

Middleware

Figure 1.1. Middleware as enabling technology
for component reuse.

development to the electronics industry, where new solutions are assembled from integrated circuits.

1.3.2.3 Perspective and Component-Based Development

Service-based reuse requires a service-based architecture.

The movement toward separation of software applications and the increasingly heterogeneous technology platforms on which the services are deployed provides the potential for an application to be physically distributed so that it services the needs of the business and not the technology. Perspective provides an overall design philosophy for realizing the vision of service-based reuse. This philosophy is expressed as a **service-based architecture**, which has evolved from the layered architecture mentioned earlier. The architecture helps shape and enhance established modeling techniques.

Modeling techniques have evolved to leverage component technology.

Components are particularly powerful types of *objects*. Therefore it should come as no surprise that many of our tried and tested object-oriented techniques still hold good! We have evolved many of Perspective's proven object-oriented modeling techniques to capitalize on the concept of services. Perspective has also been extended to provide **business-oriented component modeling, component modeling of legacy assets,** and **deployment modeling**.

A two-tier process is introduced.

Components provide a means of packaging related objects together into prefabricated pieces of software from which solutions are constructed. A special **component process** is introduced in response to the high standards of rigor, reusability, and quality demanded by such projects. However, just as a house builder does not expect to have to make every brick, timber, pipe, and tile every time a house is constructed, so the solution provider cannot be expected to build every software element from scratch every time an enterprise solution is to be delivered. We have therefore enhanced the original Perspective process to form a **solution process,** which guides the need for fast assembly of business solutions using components.

1.3.3 Legacy Software

In the real world most development is about enhancing existing systems, providing new front-ends to established back-ends, capitalizing on existing relational technology for data storage, and building interfaces to existing packages. Organizations are increasingly looking to find an effective way to reuse their investments in existing packages, databases ,and legacy systems, within the context of component technology. "Reuse before you buy. Buy before you build," we are told. Unfortunately most methods offer little advice in this area, making the implicit assumption that the component builder always starts afresh.

Most methods and tools do not integrate legacy assets into the process.

The Perspective architecture helps to take a service-based view of existing software. This allows organizations to easily wrap these services into new offerings or products. Techniques have been added that specifically address topics such as wrapping previous generation systems, packages and legacy databases. The component process brings existing software into the process as an asset, rather than ignoring it as a liability.

Perspective fully addresses legacy assets as a key part of component-based development.

1.3.4 Quality Issues

Component development is unique in that it is specifically aimed at creating **reusable** software. This requires a high level of quality that inspires trust in consumer bases that have the potential for huge growth with the Internet. What makes this more difficult with components is that the quality criteria are often conflicting: for example, maximum generality without sacrificing cohesion, maximum maintainability without sacrificing performance. This in itself is often a considerable challenge requiring skilled and thorough design. The documentation also has to indicate in very clear terms how the software interfaces to other software.

Good nonreusable software is better than bad reusable software.

The Perspective modeling techniques are primarily aimed at ensuring functional correctness at **what** a solution or component is expected to do; guidelines are also included to help with consistency and completeness of the models at various baselines. *Quality attributes* are statements about **how well** the solution or component is expected to function; examples include reliability, efficiency, usability, maintainability, testability, and portability, as well as the central concern of the component process: reusability. Introducing quality

Perspective addresses quality factors as part of the process.

templates (Gilb,1988) provides a means of measuring success of a solution or component. Guidelines are introduced into the component process to ensure that quality attributes are made explicit, allowing management to trade off quality against development time/cost, and the designer to make well-reasoned design trade-offs.

1.3.5 Planning and Building for Reuse

Services provide black-box reuse.

The move to a service based architecture is geared to facilitate black-box reuse. A service is effectively decoupled from its clients. That means a service can be shared by multiple clients. It can be repeatedly reused by different clients. As the bank of services is built up so reuse of pre-existing code increases and the need to write new code decreases. Component code can be changed without disturbing its clients, providing the interfaces are kept consistent. This is particularly important for legacy software (as mentioned previously). For example, a freight company acquiring another freight company needs to find a way to interface with its billing system. The goal is to give the customer a "unified" bill so he or she has all transport costs on a single invoice. Both billing systems are legacy systems operating on different hardware at different sites, which are not practical to integrate. By wrapping each billing system in terms of the services it provides, a new "solution" can be rapidly put together that accesses the required services.

Generic models provide white-box reuse.

Building and refining generic models is an important aspect of component-based development in which we want to leverage model reuse rather than code reuse. A model-based approach facilitates reuse at the high end of the process before any code is attempted, with correspondingly greater opportunities to save effort. The term "framework" is often used to describe large collections of class libraries organized to facilitate GUI and application development for various operating systems; examples include MacApp, NextStep, and Common Point. In Perspective we employ the concept of framework specifically to refer a generic *model*, which normally requires refinement/ extension. If we consider a component to be a black box that we can only address through its interface, then a generic model is a white box.

The religious paradigm does not encourage reuse.

However, reuse is not just about modeling. Reuse is a key cultural issue. We're continually reminded that reuse is a long-term investment, to fight Not Invented Here syndrome, to provide artificial incentives, and to preach the gospel of reuse. Our experience in the field suggests this is not a viable paradigm. We do better to concentrate on what *works* in specific organizations: To nurture the best and discard the rest. We have tried to cultivate pragmatism into the Perspective process introducing guidelines and checkpoints to keep developers reuse aware. Specific reuse team roles are also introduced to help with the organizational problems associated with reuse.

1.3.6 Retaining a Pragmatic Focus

The term RAAD (Rapid Architected Application Development) is used by Gartner, (1996) to highlight the fact that modern businesses require applications that confer early user benefits at minimum cost, leveraging existing legacy systems where possible but not at the cost of sacrificing maintainability, flexibility, and reusability. Solutions must be developed quickly but on a sound evolving architectural base. Since its beginnings, Perspective has continued to evolve in this spirit of pragmatism.

Perspective is characterized as RAAD.

Contrary to popular misconception, modeling skills are in fact becoming increasingly important as the software industry moves toward a component marketplace with a greater emphasis on quality and reusability. However, the modeling must add value, for example, in the form of good class structures and clear object collaborations. We must beware the "modeling fanatic" whose sole goal is to create overweight models that are incomprehensible to everyone else. "A picture is worth a thousand words," but not if it has a thousand words written all over it.

Creativity is needed where it helps, not where it hinders.

The potential complexities of internal implementation details can result in top-heavy complexity, especially if further notations are used to model these relationships. In fact we have witnessed some horrendous "spaghetti models" during the course of our work. Coding environments are already providing detailed design-modeling support. For example, Visual C++ has color-syntax editors, wizards for application frameworks, specialized forms of class manipulation, and overviews of systems at the class level. Such features are rapidly emerging in code-generation tools, which are seeking to provide ever more sophisticated wizard support using technology frameworks. Component modeling and deployment modeling have therefore been introduced with the goal of providing a sound architectural context in which to apply such technologies.

Addressing component modeling in this spirit presents considerable challenges.

1.4 Modeling Techniques

We have added component modeling and deployment modeling to the four original Perspective models; all six core models are based on established UML notations (UML, 1997), which we have streamlined and minimally enhanced to meet the practical needs of enterprise systems. In particular, collaboration diagrams have been added to the object interaction model for modeling scenarios.

Six core model types are based on UML.

Table 1.1. Perspective Models		
Model	**Chapter**	**Reference**
Business Process Model	3	(CSC, 1995)
Use Case Model	4	(UML, 1997)
Class Model	5	(UML, 1997)
Object Interaction Model	6	(UML, 1997)
State Model	7	(UML, 1997)
Component Model	8,9	(UML, 1997)
Deployment Model	10	(UML, 1997)
Logical Data Model	Appx. B	(CCTA, 1995)

Business process modeling is integrated into Perspective.

For business process modeling we use a notation adapted from CSC's (Computer Sciences Corporation) proprietary methodology CSC Catalyst (CATALYST)[2], which is the best established and most practical of the different notations offered (see Table 1.1, which details where the models can be found in this volume).

Data modeling is used for non-OO persistence.

Finally, we employ logical data modeling in the case in which relational (or other non-OO) databases are used for data storage, obviously a key area in legacy database wrapping.

Techniques are integrated into the process.

Chapters 3 to 10 of this book take the form of an experience library of modeling techniques, tips, and guidelines. Obviously the component model is very largely geared to component development. However, most of the techniques are applicable to both the development of specific solutions and to development of reusable components; full guidelines on when to apply specific techniques are included as part of the process definition.

Prototyping is integrated into the process.

The models described in Figure 1.2 are essentially static. Prototypes are valuable because they provide us with *working* models. Indeed it has been remarked that "if a picture is worth a thousand words then an animated model is worth a thousand pictures" (Boar, 1984). On the other hand, the dangers of prototyping have been well documented (Allen, 1991). The keynote is that prototyping is carefully integrated into the process. These issues are therefore addressed in chapters 11 and 12.

---

[2]CSC Catalyst℠ is a service mark of Computer Sciences Corporation. All rights reserved.

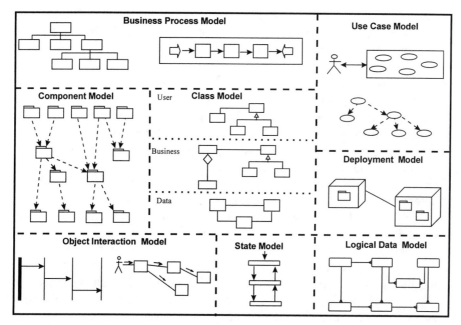

Figure 1.2. Perspective models chart.

1.5 Architecture

The shift from layered to service-based architecture largely reflects the need to capitalize on the emergence of component technology discussed earlier. The service based architecture provides a framework for modeling that assists the developer in terms of service categories (Microsoft, 1996) and object stereotypes. This facilitates business-oriented reuse and also provides an underpinning for the different types of process. A brief summary of the different *service categories* follows:

The architecture provides a framework for modeling.

- User services link together with business services in order to deliver the business capabilities to users. User services are like main-street shops that sell directly to consumers.
- Business services convert data received from data services and user services into information. A business service joins related business tasks with relevant business rules. Business services are like the service industries that supply the shops and oil the wheels of commerce; examples include brokers, insurers, credit agencies, and advertising agencies.
- Data services are used for the manipulation of data in a way that is inde-

pendent of the underlying physical-storage implementation. To continue the analogy, services provide the raw materials (goods and money) to enable commerce to be conducted; examples include manufacturers and banks.

A recent project involved a dealing system in which various *user services* provided visible functionality in the form of sets of window-based GUI forms. User services included placing deals, authorizing deals, setting up schemes, removing schemes, and so on. A set of reusable *business services* supported the user services in their function. Business services included business tasks such as checking the ability to proceed with a deal and verifying security types. The business services made use of a number of business rules, such as rules for determining a customer's credit rating or whether sufficient funds cover pending deals. The business services used *data services* to access the necessary client and security data from various legacy databases transparent to the user.

Objects are stereotyped according to whether they exhibit user interface, business, or data-storage characteristics. Objects of each stereotype work together in the form of components to provide services through their interfaces. Legacy databases are wrapped using data services. Legacy software and packages are wrapped using business services (and data services where appropriate).

The Perspective architecture is illustrated in Figure 1.3. The reader will note that there are similarities with the earlier architecture (Frost, 1995). However, the move from objects to services reflects the need to capitalize on component technology in a way that maximizes business benefits, as reinforced by the fact that it is now business processes that are served by the software. Also, we have abandoned the strict dichotomy between local and corporate levels of reuse because in reality there are degrees of reuse; it is not a binary concept. Degree of reuse is better controlled through component management tools, as discussed in section 1.7, which provide greater flexibility. A full account of the service-based architecture is provided in chapter 2.

1.6 Process

The literature contains a proliferation of advice in the area of the software process. Since Barry Boehm's work on the spiral life cycle (Boehm, 1986), a seemingly countless number of software life cycles have been postulated. It is not our purpose to discuss these here. We simply note, based on repeated experience, that most project managers seek simple and pragmatic guidelines for planning their projects in a component-based setting. Perspective uses a two-tier process to achieve an RAAD approach, with guidelines for assessing which type of process to use supplied in chapter 11. The two sub-processes are as follows:

Margin notes:

A recent project illustrates service categories.

Objects are also stereotyped.

The Perspective architecture has been enhanced.

Most methods do not integrate modeling into a clearly defined process.

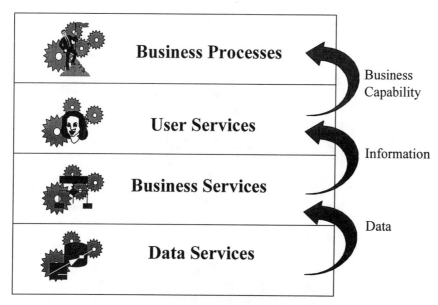

Figure 1.3. Perspective architecture.

1. The **solution process** is aimed at development of solutions, typically in terms of user services, to maximize reuse of existing services and provide early user value; chapter 12 describes this process in detail.

2. The **component process** is aimed at developing components that provide commonly used business and/or data services across different departmental systems or for use by third parties; chapter 13 describes this process in detail.

The relationship between the two processes is depicted in Figure 1.4. It is important to understand that solution and component processes are ideals: Commonly, you will need to use elements of both processes adapted to your own specific needs. Each delivery becomes a successive release of a set of evolving components.

> The two processes work in an interleaved fashion.

From organization to organization no one software process is exactly like another. We have abstracted out the commonly recurring process features and combined them into a generic process that can be configured to suit individual needs. Task catalogs provide check points to show where each technique most appropriately fits in with other activities and encourages teams to ask key questions as they seek to sow and harvest reuse.

> Task catalogs provide check points.

Teams should be multidisciplinary with a range of skills represented in one team. This is in sharp contrast to the traditional approach of an analysis team throwing requirements "over the wall" to a design team that in turn

> Recommended team roles are integrated into the process.

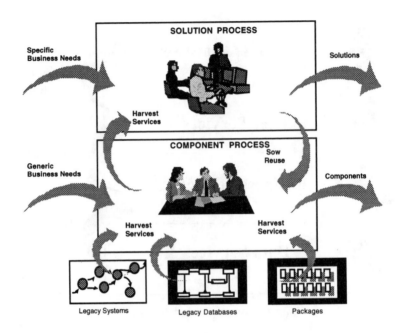

Figure 1.4. Perspective process.

throws specifications over the wall to coders, and then to testers, and so on. Techniques such as JAD (joint application development) are used to facilitate the process. These important related subjects are addressed in chapter 14.

1.7 Component Management

Component management tools provide enabling technology for software reuse.

The interplay between solution and component processes requires effective component management as illustrated in Figure 1.5. Service-based component management tools provide the ability to browse, install, and register the components in a repository. A good component-management tool enables organizations to make their components available to a wide audience via the Internet. The tool provides facilities to make the use of the component marketplace easier, by allowing users to register interest in particular catalogs of components. The repository includes definitions of component interfaces and the services supplied through those interfaces. The repository should also enable identification of models that are associated with the components and that we compose, extend, and adapt through the modeling process. Also, in practice reuse is not a binary concept: A good component-management tool

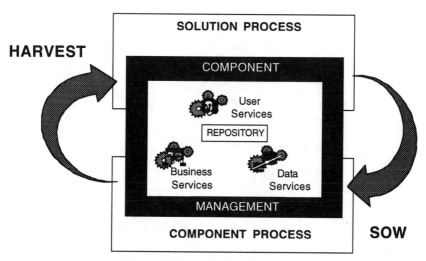

Figure 1.5. A service-based process.

should provide facilities for controlling and administering levels of reuse as described in Allen and Frost (1996).

1.8 A Road Map for Using This Book

Like all books, you can read this one from cover to cover. However, it is more likely you will want to use this book more in the manner of a reference guide. For example, "dipping in" to the experience library for modeling help at appropriate points as and when necessary. Similarly the process sections can be used to guide construction of project plans and to assist the manager in checking progress. However, we would encourage the reader to read chapter 2 first, as this supplies much of the architectural context for the remainder of the book. Similarly, it is also worthwhile to read through chapter 11, which provides a context for the succeeding process chapters. A road map is presented in Figure 1.6.

Here is a road map.

1.9 Summary

Let's summarize by means of a culinary analogy. In cooking, the goal is to create a good meal (the *model*). A classification scheme (the *architecture*) is used to structure our thinking in terms of meats, poultry, herbs, spices, legumes, and so on. There are certain rules (architectural details) that apply to this scheme, which apply to different cooking cultures (modes of software development). For example, in traditional English cooking, pork goes with apple,

This is a common-sense approach.

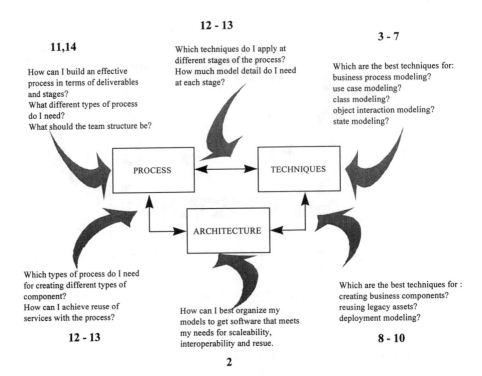

12 - 13

Which techniques do I apply at
different stages of the process?
How much model detail do I need
at each stage?

11,14

How can I build an effective
process in terms of deliverables
and stages?
What different types of process
do I need?
What should the team structure be?

3 - 7

Which are the best techniques for:
business process modeling?
use case modeling?
class modeling?
object interaction modeling?
state modeling?

Which types of process do I need
for creating different types of
component?
How can I achieve reuse of
services with the process?

12 - 13

How can I best organize my
models to get software that meets
my needs for scaleability,
interoperability and resue.

2

Which are the best techniques for :
creating business components?
reusing legacy assets?
deployment modeling?

8 - 10

Figure 1.6. A road map structured by questions.

turkey goes with cranberries. A cookery book (*process*) supplies various recipes
that can be followed. The cookery book refers to various procedures (*tech-niques*), such as simmering, baking, sautéing, stir-frying, and so on.

Ironically, we find in the course of our work that there are many organi-zations that do not seem to follow the common sense of this framework: over-rigid processes constrict developers, absence of architectural guidelines result
in systems that are unfit for today's heterogeneous environments, systems are
over-engineered through top-heavy diagrams without heed of a pragmatic
process. In eating out this situation would not be tolerable: How would we feel
about dining in a restaurant in which the cook did not understand which ingre-dients to use for which recipes or where the chef fiddled so much in the search
for perfection that the meal was cold by the time it arrived? Although I am
sure, like the authors, the reader has culinary horror stories to tell!

Common sense is
sometimes
remarkably
uncommon!

CHAPTER 2

• •

The Perspective Architecture

2.1 Introduction

Incremental releases that are developed in isolation solely to meet tight deadlines will eventually result in fragmented systems that lack consistency and fail
to provide integrated support. In enterprises with complex business processes
this presents a problem that grows out of control exponentially with the number of increments delivered. A key requirement of an incremental approach is
to base increments on a sound architecture that enables components to be
"plugged in" as service providers to the increments.

Organizations have long struggled with the sheer scale and complexity in
software development, which continues to accelerate at a terrific pace. Many
such enterprises have long surrendered hope of an overall framework that inte-
grates their legacy systems with the newer technology. Increasingly adaptive
businesses, where requirements change fast, need correspondingly flexible software. Above all else these issues call for an effective architecture. Unfortunately,
most current methods and tools fail to recognize this as a core need.

Developments in component technology and the Internet, as well as
standards such as CORBA and DCOM are opening up a new opportunity:
to architect software according to the needs of the business, not the technology. The Perspective architecture is aimed at harnessing a service-
based approach with effective object-oriented modeling to capitalize on

*Successful
incremental devel-
opment requires a
sound architecture.*

*Most current
methods fail to
recognize the
importance of
architecture.*

*Architecture is a
central concern in
Perspective.*

the increasing power of the fast-developing technology. This chapter examines some of the driving forces behind the Perspective architecture before explaining the framework and two key concepts of the architecture: *service categories* and *object stereotypes*. Finally we look at how to put the architecture into practice in terms of components.

2.2 Problem Definition

The Perspective architecture provides a framework for modeling.

There are many types of architectural models. The Perspective architecture provides a framework for effective application of the modeling techniques discussed throughout this book. Other important architectural models not discussed in detail here are the business and technical architectural models. The Perspective architecture, however, is an *architecture for model building*, which establishes definitions, rules, and relationships that will form the infrastructure for our models. Let's briefly consider three of the major goals of effective architecture:

• management of scale and complexity,
• interoperability,
• adaptability.

> *Management of scale and complexity:* In large organizations with complex business processes there is a need to manage scale and complexity in software development in such a way that the resulting software structure mirrors business needs as closely as possible. This requires a framework or architecture to establish the definitions, rules, and relationships that will form the infrastructure of models from business process to code.

> *Interoperability:* Typical system portfolios in large organizations consist of a mix of legacy systems and databases, off-the-shelf packages and newer object-oriented applications. Many IT managers long ago abandoned hope of a generic mechanism of integrating such systems and settled for limited point-to-point integration, devoid of an overall architecture to steer software evolution.

> **Adaptability:** In most organizations requirements are not fixed but fluctuate to mirror business needs. For example, Horowitz (1993) reports that 30% of development cost is attributable to changing requirements and around 70% of operations and maintenance costs are due to new requirements or changes to requirements. Adaptability is therefore a key requirement of effective architecture.

As businesses strive to capitalize on advances in technology, changes in technology architectures are paralleled by changes in business architectures. However, the speed at which technology has changed has meant that the business has always been "playing catch-up," continually reinventing itself to mirror the organization of technology. Computer systems have moved from being purely a centralized resource based on mainframe technology, toward PC-based technology that puts far greater computing power into the hands of end-users, and more recently toward the component marketplace.

Businesses have long been organized around technology needs.

In the previous chapter we saw that there is an irresistible movement toward separation of software solutions and the increasingly heterogeneous technology platforms on which the solutions are deployed. The paradox is that the developments in the technology, especially the interface standards, have opened up an important opportunity to architect software around business needs and *not* the needs of the technology!

There is now an opportunity to architect software around business needs.

2.3 A Brief Historical Survey

In this section we track the various architectures that have influenced software development in order to set the scene for the description of the Perspective architecture.

A brief history follows.

2.3.1 Application-Based Architecture: System-Driven Users

Application-based architectures are based on function decomposition methods that tightly couple different aspects of an application and make it very difficult to reuse parts of the application. Such an approach has long since become impotent to the challenges of enterprise systems development. Application-based architectures have their roots in host-based systems. With the user interface, business logic and data storage mixed throughout the host-based code, systems are inflexible, hard to use, and very slow to change. In fact, although host-based systems have long been passé, we find that the appli-

Application-based architectures have been dominant.

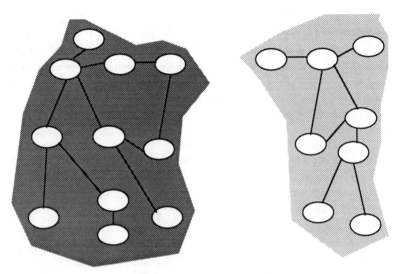

Figure 2.1. Application islands.

cation-based mind-set is so deeply ingrained that it is still pervasive today (see Figure 2.1).

2.3.2 Client-Server Architectures: User-Driven Systems

Two-tier client-server strenghts...

Key strengths of the two-tier client-server architecture include the following:

• the ability to use a GUI (graphical user interface),
• an event model that puts control into the users' hands,
• integration of enterprise data with desktop productivity tools,
• some reusability of business rules and processes.

...and weaknesses.

The primary weaknesses of this architecture are as follows:

• it's not clear whether you put your business logic code in the client or the server,
• the bandwidth of communication between client and server,
• only business logic code put into the server (implemented as stored procedures) is reusable across multiple client applications,
• the business logic code is attached to a particular database. This lowers reusability as much business logic tends to be global to a business, not local to a database.

With three-tier client-server, the business logic applying to different business processes can be supported by separate servers, independent of the client and

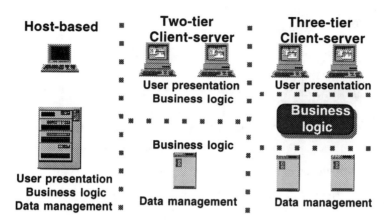

Figure 2.2. The evolution of technical architecture.

the database. This makes it possible to isolate and manage appropriate business logic from data management and user presentation logic. A three-tier architecture provides a much closer match between the architecture of the business and that of the technology that supports the business. However it is still very much a software architecture premised on the needs of the technology, not the user. The above discussion is summarized in Figure 2.2.

Many businesses are splitting their efforts between enterprise and business unit development teams—this is the hybrid approach (Gartner, 1995). This requires a mechanism for identifying and managing business logic that is local to particular users or departments and business logic that is reusable across the enterprise. Enterprise client-server architectures separate local and enterprise business logic as illustrated in Figure 2.3. Such an architecture can be successfully deployed in many different physical configurations from a single machine to a complex network of clients and servers. Despite its attractions, however, enterprise client-server is no different to its ancestors in that it implies a strict client-server interaction between software layers, which may be constricting. Users have to deal with a system optimized for the computer and not for them. Distributed object technology has the potential to address these issues, as discussed in the following section.

2.3.3 Object-Oriented Architectures: Toward Business-Driven Systems

The significance of distributed object technology is that components can be "moved around" at execution time and deployed in a way that optimizes the technology in order to deliver the most business benefit. This opens up the potential of distributing an application so that it serves the needs of the business and not the technology. Combined with Internet technology such environments explode

Margin notes:

Three-tier client-server makes appropriate business logic reusable.

Enterprise client-server architectures separate local and enterprise business logic.

Distributed object technology explodes the original concept of client-server.

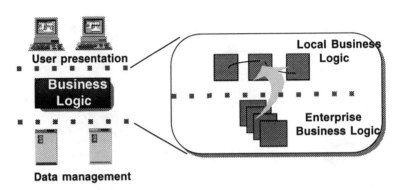

User presentation

Business Logic

Data management

Local Business Logic

Enterprise Business Logic

Figure 2.3. Toward a business-oriented software architecture.

the original concept of client-server computing as a set of workstations hooked up via a LAN (local area network) server.

Distributed object technology calls for a more flexible and business-oriented architecture that retains the value of the lessons we have been taught by maturing client-server technology; for example, "don't mix business logic code with GUI code" and "keep data storage code separate from business and interface code." In fact by giving developers *carte blanche* with such powerful and distributed technology, the dangers of hacking all the application logic to the GUI become magnified. Business logic becomes fragmented across countless different applications and there is an attendant loss of control of the business policy implemented by the software. Any opportunity for leveraging reusable business components is abandoned.

Object orientation (OO) is often presented as the key to the problems described previously: objects, we are told, reflect the "real world" in the software. Importantly, objects, so it is argued, provide the reuse, clarity, and adaptability that are lacking in client-server applications and the interoperability required by distributed technology. A prevalent approach in the use of object modeling is to foster a piecemeal approach in which the focus of attention from the very outset is on applications instead of services. Various object-oriented techniques (for example, class diagrams and use cases) are used to identify objects which are then partitioned into subsystems as shown in Figure 2.4. Experience shows there is great value in such techniques and in object orientation as a principle: however, we need to consider how this measures up as an *architecture*.

The first problem with piecemeal object orientation as an architecture is that the objects are not created as service providers, they are treated as parts of applications. This steers the developer toward point solutions that do not address the wider needs of the business as a whole. In fact we have come full

Distributed object technology itself requires an architecture.

Object orientation is often presented as "the cure" to these problems.

But we have come full circle.

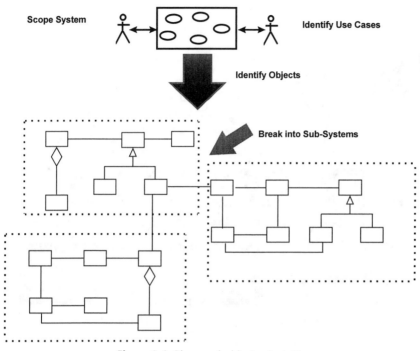

Figure 2.4. Piecemeal object orientation.

circle back to a monolithic application-based architecture. We find that in practice the application-based mind-set is indeed "alive and kicking" in many organizations today.

The second problem with this approach is that implementation dependencies are often exposed through OO programming language interfaces. Technology such as CORBA IDL can help to resolve this issue by providing clean separation between clients and implementations in terms of *interfaces*. Interfaces are separate from implementations providing isolation of changes and a compilable linkage between architecture and implementation. Although it is objects that form the underlying fabric of software solutions, it is components that provide the effective granularity of reuse through consistent published interfaces that encapsulate the implementation. Components provide a cross-functional view that is aimed at encapsulating groups of services (see Figure 2.5) that are responsive to a broad spectrum of consumers.

Encapsulation of objects is often imperfect.

A component-based approach removes the tight coupling of an application's parts and eases reuse of parts across different applications. In fact the application has disappeared: instead model items are packaged as components, which are configured in network fashion to meet business needs.

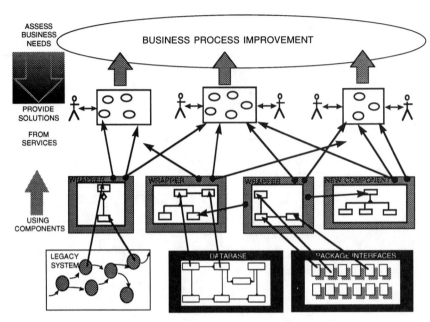

Figure 2.5. Component-based object orientation.

A component-based approach does not appear out of thin air!

Importantly, this also applies to existing systems, packages, and databases: components can be employed to wrap such applications. Use cases are still used to scope the requirement, but in relation to business needs rather than existing application boundaries. Class diagrams are still used to model the structure of the software, but in relation to business requirements and not as a by-product of the existing application structure. However, a component-based approach does not appear out of thin air. It needs to be architected properly as we are about to see.

2.4 A Service-Based Architecture

2.4.1 Services

A service is a set of functionality accessed through a published interface.

What exactly do we mean by services? Services are cohesive collections of related functionality, accessed through a consistent interface that encapsulates the implementation. Each service has a published specification of interface and behavior. Components provide the interfaces. In modeling terms, a service groups one or more operations that bind together to form a contract with consumers of the service. A service is triggered through and manifests itself as an operation: operations can be stereotyped as services. Services are provided through a special type of object known as a service object, which is described in section 2.5.5.

2.4.2 Reuse of Services

Perspective uses a service-based architecture, as described in the Microsoft Solution Framework (MSF) application model (Microsoft, 1996), to fully exploit the opportunities presented by distributed object technology, as previously described, while at the same time retaining the good sense learned from client-server experience. This addresses the shortcomings of client-server architecture by taking a business-inspired view of the component marketplace (Cox, 1986). Instead of rethinking the problem through afresh in terms of what software can be used to solve a business problem, sets of service features are examined to see which can be reused. Reuse of services has three major advantages over reuse of objects:

Services work together to serve the needs of business processes.

- Objects are usually at too low a level of useful granularity. Objects seldom stand alone in enterprise systems: they collaborate with one another to provide services. Services provide for a much more effective level of reuse based on software structures that transcend the individual object.
- Objects often contain functionality that is not required in a particular context of use. Services can be designed to be cohesive to the needs of their users in a way that avoids inheritance of the unnecessary baggage that often comes with object reuse.
- Object reuse is implemented in the form of class browsers, which tend to have a very technical implementation focus tuned in to code reuse. Service reuse is implemented in the form of browsers, which have a direct business focus geared to the needs of business processes.

In a nutshell, although it is objects that are *developed*, it is services that should be *provided*.

2.4.3 Service Categories

Service categories, from the Microsoft Solution Framework (Microsoft, 1996) are defined as follows:

Here is the set of service categories.

- **User services** are typically employed to meet specific business requirements: the needs of a particular business process or department. User ser-

vices link together with business services in order to deliver the business capabilities to users as follows:
- They provide the visual interface for presenting information and gathering data,
- secure the business services needed to deliver the required business capabilities,
- integrate the user with the application to perform a business process.

- **Business services** commonly apply to generic business requirements across several business processes or departments. Business services convert data received from data services and user services into information as follows:
  - They respond to requests from the user (or other business services) in order to execute a business task,
  - couple related business tasks with the relevant business rules,
  - secure the data services needed to accomplish the business tasks or apply the business rules.

- **Data services** commonly apply to generic data-access requirements across several business processes or departments. Data services are used for the manipulation of data in a way that is independent of the underlying physical storage implementation as follows:
  - They manage and satisfy business services' requests for data,
  - define, maintain, access, and update data,
  - provide private primitive value domains (such as TEXT or INTEGER) and their associated operations.

Services collaborate to support one or more business processes.

The application becomes a set of services that are targeted to meet business-process needs: application islands are now integrated as shown in Figure 2.6. Although the interaction between the different service types is typically client-server in nature, the service category scheme does not necessarily imply a strict (layer to layer) structure of interaction. The service-based architecture is technically neutral. The solution process (described in chapter 12) typically develops a set of use cases and produces user service components that provide the required user services through their interfaces. The user services are modeled to capitalize on other user services and the reusable business and data services developed via the component process (described in chapter 13).

2.4.4 Services and Component Management

Class browsers have been widely available for some years. However, until recently one of the major obstacles to reuse has been the absence of effective

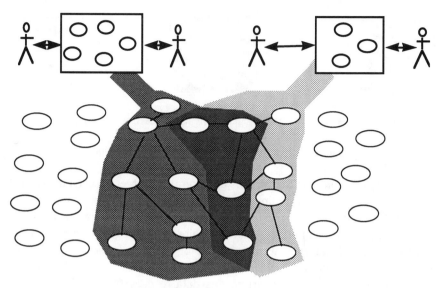

Figure 2.6. Application integration.

facilities for cataloging and retrieving components in a business-oriented way using services. Service-based component management tools provide the ability to browse, install, and register the components in harmony with a model-driven approach. Also, in practice, reuse is not a binary concept: there is a need to control and administer levels of reuse. Such component management facilities are important in enabling technology for leveraging the approach we describe; these facilities are described in Allen and Frost (1996).

Service-based component management tools are essential.

2.5 Object Stereotypes

2.5.1 Overview of Object Stereotypes

Objects are the nuts and bolts that are packaged together into components that provide services. The word "stereotype" (UML, 1997) is used in UML to denote a useful meta-classification. In fact, many methods make use of this concept, which originates from Rebecca Wirfs-Brock (1993); for example, Jacobson's entity objects, control objects, and user objects (Jacobson, 1992). The term is used here to emphasize certain basic architectural stereotypes of objects. Objects are stereotyped according to whether they exhibit external interfacing, business, or data management characteristics, as illustrated in Figure 2.7. In addition, the concept of *service object* provides an abstraction of interfaces, as described in 2.5.5.

Underlying the service-based architecture are different stereotypes of object.

USER OBJECT   BUSINESS OBJECT   DATA OBJECT

Figure 2.7. User, business, and data object stereotypes.

User and data
objects are
technology objects.

User objects provide the screens and controls that let people employ user services, as well as other noninteractive interfaces, such as interfaces to other systems or batch reporting. By assigning responsibility for interfaces in this way, changes to user interfaces that are quite common given ongoing developments in graphical user interface technology, will not affect the underlying business objects. The data objects provide data services by controlling access to database storage and converting this data to clean nondatabase-specific interfaces for use by business and user services. Again, this protects the business objects from the effects of changes to databases.

Business objects are
insulated from the
technology.

The fast pace of change of technology and the transition to open implementation architectures reinforces the need for quality business models that will outlive the environments for which they are originally implemented. Similarly, the fast-changing face of businesses requires software to be grown into the workplace and to be flexible enough to meet change. The business objects therefore represent an important investment around which software can be built and rapidly developed.

2.5.2 User Objects

A user object is
crucial to providing
the front-end of a
user service.

To provide user services a user object works in collaboration with other user objects and with business objects that provide business services. User objects are typically forms and menus, but do not have to be interactive; for example, a batch report. The communication between users and the system will actually be physically realized by several layers of abstraction that gradually shift the focus of interest from sequences of basic mechanical data into the higher level concepts actually symbolized by business objects. Clearly we do not want to model every last nut and bolt of the interface. User objects are intended to provide a *useful* level of abstraction for *modeling* communication between users and business objects, given implementation constraints.

User objects, like forms, often communicate directly with business objects. However, other "intermediate" objects may also be useful, depending on the level of abstraction chosen. In fact, user objects may be responsible for a variety of tasks depending on the environment. Examples include the following:

- direct user interfacing (for example, understanding the information and its format displayed in a window),
- batch reports,
- controlling a family of user objects in a complex transaction,
- search facilities,
- device handlers.

Attributes in user objects typically represent fields contained on forms or temporary storage items. Operations in the user object often handle form-related logic, such as edit checking. Operations may also be linked to events on a control. For example, different operations can be called when a button is subject to different kinds of events (such as a click and a double-click). It is the responsibility of the user object to interpret such events. Increasingly, with the growing sophistication of GUI tools, it is unlikely to be worth modeling the controls as objects. Pressing of controls causes messages to be directed to user objects, which will interpret the message, invoking the appropriate operation accordingly. User objects do not need to know the actual layouts of windows; only what fields and controls are on the windows. As far as the user object is concerned the window is treated just like any other object. For example, if a user does something to a window, the user object receives messages, such as "Command button pushed" or "Cancel," in exactly the same format and structure as those received from other objects, including business objects.

User objects may be local to the needs of a particular business process or department, as illustrated in Figure 2.8. Other user objects may be reusable across different business processes or departments; examples of such generic user objects are shown in Figure 2.9. Sometimes these objects are vendor supplied, such as Microsoft Foundation Classes. Generic user objects are commonly used to implement organizational standards, such as standard form layouts or message protocols. Clearly the more potentially reusable the object, the greater justification for engineering it as a component, as described in chapter 8.

At one extreme it may be tempting not to bother modeling user objects at all, taking the view that if interfaces to business objects are right then they will integrate smoothly with any set of user objects. This may be an attractive option in rapid development, using prototyping tools, where user object modeling may seem like an unnecessary and expensive academic luxury. For example, if the interface is relatively simple and can be shown directly in a GUI builder, such as Visual Basic or Delphi, the diagrams may be redundant.

> User objects come in many "flavors."

> User objects provide fields and controls.

> There are different levels of reusability of user objects.

> We need to decide how much emphasis to place on user object modeling.

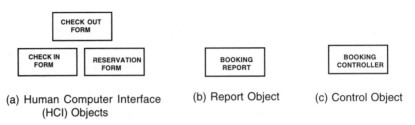

(a) Human Computer Interface
    (HCI) Objects

(b) Report Object

(c) Control Object

Figure 2.8. An example of local user objects.

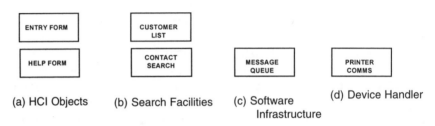

(a) HCI Objects

(b) Search Facilities

(c) Software
    Infrastructure

(d) Device Handler

Figure 2.9. An example of generic user objects.

Remember, a major goal is to avoid capturing redundant information. It must therefore be decided whether to model user objects in the context of the project. Clearly some guidance is required here and is provided in 5.4.12.

2.5.3 Business Objects

Business objects are technically neutral.

Business objects are sometimes referred to as *conceptual* objects, because they provide services that meet business requirements, regardless of technology. To provide business services a business object works in collaboration with other business objects and uses data services provided by data objects. A business object applies business rules to transform data into *information*. The data may be acquired from data services or user services.

There are different levels of reusability of business objects.

Business objects may meet the *specific* needs of business processes or parts of business processes. Such processes may well be sited in different organizational departments. This is in contrast to business objects that meet the needs of multiple business processes across different departments. Examples of local business objects for a hotel reception process are shown in Figure 2.10. Examples of business rules applied could be that a reservation cannot be canceled within 3 days of a required date without incurring a penalty or that a room cannot be occupied by more than four people. Other business objects provide business services relevant to the whole organization and are used across business process and departmental boundaries. Such generic business objects

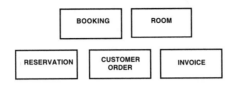

Figure 2.10. An example of local business objects.

Figure 2.11. An example of generic business objects.

meet business domain specific needs and will call for centralized administration. Examples of generic objects in a hotel system are shown in Figure 2.11. Examples of business rules applied could be that an account balance cannot drop below its credit limit or that corporate contacts receive a special service rate. Clearly the more potentially reusable the object, the greater justification for engineering it as a component, as described in chapter 8.

The gains to be made from reusing business objects are huge compared to potential gains in implementation reuse of class code from libraries. In turn we believe the gains to be made from reusing business services outweigh potential gains in reusing business objects. It is components that provide the enabling technology for achieving this goal.

Components provide the enabling technology.

2.5.4 Data Objects

To provide data services a data object works in collaboration with other data objects and by issuing calls to the underlying database software. The main aim of data objects is to insulate business objects from the effects of changes in technology by isolating data management system dependencies. Data objects therefore need to be able to translate persistent business objects into the appropriate storage units and vice versa. Although data objects can apply locally, they typically provide data services across many different business units and are therefore engineered as data service components. Importantly, this includes wrapping of databases, as described in chapter 9.

Data objects are geared to providing data services.

In the case of an object-oriented database, such as Object Store or Gemstone, the translation process is likely to be straightforward, though it should not be underestimated as the object database structure may be optimized for performance and therefore be markedly different to the business-

Data objects address relational databases in a component-based setting.

object structures. If, as is generally the case with current systems, relational technology is used, the data objects will need to deal with the "impedance mismatch" between business objects and the relational tables. Data objects provide services such as loading data from the database into objects, for saving data captured by objects to the database, and for handling referential integrity. Data objects can issue SQL, or proprietary database I/O, depending on your database type, and so on. The reader is referred to chapter 9 for a detailed treatment with examples.

2.5.5 Service Objects

Service objects are abstractions of interfaces.

Earlier we stated the importance of interfaces: Interfaces are separate from implementations providing isolation of changes and a compilable linkage between architecture and implementation. Regardless of stereotype, objects that are to provide services will need interfaces designing for them; a *service object* is a type of control object (Jacobson, 1992) that provides a mechanism for identifying and modeling where interfaces are going to be required. This is important for achieving a design that mirrors business needs. A service class, discussed in detail in chapter 8, is a class that provides one or more services, which represents an abstraction of a component interface(s). Note that the fact that a class is a service class is derived from the fact that at least one of its operations is stereotyped as a service.

2.6 Service Categories and Object Stereotypes

User services are triggered through user objects.

User objects collaborate with other user objects to realize user services. The user objects may also invoke business services and other user services. It is not possible for user services to extract information directly from data services. All information access is through business services. Example user services are Check in Customer, Accept Reservation, and Book Catering Facility.

Business services are triggered through business objects or user objects.

Business objects collaborate with other business objects to realize business services. The business objects may also invoke data services and other business services. Very often, business services are "black box" and triggered through business objects. Examples of black box business services are Check Customer Credit and Upgrade Customer Account. However, other business services can be triggered through their own user objects. These are not user services because they do not have user value employed in isolation. An example is Assess Customer Payment History, which is reusable across a range of user services (Check in Customer, Accept Reservation, and so on) but has no purpose other than in the context of those user services. Finally, note that a business service (black box or interactive) can invoke a user object; for example, if a business exception occurs it may be necessary to alert a user object so that appropriate users can be informed to take action.

Data objects collaborate with other data objects to realize data services. The data objects may also invoke other data services. Typically the data service is black box. Example data services are Get Customer Account, Read Customer Account, and Update Customer Account. Less commonly, as with business services, it is possible for a data service to be triggered through its own user object. Typically these are database administration and housekeeping procedures, such as Back-Up Customer Account. Finally note that a data service (black box or interactive) can invoke a user object; for example, if a data exception is recognized by a data service this could invoke a user object to display the exception.

Data services are triggered through data objects or user objects.

The service architecture works on the classic basis of gathering content (data), structuring and translating the content into form (information), and interpreting information (business capability). Multiple user services can all use the same business service. For example user services Check in Customer, Accept Reservation, and Book Catering Facility all make use of the business service Check Customer Credit. Similarly multiple business services can share the same data service. For example, Check Customer Credit, Assess Customer Payment History, and Upgrade Customer Account all use the data service Get Customer Account.

This presents great opportunities for reuse.

At present truly reengineered business processes tend to be the exception. Many organizations are settling for the more realistic goal of gradual process improvement, as described in the next chapter. In this situation there is a need to impose an architecture to meet current business realities as illustrated in Figure 2.12. Techniques are used to wrap legacy assets in preparation for potential later migration to fully component-based designs. For example, user services to wrap previous generation user interfaces, business services to wrap package business objects or legacy transactions, data services to wrap database transactions. Legacy component modeling techniques are described in chapter 9.

Services also help with integration of legacy assets.

2.7 Modeling Techniques Within the Perspective Architecture

As stressed in chapter 1, our approach to component-based development is evolutionary, not revolutionary: Established modeling techniques, described in chapters 3 through 7, are enhanced and employed within the framework of the service-based architecture. Perspective employs the concept of *service package,* described in chapter 8, to facilitate a business-oriented modeling process.

The Perspective architecture provides a framework.

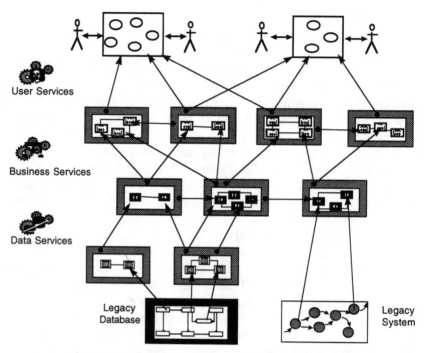

User Services

Business Services

Data Services

Legacy
Database

Legacy
System

Figure 2.12. Service category usage of object stereotypes.

A service package provides a set of services belonging to a single service category. Service packages provide a mechanism for grouping objects into units that are cohesive to the needs of a particular set of services; this is akin to the idea of subsystem partitioning using responsibility-driven design (Wirfs-Brock et al., 1990). The service package provides the required services through one or more service classes. This provides a business-oriented basis for modeling deployment of components using *component packages*: these are implementation packages of objects, which provide services through their interfaces, as described in chapter 10.

System architecture is modeled using service packages.

We map out the high-level system architecture in terms of service packages early in the process. One of the major benefits of this is that proposed reuse of legacy systems, software packages, and databases are addressed as part of architectural design, and not left as an afterthought, as in many methods.

Multiple user services share the same business service.

Let's consider a simple example to see how service reuse typically works. User service packages Book Conference Folder, Reception and Catering Folder all make use of the business service package Customer Account, which provides the business service Check Customer Credit. The corresponding user services might be Book Conference, Check in Customer, Reserve Booking, and Book Catering Facility. Such dependencies are modeled using a package

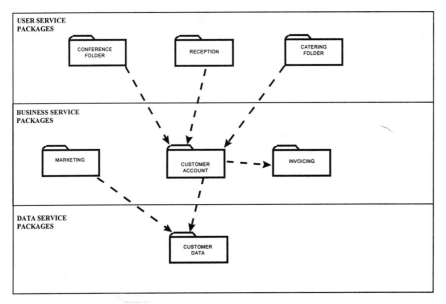

Figure 2.13. An example of a package dependency program.

dependency diagram as illustrated in Figure 2.13; the full semantics of these diagrams are given in chapter 8.

Marketing and Customer Account both use Customer Data, which pro-vides create/read/update/delete of customers from an underlying relational database. Service reuse also occurs within the same service category; for example, Customer Account uses the services of Invoicing.

> Multiple business services share the same data service.

The service packages are used to effectively wrap legacy assets. For example, Invoicing wraps an existing COBOL system, Marketing wraps a soft-ware package, and Customer Data wraps a legacy relational database.

> Legacy assets also provide services.

The service packages must be modeled in a way that makes the resulting components useful building blocks, simple to activate and inexpensive to administer. The level of granularity of a component can vary from large and complex to small and simple. Large components have the greatest potential for reuse but are often not cohesive and may be difficult to assemble into solu-tions with other components. Small components are usually more cohesive but often need to be coupled with many other components to achieve significant reuse, resulting in excessive intercomponent coupling. Clearly, settling on a good and useful level of granularity is a trade-off between these two extremes. Each organization will have an optimum level of granularity of component to best suit their own needs. General guidelines on component modeling are con-tained in chapters 8 and 9.

> The system architechture provides a context for more detailed modeling.

Component modeling also requires a rigorous process.

The more potentially reusable an object, the more it is a candidate for migration to the role of component (or part of a component). Component modeling also requires a more stringent process, focusing more on quality engineering and rigor of specification: The component process is described in chapter 13. Other objects may also be "componentized," but not to the same degree of rigor. The main role of such objects is as solution providers. This requires a process that is focused on fast delivery of business functionality: The solution process is described in chapter 12.

2.8 Summary

We build solid yet flexible model-based structures on which business solutions can be rapidly assembled.

The ultimate promise of component-based development is that software solutions can be composed from reusable components, in analogous fashion to hardware. The Perspective architecture has been designed to exploit technologies such as DCOM and CORBA within the context of the component marketplace. Flexibility is provided to distribute system functionality according to actual business requirements, rather than at some arbitrary level set by hardware and software suppliers. The business services effectively encapsulate business policy, protecting the organization from the threat of changes to business policy.

The architecture can be imposed to meet current business realities.

Business units often cannot wait for "the grand design." Costs for central teams to create reusable objects "up front" are prohibitive and the risks involved in such architectural initiatives are high: the assumptions on which reusable components are designed often change drastically before anything useful is delivered. The Perspective architecture is designed to help integrate legacy assets using wrapping techniques in preparation for possible later migration to fully component-based designs.

CHAPTER 3

• • • • • • • • • • • • • • • • • • • •

Business
Process
Modeling

3.1 Introduction

Management's need to continually reinvent businesses in the context of a changing technological and sociological world is reflected in sustained interest in business process reengineering (BPR) and business process improvement (BPI). Such initiatives, which are customer and technology inspired, flatten organizational structures through the use of empowered teams, remove redundancy, and look for new ways to leverage a business advantage.

BPR and BPI are hot-topics of the 1990s

A variety of work-flow and process diagrams have been used to model business processes and it is not our purpose here to over-elaborate on the notations used. We will use a subset of core business process modeling (BPM) concepts, adapted from CSC's proprietary methodology CATALYST (CSC, 1995) which are briefly explained before considering how they fit into Perspective. A full set of relevant definitions is included within the glossary. For reasons of scope we do not address some of the key issues of BPR and BPI such as organizational issues, location, and physical distribution, as well as cultural and political impact.

The focus in this chapter is restricted to relevant modeling concepts.

The purpose of this chapter is not to describe a complete definitive BPM methodology but to understand how BPR and BPI projects can provide the needed scope for component-based development projects. We describe a *basic*

We focus on some basic essentials of BPM techniques.

set of business process modeling concepts and diagramming techniques that are usable with as little translation or rework as possible in component-based development. For an account of how the techniques are employed within the Perspective process the reader is referred to section 11.5.

3.2 BPM Principles

3.2.1 Focus of Interest

BPR involves the radical reorganization of an enterprise.

The meaning of the term BPR has become rather vague, as it is used differently by different authors and commentators. We use the term "BPR" to refer to the radical reorganization of an enterprise along the flow of work that generates the value sought by the customer. The emphasis in BPR is that change should be radical in order that the business makes efficiency gains of orders of magnitude.

BPI involves improvement of the current processes.

Under some circumstances the radical changes envisaged with a BPR exercise are unacceptable, resulting in a drive for improvement of the current processes, however defined, rather than reengineering. We use the term BPI to indicate where improvements are sought within the current business constraints.

Both BPR and BPI encompass techniques for organizational change.

Techniques for organizational change are characterized by approaches to managing resistance to change, team building, performance measurement, and incentive compensation. These lie outside our scope. The discussion in this chapter is restricted to core BPM techniques irrespective of whether a BPR or BPI approach is taken. Current "As-Is" modeling and future "To-Be" modeling techniques are described, which provide a basis for further BPM techniques, which lie outside our current scope, such as workflow analysis, simulation, value-chain analysis, critical-path analysis, and performance measurement. A key requirement is that the business process models are readily usable in analyzing software requirements with as little translation or rework as possible. To speed development, close integration is critical between BPM and component-based development. In this chapter we will focus toward showing how to "make the connection."

A business process is crucially distinct from a function.

Some business processes might be contained within a departmental function; for example, Computer Programming. Often, however, we find that a business process crosses the "white space" between boxes on an organizational hierarchy as described in Rummler and Brache's (1990) landmark paper; for example, Order Processing spans Sales, Credit Control, Inventory Management, and Invoicing. Business processes operate "horizontally" through a company in contrast to the vertical division of labor on which traditional function decomposition approaches to business analysis are based. Each activity along the series should leave the system in a consistent state, which adds value to the business process. This feature needs to be leveraged and functional partitioning avoided.

A huge amount of learning and process improvement can result simply from modeling how the parts of business processes interconnect. In BPI we can seek to eliminate duplicate activities, introduce parallel activities, and eliminate unnecessary movement of work. In the more extreme case of BPR this can result in a totally reorganized set of functions, based on business processes; for example, the four different elements of Order Processing (Sales, Credit Control, Inventory Management and Invoicing) are rationalized into a single process-based function: Provide Customer Service. BPM is an integral part of the approach, regardless of whether BPR or BPI is used. It helps to challenge and pinpoint unnecessary interfaces and time delays within the business process and involves creative thinking as to how best the organization interfaces with its customers.

> The value of BPM should not be underestimated.

A business process often involves multiple users and activities that take place over different time-slices. Not only is it necessary to examine the activities in which inputs are converted into outputs, the correct activities must be identified in the first place! A common approach is to attempt some form of function decomposition, unpeeling the layers of the process onion, until one reaches the magical notion of a component process. Unfortunately there is an absence of criteria for establishing a bottom level process. Too often we are exulted to "find a level you are comfortable with." This is not helpful. In Perspective a business process is viewed as a family of activities that together collaborate in different event-driven groups to fulfill the business process. Groups of activities are "time-sliced" by events that denote essential constraints imposed by the business, not by technology. This allows us to identify common business activities that can act on different process threads. The approach should be "outside-in" rather than "top-down." Very few BPM methodologies seem to recognize this fact. An exception is CATALYST from CSC. Many of the concepts in this chapter are therefore drawn and adapted from this methodology.

> The anatomy of a business process is essentially event driven.

3.2.2 Direct and Indirect Business Process

Some processes produce results that directly affect the external customer. Other processes, although transparent to the customer, are nevertheless necessary for effective management of the business. Some examples of the different types of process are shown below (Rummler & Brache, 1990).

> It is useful to distinguish basic types of business process.

- Generic Customer Processes
  - Marketing and sales

- Product/service development and introduction
- Manufacturing
- Distribution
- Billing
- Order processing
- Customer service

• Industry-specific customer processes
  - Loan processing (banking)
  - Claim adjudication (insurance)
  - Grant allocation (government)
  - Merchandise return (retail)
  - Food preparation (restaurants)
  - Baggage handling (airline)
  - Reservation handling (hotels/airlines)

• Generic administrative processes
  - Formal strategic and tactical planning
  - Budgeting
  - Training
  - Facilities management
  - Purchasing
  - Information Technology management

A process may be "direct value" or "indirect value."

BPM tends to work best with processes that are essentially "value chains" (Porter, 1985) of interconnected activities. Often such processes are customer focused (for example, Claim Adjudication), though this is not always the case (for example, Purchasing). Such processes have predefinable triggering events and are referred to as *"direct-value"* **processes.** It is important not to forget other administrative processes, which though they do not add measurable business value to the customer, are nevertheless part of the life blood of the enterprise. Such "indirect-value" processes include key management information activities in which a triggering event is not predefinable; for example, Analyze Pricing Trends. Often such management activities are concerned with overall business performance; for example, Monitor Sales Activity. Also included here are infrastructure activities concerned with efficient service provision; for example, Maintain Stock.

3.2.3 BPM Concepts

There is a plethora of terminology associated with BPM. Many of the problems that we meet on real-life projects are rooted in confusions over terminology.

This section addresses the need for clarity and simplicity of definition and establishes some basic ground rules. The three main concepts are *elementary process*, *business event*, and *process thread*. Other concepts are secondary in the sense that they act as packaging constructs or terms of convenience.

3.2.3.1 Elementary Business Process

An elementary business process (EBP) is a task performed by one person in one place at one time, in response to a business event, which adds measurable business value and leaves the data in a consistent state; for example, Approve Credit or Price Order.

3.2.3.2 Business Event

A business event is a stimulus that triggers an EBP. Business events may be input or output driven. Input-driven business events are signaled by the arrival of an input information flow; they can be *external* or *internal*; for example, Customer submits order (external) or Customer-service clerk requests credit approval (internal). Output driven business events may be temporal or conditional. Temporal events are signaled by the arrival of a predefined point in time; for example, Time to issue payment reminders. Conditional events report the sensing of a particular circumstance, which triggers an elementary process; for example, Credit limit exceeded.

3.2.3.3 Process Thread

A process thread is a value chain of EBPs. It is used to model the flow of EBPs, initiated by a business event in terms of sequence dependency, iteration, conditionality and process breaks; note that alternative triggering business events are possible. A process thread normally produces some result, which represents business value. A result from one process thread is often a business event relative to another process thread. Note that process threads can be diagrammed at a higher level of granularity by clustering EBPs into process groups.

3.2.3.4 Process Group

A process group may be direct or indirect. Both types of process groups can be nested within process groups to manage complexity. A direct process group is a grouping of activities performed in response to a set of related business events; that is, a grouping of one or more related process threads. An indirect process group does not have an associated event; it denotes an "indirect-value" process, such as a management information process. Indirect process groups do not have process threads.

3.2.3.5 Activity

The generic term "activity" is used to describe a process group, process thread, or EBP.

3.2.3.6 Business Actor

A business actor is a role or set of roles that has a specific set of responsibilities relating to a business process. It could be a person, a group of persons, an organization, another system, or a piece of equipment. A business actor can be external (e.g., Customer) or internal (e.g., Credit Controller, Credit Control System) to the business.

3.3 BPM Notation

3.3.1 Notation Set

We use a notation set for our business process models based on CATALYST, summarized in Figure 3.1. Full definitions of all terms are included in the glossary.

3.3.2 Diagrammatic Views

The **Process Hierarchy Diagram** is used mainly as a graphic index, which shows the relationship between the levels of process granularity (see Figure 3.2). At the very top sits the enterprise (or part of the enterprise) under study. This is divided into a number of key business processes consisting of process groups. Process groups may be nested as necessary, depending on the size and complexity of the business under study. EBPs can be reused both within and across different process threads. Conceptually a process group consists of a number of process threads. However, it is optional to actually show process threads on this diagram. Typically the same core family of EBPs are configured in terms of several process threads within the same process group, so if process threads are shown too there will be much redundancy.

The **Process-Thread Diagram** is the major modeling tool. It is used to model dependencies between EBPs. A process thread is shown in context in Figure 3.3. However, as previously mentioned, the diagrams can be used at a higher level of granularity to include dependencies between process groups as well as EBP. A result produced by one process thread can be a triggering event relative to another process thread. An EBP could be common

NAME	SYMBOL	DESCRIPTION
Internal Business Event		Internal stimulus which triggers a process thread or activity
External Business Event		External stimulus which triggers a process thread or activity
Result		An outcome of value produced by the process
Optional Dependency		Leads to a process to indicate its optionality
Mandatory Dependency		Leads to a mandatory process
Activity		Generic Process
Exclusivity		To indicate a condition
Parallel processes	P1 P2	Each process must complete for the containing box to be complete
Iteration	For each X	To indicate a repeating process or processes
Process Break		A delay prior to another process starting (ends with an event)

Figure 3.1. BPM notation set.

to more than one process thread; it could also be used more than once in the same thread.

3.4 BPM Techniques

3.4.1 "As-Is" Process Hierarchy Diagramming

The process hierarchy diagram provides a visual focus for BPM with respect to the current set of business processes. The aim here is to understand the business process, which will often be more difficult than originally perceived, as we start to challenge assumptions about what is actually going on! This usually involves scouting ahead and doing some process thread diagramming and

A process hierarchy diagram helps determine our scope.

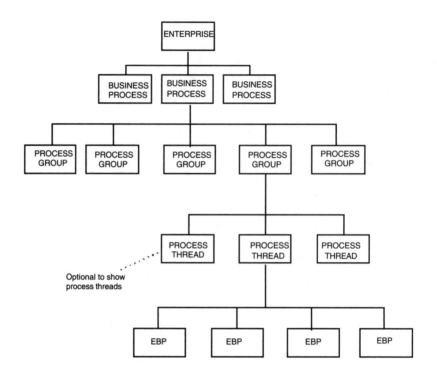

Figure 3.2. Process-hierarchy concepts.

then revisiting and evolving the process hierarchy diagram as our understanding sharpens. The process hierarchy diagram in Figure 3.4 illustrates business processes within a motor dealership enterprise. The business process Maintain Vehicle is identified as a direct-value process, as described previously in 3.2.2: It takes a collection of inputs (a customer car maintenance request) and produces an output that is of value to the customer (an improved car). This business process splits into five process groups. The process group Service and Repair Vehicle provides the context for our BPM. Note in this example, for the sake of simplicity, that the process group consists of a single process thread.

3.4.2 "As-Is" Process Thread Diagramming

Process thread diagrams are constructed for process groups. A process group responds to a set of triggering business events. Each business event triggers a

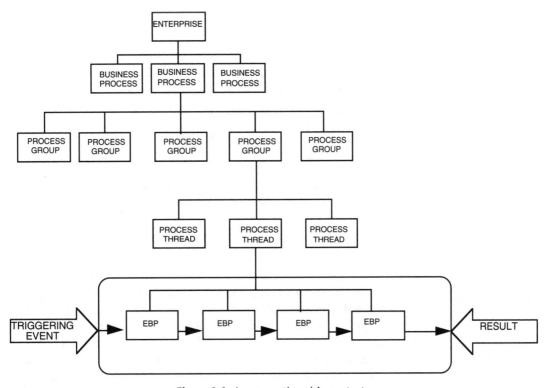

Figure 3.3. A process thread in context.

different process thread within the process group, which produces a result. The current process
First, we identify triggering business events and primary results for the process group now analyzed
group. Second, we analyze each event-result pair as a chain of activity in terms in more detail.
of a number of process thread diagrams. How many process thread diagrams
are produced is dependent on the objectives set for the BPM exercise. It is
important to concentrate on the most significant scenarios resulting from the
triggering business event first, in order to avoid getting bogged down in exceptions and minor aspects.

In our example, the process group Service and Repair Vehicle is triggered Initiating event and
by the business event Customer requests job with the eventual result that the result pairs are
job is closed with the car ready for collection. In this case there is a single identified.
event-result pair resulting in a single process thread for the process group. Note,
that in real life you can expect to find several event-result pairs, each of which
corresponds to a separate process thread.

Chains of events are tracked for each initiator–result pair. Each chain is
segmented into essential time-slices by considering the typical pattern of

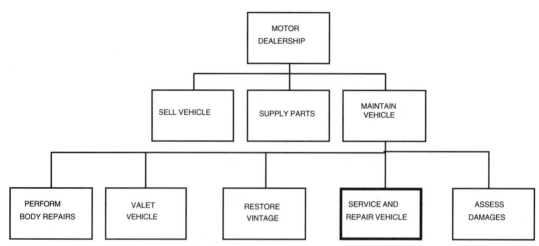

Figure 3.4. Motor dealership "As-Is" process-hierarchy diagram.

events that occurs, thus exposing constituent EBPs, each of which should end in some value that is reflected in a stable system state. First we note that our process thread is initiated by the external business event (1) of a customer requesting a car service in dialogue with the customer-service clerk. The customer-service clerk uses a service from the system, in the shape of a bookings form, to sort out the customer's requirement and work out required parts. The next event in the chain is temporal: parts requests are produced at regular times (2). If parts need to be ordered, the parts controller talks to a supplier, raising the necessary purchase order (3). At the start of day (4) a schedule of jobs is produced for the lead mechanic. On finishing the job, the lead mechanic submits job-completion details (5). The process thread finishes on receipt of the external business event (6) of the customer collecting the serviced vehicle (see Figure 3.5). We now construct a process thread diagram, as shown in Figure 3.6. **Note that internal business events Parts Controller submits parts request and Lead Mechanic completes job are not shown on the diagram to limit complexity; though they could be shown if required.**

Preconditions and postconditions must always evaluate to "true" or "false." Thus the event Parts Controller submits parts request will only trigger Request parts for job provided that the precondition Parts established for job is true. Preconditions and postconditions are important because they help to govern the behavior of required services, when we model our system use cases.

Swim-lanes are bands drawn vertically down the diagram, which represent business actors. This can help visually portray areas of business actor

Process threads are constructed for typical patterns of events.

The dependencies between EBPs represent pre- and postconditions.

Swim-lanes can be used.

Event No.	Event Type	Event Name	Elementary Business Process
1	External Business	Customer asks customer-service clerk to book a job	Book Job for Customer
2	Temporal	Time to establish parts for job	Establish Parts for Job
3	Internal Business	Parts controller submits parts request	Request Parts for Job
4	Temporal	Time to schedule jobs for day	Schedule Jobs for Day
5	Internal Business	Lead mechanic completes job	Record Job Completion
6	External Business	Customer arrives to collect serviced car	Close Job With Customer

Figure 3.5. Service and Repair Vehicle events and EBPs.

responsibility and highlight interfaces that are candidates for elimination in "To-Be" modeling.

We now elaborate the process hierarchy diagram, as shown in Figure 3.7. Notice that we have not done this by function decomposition. We have applied event analysis to expose the next level. The process hierarchy diagram simply provides a convenient graphical index.

The process hierarchy diagram is developed.

3.4.3 "To-Be" Process Hierarchy Diagramming

Process hierarchy diagramming is again used this time to scope the proposed "To-Be" solutions at a high level. Clearly, much depends on the scale of proposed changes; for example, whether our goal is to *improve* an existing process group, such as Service and Repair Vehicles or to *reengineer* across the board, which may involve considering process elements from various existing groups with a subsequent recommendation to reorganize. In our example our goal will be the former. Whether improving or reengineering, we need to consider the possible options that will move the organization toward achieving its goals. A process hierarchy diagram reflecting the required solution is produced for a selected option. The level of detail of this model depends on the extent of the

A process hierarchy diagram helps determine the scope of the changes.

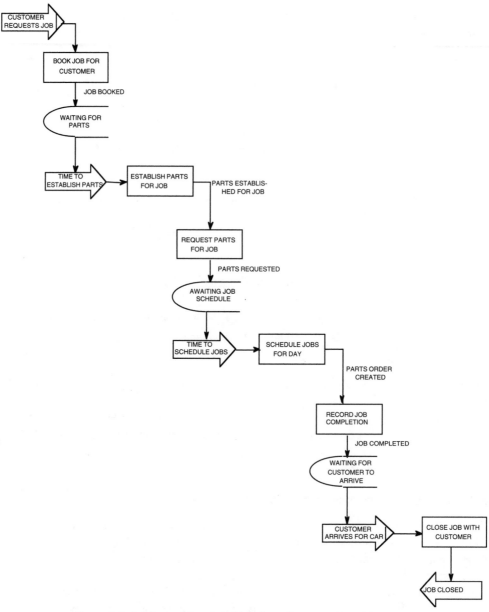

Figure 3.6. Service and Repair Vehicle "As-Is" process thread diagram.

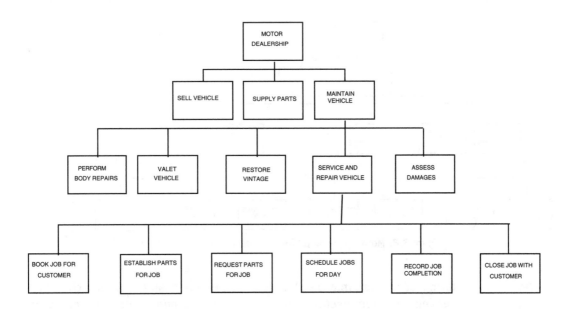

Figure 3.7. Motor Dealership extended "As-Is" process hierarchy diagram.

required change to the current business process. However, the model produced should at least be at an outline level. In our example, we note that there
is an increasing demand for a priority service for which customers are willing
to pay premium rates. This involves same-day service to alleviate pressing
problems. The Services Manager would be able to commission parts for and
schedule such jobs automatically, according to predefined algorithms. Certain
complementary tasks, such as water and battery checks would be included
and a chauffeur service would also be available as part of the deal. Let us suppose that we decide to cater for priority jobs. This results in two further EBPs:
Organize Parts and Schedule Job Item, as shown in the process hierarchy diagram in Figure 3.8.

3.4.4 "To-Be" Process Thread Diagramming

Process thread diagramming is used iteratively with process hierarchy diagramming to assess issues and possible "To-Be" solutions at a lower level. We
restrict the discussion here to diagramming techniques. However, it is important to realize that in most cases storyboarding (described below) and simulation of the process thread using relevant volumes is useful in order to highlight bottlenecks, peaks and troughs, and other problems. Process thread per-

Iteration is the
keyword.

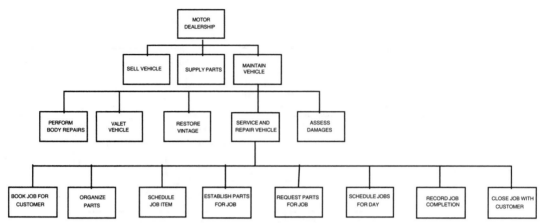

Figure 3.8. Motor Dealership "To-Be" process hierarchy diagram.

formance analysis may also be useful to measure characteristics such as processing time from event to outcome, processing and capital cost, and error rates. Such measures provide a baseline against which to assess proposed solutions.

Issues are raised.

Process thread diagramming raises issues about the necessity of any events associated with internal business actors. For each internal business event we ask "Is the event **essential**?". For example, although the interfaces with the lead mechanic and customer services clerk are probably necessary, we might question the interfaces with the parts controller. For example, could the related work carried out by the parts controller be effectively automated?

The necessity of process breaks is questioned.

We also recognize that the two EBPs Establish Parts for Job and Request Parts for Job could be combined and triggered automatically on booking a job. This removes the time delay Waiting for Parts of anything up to half a day and also removes the need for manual intervention by the parts controller in requesting parts. However, after much deliberation, it is decided to leave things as they are. This is in order to take advantage of bulk discounts and delivery procedures, by keeping the temporally triggered Establish Parts for Job. Also, complete automation of part ordering is not yet possible due to the level of human expertise needed in choosing best suppliers for specific requirements and conditions. Improvement is therefore limited to simply enhance the process thread diagram, as shown in Figure 3.9, to cater for priority jobs. Note that the EBPs Establish Parts for Job and Request Parts for Job are potentially reusable by Organize Parts.

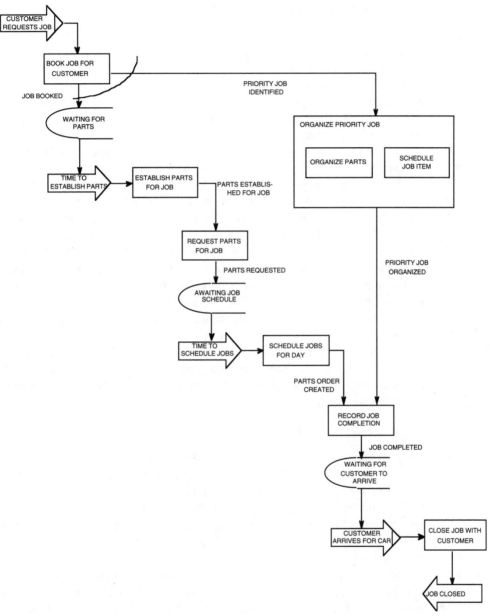

Figure 3.9. Service and Repair Vehicle "To-Be" process thread diagram.

3.4.5 Process Thread Storyboarding

Storyboarding helps
in business process
redesign.

Storyboarding provides an excellent mechanism for interactively developing the process threads and EBPs that are affected by the proposals for business improvement. A storyboard can take various forms, from simple white-board sketches to much more sophisticated simulations using different performance parameters. This approach ventilates discussion, and helps to challenge assumptions. As there are potentially thousands of scenarios within a business process, it is important to be selective and concentrate on key ones.

This is not the same
as systems analysis.

We need to consider all aspects of a business process including human interaction within the business context as well as automated activities. This is also a major difference to conventional systems analysis, which suspends judgment of how a process is to be supported by computer-based activities until after a "pure" logical model has been built. Some "how" questions have a significant impact on how the business actually works, and simply cannot be left until later. Nevertheless it is important not to become entangled in the mechanics of interface design. The principle is to get a feel for those aspects of the design that have an impact on the identification of EBPs and not to embark on detailed screen designs.

A storyboard is
constructed for the
example process
thread.

An informal picture of how we might model the standard job path through the Service and Repair process thread is shown in Figure 3.10. After much discussion we confirm the EBPs shown down the left-hand side of the diagram. (Both customer and customer-service clerk are business actors denoted by stickmen; we use a boxed stickman to denote business actors, which are internal to the business).

3.4.6 Analyzing EBPs

Each step in an EBP
represents a
potential service
need.

We address details of how a particular EBP may be carried out in terms of external and internal business actors in collaboration with services provided by a computer system. Remember, from our earlier discussions in chapters 1 and 2, that user services are key service categories within the Perspective architecture. User services integrate the user with an application to perform an EBP and emerge out of further analysis of what the system must do to support the required steps of the EBP.

It is necessary to
break each EBP into
steps.

An EBP is analyzed into sets of business activity, thinking of the system as a black box that consumes events and information and provides services. We need to keep the focus on the user's task, concentrating on chunks of business activity and taking care not to become too preoccupied with the mechanics of the user interface, which we envisage will become part of the solution: We identify the services once we have an understanding of the steps involved in an EBP.

Also it may well be the case that the same EBP is implemented using

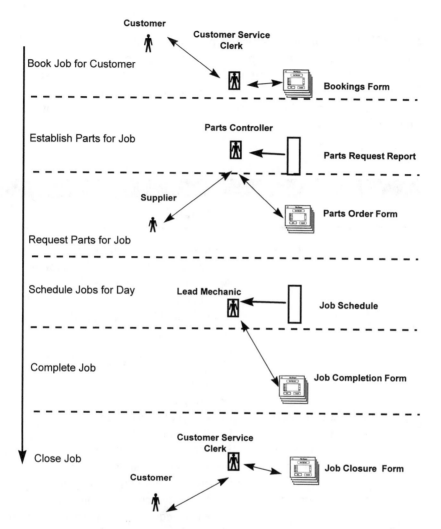

Figure 3.10. Service and Repair Vehicle storyboard.

several different user services. For example, an EBP of Provide Account Balance might be implemented using an ATM (Automatic Teller Machine) interface or a GUI PC interface (via a bank teller). Such user interfaces can change rapidly. The principle here is to provide business solutions that are insulated from changes in technology. The focus on business steps also avoids becoming embroiled in the design of the user interface before we have understood what the system is actually for in the first place.

Our analysis results in the set of EBPs, within the Service and Repair Vehicle process group, shown in Table 3.1. Preconditions and postconditions,

We keep the focus on business requirements.

Cataloging EBPs helps with reuse of services.

from EBP interdependencies, will help to govern the behavior of the services. Different EBPs might use many of the same steps but in different combinations and contexts. By cataloging EBPs we can readily harvest existing steps into new EBPs. Each step provides a potential service request, providing a foundation for service reuse that is central to Perspective and that we shall build on in succeeding chapters.

Table 3.1 Service and Repair Vehicle EBP Steps	
EBP	**EBP Step**
Book Job for Customer	Establish customer and vehicle details
	Agree on service type with customer
	Agree on repair estimates
	Standard Jobs:
	Find a suitable bay slot for the job
	Book the job
	Priority Jobs:
	Check feasibility of priority job
	Raise Priority Job
	Arrange Chauffeur
Establish Parts for Job	Identify parts needed for job
	Create part requests for job
	Produce part-requests report
Request Parts for Job	Reserve parts in stock for jobs
	Order outstanding parts for jobs
Schedule Jobs for Day	Produce jobs scheduled bill of materials
	Organize acquisition of parts for each job
Complete Job	Manage job to completion
	Record job labor
	Record service history
	Produce Highlight report
Close Job with Customer	Establish job
	Produce invoice
	Warn customer of highlights
	Receive payment for the job

In a full BPM exercise, business-task design is used to establish the exact details of EBPs. This focuses attention on two key types of interaction: between business actors (specifically between external and internal business actors) and between the business actors and services to be provided by the proposed computer system.

This is a simplified account.

3.4.7 Identifying Indirect Processes

Because indirect processes are not value-chain driven, process thread diagramming is generally much less applicable. For this reason there is a prevalent tendency to skip over this area in BPM. Nevertheless, indirect processes can and should be documented for reference and may be shown on process hierarchy diagrams. This is important for the component-based approach, as many indirect processes provide *generic requirements* for the component process, particularly in business-oriented component modeling, which is described in chapter 8; indirect processes are also an important source of business rules, which are often implemented as class invariants. Note that very often indirect processes do not change significantly from an "As-Is" to "To-Be" model. Often, therefore, these can be addressed directly as part of "To-Be" modeling.

Indirect processes are often overlooked or underestimated.

Many indirect processes have no triggering external business event. Typically indirect processes are associated with infrastructure maintenance activities (e.g., Maintain Stock) and information provision (e.g., Analyze Pricing Trends). Also nonfunctional constraints (e.g., geographical distribution of functionality, levels of performance, and availability) give rise to indirect processes (e.g., Implement Network, Monitor Utilization, etc.).

Indirect processes are often not externally triggered.

Other indirect processes have no corresponding business actor and the initiating business event will be a temporal or conditional trigger. A technique that helps in identifying indirect infrastructure processes is to consider them as the means by which the business ensures that required business rules are adhered to. The business rules could be imposed from outside (e.g., financial regulations or rules imposed for fitting of new parts) or internally imposed (maximum credit limits to manage cash flow, stock level constraints and monitoring to facilitate speed of delivery to client, etc.). Having identified the business rules, these can be translated into the associated checking processes; for example, Assess New Part Charge or Manage Stock Level. Note that the associated business rules help to shape class modeling and component modeling; often they are implemented in terms of class invariants.

Indirect processes impose business rules.

3.5 Business Processes and Component-Based Development

BPM usually arises from a compelling business need or opportunity. Often this requires software solutions to be rapidly developed. Information from BPM

The notion of a process object is not used in Perspective.

must therefore be usable in systems analysis and design and software development, with as little translation or rework as possible. Various attempts have been made (Jacobson, 1994) to model business processes as objects in order to streamline the process and ensure solutions that are rooted in business needs. Although we accept the concept of a business process viewed in terms of an object, experience on real projects has taught us that the process view is more pragmatic. This is partly because senior executives and users are simply more comfortable with the notion of process. And partly it is because any development process is always faced with the problem of how to model the boundary between the business and the software. We have found that from a practical point of view it makes more sense to "make the break" at the most natural point (between processes and objects) using a service-based approach, as shown in Figure 3.11.

Our approach views components as service providers to business processes.

Perspective views a business process in terms of layered activity, which requires services provided from within the Perspective architecture. The external business layer consists of external business actors that are "given" by definition of the business itself; examples include customers, suppliers, government departments, and competitors. The internal business layer consists of internal business actors that are part of the business and that perform roles within that business; examples include users, operators, and managers. (Strictly speaking it is *system* actors that interface with the system as described in section 4.2 and in the Glossary; however, this does not affect the principles illustrated here.) The Perspective architecture provides a set of service categories, which can be considered relative to the business, supporting actors in their role of executing business processes. Services are provided to business actors using collaborating components. The human–computer boundary is indicated by the heavy line.

EBPs provide a starting point for identifying use cases.

System use cases are essentially the ways in which users are going to use the proposed system. They will correspond to the user–system interaction parts of EBPs and exclude any interaction between users. System use cases, described in chapter 4, provide an excellent route to finding user services and business services. Components provide the enabling technology for providing these services.

3.6 Summary

This chapter has presented a simplified account of BPM techniques.

Our approach to BPM is designed to provide as smooth a transition as possible into business inspired component-based development. We have not yet addressed the BPM process, an account of which is provided in section 11.5. A business process is a family of activities that together collaborate in different event-driven groups to fulfill the business process. Groups of activities are "time-sliced" by events that denote essential constraints imposed by the business, not by technology. This allows us to identify EBPs that can act on different process threads. Process hierarchy diagrams are used mainly for presentation and indexing purposes. Process thread diagrams are the major modeling tool. The resulting EBPs provide key input to the solution process described in chapter 12. It is also important not to lose sight of indirect processes, which provide generic requirements for input to the component process discussed in chapter 13.

The EBP provides a unit of BPM that is readily translatable into use cases, as described in chapter 4. Identification of services, which integrate the user with the system, should be in support of the steps of the EBP. This provides an excellent business foundation for component-based modeling techniques centering on the reuse of services, as described throughout this book. The overall approach is summarized in Figure 3.12.

Our overall goal is to give a basis for assembling, not coding, business solutions.

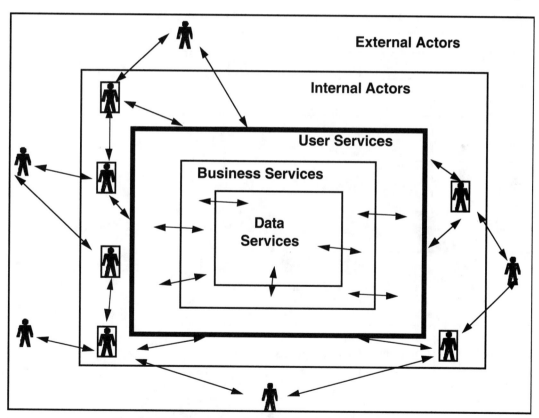

Figure 3.11 Service categories in relation to business processes.

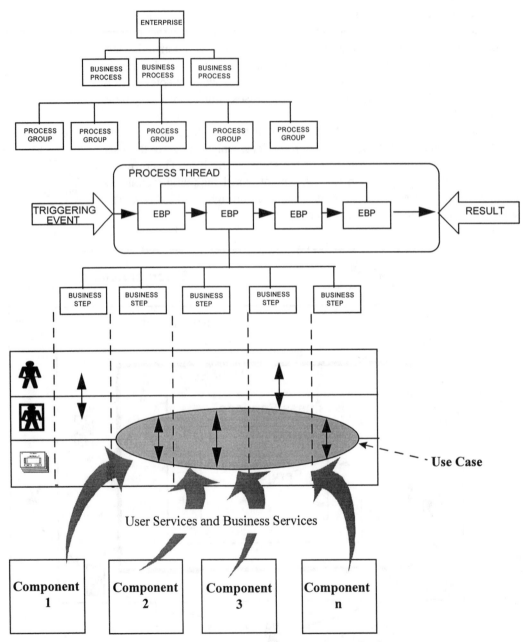

Figure 3.12. Business processes to components: Road map.

CHAPTER 4

• • • • • • • • • • • • • • • • • • • •

Use Case
Modeling

4.1 Introduction

Use case modeling has become a very popular object-oriented analysis technique, since Jacobson (1992) first published his ideas on the subject. The "nontechnical" nature of use cases allows users to participate in a way that is seldom possible using the abstractions of object modeling alone. It also helps the analyst get to grips with specific user needs before analyzing the internal mechanics of a system. Use cases also fit particularly well within an evolutionary and incremental process, such as that provided by Perspective, in that they provide a basis for early prototyping and provide a means of driving units for incremental delivery. They also provide a means of traceability for functional requirements upstream in the process and for constructing test plans downstream in the process.

> The strength of use case modeling is in its nontechnical simplicity.

    In this chapter we look at the principles behind use cases before explaining the notation to be used and describing the techniques involved. Despite the apparent simplicity and the many attractions of use cases, we have found in our work on many projects that very real problems can occur if one is not careful in understanding what are sometimes subtly different applications of the same concept. We conclude the chapter by considering the pragmatics and dangers of use cases on real-life projects with some recommendations, based on the authors' experience, for applying the technique "in the large." The reader

> However, we need to take care in applying use cases.

should note that for reasons of scope the focus of this chapter is restricted to use case *modeling* techniques. There are many closely associated activities, such as JAD, prototyping, and storyboarding, which though not considered in this chapter would nevertheless form part of the day-to-day context in which use case modeling is employed.

4.2 Use Case Modeling Principles

4.2.1 Focus of Interest

There is a need to capture a system's functional requirements before detailed design work starts.

The rationale behind use case modeling is that we should not start to work out how to design a system in detail until we have worked out what the system is for in the first place. Jacobson distinguishes two levels of use case: requirements analysis and system design. At requirements analysis a use case consists of a use case diagram plus a set of descriptions usually combined with illustrations of prototype screens. At system design a use case consists of a structured set of formal descriptions, in the form of structured language (using sequence, choice, and repetition constructs), which are placed in the left-hand margin of a sequence diagram. In Perspective the term "use case modeling" is confined to the former. We treat the latter as part of object interaction modeling (see chapter 6).

4.2.2 Key Concepts

4.2.2.1 Use Cases

Use cases are illustrative.

Jacobson (1994) describes a use case as "a behaviorally related sequence of interactions performed by an actor in a dialogue with the system to provide some measurable value to the actor." In short, use cases represent ways of using the system in terms of sets of scenarios; actors represent roles that have specific sets of responsibilities relating to use cases. A well-respected methodologist once said that use cases do not work in practice because there were too many in actual systems. His example of this was a system that had *17 million* use cases. On further investigation, it turned out that he was counting the number of possible paths through the system—otherwise known as scenarios. When it was clarified that a given scenario was an instance of a particular use case (i.e., use case is the class, scenario is the instance), it was finally agreed that the system had only 34 use cases—a much more manageable number.

Use cases are self-contained units of interaction.

In Perspective we place emphasis on treating each use case as a self contained unit of interaction with no intervening time delays imposed by the system environment. This is in contrast to some methods, which allow a use case to span several external system events (see below) resulting in over-complex use cases. Our approach helps with managing such complexity and introducing the flexibility that adaptive businesses are looking for: A family of use cases might be configured in different ways, depending on patterns of external system events, to meet the needs of a business process. An additional use case, designed to meet business competition, can be "borne into the family" and configured with other family members to provide a competitive edge.

4.2.1.2 System Actors vs. Business Actors

Business actors often correspond one to one with actors but this need not always be the case. For example, if sales took place in different ways depending on whether a sales agent took the booking using a laptop on the client's site or a sales administrator took it at the head office using a desktop, the single business actor "salesperson" could correspond to two different system actors: "sales agent" and "sales administrator." Conversely the business might work differently for permanent and temporary sales administrators, because of the different business rules involved. The two business actors could correspond to a single "sales administrator" system actor if they both played the same role with respect to the same system interface. From this point we abbreviate " system actor" to "actors" unless the context demands otherwise.

Actors of a use case are system actors as opposed to business actors.

4.2.1.3 Use Cases vs. EBPs

In the previous chapter we saw that business processes are broken down into process threads. A process thread consists of a number of EBPs. The relationship between EBP and use case is potentially many to many. In the majority of situations we have found that providing the use case granularity is correct, an EBP corresponds to one (or occasionally two or three) use cases. A use case is formed from the subset of actor–system interactions from the EBP.

EBPs provide a good basis for identifying use cases.

4.2.1.4 External System Events vs. Business Events

Use cases are triggered by *external system events*, which assume the existence of a human–computer boundary. In the previous chapter we encountered *business events* that obtain regardless of the choice of human–computer boundary and that trigger elementary business processes. A business event may give rise to a number of external system events. For example, the business event Customer orders product may give rise to a number of external system events of the form Salesperson submits order for product X, once the order has been manually interpreted prior to submission at the system boundary. Conversely, an external system event may result from a number of different business

External system events are used to help drive the use case modeling.

events. For example, the external system event Administrator submits change of address may arise in a variety of different business contexts. For more detail, see "business event" and "system event" in the Glossary and comments on identifying the right event at the right time in section 7.5.

4.2.1.5 Use Cases vs. Services

Use cases fit very well with service categories.

A use case is supported by one or more user services and business services. Despite the strong connection between use cases and user services it is important not to make the common mistake of equating the two. Table 4.1 summarizes some of the key features of each .

A use case may reuse existing user and business services.

The last row in Table 4.1 is very significant for a component-based approach such as Perspective: **a use case may reuse existing user and business services**. If existing services can be pinpointed early in the process this can represent dramatic savings in development time as well as a better quality solution based on established components. Effective component management tools therefore become a key part of the equation in facilitating early sighting of reusable services.

4.3 Use Case Modeling Notation

4.3.1.Notation Set

Our notation set is based on Unified Modeling Language (UML, 1997), shown in Figure 4.1, with some minimal enhancements, as follows:

- "Boxed" actors represent actors internal to the enterprise (for example, clerks and operators), as opposed to "unboxed" actors, which represent actors genuinely external to the enterprise (for example, customers and competitors).

Table 4.1. Use Cases vs. Services

Use Case	Service
Modeling technique	Computing capability
Incomplete: set of scenarios	Complete: working code
Partially outside system boundary	Inside system boundary
Supported by set of services	Provided through component interface
Drives incremental design	Delivered through incremental design
User focus	Design focus
Reuses services	Reuses services

• Uses and extends are modeled as dependencies, which we have found are both intuitive and semantically sound.

Note that directed associations are used for outputs to passive actors not involved in the system interactions of a use case; these are quite common, for example, a packing list is sent to a storeman as a result of a cashier recording an order. Similarly directed associations are used for inputs from external systems (for example, receiving a file transmitted over a network); however, these are rare as there is usually a need for a dialog, even if it is simply to acknowledge receipt.

Use case modeling involves building external views of the system in terms of actors and use cases. Collectively, these views, together with their underlying definitions, are referred to as the "use case model." These views can be textual or diagrammatic.

NAME	SYMBOL	DESCRIPTION
Use Case	 ⬭	A way in which an actor uses the system.
System Border	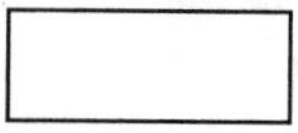 ▭	Scoping boundary for group of use cases
Two Way Association	——	Abstraction of interactions between an actor and a use case
One way Association	⟶	An information flow from a use case to an actor (or vice-versa)
Extends Relationship	Extends ⇢	Extending use case points to extended use case
Uses Relationship	Uses ⇢	Using use case points to used use case
External Actor	🧍	Actor external to the enterprise
Internal Actor	 🧍	Actor internal to the enterprise

Figure 4.1. Use case modeling notation set.

4.3.2 Diagrammatic Views

Diagrammatic views consist of use case diagrams, which employ the notation previously described, to show the *interactions* between actors and use cases and also the *structure* of use cases in terms of uses and extends relationships. Use cases are shown inside a box representing the system boundary with interactions to actors external to the boundary. Any number of use case diagrams can be used for a single system, each box representing part of the system boundary.

4.3.3 Textual Views

Textual views consist of a statement of purpose for the system, lists of actors and use cases (which also include cross-references to each other), and actor and use case descriptions (which define individual actors and use cases). The lists are sometimes referred to as the "actor catalog" and the "use case catalog," respectively.

4.4 Use Case Modeling Techniques

The essence of the exercise is to scope our project in terms of specific user requirements.

We deliberately restrict the focus to functional requirements expressed in the users' language: This counteracts the tendency that we often have as analysts to "dive in" and work out the internal mechanics of the system before we have understood what the system is meant to actually achieve. This is in contrast to traditional top-down function decomposition approaches, which result typically in very vague scopes that often lead to early project inertia and disastrous consequences. The approach can thus be pictured as very much "outside-in" as opposed to "top-down" or "bottom-up."

Once we have established what the actors and use cases are we can start to describe them.

This gives us an external view of the system: a business base, from which we can project system behavior in terms of required object collaboration. A use case is typically built up by focusing first on business requirements and then on required business services, some of which may of course be provided through existing user services. Once the use case has stabilized, a user service is often introduced (or reused) to "design" the use case.

The "black-box approach" starts from a system viewpoint.

The "black-box approach" begins with a statement of purpose, and treats the system as a black box that responds to events, triggered by actors, along various system cycles. Use cases represent different ways the actors use the black box with respect to different events. This is akin to event-partitioning approaches as described by McMenamin and Palmer (1984) and Allen (1991), as Larry Constantine observes in his introduction to Jacobson (1992): "Use case driven analysis is clearly akin to the event partitioning methods pioneered by McMenamin and Palmer."

The "business process approach" starts with EBPs produced as a result of business process modeling, which is described in the previous chapter. Use cases represent the actor–system-interaction subsets of the EBPs. Clearly the amount of work to be done here depends on the level of detail contained within the EBPs. However, we should not fool ourselves into thinking this is a mere extraction exercise: It may well be that there are many assumptions contained within the EBPs that we want to challenge as a result of our specific concern with the system interactions.

The "business process approach" starts with a set of EBPs.

If starting from a system perspective, it is useful to cast the net a little wider to examine the business context of the system in order to combat the risk of premature system design; this may well affect the scope. A key point about use cases is that, like business processes, they often cut across organizational boundaries in their mission to add value for the customer. Business processes operate "horizontally" through a company in contrast to the vertical division of labor on which traditional function decomposition approaches to business analysis are based. Each use case along the process thread should leave the system in a consistent state, which adds value to the business process. We want to partition around this feature and guard against functional partitioning. This is exactly how the black-box approach works best, by challenging and pinpointing unnecessary interfaces and time delays and applying creative thinking as to how best the system interfaces with its actors (see Figure 4.2).

The two approaches are complementary.

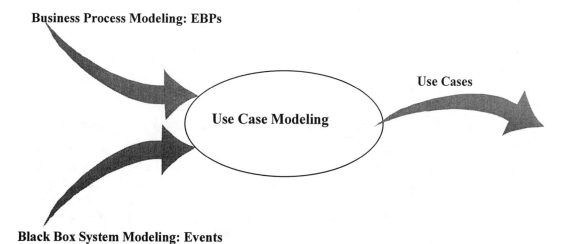

Business Process Modeling: EBPs

Use Case Modeling

Use Cases

Black Box System Modeling: Events

Figure 4.2 Different routes to use case modeling.

4.4.1 Determining the Statement of Purpose

The statement of purpose is a concise statement of rationale for the system.

The statement of purpose should answer the question "Why are we building a system?" and is intended primarily for senior management, including the visionary who acts as the driving force behind the project. The statement of purpose should be kept deliberately short (around a page maximum) and also include a list of exclusions. The reader should note that the statement of purpose would be included as part of the executive summary within a Feasibility Document (see Appendix A).

4.4.1.1 Identifying the Statement of Purpose Using a Black-Box Approach

With a black-box approach we look to the visionary for the statement of purpose.

It is important to establish the business objectives of the proposed system, as opposed to specific user goals. The former (e.g., make larger deals) may be in conflict with the latter (e.g., make as many deals as possible). We look therefore to the visionary (see chapter 14) to concentrate on how the envisaged solution meets the perceived business requirement. This minimizes the risks involved in developing a system solution for the wrong problem. The statement of purpose for an Order Shipping System, is shown in Figure 4.3.

> The purpose of the system is to provide the mechanism for recording order information and tracking the progress of orders. The system must provide the following facilities:
>
> recording of orders
> notification of packing instructions
> progressing of orders to shipment
>
> Exclusions: Inventory management.

Figure 4.3. Statement of purpose for Order Shipping System.

4.4.1.2. Identifying the Statement of Purpose Using a BPM Approach

With a BPM approach we look to the process group for which a system solution is recommended.

Again the visionary provides the driving force. However, the purpose of the supporting system is gleaned from the purpose of the process group, as documented within the business process model. We consider the goals of the proposed system in providing support for the process group. Consideration of the goals of the process group Service and Repair Vehicles might, for example, result in the statement of purpose shown in Figure 4.4.

> *The purpose of the system is to enable effective management of all aspects of the servicing-and-repair cycle from identification of appropriate jobs for customers to the closure of jobs. The system must provide the following facilities:*
>
> > *booking of jobs (both repairs and services)*
> > *parts identification and requisition*
> > *scheduling of jobs*
> > *recording of finished job details*
> > *closing of jobs*
>
> > *Both standard and priority jobs are to be supported.*
> > *Exclusions: Servicing of industrial or heavy goods vehicles.*
> > *BPM Reference: Service and Repair Vehicles*

Figure 4.4. Statement of purpose for Vehicle Servicing and Repair System.

4.4.2 Identifying Actors

We hold JAD sessions (August, 1991), as described in chapter 12, with project visionaries to elicit the actors. Sometimes actors can be found simply by reference to the statement of purpose. However, we assume we do not have that luxury.

Group dynamics are used to identify actors.

4.4.2.1 Identifying Actors Using a Black-Box Approach

Consider the statement of purpose for the Order Shipping System. We find that orders are sent for packing at predefined intervals; once packing is confirmed orders are shipped. The first question to ask is whether the customer is going to interact directly with the system or whether there is an internal user involved. In this case it is established with the business users that customers in fact request orders through sales people who are responsible for submitting orders to the system. **Salesperson** is therefore our first actor. The next question might be to ask who is responsible for packing the order. After some investigation we find that orders are to be packed by a **Stockperson** on instruction from the system. Once the orders are packed the stockperson is responsible for recording the details but not for sending the goods out to the customer. Further investigation reveals that this is done directly by the external **Shipping Agent** via an electronic link once orders are recorded as packed. We now have an initial view or "black box" (see Figure 4.5).

A useful strategy is to establish relevant responsibilities external to the system.

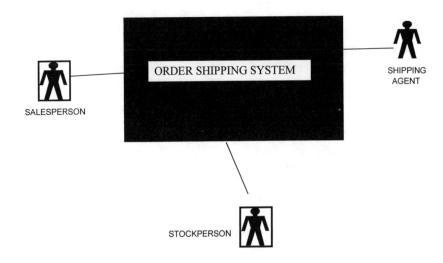

Figure 4.5. Initial black-box view of the Order Shipping System.

4.4.2.2 Identifying Actors Using a BPM Approach

The relevant
information should
be readily available.

In the previous chapter we identified business actors when we modeled the Service and Repair Vehicles process group. The business actors were: Customer and Supplier (external), Customer-Service Clerk, Parts Controller, Lead Mechanic (internal), and the system itself. We extract the actors who are to interface directly with the system: **Customer-Service Clerk, Parts Controller,** and **Lead Mechanic**. System actors can be listed as shown in Table 4.2.

4.4.3 Identifying Use Cases

4.4.3.1. Identifying Use Cases Using a Black-Box Approach

Use cases are
identified along
chains
of event-related
activity.

The system is a black box that responds to events occurring along a chain of activities, representing a typical system cycle producing some result of measurable business value. Each use case is a self-contained unit of interaction with no intervening time delays. It must be performed by a single actor in a single place, although it might result in output flows that are sent to other passive actors. The use case must also leave the system in a stable state; this may result in some measurable value to its user, which may be a measurable business value if it is the last along the chain of activities. Customers request orders, which are then sent for packing at predefined intervals. Once packing is confirmed, orders are shipped. This is triggered by an external business event (outside our system scope): Customer requests order. There are four subse-

Table 4.2. Actor Catalog for Vehicle Servicing and Repair

Actor	Description
Customer-Service Clerk	Overall responsibility for customer facing tasks related to services and repairs.
Parts Controller	Responsible for maintaining and monitoring optimum numbers of parts in relation to all potential needs.
Lead Mechanic	Responsible for day-to-day scheduling and satisfactory completion of jobs.

quent system-related events with associated use cases that occur in sequence. Note that the end result of the system cycle is some measurable business value: the customer order is satisfied.

1. Salesperson submits order.
   Providing the customer's credit is good and there are sufficient items in stock, record the order and notify the customer of acceptance or rejection.

2. Time to issue packing order.
   At the end of the day notify the stockperson to pack the order, updating the status of the order accordingly.

3. Stockperson packs order.
   Confirm that the order has been packed, notify the shipping agent to ship the order to the correct address, and update the status of the order accordingly.

4. Shipping Agent ships order.
   Record the order as shipped.

More formally we can document the system cycle in terms of a table (see Table 4.3).

4.4.3.2 Identifying Use Cases with a BPM Approach

A use case is formed from the subset of actor–system interactions from an EBP. In the previous chapter we analyzed EBPs for the process thread Service and Repair Vehicles, as shown in Table 4.4. Generally, a single use case is cre-

EBPs are used to drive identification of use cases.

Actor	System Event	Use Case
Salesperson	Salesperson submits order	Record Order
Stockperson	Time to issue packing order	Issue Packing Order
Stockperson	Stockperson packs order	Record Packed Order
Shipping Agent	Shipping Agent ships order	Record Shipment

Table 4.3. System Cycle for Order Shipping System

ated for each EBP that requires system interaction. Where the EBP is complex enough it may be analyzed in terms of more than one use case, though in our experience more than two or three suggests the EBP is probably too high level and that further analysis of EBPs is needed.

4.4.4 Creating a Use Case Diagram

Diagramming and identification of use cases are iterative.

A use case diagram for the Order Shipping System is shown in Figure 4.6. Note the output flows from use cases for showing outputs to actors from temporally triggered use cases (Issue Packing Order) and for showing outputs to actors, not actually participating in, but nevertheless interested in, the results of any type of use case (Record Packing Order). Returning to the Vehicle Servicing and Repair System, the resultant family of use cases is shown in Figure 4.7. Two use cases, Establish Parts For Job and Schedule Jobs For Day, are actually carried out by the system which produces outputs that effectively trigger subsequent use cases.

4.4.5 Describing a Use Case

Use cases must be described using "external" language.

We concentrate on describing what the actor, using the system, is doing and not describing what the system is doing! This is very important as it is part of the outside-in philosophy of the approach. The use case descriptions shown in this chapter are based on conventional narrative. A useful alternative representation, which separates user from system actions is employed in the case study in chapter 15.

Use case modeling focuses on basic courses first.

A basic course is "the most important course of events giving the best understanding of the use case. Variants of the basic course are described in alternative courses. Normally a use case has one basic course, but several alternative courses" (Jacobson, 1992). Use case modeling focuses on the basic course before addressing the alternative courses in order to limit complexity and to leverage the "80:20 rule," which is described in section 4.5.

EBP	**EBP Step**
Book Job for Customer	Establish customer and vehicle details
	Agree on service type with customer
	Agree on repair estimates
	Standard Jobs:
	Find a suitable bay slot for the job
	Book the job
	Priority Jobs:
	Check feasibility of priority job
	Raise Priority Job
	Arrange Chauffeur
Establish Parts for Job	Identify parts needed for job
	Create part requests for job
	Produce part-requests report
Request Parts for Job	Reserve parts in stock for jobs
	Order outstanding parts for jobs
Schedule Jobs for Day	Produce bill of materials for jobs
	Organize acquisition of parts for each job
Record Job Completion	Manage job to completion
	Record job labor
	Record service history
	Produce Highlight report
Close Job with Customer	Establish job
	Produce invoice
	Warn customer of highlights
	Receive payment for the job

Table 4.4. Service and Repair Vehicle EBP Steps

4.4.5.1 Describing Use Cases Using a Black-Box Approach

To describe the use cases in our "black-box" example we follow through the consequences of the related event. This usually involves white-board sketches or storyboards to elicit the information from users in JAD sessions. In the case of Record Order the related event is Salesperson submits order.

    The purpose of the use case is summarized in the intent section. The use-case description effectively talks us through the normal sequence of interactions as shown in Table 4.5. Note that the use case cannot be left "half done"; we have

Start with the basic course.

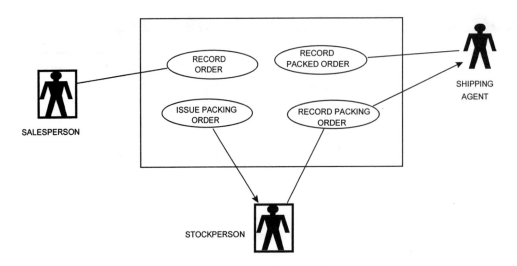

Figure 4.6. Use case diagram for Order Shipping System.

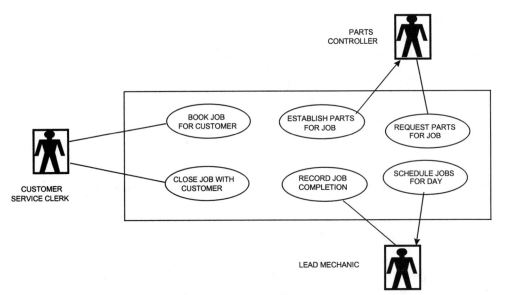

Figure 4.7. Use case diagram for Vehicle Servicing and Repair System.

Table 4.5. Use-Case Description for Record Order

Use Case Name	Record Order
Use Case Intent	To allow a salesperson to create shipping orders for customer-specified quantities of different products.

Use Case Description

1. Verify customer details
2. Check customer's credit
3. For each product ordered:
   3.1 Ensure there is sufficient stock
   3.2 Enter the details as an order line
4. Record shipping destination for the order

5. Close the order

to continue right through to closing the order, at which point the system returns to a stable state, waiting for a further event and its ensuing use case.

Questions arise concerning errors and exceptions. It is unwise to model these, as this results in a flood of use cases. We simply list such "alternative courses" at the bottom of the use case description. For example, if a service type is not available for the make and model of vehicle, the user adjusts service details from the nearest match to meet the customer's requirements.

The focus is on the mainstream requirements.

4.4.5.2 Describing a Use Case Using a BPM Approach

In describing the use cases in our BPM example we have something of a "flying start": the EBP descriptions provide a ready starting point, especially if they are phrased in terms of simple steps, as suggested in chapter 3. The EBP steps for Book Job for Customer are shown in Table 4.4.

Again start with the basic course.

Ninety percent of jobs are standard. Standard jobs therefore form our basic course and priority jobs are identified as an alternative course. A table can be used to assist in creating a use case from an EBP (see Table 4.6). The shaded rows indicate actor–system interactions. We can also use the table to have a tentative attempt at identifying likely services to support the use case. This also provides for good traceability. Book Job for Customer is described in more detail in Table 4.7. It is important to first clearly state the intent of the use case. Each business step is expanded to bring out the main intent of the actor–system interaction.

Basic course steps are analyzed.

Table 4.6. EBP Steps for Basic Course of Book Job for Customer

EBP Step	EBP Step Detail	External Actor	Internal Actor	Candidate Service
Establish customer and vehicle details	Requests to book job	Customer		
	Request customer details		C.S. Clerk	
	Supplies identification details	Customer		
	For existing customer use fuzzy list to match customer and vehicle		C.S. Clerk	Find Customer
	For new customer add customer and vehicle details		C.S. Clerk	Add Customer
Agree service type with customer	If service required find available service types		C.S. Clerk	Find Services
	Ask for confirmation		C.S. Clerk	
	Agree service requirement	Customer		
Agree repair estimates	If repair required find estimates		C.S. Clerk	Find Repairs
	Ask for confirmation		C.S. Clerk	
	Agree repair requirement	Customer		
Find a suitable bay slot for the job	Assess dates/times service bays available		C.S. Clerk	Find Bay Slots
	Agree date/time with customer for identified bay	Customer		
Book the job	Book job to include services/repairs agreed at bay		C.S. Clerk	Book Job
	Confirm job with customer	C.S. Clerk		

Table 4.7. Sample Use Case Description
for Book Job for Customer

Use Case Name	Book Job for Customer
Use Case Intent	To achieve identification of the most appropriate job to meet the customer's needs and to schedule the job at a mutually convenient time.

Use Case Description

1. Establish customer and vehicle details:

1.1 Where this is an existing customer match customer and vehicle.

1.2 For a new customer enter details to file: name and address, vehicle registration, number, make, and model.

2. Where service is required find the available service types for the make and model of vehicle.

3. Where repairs are required, find the estimated price for agreement with the customer.

4. Establish date/times service bays are available for duration of job for agreement with the customer.

5. Enter the job to include services and repairs identified, booking required bay slots.

4.4.6 Identifying User Services and Business Services

In Perspective the approach to use case description is by assembly from existing services wherever possible. This is very much in the spirit of business-inspired component reuse. One of the goals of use case modeling is to expose the need for user services and business services in a way that facilitates reuse of services. Ideally user services and business services should therefore be catalogued for ease of reference and retrieval. Component management and browsing tools (Allen & Frost, 1996) are used to assist in the identification of the candidate services. Returning to our example, we list candidate services for each use case; normally these are business services as shown in Table 4.8, though it is also pos-

Candidate reusable services are declared for each use case.

	Table 4.8. Example Services for Service and Repair Vehicles		
Use Case	**Use Case Step**	**Candidate Service**
Book Job for Customer	Establish customer and vehicle	*Add Customer, Find Customer*
	Agree on service type with customer	Find Services
	Agree on repair estimates	Find Repairs
	Standard Jobs:	
	Find a suitable bay slot	Find Bay Slots
	Book the job	Book Job
	Priority Jobs:	
	Check feasibility of priority job	
	Raise Priority Job	Book Job
	Arrange Chauffeur	
Establish Parts for Job	Identify parts needed for job	*Find Parts*
	Create part requests for job	Add Part Request
	Produce part-requests report	Report Part Requests
Request Parts for Job	Reserve parts in stock for jobs	*Reserve Part*
	Order outstanding parts for jobs	*Order Part*
Schedule Jobs for Day	Produce jobs bill of materials	*Report Jobs Bill of Materials*
	Organize parts for each job	
Record Job Completion	Manage job to completion	
	Record job labor	Modify Job
	Record service history	Add Service History
	Produce Highlight report	Report Service Highlights
Close Job with Customer	Establish job	Find Job
	Produce invoice	*Add Invoice*
	Warn customer of highlights	
	Receive payment for the job	*Record Payment*

sible to identify user services too. Those shown in italics are services that are likely to be provided from outside the context of the Service and Repair Vehicles solution, as described in chapter 8.

4.4.7 Developing User Services

Alternative courses can be modeled as use case extensions, which are potential user services. Extensions are commonly used to partition error and exception functionality as identified in the alternative courses. Normally there would be no more than one use case that was extended, otherwise a uses relationship would be used. For example, Book Priority Job was identified as an alternative course for Book Job for Customer. This can be modeled on a use case diagram as shown in Figure 4.8. Similarly, commonly used pieces of use-case functionality can be modeled with "abstract use cases," which are examples of potential *user services*. For example, Order Part might be common to both Book Job for Customer and Sell Spares to Customer as shown in Figure 4.9. Note that it is not advisable to mix these diagrams with the other diagrams (showing actors and use cases) that we have already created. This can result in a veritable jungle of a diagram with countless crossing lines.

Use case diagrams can be used to help identify user services.

4.4.8 Developing Business Services

Commonly used pieces of business functionality can also be modeled with uses use case relationships. These are examples of potential *services*. The difference between such business services and user services, which are similarly reused (as in Figure 4.9), is sometimes a fine one. A user service normally implements a significant part of a use case if not a whole use case, confers some direct business capability, and involves significant user-interface design. In contrast a business service normally only exists to support other services and is largely "black box." For example, Check Customer Details does not have a purpose in isolation from the use cases it supports, Book Job for Customer and Sell Spares to Customer, as shown on Figure 4.10. Also it is black box in that it receives a set of input parameters and returns a parameter that shows customer credit = good or bad.

Use case diagrams can also be used to help identify business services.

Another example is Find Repairs, which is common to both Book Job for Customer and Assess Body Repairs, as shown in Figure 4.11 Although Find Repairs involves using a search index typically supplied through a user object, this service has no purpose other than in the context of the use cases through which it is employed. Therefore it is considered a business service.

Business services can exhibit a user interface.

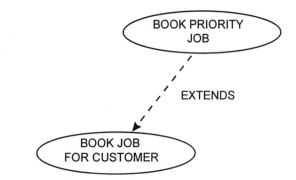

Figure 4.8 Use case extends relationship showing user service.

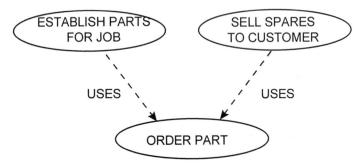

Figure 4.9. Use case uses relationship showing user service.

4.4.9 Completing the Use Case Descriptions

Each use case description, is usefully augmented using a template.

Some suggestions for augmenting the use case descriptions using a template are included here although this is not a definitive list as specific requirements are likely to vary from project to project:

- **Preconditions and postconditions:** the states of the system before and after successful execution of the use case; they correspond to process dependencies where business process modeling has been used.

- **Nonfunctional Requirements:** these include implementation constraints, such as platform and operating environment, as well as quality attributes, such as response time and mean time to repair.

- **Business Rules:** business conditions governing the behavior of the use case; this would include validation criteria. Such business rules must relate

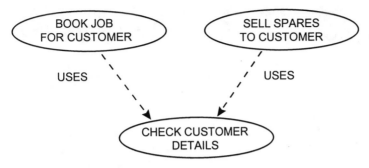

Figure 4.10 Use case uses relationship showing common "black box" business service.

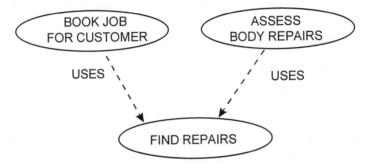

Figure 4.11. Use case uses relationship showing common interactive business service.

to the user interface. Other business rules are attributed to appropriate model items; for example, the rule "bay slots must not exceed 3 hours" is attributed as an invariant to the appropriate class (Bay Slot) in the class model.

- **Alternative Courses:** a selection of alternative courses can be listed.

- **Sample screen layouts:** Illustrations of screens associated with the use case, including sample user data where available.

A formatted example template is shown in Table 4.9.

Example links to other model items include *business requirement references, user services, business services, actor,* and *triggering event.* Business requirement references are used to ensure traceability back to the original business require-

Use cases link to other model items.

Table 4.9. Use Case Additional Information: Book Job for Customer	
Use Case Feature	**Feature Description**
Precondition	None
Postcondition	Job Booked
Nonfunctional Requirements	Response time less than 5 seconds
Business Rules	Where services and repairs are entered together, services should be booked first by default
Alternative Courses	Book Priority Job.
Example Screen	As in Figure 4.12

ment, which should exist in some form of requirements definition document. Where BPM has been used this may be included within an EBP or process-thread definition (see Table 4.10).

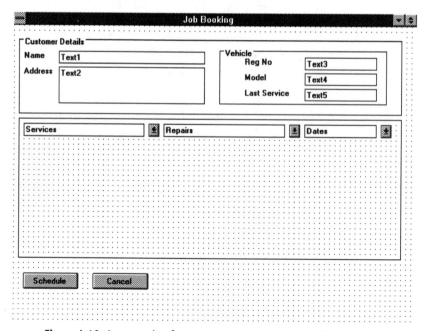

Figure 4.12. An example of a prototype screen: Book Job for Customer.

Table 4.10. Sample Use Case Cross-Reference Information: Book Job for Customer

Use Case Feature	Feature Description
Actor	Customer-Service Clerk
Triggering System Event	Customer-Service Clerk requests to book a job
Requirement Reference	BR1342
Business Process Thread	Service and Repair Vehicles
User Services	
Business services	Find Customer
	Add Customer
	Find Services
	Find Repairs
	Find Bay Slots
	Book Job

4.5 Practical Guidelines for Use Case Modeling

4.5.1 Why Bother with a Use Case Diagram?

The use case diagram may seem somewhat trivial, and there are certainly those who prefer not to bother! After all, it is argued, a use case catalog or table shows the same information in a more succinct manner. However, the diagram is often very useful in open discussions, especially scoping sessions, where we want to make it transparently obvious who (and who is not) responsible for interacting with the system. This may sometimes be a matter of some debate. We want to encourage such political issues out into the open at an early stage and not leave them to fester with possibly disastrous consequences later on, when a great deal of time and money might have been wasted. Use case diagrams have an impact at the front of specifications and tend to call the attention of senior managers who may well not be interested in the detail.

A use case diagram has a visual impact.

4.5.2 Use Case Diagram Scale

On a system of any size there may be up to 20 or more use cases that are impossible to absorb on a single diagram. We would prefer around five to nine use cases to a diagram as a rough rule of thumb. In such situations therefore it is necessary to partition the diagram. We can do this by actor or by functionality. For

Use case diagrams are usefully partitioned.

example, if there were 20 use cases in the Order Shipping System we might split into separate diagrams for Shipping Agent, Salesperson, and Stockperson. On the other hand , it is often useful to split the diagram by project, once we have decided on a development plan. However, remember that this is very much a presentation issue and indeed alternative views are possible.

4.5.3 System Scale

A manageable number of use cases on an "average" project tends to be between 10 and 20.

However, one of the authors is reminded as he writes this sentence that only last week he was working on a simple order-entry "mini" project with only 5 use cases at feasibility stage and earlier in the year on a complex project with 38 use cases. Such cases are acceptable given the relative complexity of the problem. Of major concern, however, are 200-page-long specifications of use cases that swamp the reader. If you have a such a "large" project we suggest you either partition the project or perhaps your level of granularity is too low. On the other hand, we have seen situations where the functionality of a complex system has been bundled into two or three use cases. It could just be that you have a tiny scope! More likely, however, your level of granularity is just too high.

4.5.4 Granularity

Apply the use case definition to achieve good granularity.

Granularity is the functional level of a use case. A very high level would be functions such as Purchasing and Accounting. A very low level would be specific atomic tasks such as Find Customer Address and Validate Stock Level. To find the right level of granularity for a use case we need to again consider the definition: "A behaviorally related sequence of interactions performed by an actor in a dialogue with the system to provide some measurable value to the actor" (Jacobson, 1994). There are four rules of thumb that are usefully applied with respect to this definition.

Four rules of thumb are helpful.

1. "Behaviorally related" means that the interactions as a group should be a *self-contained* unit, which is an end in itself with no intervening time delays imposed by the business.
2. The use case must be performed by a *single actor in a single place*, although it might result in output flows that are sent to other passive actors.
3. "Measurable value" means that the use case must achieve some business goal. If we cannot find a business-related *objective* for the use case then we should think again.
4. The use case must leave the system in a *stable state*; it cannot be left half done.

For example, Purchasing and Accounting would clearly fail on all four counts; Find Customer Address and Validate Stock Level fail on the first and third counts.

4.5.5 "80:20" Rule

It is important to focus on the basic courses of use cases that comprise 80% of the systems and not get entangled in the details of the more unusual cases, such as errors and exceptions. Experience teaches that on traditional projects we spend 20% of our time focusing on 80% of the system functionality, only to spend a further 80% of our time on the remaining 20%. This is witnessed by the infamous 99% syndrome of software development, whereby team members race to "nearly there" in a few weeks and then report back "nearly there" for the next few months. A key principle of Perspective is to avoid this situation and encourage rapid development of useful functionality.

The focus should be on significant functionality.

4.5.6 Applicability

Use cases apply well to systems that involve transaction or event-driven processing. They are much less well suited to batch processing, general maintenance, and management information requirements. One of the authors recounts the case of a major telecommunications company that had reached 400 use cases, with the number still rising, on one of their projects. On closer investigation it was revealed that this was a management information system involving flexible inquiries over a range of varied telephone network information. Thinking of the possible inquiries for such a system was like an open-ended shopping list! And yet the team had not even started building a class diagram, which would have provided useful insights into the required information structure.

Use case modeling is very well suited to interactive operational systems.

Although it is possible to construct use cases for such requirements there are more suitable techniques that can be employed; for example, class modeling, object-message diagramming, and prototyping. The exception to this is operational batch processing where some use cases might actually be useful, especially where the system responds to temporal events that trigger key operational reports. In other cases a single aggregate use case can be diagrammed entitled "Batch Processing," "General Maintenance," or "Management Information," as appropriate and with a general description of each included.

Less applicable requirements can be earmarked for further investigation.

4.5.7 The User Interface

A difficulty often experienced with use cases is that because they model sequences of transactions, there can be a tendency to become hung up on the mechanics of the user interface before we have really understood what the

Our approach avoids becoming embroiled in user interface design.

business requirements are. By focusing initially on cycles of business-related activity and patterns of events we help keep the intent of use cases external. We break the use case into business steps, thinking of the system as a black box that consumes events and information and provides services. Prototype screens are usefully appended to the use case description but these should be functional prototypes that bring out essential details of the interaction in terms of information and events. They should not be usability prototypes, which focus on cosmetics or ergonomics.

4.5.8 Use Cases and the Internet

Use cases can counter the risk of "throwing technology at the problem."

Increasingly, we also need to consider the use of distributed services, exemplified by the fast maturing World Wide Web, in our use cases. Intranets use the infrastructure and standards of the Internet and the World Wide Web, but are partitioned from the public Internet through software programs known as "firewalls." Applications commonly include employee manuals, user guides, company and industry news, and customer-contact information. The sophistication of this application set is maturing fast. Programming languages such as Java from Sun Microsystems provide a way of writing small software "applets" that can be zapped across the Net to perform discrete simple services such as displaying share prices or compiling an expense report. Applets and the like will become increasingly sharable as they mature from research technology to part of the fabric of day-to-day commercial applications. As this application set increases in complexity, the risk grows of "throwing technology at the problem." As Ed Yourdon points out "You need to find out what your users could *do* with the information you could provide to them on the Web. This strongly suggests of course that you actually *talk* to your users, rather than just assuming it would be "really cool" to surprise them with a hot new Web site " (Yourdon, 1995). Use case modeling provides an effective and simple means of addressing this problem, especially when combined with prototyping and iterative development. Not only is use case modeling helpful for modeling detailed workflow sequences that help develop good interface design, it also allows us to identify the services required. This also helps with control: We counteract the tendency to mushroom lots of overlapping applets, which may result in a jungle of duplication and inconsistency.

4.5.9 Keeping a Project Log

In our experience it is good practice to keep a "project log."

Use case modeling raises all sorts of questions and issues that are not always directly relevant to the subject under study, but nevertheless represent important information such as alternative courses and business rules. This can swamp a project especially in the earlier stages when we want to restrict the model to basic courses. Such items can also often fluctuate as our understanding deepens and clearly we want to avoid rework wherever possible. A "project log" provides a place to record such details, which are regularly reviewed prior to formally committing them to the model.

4.5.10 Dangers of Use Case Modeling:

Finally, we make some cautionary remarks regarding the dangers of use cases as witnessed on different projects, with suggestions for counteracting the dangers shown in Table 4.11.

Table 4.11. Sample Use Case Dangers and Countermeasures

Use Case Danger	Countermeasure
Do not cover all aspects of a system; for example, algorithmic processing, ad hoc inquiries, real-time state changes.	Apply use cases to key interactive operational requirements. Identify other types of requirement using class diagramming and object messaging to elicit system features.
Use cases lead to functional analysis if used as sole driver. This often occurs when use cases are equated with processes on a data-flow diagram, leading to functional decomposition.	Use black-box events or process threads. Use cases are a means of identifying the responsibilities of objects and we should constantly bear in mind the object-oriented architecture of the system being developed.
Difficult to assess completeness, without overcluttering.	Concentrate on 80% major requirements. Identify other 20% through incremental development.
Problem of overlapping use cases causes duplication.	Needs careful management. Identify reusable use cases and services.
Too many use cases.	Model batch processes, ad hoc inquiries, general maintenance as single aggregate use cases. Use a project log to record alternative courses.

(continued on next page)

Table 4.11. (Continued)	
Use Case Danger	**Countermeasure**
Not knowing when to stop.	Apply 80% rule. Concentrate on interactive operational requirements.
No means of identifying inter-use case dependencies.	Use pre- and postconditions.
Incremental development results in partial variant classes appearing, corresponding to use cases.	Incremental base should be complete classes not "bits of classes."
Use cases not always of equal value; planning and estimation problem.	Use cases need to be prioritized according to business importance.
Lack of formality.	Introduce standard format for use case descriptions.

4.6 Summary

The BPM and black-box approaches share a common process.

Although the BPM and black-box approaches vary in application, both share the same basic steps, namely, to

- determine the statement of purpose for the software solution,
- identify the actors,
- identify the use cases,
- create a use case diagram,
- describe the use cases,
- identify user services and business services,
- develop user services and business services,
- complete the use case descriptions.

Use case modeling is iterative.

Although this looks like a sequential list, do not be mislead into thinking that application of the techniques follows a simple sequence. The process is essentially iterative. Identify and understand the mainstream use cases before describing them in any detail and before addressing less common and alternative use cases. It is important also to understand that use case modeling and class modeling are done very much in parallel. If you get overburdened with detail in one model then switch to the other model for a fresh perspective.

CHAPTER 5

• • • • • • • • • • • • • • • • • • • •

Class Modeling

5.1 Introduction

If the use cases contain errors, then all is not lost. If the class model contains errors then all may well be lost. The quality of the resulting system in component-based development is essentially a reflection of the quality of the class model. This is because the class model sets the underlying foundation on which objects will be put to work. A quality class model should provide a flexible foundation on which systems can be assembled in component-like fashion. A poor class model results in a shaky foundation on which systems will grind to a halt and buckle under the threat of change.

Business process modeling (BPM) is the ideal forerunner to component-based development. Perspective employs business objects, insulated from the threat of changes in technology, to provide business services. This chapter therefore focuses on business class modeling, although some guidelines are also included on user class modeling, as this is a critical activity particularly in component-based development where the traditional distinction between business analysis and external design ceases to apply.

We concentrate on the more pragmatic techniques that we have found to work well on real projects. These are explained using a step-by-step guide with reference to an evolving example. Where more detail could be useful salient references to the appropriate texts are provided.

Class modeling is a key activity in component-based development.

It is important that the eventual implementation mirrors business needs.

The literature is rich with advice on class modeling.

5.2 Class Modeling Principles

5.2.1 Focus of Interest

Classes, not objects, are modeled on the class diagram.

Class modeling focuses on static system structure in terms of classes, associations, and on characteristics of classes (operations and attributes). This does not mean to say that thinking about objects is not useful in class modeling. Indeed many of the techniques stem from discovery and consideration of objects. The term "class" is used throughout this chapter unless specifically referring to objects.

Most of our attention is given to business classes

Business classes are "technically neutral" classes that provide business services to meet the needs of business processes, as described in chapter 3. Object orientation has the potential of seamless engineering of business concepts into implementation through a single representation, without the need for translation of one model to another. This is in contrast to structured approaches that are prone to "midlife-cycle crisis" as developers struggle to "convert" data-flow diagrams into structure charts. In object orientation it is the class model that forms the major vehicle for seamless engineering. The essence of the exercise in Perspective is to construct business class models that are formal reflections of business policy. Implementation classes form a "skin" around the essential "core" of business classes.

5.2.2 Key Concepts

A class is a set of objects that share a common structure and a common behavior. An object is something you can do things to. An object has state, behavior, and identity; the structure and behavior of similar objects are defined in their common class. Similarly an association between classes is an abstraction of its constituent links between objects. Classes are described in terms of attributes (data) and operations (function). An object takes attribute values for each of the attributes of the class of which the object is a member. Operations are defined once, in their class, but executable on any object which is a member of the class.

5.3 Class Modeling Notation

5.3.1 Notation Set

The class modeling notation set is shown in Figures 5.1–5.3. It is based on the Unified Method (UML, 1997), with the minimal enhancement of a "double-lined" box to represent external classes. An external class provides a reference to a class outside the project, in a separate work space. Static associations may

NAME	SYMBOL	DESCRIPTION
Class	Class Name / Attribute Name 1 / .... / Attribute Name n / Operation Name 1 / .... / Operation Name n	Class name / Attribute names (optional) / Operation names (optional)
External Class	Package Name :: / Class Name / Attribute Name 1 / .... / Attribute Name n / Operation Name 1 / .... / Operation Name n	Class name / Public attribute names (optional) / Public operation names (optional)

Figure 5.1. Class modeling: class and class.

be drawn from a class within a project to the external class. Full definitions of all the terms are included in the Glossary. The notation set is very rich particularly in the area of associations. For most practical purposes a subset or "lite" notation is adequate. The minimum required model items have their names highlighted.

Associations are assumed to be bidirectional unless specified as directed; directed association arrows represent traversal direction. Name direction shows the direction in which the association is to be read. Sometimes this is obvious and can be omitted. Each association must have a role for each end of the association. It is not necessary, however, to name the role and hence show the role on the diagram. Role names are similar to association direction names except that nouns are used instead of verbs, for example, "Controller" instead of "Controls." Use of role names and direction names on the same diagram are not recommended as this clutters the diagram with overlapping information.

5.3.2 The Class Model

Class modeling involves building structural views of the system. Collectively these views together with their underlying definitions are referred to as the "Class Model." These views can be textual or diagrammatic.

NAME	SYMBOL	DESCRIPTION
Association	————————	Static relationship between classes
Multipicity	————————— *	Any number
	————————— 1	Exactly one
	————————— 0..1	Zero or One
	————————— 1..*	One or More
	————————— X..Y	From X to Y
Name Direction	ASSOC NAME ▶ —————————	Name reads in direction of arrow
Role Name	——————— ANYCLASS ROLE NAME	Name of Association End (attached to class)
Qualifier	——————— Q.NAME ANYCLASS	Qualifier Name (boxed on to class)
Traversal Direction	——————————▶	Association traversed only in direction of arrow
N-ary Association	—◇—	Associates any number of classes

Figure 5.2. Class modeling: associations.

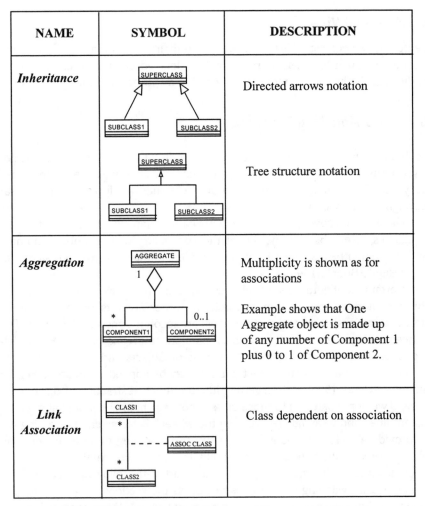

NAME	SYMBOL	DESCRIPTION
Inheritance		Directed arrows notation
		Tree structure notation
Aggregation		Multiplicity is shown as for associations
		Example shows that One Aggregate object is made up of any number of Component 1 plus 0 to 1 of Component 2.
Link Association		Class dependent on association

Figure 5.3. Class modeling: association constructs.

5.3.3 Diagrammatic Views

Diagrammatic views consist of class diagrams, which employ the notation shown in Figures 5.1–5.3, to show classes, their associations, and the various association constructs. All associations on class diagrams are static. Any number of class diagrams can be used for a single system. Examples can be found throughout this chapter.

5.3.4 Textual Views

Textual views consist of lists of classes and their associations, attributes, and operations. Such lists can be more or less detailed depending on the target audience. The lists are sometimes referred to as the "class catalog."

5.4 Class Modeling Techniques

We adopt a broad-based approach.

Techniques can be mixed and matched according to your own needs, including your user's perspective. Mainstream techniques that we have found practically useful are included in this section. References to further work appear throughout this section.

Discovery generally precedes abstraction.

Generally discovery of classes occurs earlier than invention or abstraction of classes; "Key abstractions reflect the vocabulary of the problem domain and may either be discovered from the problem domain, or invented as part of the design" (Booch, 1994).

Patterns should be applied to help graduate from discovery to abstraction.

Certain configurations of classes typically recur as common themes throughout development. For example, an order consists of order lines, a transaction consists of transaction lines, an account consists of entries. The concept of a *pattern* is built on this simple concept: reuse of the best modeling ideas. Patterns are "reusable templates of objects and associations with stereotypical characteristics; the template may be applied again and again by analogy" (Coad, 1995). Before getting into too much abstraction of discovered classes we apply patterns to those classes both to channel thinking along consistent lines and to avoid "reinventing the wheel." Patterns can be catalogued to provide a "reference book" to assist in the modeling process. In the long term an organization should look to build its own pattern catalog.

The techniques sections are arranged in increasing levels of abstraction.

The discovery techniques appear at the start of the following sections, with the emphasis switching more to abstraction as the sections progress. The discovery techniques are best applied using interactive JAD sessions with users, which will include regular reviews. Abstraction techniques are often best approached using smaller groups of analysts and designers. Detailed documentation is usually best applied in isolation for subsequent review by a JAD group.

5.4.1 Discovering Classes

There are two basic strategies for discovering classes.

The two basic strategies for discovering classes are business-semantics driven and service driven. A balanced approach works best as excessive reliance on either approach leads to a distorted model.

The **business-semantics driven approach** is ubiquitous in the literature (Booch, 1994; Coad-Yourdon, 1991; Coleman, 1994; Shlaer-Mellor, 1988).

Business requirements statements are analyzed for nouns, particularly collective singular nouns. The nouns provide candidate classes or attributes. A potential hazard with this approach is that because of the emphasis on attributes it is very easy to end up with a relational data model dressed as a class model.

The business-semantics-driven approach looks for business concepts.

The **service-driven approach** echoes much of the criteria used in the responsibility-driven approach, which is most eloquently described in the work of Rebecca Wirfs-Brock (1991) and more recently in Lorenz (1993). Candidate classes should provide cohesive sets of services with minimal interfaces. The approach is often used in conjunction with a method of documenting objects known as class-responsibility-collaborator cards (CRC cards), originally introduced and developed by Kent Beck and Ward Cunningham (Beck, 1993; Beck & Cunningham, 1989). The CRC approach lends itself well to an interactive JAD-like approach, as described in Wilkinson (1995). Identifying the responsibility of an object is another way of asking what functions it performs. This often leads to discovery of operations on existing classes as well as discovery of new classes to provide the services. The focus on functions leads one to focus on verbs in a business requirements statement, rather than nouns, and is very useful for identifying operations. A potential hazard with this approach is that because of the emphasis on operations it is very easy to end up with a functional model dressed as a class model.

The service-driven approach asks what business services are required.

Associations, like operations, can be found by looking for verbs in source documents. Whereas operations reflect required functionality, associations reflect required structural relationships between classes. Associations can also be found by considering all combinations of pairs of classes and asking if a meaningful relationship exists between the two.

Associations identify good paths for communication between objects.

Two of the most useful sources are use cases and event patterns, which are discussed in the next section. A final word of caution: Do not restrict yourself to a pure grammatical analysis, otherwise you will end up swamped with classes. It is important to apply the definition of a class carefully and to check for genuine semantic significance within the business domain.

The base techniques should be applied pragmatically.

5.4.2 Examining Use Cases for Classes

Let us return to the use case description for Book Standard Job for Customer, which is shown in Table 5.1. First we apply the business-semantics approach to the text, searching for nouns that represent key business concepts having significant meaning within the business domain and fulfilling the definitions of class and object. Semantic analysis of the system use cases suggests the following candidates: Customer, Vehicle, Service, Repair, Job, Bay. They are important concepts in their own right about which information could be kept

The business semantics approach is applied to use cases.

Table 5.1. Sample Use Case Description: Book Standard Job for Customer

Use Case Name	Book Standard Job for Customer

Use Case Description

1. Establish customer and vehicle details:
   1.1 Where this is an existing customer match customer and vehicle.
   1.2 For a new customer enter details to file: name and address, vehicle registration, number, make, and model.

2. Where a service is required find the available service types for the make and model of vehicle.

3. Where repairs are required, estimate the price for agreement with the customer.

4. Establish date/times service bays are available for duration of job for agreement with the customer.

5. Enter the job to include services and repairs identified, booking required bay slots.

and from which services could be provided. Name and Address looks like an attribute of Customer; Vehicle Registration Number, Make, Model are probably attributes of Vehicle; Service Type looks like an attribute of Service; Bay Slot looks like an attribute of Bay. There are no explicit associations but it is noted, for verification with the user, that a customer *owns* a vehicle and a bay *is booked for* a job. Also by implication a vehicle *receives* a job and job *involves* either or both a *service* or *repair*.

The service-driven approach is applied to use cases.

The second strategy is to examine the use cases for verbs that suggest particular objects that might be appropriate business service providers. If the use case is formatted along the lines suggested in chapter 4, business services will be conveniently listed for each use case. The extracted business services for the example given in Table 5.1 are shown in Table 5.2. Do we have a candidate class for each business service? Actually in this case we do, from our earlier analysis. Each business service will correspond to an operation on the classes shown.

We might have modeled some of the verbs directly as new classes.

Table 5.2. Business Services of Book Standard Job
for Customer

Business Service	Feature Description
Find Customer	Customer, Vehicle
Add Customer	Customer
Find Services	Service
Find Repairs	Repair
Find Bay Slots	Bay
Book Job	Job

Sometimes this can work well. However, care is needed. In this case this turns out to be a bad idea, as we shall explain. For example, we might have chosen to introduce a Scheduler class to book jobs. Scheduler objects would have to message Bayslot (to ensure there was an available slot) and Job (to set up the job details). Also, Bay Slots might be scheduled for tasks other than Jobs. It is more in the spirit of the responsibility-driven approach to allocate business services such that coupling between objects is minimized and to ensure that the business service is localized to its subject matter. In the example, Scheduler may well end up as a collection of dissimilar behaviors (Book Job, Schedule Bay Slot, Schedule Work Tasks...Book Holidays!) disguised under the banner of commonality. The trap here is the same trap that analysts following functional decomposition have fallen into many times during the past.

Particular care is needed with the service-driven approach.

Finally in the example given in Table 5.2 most business services have been allocated to existing classes: Each class has a responsibility to provide the required business service although it may need to message other classes to ful-fill that responsibility. However, this is very often not the case. A special type of control class known as a *service class* can be introduced to provide services that do not sit comfortably within any of the existing business classes. Control classes, which do not appear on a class diagram, are discussed in chapter 6 and service classes are covered in chapter 8.

Note: Service classes are critically important!

5.4.3 Examining Events for Classes

The event-driven approach to finding classes centers on how objects commu-nicate, and in particular on how they communicate with the outside world. This is particularly applicable to real-time systems where the natural focus is on messages, signals, and interrupts. Essentially the system is pictured as a set of objects that collaborate through event passing. Each set of collaborations is

Events form a rich source of classes, operations, attribut-es, and associations.

Business events can
be used to drive
class modeling
directly.

a response to an event occurring in a different pattern of events and life cycles. Such an approach is exemplified in Shlaer and Mellor (1992). Others (Page-Jones, 1995; Yourdon, 1995) also emphasize the importance of events.

Business events from business process modeling can be used to help identify classes as well as use cases. Table 5.3 shows a typical pattern of events that occurs in the Service and Repair Vehicles business process. Analysis of business events suggests the following further candidate classes: Customer-Services Clerk, Part, Parts Controller, Part Request, and Lead Mechanic. Customer-Service Clerk, Parts Controller, and Lead Mechanic can be discounted because, although key actors, they provide no services or information. This leaves the candidate classes, Part and Part Request, and the implied association Part Request *requests* Part. It is further supposed that additional analysis of individual use cases leads to the discovery of business services Allocate (on Part Request) and Order (on Part).

5.4.4 Creating a First-Cut Class Diagram

A first-cut class diagram is created as shown in Figure 5.4. Note that only a single use case and a single chain of events has been examined in detail. The exam-

Table 5.3. Service and Repair Vehicle: Events and EBPs

Event No.	Event Type	Event name	EPB
1	External Business	Customer asks customer-service clerk to book a job	Book Job for Customer
2	Temporal	Time to establish parts for job	Establish Parts for Job
3	Internal Business	Parts controller submits parts request	Request Parts for Job Parts Request
4	Temporal	Time to schedule jobs for day	Schedule Jobs for Day
5	Internal Business	Lead mechanic completes job	Record Job Completion
6	External Business	Customer arrives to collect serviced car	Close Job with Customer

ple is deliberately simplified to illustrate the basic techniques. Also it is generally useful to suppress basic housekeeping operations such as get and set for attributes and create/read/update/delete for classes. Unless specifically identified as a service request from a use case, such operations are treated as implied.

A first-cut class diagram is created.

A common *problem* with class modeling is the discovery of too many classes, especially if grammatical analysis is applied too naively, for example, by making every noun into a class. Sometimes a "more is better" mentality can lead analysts to naively create many classes that do not merit existence. It is better to concentrate on business semantics and responsibilities and apply the definition of class carefully. Notice, for example, that each class in Figure 5.4 at least has one clear responsibility. Further checklists to assist are provided at the end of chapter.

Each class should have at least one clear responsibility.

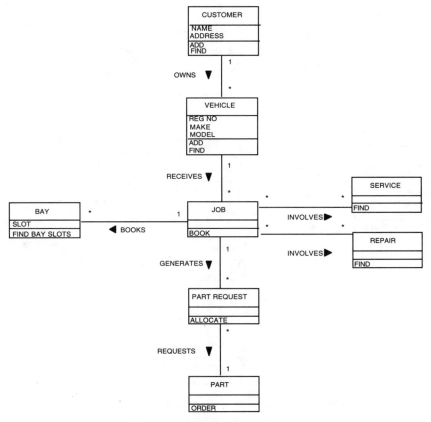

Figure 5.4. First-cut class diagram.

5.4.5 Developing a First-Cut Class Diagram using Attributes and Operations

Further attributes
and operations are
added to the
diagram.

A JAD session helps identify attributes for Part, Part Request, Job, Service, and Repair (see Figure 5.5). Further attributes are identified for Bay. A Job Type attribute is added to distinguish standard and priority jobs. An additional operation on Part is Reserve Parts, which services part requests. Many operations also arise as a result of object interaction modeling, as described in chapter 6.

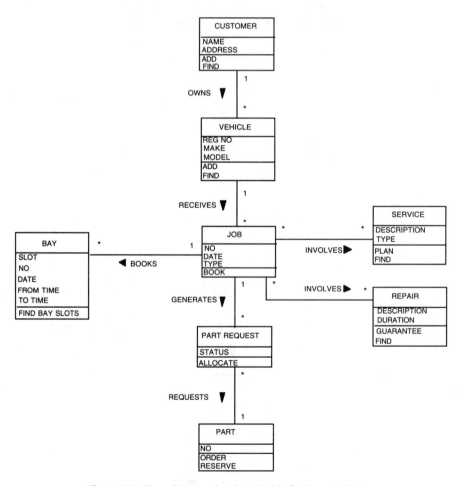

Figure 5.5. Class diagram developed with further attributes and operations.

5.4.6 Applying Patterns to Develop the Class Diagram

Patterns continue to receive much attention in the literature. We only touch on their use here; the reader is referred to Coad (1995) and Fowler (1997) for detailed accounts of their use in analysis. In chapter 8 we return to the subject of patterns for developing reusable enterprise components. For the present purpose of developing an initial class diagram, patterns are extremely useful because they provide common solutions to problems in specific contexts.

Patterns can be applied repeatedly by analogy alongside the other techniques.

Once an initial understanding of classes, attributes, and operations has been built up, patterns are very useful to fashion the initial class diagram along consistent lines. This should not be done "blindly," it should be done in harmony with consideration of business policy, as depicted in Figure 5.6. The patterns applied here are from Coad (1995).

It is important not to apply patterns prematurely.

First, closer inspection reveals that make and model are more correctly attributed to a separate class: Model. The Model class is interesting in its own right because part of the booking process involves finding out which tasks (services or repairs) are appropriate for a particular model of vehicle. Another point is that there can be many vehicles classified under one model, and maintenance of model details is best localized to one class; we do not want to have to change every vehicle of a particular model if the model details change. Therefore a Model class is introduced.

The "Item-Specific Item" pattern is applied.

A second issue concerns user policy regarding scheduling of bays. Business process modeling has revealed the need to organize bay usage around bay slots, which have scheduled start and end times. It is therefore decided to split out the bay, which can have a number of bay slots and, and create a new Bay Slot class to do its own work (i.e., schedule itself) and keep its own information (i.e., date, from time and to time). Job–Bay is an example of the "Plan–Plan Execution" pattern. Bay–Bay Slot is an example of the "Place–Transaction Execution" pattern.

Two Execution patterns are applied.

A third point is that there are standard services and repairs for different models of car. The users would like to be able to reference this as standard information. Model–Service and Model–Repair are examples of the "Associate–Other Associate" pattern. Other patterns are as follows:

The "Associate–Other Associate" pattern is applied.

- Job-Service and Job-Repair are examples of the "Plan–Plan Step" pattern.
- Customer–Vehicle is an example of the "Associate–Other Associate" pattern.
- Vehicle–Job is an example of the "Participant–Transaction" pattern.
- Job–Part Request is an example of the "Transaction–Subsequent Transaction" pattern.
- Part–Part Request is an example of the "Specific Item–Transaction" pattern.

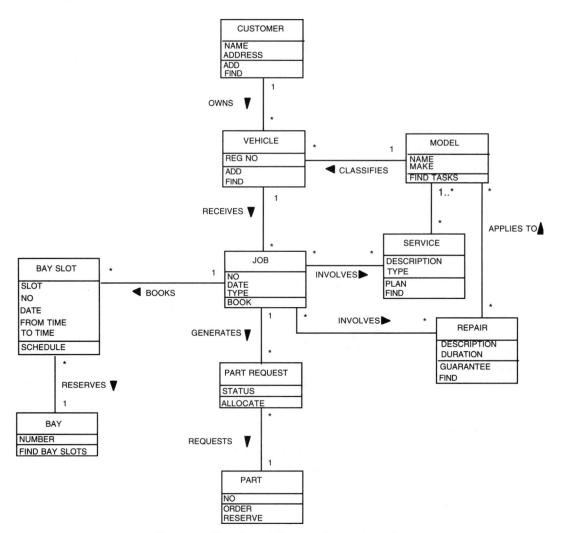

Figure 5.6. Class diagram (after applying patterns).

5.4.7 Using Association Classes

Associations can be classes.

Where an association has operations or attributes, a class can be introduced to model the dependency of these characteristics on the association itself. Such an "association class" has no separate existence apart from the association. Often such associations are many to many. For example, the association

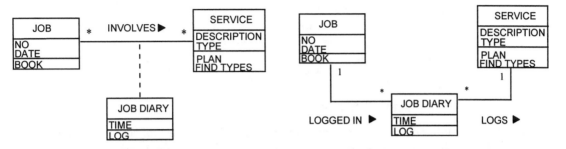

Figure 5.7. Association class example alternative notations.

between job and service might "hide" the fact that it is necessary to record the time the service was completed for the job and the fact that it is important to keep a diary of the service. An association class Job Diary can be used to hold a time attribute and provide a diary of the operation, as shown in Figure 5.7(a).

The above situation could have been modeled by treating Job Diary as a straightforward class and introducing two one-to-many associations from the original classes to the new class as shown in Figure 5.7 (b). One argument is that this solves the problem without the need for new notation and hence is a simpler representation; also the association class is, in any case, not directly implementable without such resolution. The counter to this is that the association class is more semantically accurate as it is essentially a property of the association. The authors' experiences suggest that for all practical purposes association classes are something of an academic luxury. However, we also recognize that association classes do have their adherents. We leave it to the reader to make up his or her own mind about whether or not to use association classes. As far as notation is concerned it is clearly necessary to standardize one way or the other. To have some teams using association classes and others not using them is a recipe for confusion.

Each association should be examined to see if it is in fact a class. Ask if it provides services and whether there is information that applies to it. Be especially wary of many-to-many associations, as they often hide information. Such information often takes the form of temporal attributes, such as start and end dates. Therefore ask if the association is relevant over time. Do not, however, introduce classes that are equivalent to relational link tables with concatenation of foreign keys. The new class must be semantically meaningful in a business context. Therefore look for semantically valid names. For example, the many-to-many association between Job and

The organization should standardize one way or the other on notation.

The important point is to apply the thinking that comes with association classes.

Service might have been factored into a class Job-Service containing the identifiers (as foreign keys) of Job and Service, in the manner of a relational join table. This would not be a valid approach as reflected in the artificial, hyphenated join name. However, Job Diary is valid because it reflects business semantics; that is, the need to keep a diary of the time it took to perform a service as part of a job.

5.4.8 Using Inheritance

Inheritance centers on the activity of classification.

Inheritance is a mechanism that permits classes to share characteristics through a tree-structure association between a superclass (which contains common characteristics) and its subclasses (which contain the specific characteristics); subclasses are said to inherit characteristics of the superclass. It is important to understand that inheritance operates at the class level and not the object level. It is worth remembering that a **single** object is classified in many different ways within an inheritance structure; there are not separate objects for each class within the structure.

We take a pragmatic approach to inheritance.

In the spirit of Perspective rather than dwell on the theory often associated with inheritance we explain the most important aspects for practical project use. Because it is such a centrally important topic the more pressing issues are discussed at some length. In particular a good understanding of inheritance, is vitally important in subclassing from hierarchies in generic models in analogous fashion to framework refinement. However, we recognize that for reasons of scope we are only able to treat the tip of the iceberg, and provide salient references to the useful discussions throughout this section.

The following situation requires modeling.

Services and repairs both have a description and can provide a find service. Additionally it is found that both can have a base price. However, services, unlike repairs, additionally have a type and can be planned. Services also have an associated mileage that does not apply to repairs. Also repairs, unlike services, have an average duration and can provide a guarantee. We would like to define the common characteristics just once and then add details for service and repair. Figure 5.8 shows how this policy can be modeled using inheritance.

It is important to understand the basis for modeling inheritance.

Task is introduced as a superclass of Service and Repair, which are both subclasses of Task. The inheritance itself is represented by the unfilled triangle, which points up to the superclass. The superclass is said to "generalize" the subclasses, which in turn are said to "specialize" the superclass. The triangle represents the basis on which the generalization/specialization is made; this is documented as a "discriminator," which describes the business relevance of the specialization. In the example, Service and Repair are discrimi-

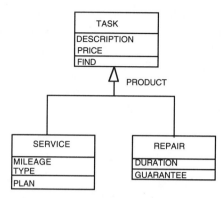

Figure 5.8. Example of Inheritance.

nated on the basis of product; the discriminator "Product" is shown next to the arrow. The following constraints (UML, 1997) can be applied: overlapping, disjoint, complete, and incomplete. This is an example of subclasses, which are disjoint (a task cannot be both a service and a repair) and complete (there are no further subclasses within the specialization).

Specialization involves examining a particular class for different ways in which its member objects can be split into subclasses, which have their own specific characteristics. Generalization involves searching for different classes that have some characteristics in common and grouping those characteristics into a superclass. In Figure 5.8 we used generalization to abstract common characteristics of services and repairs into a task superclass.

Inheritance can be approached in two ways.

For example, Service might be specialized into Gold Service and Standard Service on the basis of quality, should there be sufficient special characteristics of those subclasses. A Gold Service would inherit characteristics of Service and transitively it would inherit characteristics of Task.

Inheritance is transitive across many levels.

5.4.8.1 Adding Subclasses to the Inheritance Hierarchy

There can be any number of subclasses that specialize a superclass, although again it is important to limit "fan out" and also the depth of the inheritance hierarchy, as described in section 5.5. We might choose to add the subclass Valet on the basis that there are different levels of valet (one star to five star) and that valets, unlike other types of task, can be contracted out to external suppliers (see Figure 5.9).

Subclasses can be added.

5.4.8.2 Using Inheritance to Simplify the Class Diagram

The class model can be simplified by abstracting separate identical associa-

Subclasses also
inherit the
associations,
of the superclass.

tions from the subclasses to single common associations from the superclass. For example, the two associations from Job Diary to Repair and from Job Diary to Service are both "involves" associations. Figure 5.10 shows these are abstracted into a single association between Job and Task.

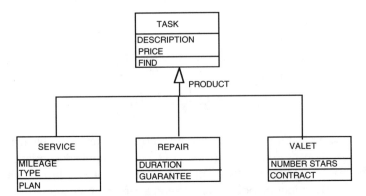

Figure 5.9. Adding a subclass to an inheritance hierarchy.

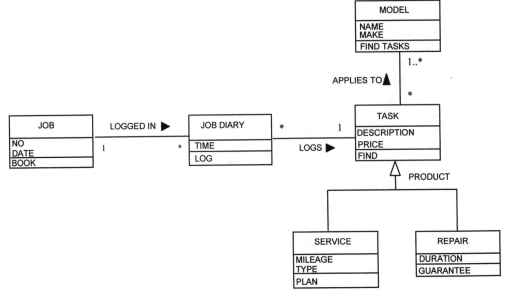

Figure 5.10. Abstracting associations to a superclass.

5.4.8.3 Dealing with Parallel Inheritance

Suppose, for example, that we are also interested in the degree of difficulty associated with tasks. We might further classify tasks into easy, average, and complex as shown in Figure 5.11. This is sometimes referred to as parallel inheritance and can sometimes be usefully applied to central classes that can be viewed from multiple dimensions.

A class can be specialized in multiple ways.

In this case we chose not to add the further hierarchy because the candidate subclasses do not have any attributes or operations of their own. This illustrates a fundamental point about inheritance. It is always possible to think of many different ways of introducing inheritance into the model; a cake after all can be cut in multiple ways. However, like most powerful concepts, inheritance should be used sparingly.

If in doubt, keep it simple.

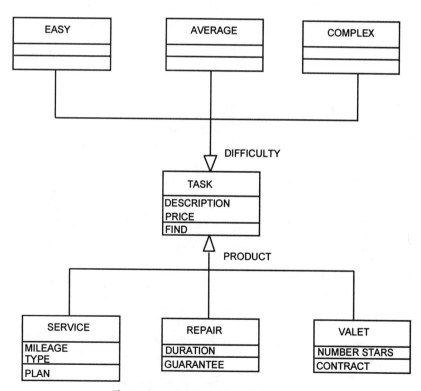

Figure 5.11. Example of parallel inheritance.

5.4.8.4 Dealing with Multiple Inheritance

A class can inherit from more than one superclass.

Suppose there is a special type of service that allows a valet to be included at a discount rate. We might introduce a new class, Valet Service, to inherit from both Service and Valet as shown in Figure 5.12. Note that this implies that subclasses within the Task generalization are overlapping.

We caution against the use of multiple inheritance.

Multiple inheritance is often a clumsy way of modeling inclusive hierarchies, which introduces unnecessary complexity and leads to designs that are difficult to maintain. This is reflected in the absence of characteristics of Valet Service and the use of the artificial discriminator "usage" for the Valet generalization.

Multiple inheritance can always be avoided.

A common strategy is to introduce roles as aggregate parts of the original superclass and specialize the role class accordingly, as shown in Figure 5.13. Aggregation is discussed in the next section. Although this could be criticized on the basis that the role class is a pure abstraction without business significance, the big advantage of this technique is that it is much more flexible in the face of change: it is far easier to introduce a further role subclass than to introduce a subclass that inherits from several superclasses. There are many

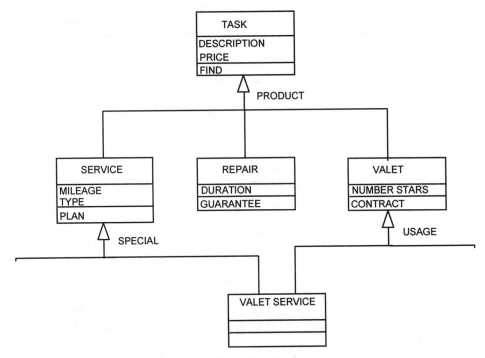

Figure 5.12. Example of multiple inheritance.

other techniques that can be used to combat multiple inheritance; the reader is referred to Rumbaugh (1991), but remember: no technique is perfect.

5.4.8.5 Using Abstract Classes

An abstract class allows behavior common to a variety of classes to be factored out in one place, where it can be defined once, and reused repeatedly. Task Role, as shown in Figure 5.13, is an example of an abstract class. All the objects belong to subclasses. As abstract classes are used solely for inheritance, definitions in an abstract class do not have to be complete. Definitions are supplied in the subclasses, which inherit from the superclass. Abstract classes are often used to implement polymorphism. For example, suppose services and repairs both involved calculations of time taken based on different algorithms. A Calculate operation might be introduced in each subclass, implemented by a different method for each algorithm. An abstract Calculate operation is introduced in the Task Role class. This operation has the same interface (or "signature") as in the subclasses. A calling object that is required to calculate time does not need to know the implementation: it simply asks Task Role to calculate.

An abstract class is a class without objects.

5.4.8.6 Overall Inheritance Guidelines

Inheritance has an important influence on future reusability of the design and robustness in the face of change. For example, if an operation is altered or introduced to a class, what is the impact of this on classes that inherit the operation? If the inheritance hierarchy is a good one, there should be little "ripple

Building good inheritance hierarchies is a key activity.

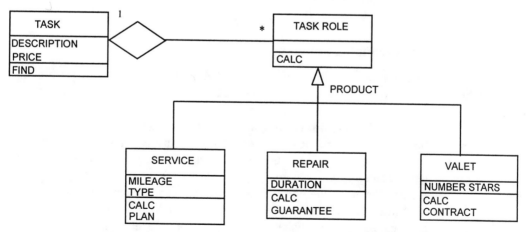

Figure 5.13. Using aggregation of roles to avoid multiple inheritance.

effect." Conversely, if the inheritance hierarchy is badly modeled the ripple effect could be far reaching and expensive to deal with.

Changing the structure of the class model, for example, by adding a new class, is akin to changing the geography of the map by adding a new road. The idea is to localize change without changing the geography. Inheritance offers a way of building change into the road map with a minimum of impact, for example, by adding new subclasses that inherit the behavior of existing superclasses. However, if changes are made to a superclass, subclasses inheriting from the superclass are also affected. Therefore, in an important sense, inheritance violates the principle of encapsulation. This means that care needs to be taken in identifying stable superclasses.

Superclasses need to be especially resilient.

Particular care is needed where a subclass is introduced solely as a mechanism to reuse another definition, without consideration of shared semantics or substitutability. This is sometimes known as "implementation inheritance" an example of which would be the definition of Binary File as a subclass of ASCII File simply because it was convenient to reuse some of the definition implemented for ASCII File. There is now almost universal consensus that this type of inheritance should be avoided. It is ultimately an abuse of inheritance, which is likely to return to haunt developers when further maintenance is required or when the inheritance hierarchy needs extending for semantically valid reasons.

Implementation inheritance should be avoided.

Finally, the guiding principle in using inheritance is that the semantics of inheritance hierarchies must be clear. This means that the criteria used as the basis of an inheritance structure must be clearly communicated through the discriminator. For further guidelines the reader is referred to Yourdon (1995) and Page-Jones (1995).

An inheritance hierarchy should be a formal reflection of business needs.

5.4.9 Using Aggregation

Aggregation is used to model whole-part relationships between objects.

Aggregation centers on the activity of **decomposition**. An aggregate object is said to contain component objects. It is important to understand that aggregation operates at the object level, unlike inheritance, which operates at the class level. Confusion often arises between aggregation and inheritance because both are modeled as trees through transitive closure. An aggregation tree is composed of objects that are part of an aggregate object, whereas a generalization tree is composed of classes that describe a single object. Aggregates are made up of objects belonging to different classes as depicted in Figure 5.14. A diamond is placed adjacent to the class representing the aggregate object; a vehicle is composed of one engine, one chassis, four wheels, and any number of interior components and exterior components.

It is also possible to use aggregation to model conceptual composition. Note further that an object can be contained within more than one parent aggregate object. For example, a service is composed of any number of activities. Each activity may be part of more than one task (see Figure 5.15).

> Aggregation does not have to operate at the physical level.

Aggregates allow us to bring together different objects in a manner, which makes those objects appear externally as a single object. An operation on the aggregate can be propagated to its constituent objects. For example, a copy operation on a document could be propagated such that its constituent paragraphs and graphics are also copied.

> Propagation is a powerful feature of aggregation.

Aggregation is a common technique in manufacturing applications for modeling parts explosions. However, in more general terms, when is it useful to employ aggregation? First it is important to understand that aggregation is a flavor of association, but unlike inheritance it is not an independent concept. Therefore guidelines are needed for when to actually use aggregation as opposed to a association. It is seldom a clear-cut decision and it is often a matter of some discretion. However, some criteria follow:

> The difference between an aggregate and an association is often one of degree.

- the components are essentially part of the aggregate object.
- the aggregate object is often used as a whole, together with its components.

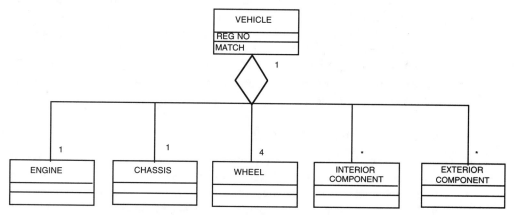

Figure 5.14. An example of aggregation.

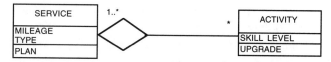

Figure 5.15. An example of many-to-many aggregation.

• there is propagation of operations and attributes from the aggregate object to its components.

5.4.10 Harvesting Business Services

Business services can be reused by the class model being developed.

An external class is used to declare a class external to the project that is to be used within the model under development. Clearly good component management facilities (Allen & Frost, 1996) are essential for identifying such classes, which may be implemented as interfaces of components, as described in chapter 8. In our example it is found that Part is in fact a class that can be readily reused from the Parts Inventory package. This is shown in Figure 5.16, which also reflects the changes made as a result of thinking about inheritance and aggregation, that were discussed previously.

5.4.11 Sowing Business Services

As classes mature, they become candidates for engineering as components.

In Figure 5.16 it is noted that Model, Task, and Activity are possible components. All these classes cluster around the enterprise theme of work breakdown. They are reference classes which might provide business services across a range of applications. We return to develop these classes in chapter 8. Both Model and Task appear as external classes within the class diagram shown in Figure 5.17. Also note that the association between Model and Task has apparently disappeared. Also, Task's subclasses and the aggregation of Activities are no longer present. This is because for the purposes of the local class diagram it is not necessary to know this. The public interfaces of Model and Task are quite sufficient. In line with the principle of encapsulation, it is not necessary to know "what goes on behind the scenes."

5.4.12 Modeling User Classes

We need to decide on how much emphasis to place on user class modeling.

We have seen in chapter 2 that user classes provide user services; they sit on the boundary between business services and users. However, as yet we have said little about user classes. In fact the literature as a whole offers little advice in this area. On many recent projects we have encountered a negative view of user class modeling. Common reactions to the idea include the following:

• Why should we bother when our interface is changing as a result of user feedback from prototyping sessions; as soon as we document user objects in the model they change again.
• Providing we get our interfaces to the business classes right, user interface modeling is an academic waste of time; a well-designed set of business objects should be "pluggable" into any user interface.
• We are using a rapid development approach and simply have not got time.

Certainly, Perspective is a light-weight approach that advocates using prototyping tools to establish not only the user interface, but also to assist in eliciting requirements. So where does user object modeling fit in?

Here are four reasons for user class modeling.

1. **Reuse of user classes:** Commonly used interface operations such as opening a window are usefully abstracted into superclasses from which form classes are specialized, enabling inheritance of common characteristics. We return to this subject in chapter 8 where the subject of reuse across projects is addressed in the shape of components. Returning to our example of booking jobs for customers we could have implemented the booking

...to identify reuse

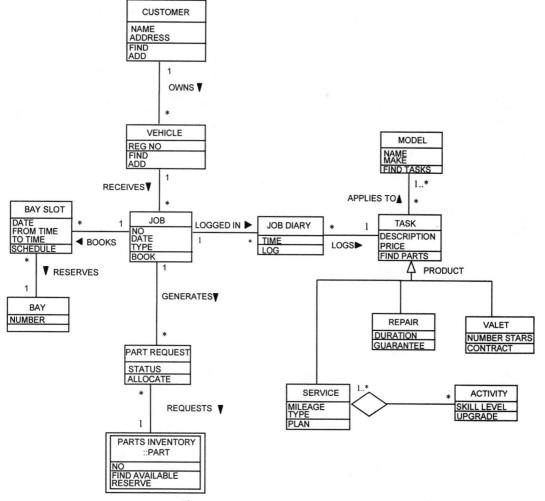

Figure 5.16. Enhanced class diagram.

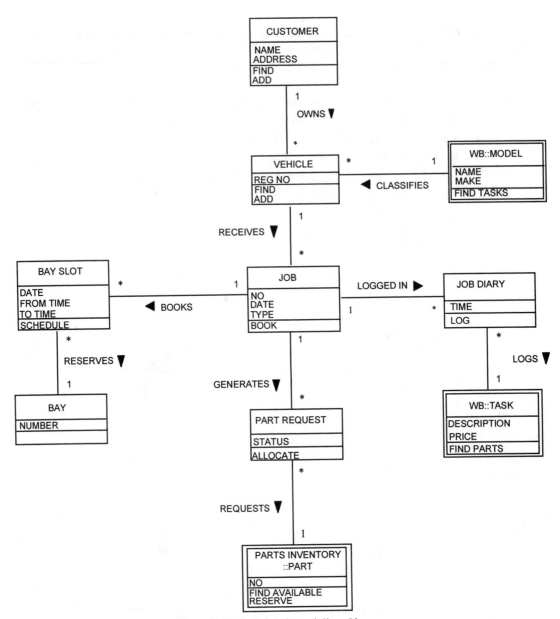

Figure 5.17. Completed Local Class Diagram.

form (in chapter 4) as a single class. Clearly this would be very shortsighted in that the elements on the form can clearly be reused elsewhere. For example, the customer and vehicle information is required by many other applications from market analysis to customer care and the drop-down list of service types might be used by sales and customer inquiries applications.

2. **Scope of user classes:** It is important to consider the behavior of *objects* as members of a class. In their mission to provide user services, user objects often communicate directly with both the user (as servers) and with business objects (as clients), but there are other "intermediate" objects that are often useful, depending on the level of abstraction chosen. A common example is when frequently used features of a business object (such as validating a customer number) are placed in an intermediate user object, invoked by many form objects, for performance reasons. Such intermediate user objects can also be employed to house temporary storage; for example, for totaling values fed by a family of forms in a dialog. Also user objects may be responsible for a variety of other tasks, depending on the environment. Examples include batch reports and control objects that coordinate the behavior of families of user objects in a complex transactions.

...to explore options

3. **User interface structural principles:** Perhaps most important, user class modeling can often be used to explore structural issues at the start of a project, to help us understand the best way to exploit the development environment chosen for implementation. This is especially relevant where there is considerable scope and variety of choice in interface design.

...to examine architecture

4. **Trailblazing projects:** Issues such as those listed previously are typical concerns on vanguard projects addressing the complexities of the user interface for the first time. If a purely project focus is taken, this leads to inconsistent user interfaces, lack of reuse ,and eventually much unnecessary maintenance because of duplication. User modeling therefore becomes imperative on early projects that are effectively trailblazing standards for future use. On later projects user class modeling will become much less important as the lessons from earlier projects are harvested into the resulting user-interface designs.

...and on early projects

Architectural guid-
ance and support is
imperative.

It is vital that projects do not become bogged down in user class model-ing, as witnessed by the concerns just listed. Component modeling of the user interface provides architectural guidance to ensure consistency with the most appropriate standards for the organization. This also helps develop compo-nents for maximum reuse. The example, shown in Figure 5.18, is further explored in section 8.4.10, which deals with this subject.

5.4.13 Documenting Classes, Operations, and Attributes

Diagrams alone
cannot form a
basis from which
code can be
generated.

Ultimately it is necessary to provide a rigorous specification for all classes, opera-tions, and attributes. This should remove all ambiguities from the model in that it should provide a specification that reflects business requirements and can be test-ed. Also, if you are generating and regenerating code, it is important that this is based on a consistent underlying repository with clear unambiguous definitions.

5.4.13.1 Classes

Each class should be specified in terms of a clear and concise description and in terms of its operations and attributes (see below). It is also important to

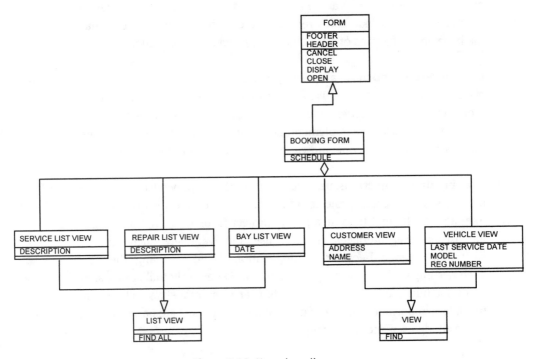

Figure 5.18. User class diagram.

document invariants of the class. Invariants (Meyer, 1988, 1995) are integrity conditions that govern all object members of a class regardless of state. Invariants often reflect business rules that emerge as a result of modeling indirect business processes, as described in section 3.4.7.

Class specifications are required.

5.4.13.2 Operations

It is important to allow the class model to stabilize before attempting to specify operations, because the early view of operations may change drastically as understanding deepens and the model matures. Also many operations will arise as a result of object interaction modeling, as described in chapter 6. However, in the final analysis all operations must be specified. An operation should be specified in a way that is independent from its internal implementation specification as follows:

Operation specifications are required.

Intent: A clear concise statement of objective for the operation.

Stereotype: The stereotype should indicate whether the operation is a service (see chapter 8).

Specification: The specification of an operation must include a description of its semantics. This is important in assisting all potential users as to whether they can use the operation for a given purpose. This may be expressed as a simple textual statement of objective, decision tables, structured language, or pre- and postconditions, depending on the level of detail required. Pre- and postconditions (Meyer, 1988, 1995) provide a means of specifying assertions that describe software contracts. This is an ideal mechanism for clear "black-box" specification, which is particularly important for component-based development that hides internal specification details and relies on external description. The precondition asserts the conditions a client should satisfy to be allowed to invoke the operation; the postcondition asserts what is true on successful completion of the operation.

Signature: Each operation must have a clearly defined signature: a signature (UML, 1997) consists of a number and type of input arguments and return values of the form (parameter-list): return type expression.

Finally we also find it useful to document called operations, transmitted events, set attributes, and nonfunctional requirements, as shown in Table 5.4.

A powerful feature of object orientation is that the same operation may apply to several different classes. This allows an operation to be implemented by different methods in different classes. Such an operation is said to be *polymorphic*; that is, it takes on "many forms." Polymorphism requires that the

Polymorphism requires consistent signatures.

Table 5.4. An Example of Operation Specification

Operation Name	Model:: Find Tasks
Intent	Reports all tasks applicable to specified model.
Stereotype	Service
Signature	(Model Name:Char): (Task: Class*)
Pre/post conditions	Pre: Valid Model name
	Post: All Task objects for this Model returned
Called Operations	Task: Get
Transmitted Events	None
Attributes (Set)	None
Nonfunctional requirements	Response time less than 3 seconds

same named operation has a single defined signature, making its interface consistent for its potentially many implementations.

5.4.14.3 Attributes

Attribute specifications are required.

Each attribute should be elementary in the sense that it takes a single value for a particular object, or a group of values that belong together; for example, address. Again, as with operations, it is important to allow the class model to stabilize before attempting to specify attributes.

Attributes are specified in terms of semantics and data type. Semantics are specified in terms of a textual definition where this is not obvious from the name. Often a simple qualification is necessary. For example, Task Description is obvious but Task Price needs qualifying as "base price without unforeseen extras." Data types should be to standard, such as boolean or character.

5.5 Practical Guidelines for Class Modeling

Two checklists follow.

Two checklists are provided in this section: the first gives some help for identifying good classes; the second gives some overall guidelines for assessing the broad quality of the class model.

5.5.1 Class Identification Checklist

Here are some suggested sources

Apart from use cases and events, there is a wealth of information sources that can be used to assist in class modeling, including the following:

- business process models (described in chapter 3),
- business strategy documents,
- policy documents,
- corporate business plans,
- organizational procedures,
- product descriptions,
- existing application documentation,
- existing models.

Many classes will be fairly obvious and perhaps typical of any type of enterprise. Examples include Customer, Product, and Order. Similarly, many classes will be common across industry-specific enterprises. Examples include Policy, Claim, and Proposal in the insurance industry. Indeed the concept of class frameworks is built on this feature. However, other classes are less obvious and more specific to the needs of individual enterprises. Uncovering such classes requires considerable analytical skill. It is also worth noting that very often a part of the reason for choosing a component-based approach is to glean competitive advantage. Frameworks alone actually run counter to such a goal. Creative thinking is needed in identifying classes, but this will require control. We find it useful to categorize classes to channel thinking toward discovery of business classes.

Class identification guidelines help channel creative thinking.

Actors: Actors sometimes, though not always, map to classes. Examples: Sales Manager, Automatic Teller Machine, Broker.

People: As well as people who are actors (above) there may also be people who are relevant for other reasons. For example, an Employee might not interact with the system, but might be something we need to keep information about (number and name) and do things to (promote, retire).

Locations and Places: Examples: City, Airport, Region.

Organizations: As well as organizations that are actors (above) there may also be organizations that are relevant for other reasons. For example, a Division might not interact with the system, but might be something we need to keep information about (budget) and do things to (transfer).

Interactions and Events: Interactions with the system might be of interest in their own right. Often these are transactions such as Withdrawal or Deposit. Events are a rich source of information as described in section 5.4.3. However, they might be interesting in their own right. Examples: Product Launch, Weekly Planning Session, Sale.

Standards: Rules that govern business policy. Examples: Recipe, Product Rule.

Business Concepts: These are abstractions that do not correspond with any physical thing but that are important to the enterprise. Sometimes attributes are of interest in themselves and can be usefully abstracted as classes depending on business context. For example, Color is an attribute of Car. In the context of a Car Sales enterprise, this might be sufficient. But in the context of a manufacturing enterprise Color itself has attributes, such as optical index and durability, that are of interest and operations that can be performed on it, such as analyze and brighten.

Invented Concepts: Other abstractions are invented as a result of generalizing the class model. Often the objective is to make the model more reusable or flexible in the face of possible business changes. Examples: Product Type, Customer Role.

A template is useful.

The above headings are not intended as an exhaustive list. Rather, they are intended as examples . Each organization will have its own needs. The suggestion here is that it is useful to construct such a template based on your own needs.

5.5.2 Class Evaluation Checklist

Here are some rules of thumb.

Class models effectively form the heart of the resulting system. Both authors have witnessed projects that have run out of control as a result of no class modeling. Other projects have run out of control because although modeling was used there were no quality guidelines. Different developers approached things "their own way." As mentioned earlier, for example, if care is not taken the class model can grow to literally thousands of classes. To address such problems we are not suggesting a large set of standards are required. Such efforts inevitably end up as shelf-ware. It is rules of thumb in the form of checklists that are useful. Pointers are therefore offered below based on our experiences on real-life projects. The checklists apply primarily to business classes unless specifically stated otherwise.

Essential Properties: Classes, attributes, and operations must be essential to business needs. This means that they must be relevant regardless of the hardware and software technology used to implement the system. Otherwise, the proposed class (attribute or operation) is a design or implementation class (or attribute or operation), and should be deferred until the appropriate phase. Examples of implementation classes are lists, containers, and communications controllers. Examples of implementation attributes are pointers, protocols, and report codes. Examples of implementation operations are save, restore, and initialize.

Attributes: Make sure that the class has some data that must be remembered. Usually a class will have more than one attribute. If a class has a single attribute, then often that is exactly what it is: the attribute of another class. This is not to say that there are never classes with single attributes. The important feature of an attribute is that it does not have an independent existence. If the attribute can exist in isolation in its own right then it describes a class with a single attribute; an example might be an external organization for which an identification code is needed but all other details are not relevant or perhaps even secret. To summarize, from the point of view of enterprise commercial systems, all diagrammed business classes should have attributes, and preferably more than one.

Various studies report differing data on numbers of attributes per class (Henderson-Sellers, 1996). We have found that typically in excess of 15 business attributes is unusual.

Operations: Make sure that the class has at least one operation that performs a business service. The class must provide business services to justify its existence, if only to maintain its attributes. If all housekeeping operations (for example, Get, Set, Update attributes and Get, Create, Update, Delete objects) are modeled explicitly the class model becomes top heavy; you cannot see the wood for the trees. Generally there is little value in modeling such operations. Therefore in business class modeling housekeeping operations are best considered *implied*. The business services that are of key relevance are connected to the purpose of the system as a whole. Each class must be assigned clear responsibilities that fulfill business needs. Such business services will be directly traceable to business requirements and identified as part of a business task; for example, Book Job and Schedule Bay Slot. Operations within a class should also be internally cohesive: that is, they should contribute toward the same overall business goal. Various studies report differing data on numbers of operations per class (Henderson-Sellers, 1996). We have found that typically in excess of seven business services is unusual. Again, with size of eventual methods there is an increasing emergence of data. A rough rule of thumb is to aim for no more than 10 to 20 lines of code per method, depending on the implementation environment.

Common Properties: All the attributes or operations of a class should apply to each and every object that is a member of the class. Optional properties should be factored into separate classes. Often this may involve introducing a subclass.

Interclass Coupling: Clearly each class must not be overburdened with associations to other classes. At the other extreme of course, a system without any coupling is useless. It is important to aim for a compromise between these two extremes. Certainly, elimination of unnecessary coupling is imperative in a good design. This also reduces reusability of classes as emphasized by Page-Jones's (1995) concept of "connascence" and its associated guidelines. Coupling is also created by inheritance in class hierarchies but this is usually treated as a separate issue, as of necessity classes in an inheritance hierarchy are more closely related.

Depth and Width of Inheritance Hierarchies: There is a trade-off between reuse of inherited characteristics and design complexity. It is important to control nesting of different levels (depth) and numbers of subclasses that fan out from a superclass (width). Chidamber and Kamerer (1991) report that a medium-sized system with approximately 100 classes is likely to have class hierarchies of seven plus or minus two levels of inheritance and aggregation structures (Chidamber & Kamerer, 1991). Rumbaugh (1991) states "An inheritance hierarchy that is two or three levels deep is certainly acceptable; ten levels deep is probably excessive; five or six levels, may or may not be proper." Similar considerations apply to width, although most authors agree that width should be less than depth.

Control Classes: There can be classes with no attributes at all especially in real-time embedded and digital control systems. Such classes are referred to as *control classes*. They are not shown on the class diagram, as they have no static associations. They would just appear as isolated boxes with no connections, which would be somewhat self-defeating on a diagram, the main purpose of which is to model static structure. Control classes are important in object interaction, which is discussed in the next chapter. Do not include them on your class diagrams.

Unique Classes: Classes should be checked for duplication of properties. Sometimes there are classes that overlap and are best treated as subclasses of a superclass, which should be introduced to house the common properties. Sometimes this technique is referred to as *generalization*, as mentioned in section 5.4.8.

Reality Check: Finally it is worth checking the model from time to time to make sure that it does reflect the semantics of the business. Sometimes classes may be added, which though they seemed "a good idea at the time" actually do not make a lot of sense when tested against reality. Relational link tables masquerading as association classes are a prevalent example, as mentioned in section 5.4.7. Brian Henderson-Sellers (1996) gives an example of a person-car as a case in point: "It is possible to have a class with high internal, syntactic cohesion but little semantic cohesion. For example, imagine a class that includes features of both a person and the car that the person owns. Such a class could be internally highly cohesive, yet semantically *as a whole seen from outside* the notion expressed (here of a thing known as person-car) is nonsensical." Certainly our experience is that the classes identified early in the process tend to form the semantic heart of the model and stay through the entire design process. Perhaps this is simply a consequence of the principle that the products of object-oriented development should directly mirror our model of reality.

Software metrics, let alone object-oriented metrics, is still in its infancy. Most studies are based on implementation data, rather than on data describing different model items, such as classes or operations. Research is rapidly emerging, however and the reader is referred to Henderson-Sellers (1996) and Lorenz and Kidd (1994) for detailed information. However, there is no magic panacea: Organizations can use metrics frameworks to get started but ultimately must invest time and money in building metrics databases geared to their own requirements, adapting and tuning the framework, if they are to glean the full benefits of object orientation. The irony is that this was eloquently recommended by Tom DeMarco (1982), long before objects hit the mainstream. The reality is that the potential power of a component-based approach reinforces DeMarco's basic message several times over: "You can't control what you can't measure."

> Effective software metrics require significant investment.

5.6 Summary

Class modeling forms a fundamental set of techniques within Perspective. Although the class model is static, in the sense that it models class structure both in terms of characteristics and associations, it nevertheless governs the dynamics of objects by providing a framework within which objects will eventually be put to work. If the tracks are badly designed the trains that run on them may well crash, causing loss of life. Similarly a poor class model results in a shaky foundation on which objects will fail to deliver the goods.

> Class modeling is a critical activity in component-based development.

CHAPTER 6

• • • • • • • • • • • • • • • • • • • •

Object
Interaction
Modeling

6.1 Introduction

The object interaction model represents the messaging between objects that is required to realize required behavior. This is in contrast to the class model, which represents the static structure on which system behavior will be based, but says nothing about the behavior itself. A class model focuses on a single stereotype from the Perspective architecture (for example, business classes or interface classes but not a mixture of the two). In sharp contrast an object interaction model typically includes objects of different stereotypes. Also, there are further objects, with key behavioral roles, that do not lend themselves to class modeling but that must be explored if we are to do justice to the system's behavior. Clearly it is important to have a mechanism for addressing such issues.

Object interaction models lend themselves very well to modeling the service categories of the Perspective architecture. In this chapter we explain how to leverage this feature, which receives more detailed treatment in chapters 8 and 9.

The notation for object interaction diagramming is a little more complex than with the other techniques. In particular there are two diagrams, sequence

Object interaction modeling explores how objects work together to meet requirements.

Object interaction modeling helps with design of services.

There are two types of diagram.

diagrams and collaboration diagrams, which are useful. We therefore spend rather more time on notation than in other areas as it is important to understand the strengths and weaknesses of the two diagrams for practical usage.

Our main focus is on practical techniques.

As in other areas the literature is rich with advice on object interaction modeling (Booch, 1993; Coleman, 1994; Jacobson, 1992) and it is not our intention to repeat it. Our main focus is on techniques that are explained using a step-by-step guide with reference to an evolving example. Although the techniques are presented in a sequential order it is important to appreciate that on a real-life project there would be considerable iteration between techniques. Where more detail could be useful salient references to the appropriate texts are provided. Finally we include some pragmatic tips that we have found useful from our work on real projects.

6.2 Object Interaction Modeling Principles

6.2.1 Focus of Interest

Business objects must be kept as technically neutral as possible.

A key principle with object interaction modeling is to preserve implementation independence of business objects. We want different business services to be "plugged in" to user services with minimal change to their interfaces. Implementation objects, such as user objects, form a skin around the core of business objects. Coupling between user objects and business objects must be minimized. It is vital to keep this principle in mind in working out the required messaging between objects.

Start simple!

Prototyping also has a key role to play, as we show later in this chapter. If we are not careful we can find ourselves in the classic situation of having a brilliant design for the *wrong* business problem! We therefore recommend starting simple and focusing on key functionality, before getting to grips with detailed issues, which might otherwise overwhelm the project.

Object interaction modeling is useful in both analysis and design.

Most authors, including Jacobson (1992) and Coleman (1994) present object interaction modeling as a design activity. While accepting the undoubted usefulness of object interaction modeling in design, we have found it also to be useful in analysis on many projects. A summary of the purposes of object interaction modeling within Perspective follows:

In analysis:

- it helps in problem understanding,
- it finds and confirms classes and operations,
- it verifies that the use cases can be supported by new operations and existing user services and business services.

In design:

- it explores alternative designs,
- it helps to assess technical feasibility and to validate proposed designs,
- it aides design of user services and business services.

6.2.2 Key Concepts

6.2.2.1 Messages

A message is a request for an operation or notification of an event that is sent to an object or class. A message may have associated parameters. For an operation these may be both input arguments and return values; an event may have input arguments but does not have associated return values. In Perspective, messages can also be used to transmit events out of the system, for example, to denote production of outputs.

It is important to understand that message passing using operation calls is, for practical purposes, assumed to be *synchronous* whereas message passing using events is assumed to be *asynchronous*; for a more detailed discussion on this see section 6.5. Finally, note that messages use links between objects that may be static (instances of associations defined on a class diagram) or dynamic.

6.2.2.2 Probes

A probe is a stimuli to a "used" or "extends" use case, which is used both to partition complexity and to identify potential services (often user services). This reflects the distinction made in section 4.4.6 between uses and extends relationships between use cases.

6.2.2.3 Pre- and Postconditions

In chapter 5 we used pre- and postconditions to help specify operations. The two concepts are also applicable to use cases and scenarios. The object interaction model defines sequences of messages that occur between collections of objects to realize particular use cases (groups of scenarios) or scenarios. Such behavior is prototypical; it is not complete. Therefore it is important to stipulate under what circumstances the behavior occurs (the precondition) and what the results of the behavior will be (the postcondition).

Preconditions and postconditions correspond to process dependencies where business process modeling has been used. Object interaction modeling may reveal that these correspond to attribute values, links, or states on state diagrams. Therefore any state diagrams should be verified accordingly. This is discussed in more detail in chapter 7.

6.2.2.4. Control Objects

Jacobson (1992) distinguishes a *control object,* which manages the other objects participating in a use case and contains behavior that does not naturally belong in business and user objects. Control objects are usually transient: Typically they only survive during the execution of their associated use cases. One of the reasons that control objects are important in object interaction modeling is because they help isolate user objects from business objects. This in turn helps insulate business services from user services (and data services). Business services must be as portable as possible across different user interface environments and data management systems. Control objects are generally restricted to dynamic links with user, business, or data objects.

6.2.2.5 Integration with State Model

State modeling should be used for addressing the complexities of event-related conditional behavior and concurrency, as described in chapter 7. A state diagram (or set of state diagrams) acts as a template for the event-driven state-dependent behavior of objects belonging to a *single class,* for which it specifies the *complete* set of possible behaviors. This is in sharp contrast to the object interaction model,which stretches across a *network of objects* and is essentially *prototypical*. **Given that we have chosen to use a state diagram**, the following integration rules are applied:

1. An event inbound to/outbound from an object in the object interaction model must correspond to one or more inbound events/outbound events on the state diagram for the object's class.

2. An operation call made to/by an object in the object interaction model may correspond to inbound/outbound operation calls on the state diagram for the object's class. Returns on outbound messages may also correspond to inbound events on the state diagram.

With a use case there can be multiple scenarios involving complex conditional behavior. Our view is that trying to "balance up" all the potential intermediate pre- and postconditions with different states is a fruitless exercise. This is reinforced by the fact that a use case or scenario cannot be left "half done": it either executes completely or not at all. Therefore the following guideline applies to preconditions/postconditions obtaining at the start/end of a scenario or use case.

1. A precondition on the object interaction model that relates to a particular object may include one or more possible source states and/or guard conditions on a state diagram for the object's class.

2. Where such a precondition exists, the corresponding postcondition on the object interaction model that relates to the same object may include one or more possible target states on a state diagram for the object's class.

6.3 Object Interaction Modeling Notation

6.3.1 Notation Set

There are two diagram types used for object interaction diagramming: sequence diagrams and collaboration diagrams. The notation set for both is based on the Unified Modeling Language (UML, 1997) with some minimal additional enhancements.

Sequence diagrams: An abstract sequence diagram is shown in Figure 6.1. A sequence diagram can be used to describe a use case (including probes; see Figure 6.1) or operation and is named accordingly. The use case (or operation)

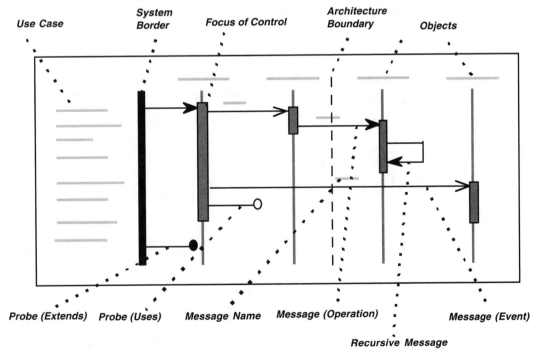

Figure 6.1. Object interaction modeling notation set: Sequence diagram.

description is formalized down the left-hand margin of the diagram using structured language based on the three basic constructs of sequence, choice, and repetition. An invisible "time axis" runs downward through the diagram.

Objects are declared across the top of the diagram and modeled as vertical lines. Following (UML, 1997) objects can be abstract (:CLASS NAME) or actual instances (INSTANCE NAME:CLASS NAME). Additionally the architecture borders (between service categories) are shown as vertical dashed lines that separate user objects (to the left) from business objects, and business objects from data objects (to the right). Vertical bars over the top of the object lines represent focus of control, "the period of time during which an object is performing an action either directly or through a subordinate procedure" (UML, 1997). An open arrow depicts an event. A closed arrow represents an operation call. A probe "lollipop" symbol acts as shorthand for a use case. The probe itself can be described, in nested fashion, using another sequence diagram.

A message may have associated parameters, which may also be shown on the diagram next to the message name as will be described for collaboration diagrams. However, such adornments should be used sparingly so as not to clutter the diagram. After all, this information should always be readily accessible from the operation or event definition if you have good supporting software.

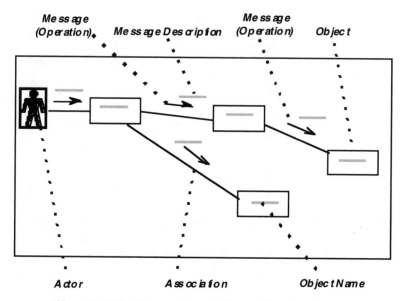

Figure 6.2. Object-interaction modeling collaboration diagram.

Collaboration diagrams: An abstract collaboration diagram is shown in Figure 6.2 . In Perspective we allow actors to be optionally included on the diagram. A collaboration diagram can be used to describe a use case, scenario, or operation. In the case of a use case or operation the collaboration diagram name is the same as the use case or operation. In the case of a scenario the collaboration diagram name is qualified with its precondition to indicate the scenario. In fact, in Perspective, this latter use is encouraged, although it is possible to use collaboration diagrams for modeling whole use cases they are somewhat cumbersome for modeling conditional behavior and complex time-related logic. This is because collaboration diagrams are in essence time-lapse snapshots of configurations of objects; there is no time axis as there is with a sequence diagram.

Following (UML, 1997) objects are modeled as rectangles; objects can be abstract (:CLASS NAME) or actual instances (INSTANCE NAME:CLASS NAME) as shown in Figure 6.3.

For specific instances the rectangle may be divided into two compartments, as shown in Figure 6.4 .

The message notation is, of necessity, more complex if you wish to specify the sequence, choice, and repetition that is modeled using structured language on a sequence diagram. Message description can be structured as described in UML (1997) as follows:

1. A sequence number using Dewey decimal notation. The triggering message has no number. The numbers are separated by dots to represent nested procedure calling sequence. For example, message 3.1 is part of the procedure invoked by message 3 and follows message 2 within that procedure . Note that "*" indicates a potentially iterative message. Letters can be appended to indicate concurrency of messages; for example 2.1a and 2.1b. Also a question mark, optionally followed by a boolean expression can be used to model conditionality.

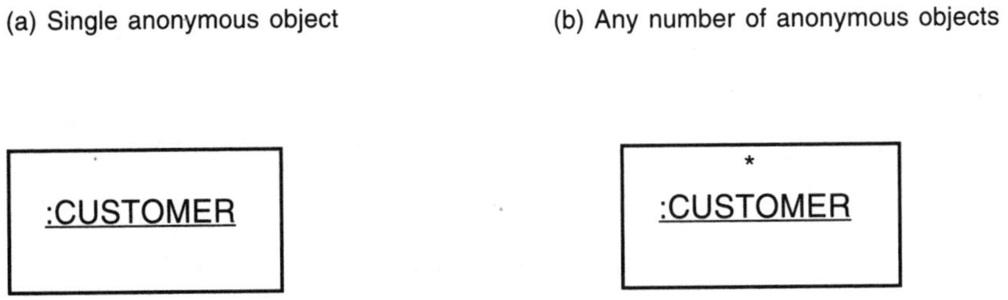

(a) Single anonymous object   (b) Any number of anonymous objects

```
┌──────────────┐              ┌──────────────┐
│              │              │      *       │
│  :CUSTOMER   │              │  :CUSTOMER   │
│              │              │              │
└──────────────┘              └──────────────┘
```

Figure 6.3. Notation for abstract object.

2. Return value name(s); followed by assignment sign (:=). This is optional.

3. The name of the message which may be an event or an operation.

4. Arguments; contained in brackets. This is optional.

Incidentally, if this level of detail is really needed then it is likely that a sequence diagram is a much more appropriate tool for tackling the problem. If collaboration diagrams are reserved for modeling scenarios then you can avoid the need to model conditionality and keep the diagram much simpler.

6.3.2 The Object Interaction Model

Object interaction modeling involves building views of the dynamic interplay between objects that are required to realize required behavior. Collectively, these views together with their underlying definitions are referred to as the "Object interaction model." These views can be textual or diagrammatic.

6.3.2.1 Diagrammatic Views

Diagrammatic views consist of sequence diagrams and collaboration diagrams, which employ the notation previously shown, to show message passing between objects. Clearly there is a significant overlap between the two diagrams in that both show objects and message passing. In Perspective the guideline is to use sequence diagrams for modeling use cases and operations, and to use collaboration diagrams for modeling scenarios; that is, specific threads through a use case or operation.

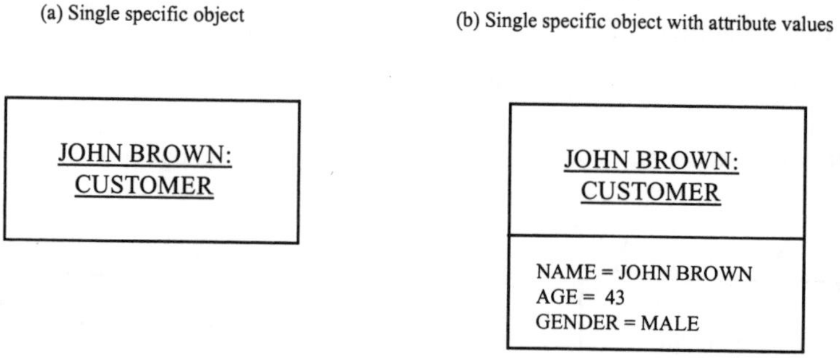

(a) Single specific object   (b) Single specific object with attribute values

Figure 6.4. Notation for specific object.

6.3.2.2 Textual Views

The only textual views exclusive to the object interaction model are message definitions, as described previously. Other textual views are already catered to by other parts of the model; for example, use case descriptions and operation specifications.

6.3.2.3 Nesting of Services

We have seen that sequence diagrams can effectively be nested as probes. This feature of sequence diagrams is also used to model the relationships between the different categories of service provided by the Perspective architecture, by using nested operations, as illustrated in Figure 6.5.

6.4 Object Interaction Modeling Techniques

Object interaction modeling for a system of any size is potentially overwhelming: Typically there could be millions of possible combinations in which objects may be put to work. Aim at understanding the basic courses of main use cases first and avoid being swamped with detail. A **"white-box"** approach models interactions between objects and is often most useful in analyzing detailed object collaboration in early design. A **"black-box"** approach models interactions at a high level between collections of objects implemented as components and is most useful in harvesting reusable services in later design. In this section we assume a white-box approach; the black-box approach is used in chapters 8 and 9, where we focus on reuse of services provided by service packages.

Start off simple and gradually introduce complexity.

The general approach is to concentrate on collaboration between business objects first, gradually introducing implementation objects as you scout ahead into design, but preserving the technical neutrality of your objects as you iterate back into analysis. We use collaboration diagrams for focusing on scenarios early in the process. This helps in problem understanding before getting involved in too much detail. Collaboration diagrams are also used to explore and validate alternative designs. Early sequence diagrams are used to understand basic courses in terms of operations required from business objects only. You can gradually introduce alternate courses as your understanding sharpens. As you progress into design so you can add implementation objects, such as user objects. Once your design starts to "gel" you can firm up on services using sequence diagrams to *assist* in specification and documentation.

The two diagrams have different strengths.

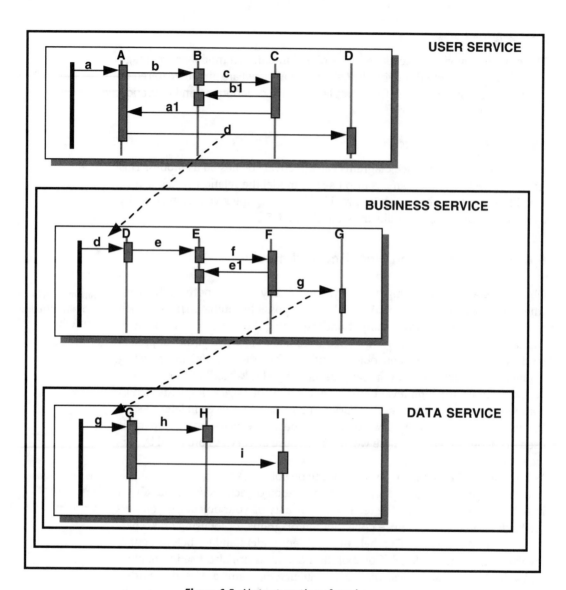

Figure 6.5. Abstract nesting of service categories through sequence diagrams.

6.4.1 Creating a First-Cut Business Sequence Diagram

A use case is selected for "playing through" the class model: The required objects are declared across the top of the sequence diagram. This involves examining the class diagram in relation to the needs of the use case and looking for candidate objects. This is illustrated for the use case Book Standard Job for Customer in Figure 6.6.

First focus on the basic course of a use case.

Notice that there are no objects to the left of the dashed vertical line representing the boundary between the interface and business objects. User interface mechanisms that deal with how actors invoke operations are abstracted out. The main purpose is to find or confirm business operations in the class model and to make sure that there are *sufficient* operations to fulfill the needs of each basic course.

Restrict a first-cut diagram to business objects.

Steps of the use case are expressed in structured language down the left margin of the sequence diagram, as shown in Figure 6.7. It is common for each request to correspond to one service request; note that in the example there are five steps in the use case and five corresponding service requests from the system boundary in the sequence diagram.

Examine each step to see which objects are required.

We try to name what the user is doing or what the user wants, not what is happening inside the system. Some statements may not be associated with a message, but are included to clarify a related user action. For example, the Model object provides the Find Tasks operation in response to the request for a list of services. The next step, "choose service type" does not cause an immediate system response as the user choices are dealt with collectively at the end of the use case. Nevertheless it is an important part of the dialog that we will need to address later when designing the interface.

Each statement in the structure should be "externally" phrased.

There may well be aspects of the interaction that cannot be modeled at this stage. For example, it will be necessary to keep a running total of time required to complete the job. This would be held in temporary storage, but is not an attribute of any business object. Such characteristics are considered part of the implementation and not modeled on the business sequence diagram.

Keep it simple and clear.

The user calls the Customer::Find operation, which calls Vehicle::Find. Customer::Find waits for a return before returning information to the user and then completing. The "returns" are implied; there is no need to show separate message arrows going back to the caller unless the message passing is asynchronous, although there are circumstances when this is useful, as discussed in section 6.5.

Add pre- and postconditions.

At present the precondition is blank; the postcondition "Job Booked" corresponds to the state "Booked" on the Job class; see chapter 7.

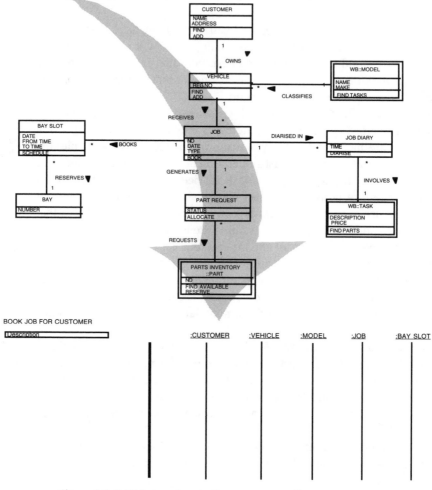

Use Case Description

1. Establish customer and vehicle details:
   1.1 Where this is an existing customer match customer and vehicle.
   1.2 For a new customer enter details to file: name and address, vehicle registration, number, make and model.

2. Where a service is required find the available service types for the make and model of vehicle.

3. Where repairs are required, estimate the price for agreement with the customer.

4. Establish date/time service bays are available for duration of job for agreement with the customer.

5. Enter the job to include services and repairs identified, booking required bay slots.

Figure 6.6. Initial steps for creating a sequence diagram.

6.4.2 Creating a First-Cut Collaboration Diagram

Experience shows that collaboration diagrams become overcomplex and awkward to evaluate if used at the use case level. In Perspective we do not legislate against this but prefer to reserve collaboration diagrams for specific threads through the use cases. Note that often it may be preferable to start with some collaboration diagrams and move on to sequence diagrams. There is no hard and fast rule as to which comes first.

To begin with focus on key scenarios.

   Use collaboration diagrams to bring out **different** aspects of the problem. For example, it is better to focus on one for a simple data entry, one for a complex update, and one for a report, rather than studying six similar data-entry scenarios. Here we are not so much interested in detailed sequences of interactions as in the overall object collaboration required to meet business requirements.

Focus on a useful cross-section of scenarios.

A collaboration diagram for Book Standard Job for Customer is illustrated in Figure 6.8. Messages are drawn clockwise in order of time from top right to bottom left, which aids readability. This example is based on the precondition of an existing customer requesting a standard service where there is an available

Declare pre- and postconditions.

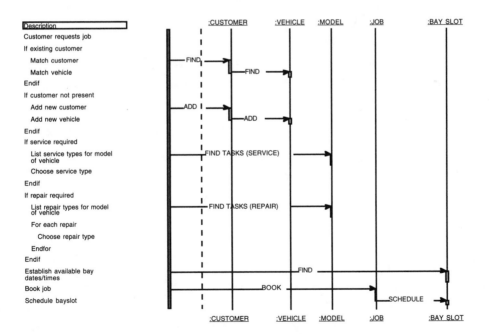

Figure 6.7. First cut example business sequence diagram for
Book Standard Job for Customer.

bay slot. The postcondition is that the job is booked. Other collaboration diagrams could be drawn, for example, involving repairs and new customers, should they be significantly different.

The collaboration diagram addresses a shortcoming in our first sequence diagram. Job cannot simply message bay slots to find out which ones are free. It is more complicated than that! First it is necessary to know how much time is required to do the job. Second it is necessary to work out when this amount of time is available. Third, this means looking at pairs of adjoining bay slots for a bay to see if there is sufficient time between and then reporting this free time range back for display to the user. Each bay knows its slots and is capable of making the required calculation. An operation Find Avail is introduced to Bay as the responsible object. Here we started with an abstract collaboration diagram. Note that examples are also usefully "simulated" through the collaboration diagram using actual instance values as discussed in section 6.4.5.

The collaboration diagram provides another angle on the problem.

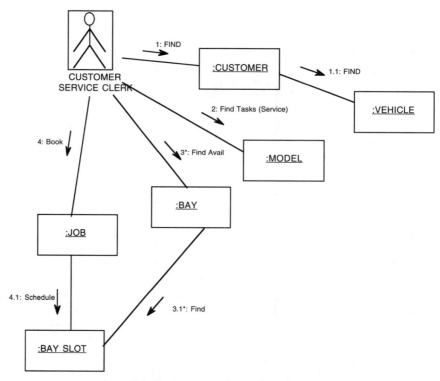

Figure 6.8. First cut example collaboration diagram.

6.4.3 Developing the Initial Collaboration Diagram

Collaboration diagrams allow us to experiment with different configurations of objects reasonably quickly simply by moving one symbol here and another symbol there, especially in exploratory discussions using a whiteboard. This is not the case with sequence diagrams, which can get very complex and take considerable time to draw and redraw, even with the best of modeling tools.

Collaboration diagrams facilitate an RAAD approach.

A problem with promoting a business object to perform the role of controller is that the object now becomes closely coupled to the user interface. A key principle is to minimize coupling. Also the business object will need to have some knowledge of the user objects that run counter to its role as a server to user objects. As the user interface for Book Standard Job for Customer involves several interactions within a dialog (entering a customer search key, choosing a service, specifying a range of suitable dates, choosing available dates) the associated coupling will be high. We therefore introduce a Job Control object, as shown in Figure 6.9.

Decide whether to introduce a separate control object.

The above situation often occurs with complex transactions. However, in other situations involving less interaction, or no user interaction at all, responsibility for control can often be delegated to a business object. For example, a requirement to print out a daily list of jobs for each bay could be delegated to the Bay object, as shown in Figure 6.10. The Bay object is capable of gleaning all the information it needs on initial invocation, to carry out the overall responsibility of providing the list. To summarize, using business objects as controllers works better with "fixed" processes with little flexibility or user interaction; for example, producing a report. Separate control objects are more intuitive and flexible with interactive processes. A more detailed account of the appropriate use of control objects is given in section 6.5.

Sometimes responsibility for control can be delegated to a business object.

6.4.4 Developing a Sequence Diagram

Our sequence diagram now includes a control object and a message to Bay to find available bays (see Figure 6.11). At this point the diagram is left deliberately simplistic at the user interface; there is a single message that invokes the controller and nothing more. Clearly there are several user interactions that will need to be catered to when it comes to modeling the user interface. The Job Control object is responsible for managing these interactions and shielding the business objects from the threat of any future changes in interface design.

The Job Control object is introduced on the sequence diagram.

6.4.5 Developing an Example Scenario

We apply a specific scenario to the collaboration diagram, as shown in Figure 6.12, which is developed to reflect the use of a control object, as discussed

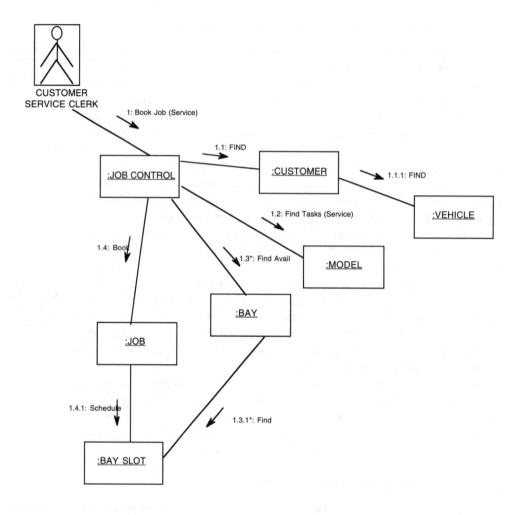

Figure 6.9. Collaboration diagram showing control object for Book Job for Customer.

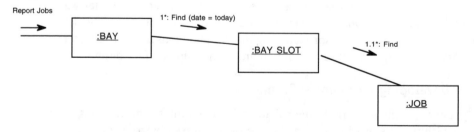

Figure 6.10. Example collaboration diagram for Report
Today's Jobs by Bay showing delegated control.

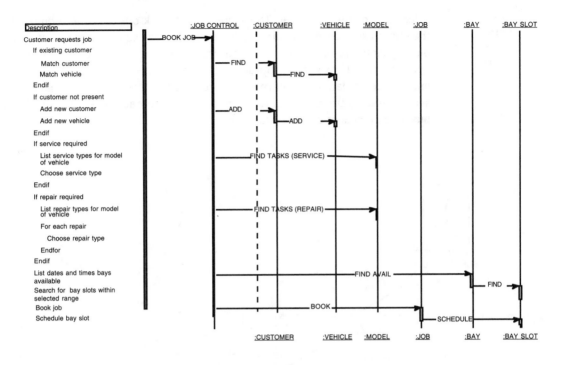

Figure 6.11. Example business sequence diagram with control object for Book Standard Job for Customer.

previously. This is analogous to prototyping of individual cases at the diagram level. Indeed animation facilities showing the activation of objects, step by step, through a collaboration diagram are most useful. Although prototyping is not formally part of object interaction modeling, we have found on many projects that the two activities are intimately connected. There are some important issues that surround the subject of prototyping and object interaction modeling, which are further discussed in section 6.5. In particular the collaboration diagram is usefully employed to rapidly check technical feasibility of proposed design ideas before committing to prototypes, let alone starting to develop sequence diagrams to model the design, which can be a time-consuming activity.

Having examined some example scenarios, a prototype for the Book Job for Customer use case can be developed on the basis of the outline screen layout as shown in chapter 4 (see Figure 4.10). Drop-down menus are provided for available services and repairs to assist the user in making the appropriate

Example scenarios are used to test out assumptions.

A prototype is usefully developed on the basis of our early diagrams.

selections for the customer. The system must work out the time required for the chosen service and repairs and find possible bay slots. The dates of possible bay slots are displayed in a third drop-down menu. The user chooses an appropriate date from the drop-down list. The selected service and/or repairs and choice of date are confirmed by pressing the "schedule" command. The sequence diagram allows us to verify that this approach is feasible given the business objects at our disposal.

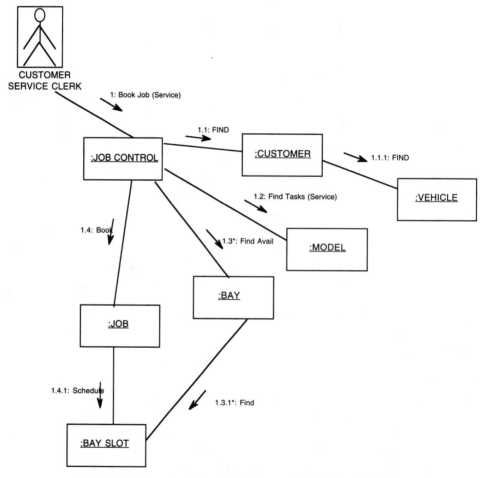

Figure 6.12. Example collaboration diagram for Book Standard Job for Customer showing specific scenario.

6.4.6 Developing a User Service Using a Sequence Diagram

Knowledge of the user-interface structure, which may be gleaned from proto-typing as described previously, is applied to the sequence diagram in order to design a user service. In this case a single Booking Form suffices, at least for now. Interactions between the user object and control object are introduced to handle the different user inputs as shown in Figure 6.13. The Job Control object is responsible for providing the user service Book Job; in fact it is an example of a *service object*, discussed fully in chapter 8.

User objects are introduced to the sequence diagram.

Note that for clarity and simplicity of explanation repairs have been tem-porarily omitted from the diagram. It is an important feature of the design that the technical neutrality of the business objects is preserved. Finally this sequence diagram is near the limit in terms of manageable size and complex-ity. We return to this subject in section 6.5.

Business objects are kept technically neutral.

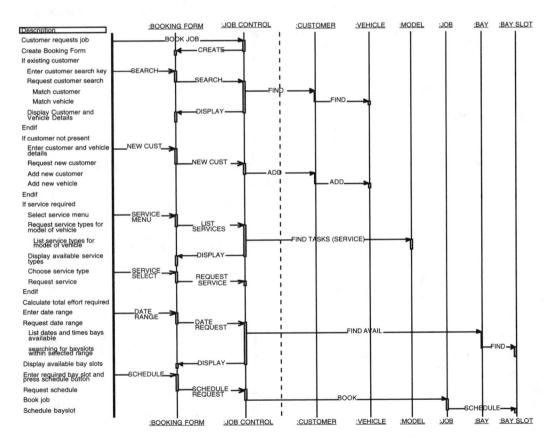

Figure 6.13. Example initial design sequence diagram for Book Standard Job for Customer.

6.4.7 Identifying Further Services

Identify potential business services...

Both Search for Customer and Add Customer are modeled as "white lollipops," which indicate used use cases, as shown in Figure 6.14. We return to design business services for these using a legacy system wrapper in chapter 9. Search services for repairs and services are dealt with in section 6.4.8.

...and user services.

We find that there is an alternative course "Capture problem details," which is used for entering an estimated time and problem description for non-catalogued jobs. This is modeled using a "black- lollipop" probe as shown. We can choose to develop this as a separate user service if required.

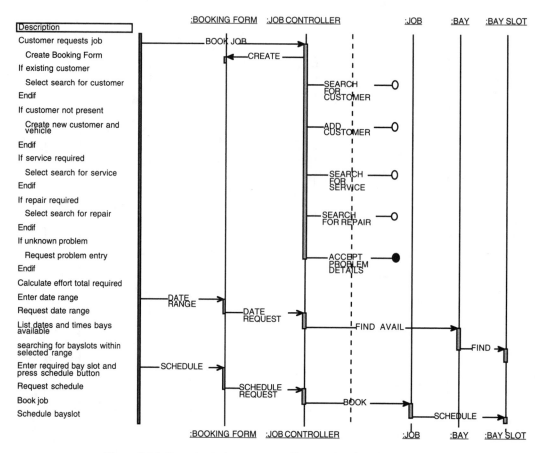

Figure 6.14. Example design sequence diagram showing user services.

6.4.8 Reusing Business Services

A sequence diagram is used to model the Search for Repair probe shown in Figure 6.15. This represents a business service, implemented through its own user objects, usable by many different use cases.

Design business services.

Note the business service, Find Tasks, which is invoked on the Model object. This is a simple service that would not normally justify modeling, but its sequence diagram is included here, in Figure 6.16, to illustrate the layering of services. Notice that the "Find" operation on Task is abstract. It is used to implement polymorphism. In the example, it is services as opposed to repairs that are requested, but the sender does not need to target the Service subclass of the Task supertype. It simply sends a message to Task and leaves it to Task to delegate to the appropriate subclass, in this case Service. Objects, such as Model and Repairs Searcher, which provide business services are examples of service objects, which are discussed in chapter 8. Again, note that interfaces to the business objects are preserved right through the process.

Layer business services.

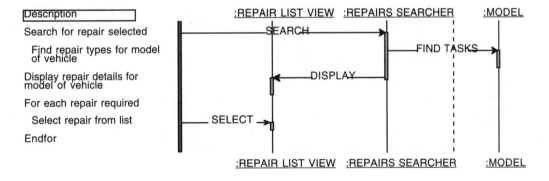

Figure 6.15. Example design sequence diagram for Search for Repair service.

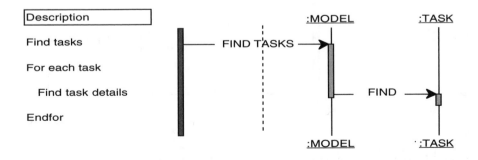

Figure 6.16. Example design sequence diagram for Find Tasks System service.

6.5 Practical Guidelines for Object Interaction Modeling

Some guidelines follow.

There are certain questions that seem to come up continually in the arena of real-life projects. A summary of how we have dealt with some of these issues is included in the text that follows.

6.5.1 How to Show Outputs

Events are especially useful for showing system outputs.

We have already seen that information can be returned back up the chain of a set of nested operation calls to the original sender, without the need to show a separate arrow traveling back across the diagram; return is implied in all operation calls. However, there are circumstances where it is useful to show arrows traveling right to left in such fashion. Events are useful for this purpose as they can be shown transmitted out of the system without the need for a target object. For example, suppose that the system needs to produce a list of tasks pertaining to each model. We might ask Model to list its related tasks as part of the Find Tasks service (see Figure 6.17). The business requirement pertaining to the report is referenced from the definition of the event "Task List"; the data items contained in the report are defined as parameters for the event.

6.5.2 Forks and stairs

A fundamental decision is whether to use a centralized or a decentralized structure.

A centralized structure is reflected in a "fork-sequence diagram" in which messages are transmitted by a central object, which assumes responsibility for flow of control within the use case. A decentralized structure is reflected in a "stair-sequence diagram" in which messages traverse a family of objects each of which has delegated responsibility for carrying out part of the use case. Of

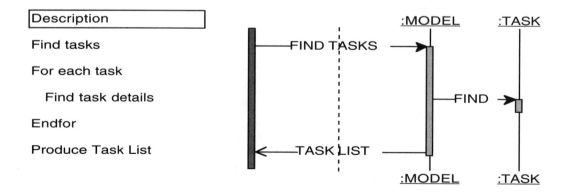

Figure 6.17. Example sequence diagram showing production of system output.

course in real life a sequence diagram may exhibit a combination of fork and stair features. The two extremes are illustrated in the abstract shown in Figure 6.18.

An object-oriented purist's answer is that the stair structure is better as responsibility is distributed evenly across objects; each object collaborates just with those objects that can help with a specific behavior. Fork structures, it is argued, are structured programming (where control is centralized in control modules) in object-oriented clothes. This leads to a structured functional architecture in which most objects become no more than dumb data transformers under a function blob. A nonpurist answer is that the fork structure is better as it is more flexible in catering to change, particularly changes to the ordering of tasks. Stair structures, it is argued, lead to convoluted and messy designs that are difficult to unpick and prone to hacking in the face of change.

The question is, "Which structure is better?"

The authors have witnessed the excesses of taking both approaches to their extreme. It is better to think of centralized and decentralized structures as extremes, both of which have their advantages and disadvantages that need to be weighed up according to individual circumstances. In our experience the most important criterion is to place responsibility for an action at the point of natural ownership for that action. Where several objects are involved in a use case and results need to be compared from several sources, there is often no natural point of ownership. Generally, a fork structure using a control object works best for such situations. In fact the examples from earlier in the chapter were largely based on centralized structures. However, this is not always the case. For example, suppose we want to know whether a vehicle is due for a ser-

The answer lies somewhere between these two extremes.

(a) Fork Structure

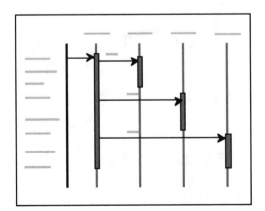

(b) Stair Structure

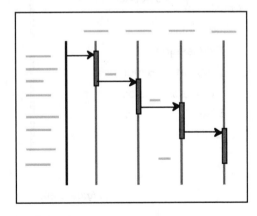

Figure 6.18. Abstract fork and stair structures.

vice. One approach might be to centralize invocation of all required objects from a Request Control object, which also makes the decision on whether a service is due and reports that decision, as shown in Figure 6.19. A second approach would be to use a stair structure, delegating invocation, as shown in Figure 6.20, and localizing responsibility for making the decision on whether a service is due to the Vehicle object.

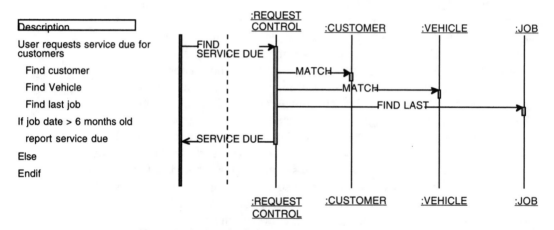

Figure 6.19. Use of a fork structure for Find Service Due.

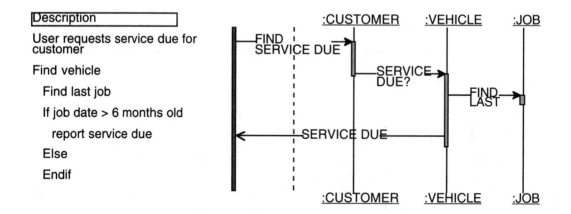

Figure 6.20. Use of a stair structure for Find Service Due.

In this example the fork structure treats the business objects as pure data handlers; the control object assumes the role of a function blob. The stair structure is preferred because responsibility for making the decision is at the point of natural ownership for that action: That is, Vehicle is naturally responsible for working out whether it is due for a service. It is after all the subject of that decision. Notice also that some of the message names have changed subtly. This reflects an important conceptual point. In the fork example a Match message is sent to Customer, whereas in the stair example the Find Service Due message is sent to Customer. In the latter case, it is Find Service Due that calls the match operation recursively on Customer; we could have included this on the diagram but suppressed it for clarity. Find Service Due then delegates responsibility for actually making the decision and reporting the result to Vehicle. Notice that in the stair example, if Match Customer is retained for doing the job of Find Service Due, then Match Customer is compromised and extended with deadweight logic that would be unused in most circumstances.

In this example the stair structure is preferred.

Our experience in fact echoes the advice given by Jacobson (1992). First it is important to examine the strength of association between the collaborating objects. At one extreme there are objects that are very strongly connected such as aggregation and inheritance hierarchies; at the other extreme there are objects that are only dynamically related; in between are objects that have optional static links. A stair structure is appropriate where the collaborating objects have strong static connections exhibited in the class model and where order is fixed. A fork structure is appropriate where the collaborating objects have looser links, which might well be dynamic, where order is flexible, and where there is a likelihood that operations may be added and/or removed.

Place responsibility for actions at the natural points of ownership.

6.5.3 Use of Patterns

We are increasingly asked about the role of patterns in object interaction modeling. In fact throughout this chapter we have had recourse to the fork and stair structures, which in a sense represent very high-level design "patterns." For example, a fork structure is exhibited by the formally defined "observer" and "mediator" patterns; a stair structure is reflected in the "chain of responsibility" pattern (Gamma, 1995). In progressing into more detailed object interaction modeling such detailed behavioral patterns become immensely useful for furnishing designs that are both optimized and consistent.

Behavioral patterns can be used to assist in object interaction modeling.

6.5.4 Operations vs. Events

It is important to understand that message passing using operation calls is, for practical purposes, assumed to be *synchronous*: each time a message is sent to an object it results in the invocation of a method. The thread of control pass-

Operations are synchronous, whereas events are asynchronous.

es from the sending object to the receiving object. The method call completes before control is returned to the caller. In contrast, message passing using events is assumed to be *asynchronous*: The sender of an event simply transmits the event and continues its behavior independently; it does not have to wait for the receiver of the event to complete its response before continuing. Sender and receiver have separate threads of control that do not synchronize during message passing. This is why it makes no sense to specify return values for an event.

Object interaction modeling is prototypical as opposed to state related.

Object interaction modeling generally works much better on the synchronous message-passing paradigm. This is because the focus of interest with asynchronous processing is on state-related conditional behavior. Typically a system responds to an event in different ways depending on the state it is in. In contrast, object interaction modeling focuses on scenarios and use cases (groups of scenarios) where for practical purposes certain assumptions have to be made regarding the state of objects. If we try to model every conceivable scenario depending on every conceivable object state we rapidly disappear under a sea of sequence diagrams and collaboration diagrams. As the old saying goes, "if your only tool is a hammer, the whole world looks like a nail." We recommend state modeling for addressing event-related conditional behavior and for specifying complete behavior, as described in chapter 7. This is not to say that events are never to be allowed in the object interaction model. Events are actually particularly useful for modeling system outputs as described previously. However, events should be used sparingly and certainly not without good justification in the object interaction model.

6.5.5 Specification

Operation specifications are needed.

A well-designed set of sequence diagrams and collaboration diagrams, though very valuable for guiding program design, is not a substitute for a well-defined set of operation specifications; see section 5.4.13.

6.5.6 Refining Use Case Descriptions

Use case descriptions may change.

Use case descriptions are refined as a result of object interaction modeling. A template is useful for channeling the information in a consistent and effective way, which promotes traceability, as described in section 4.4.9. For example, detail may be added or changed on nonfunctional requirements, which include implementation constraints, such as platform and operating environment, as well as quality attributes, such as response time and mean time to repair. Perhaps response time requirements for Book Standard Job for Customer reduce from 5 seconds as originally recorded, to 4 seconds.

6.5.7 Refining Business Rules

Business rules should be examined to see if they apply to model items other than the use case to which they were originally assigned. For example, "bay slots not to exceed 3 hours" was a business rule originally captured in the Book Standard Job for Customer use case. It is now assigned to the Bay Slot class as an invariant stating that the attribute To Time must not exceed From Time by more than 3 hours. Such business rules must now be removed from the use case to avoid duplication.

Certain business rules may be assigned to classes as invariants.

6.5.8 Managing Complexity

Too often we find developers falling into the traps of wide and deep diagrams that no one can understand. Around a page (or screen) of readable text is a reasonable limit. One of the authors was recently asked to review a sequence diagram with 13 classes and was soon reaching for aspirin! Width-wise try not to exceed seven classes; Figure 6.13 has eight classes and is looking complex!

Depth and width of sequence diagrams need to be considered.

Sometimes, however, a complex diagram may simply be an indication that you have a complex system, despite all your best efforts to aim for a cohesive set of objects. In such cases partition the sequence diagram using nesting of child sequence diagrams. Clearly a certain amount of discretion is required. If you take the nesting strategy to its ultimate conclusion you could end up with seven or more hierarchical levels of sequence diagram, which are impossible to absorb as a unit simply because you have to flip back and forth between diagrams so much. And yet this does sometimes occur on real projects because of an obsession with one strategy to the exclusion of all others! Our advice is to adopt a balanced approach.

Nesting of sequence diagrams is useful for partitioning complexity.

6.5.9 Prototyping and Object Interaction Modeling

It is important to establish a strategy for when to prototype and when to model object interactions. This was less important in the days when rapid prototypes were used as a means of exploring requirements and then "thrown away." However, today the chances are that if you begin building a prototype in Visual Basic or Smalltalk, that prototype will evolve through optimization into the implementation environment. The distinction between prototyping as a requirements capture tool and prototyping as an interface design tool is becoming more blurred because of the flexibility and power of today's GUI builders. We recommend not to construct design sequence diagrams until **after** at least some prototyping has been done. We also recommend collaboration diagrams for playing individual cases through the model, independently of prototyping, to examine internal design issues and assess

Evolutionary prototypes are increasingly common.

technical feasibility **before** prototyping. Salient comments on the prototyping process are provided in chapter 9 but we do not attempt to discuss prototyping techniques in any detail for reasons of scope; the reader is referred to Connell and Shafer (1995) for a detailed account.

6.6 Summary

Object interaction modeling is highly iterative.

It is necessary for users to see *how* a system is going to be used, *how* it will appear, and *how* it will affect them before committing to what objects are needed. This means scouting ahead into design to better understand requirements as well as to get a feel for appropriate design shape or architecture. This means that object interaction modeling is highly iterative in practice. It is easy to get lost without some clear "sign posts."

We take a graduated approach.

It is important to start simple and gradually introduce complexity. Object interaction modeling can operate at a pure business level in the very early stages with design techniques gradually introduced based on the following steps:

- start with simple first-cut business sequence diagrams and collaboration diagrams,
- use the collaboration diagrams to explore the problem,
- gradually improve the diagrams,
- introduce some specific examples,
- carry out some prototyping,
- add user objects to the sequence diagrams,
- design user services, refine and improve the design,
- look for reusable services throughout!

This last point is particularly important: We develop it in chapters 8 and 9.

CHAPTER 7

• • • • • • • • • • • • • • • • • • • •

State Modeling

7.1 Introduction

State modeling examines the different events and associated state changes that can happen to an object through different periods of time. The "period of time" may be as specific as a single use case but may also be a period of several years! This is in contrast to object interaction modeling, which *always* takes use cases and scenarios as its point of departure.

State modeling addresses the dynamic behavior of objects.

The literature is rich with advice on state modeling and it is not our intention to repeat it. A problem with state modeling, no less than the other types of modeling discussed in this book, is that it is a wide subject with a potentially rich depth of coverage. A common reaction is "We'll leave state modeling to the real-time techies and concentrate on class diagrams and object interaction models." Certainly we agree that some of the notations tend to be over elaborate. However, if state modeling is ignored there are three risks that result.

State modeling tends to be underused and undervalued.

1. Undue strain is placed on other diagrams to model state-related behavior.
2. It is virtually impossible to arrive at a complete and definitive specification of behavior for each class.
3. Errors that would have been "designed out" using state diagrams are left for testing, or worse still, for irate users to discover.

We therefore spend some time explaining the driving principles behind state modeling to demonstrate its applicability before describing the notation to be used. For example, there are important connections between state modeling and object interaction modeling that are often misunderstood.

Driving principles are therefore key.

151
• • • • • • •

7.2 State Modeling Principles

7.2.1 Focus of Interest

A state diagram is a template for a class.

A state diagram shows allowable states that may exist for objects of a specific class and the permitted transitions between states: It shows all possible ways in which the objects can respond to events either from other objects or from outside the system. A state diagram can be pictured as a template for a class that governs the behavior of its member objects.

State modeling is selective.

State modeling should only be applied to classes whose objects exhibit interesting, complex, or problematic state-related behavior. Many objects are "modeless": They always respond to events in the same way regardless. Such objects may only have "Created," "Amended," and "Deleted" states. There is no value in applying state modeling to them. Rather, look for classes whose objects may be in one of a variety of different states when they receive given events and where the actions taken in response to events may vary depending on state. Such "interesting" objects fall into two broad categories.

First, there are objects that exhibit definite life-cycles.

A sale object may be proposed, negotiated, reviewed, agreed on, and eventually closed. Often there are cycles of events associated with such objects; for example, a sale is proposed, then negotiated, then reviewed, then negotiated again, then reviewed, and so on until agreement is reached. Conditional behavior is also common in such cases; perhaps if a sale is under a certain value it does not need review. State diagrams are very useful for addressing the patterns of sequential, repeatable, and conditional events. This aspect is mainly applicable to objects that model information and behavior associated with the system that persists beyond the completion of a single use case. The life-cycle approach to state diagrams echoes the techniques of entity life histories (Martin & Odell, 1992) and entity state transition diagrams (Allen, 1991).

Second, there are objects that exhibit interesting dynamic behavior.

A Transaction Controller object may be waiting for user input, scanning prices, transmitting to a database, and so on, until the transaction completes. As with life-cycle states, there are often sequences and cycles of events and conditional event-driven behavior associated with such objects. However, the majority of such events tend to be low granularity physical events (such as key presses, interrupts, and call returns) and not high granularity external system events (such as Customer requests order). At the user interface, the meaning of different events (key presses and mouse clicks) may be very context dependent. State modeling can be useful to expose and clarify the associated complex behavior patterns. Such behavior is usually dynamic in the sense that it does not span several use cases but is confined to different types of system behavior exhibited within a single use case. This aspect is mainly applicable to *control objects*, which manage the other objects participating in a use case and contain behavior that does not naturally belong elsewhere. They are usually transient: Typically they only survive during the execution of their associated use cases. The technique of event-related behavioral analysis echoes the event-partitioning technique of state transition diagramming (Allen, 1991; Ward Mellor, 1985).

As a general rule analysis-oriented state modeling is applicable to life-cycle state diagramming of business objects and high-level modeling of control objects, whereas design-oriented state modeling is more applicable to control objects, though this also depends on the proposed design structure, as discussed in section 7.5. Many authors, including Jacobson (1992) present state modeling as a design activity. While accepting the undoubted usefulness of state modeling in design, we have found it also to be useful in analysis on many projects. A summary of the purposes of object interaction modeling within Perspective follows:

In analysis:

- it helps in understanding requirements for different cycles of business activity,
- it finds and verifies business events,
- it finds and confirms operations and attributes,
- it verifies completeness of object behavior.

In design:

- it specifies control objects,
- it finds and verifies physical events,
- it helps to assess completeness of proposed designs,
- it helps establish message definitions, including operation signatures,
- it provides a template for program design (in event-driven design).

The techniques are markedly different according to which of the two approaches is used.

7.2.2 Key Concepts

7.2.2.1 States

A state is a time window that represents a condition or situation, obtaining during the life of an object, which helps govern the behavior of an object. A state is often associated with waiting for a stimulus to occur that may cause transition to another state. States may be behavioral, in which case the state name takes the form of present participles, such as "waiting," "finding," or "transmitting." On the other hand, states may relate to information content, in which case the state name takes the form of past participles such as "proposed," "overdrawn," or "paid."

An object's state can be thought of as an abstraction of a particular set of attribute values and links to other objects. The state is derivable from the attributes and links but is of sufficient interest in its own right as to be worth modeling separately. For example, it may be possible to derive the fact that a patient is "dangerously ill" from a combination of blood pressure > 200, temperature > 100, and links to certain treatment types. However, "dangerously ill" is a sufficiently interesting *state* in its own right because there are certain events that are permissible in this state, like "blood transfusion required," and other events that are not permissible in this state, like "hair wash and manicure required." The permissible transitions between this and other associated states, "critically ill," "stable," "recovered" embody different business rules. For example, it is allowed to change state from "dangerously ill" to "critically ill" but not to "stable."

7.2.2.2 Transitions

A transition is a change of state triggered by a stimulus. The stimulus may be an operation request, an event, a guard condition(s), or a combination of an event or operation request plus a guard condition(s). Transitions may invoke operations or transmit events. Refer to section 7.5 for more information on different types of event.

7.2.2.3 Guard Conditions

A guard condition is an assertion that must be satisfied in order to cause an associated transition to be triggered.

7.2.2.4 State Variables

States are held in attributes known as "state variables." A single state diagram has a corresponding state variable; for example, patient state. A state variable contains the value of a state for a particular object; for example, the object Fred may have a state variable value of "critically ill" and Jim may have a state variable value of "stable." A class may have more than one state attribute with separate state diagrams for each; for example, patient condition and patient insurance.

7.3 State Modeling Notation

7.3.1 Basic Notation Set

The notation set for state modeling, which is derived from Harel (1987), follows the Unified Modeling Language (UML, 1997). As with other diagrams, Perspective advocates a lightweight approach restricted to the concepts that we have found useful on real projects.

The basic building blocks of the diagram are states and transitions, as shown in Figure 7.1. The initial state indicates the birthpoint for an object from which a transition takes an object to the state that it first acquires on instantiation. A class can have multiple initial states associated with different events causing instantiation. The final state indicates than an object ceases to exist. A class can also have multiple final states associated with different events causing deletion.

A transition is labeled with a transition string, which has the following format:

EVENT-NAME (Parameters) [GUARD CONDITION]/ ACTION EXPRESSION

In Perspective we use "EVENT-NAME" to cover both actual events and requests for/returns from operations on the host object, which is expedient for

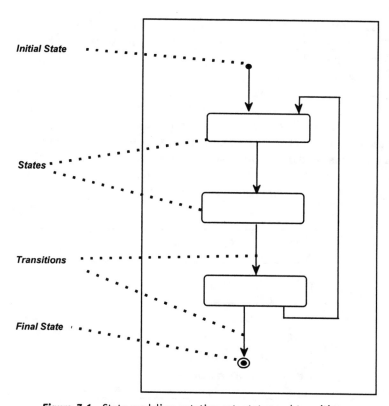

Figure 7.1. State modeling notation set: states and transitions.

integrating with the object interaction model (see 6.2.2). Parameter values and guard conditions can be used to qualify the event or operation. A guard condition is a boolean expression that may include attribute and/or parameter values. If the event occurs and the guard condition is true, then the transition occurs. Note also that a guard condition may trigger a transition without an associated event.

An action expression executes when the transition is triggered. It is used to trigger an operation on the host object. Note that there can be several action expressions, each executing a complete operation in sequence. A send clause is a special type of action expression. It is used to send events to other objects in the form CLASS NAME. EVENT NAME. Again for expediency we use "EVENT-NAME" to cover both actual events and calls to/returns from operations on the other object, which is expedient for integrating with the object interaction model (see 6.2.2). Also, the target object may be omitted where the target is not known or where the event is transmitted outside the system boundary.

A state may have further optional compartments, as illustrated in Figure 7.2. The middle compartment can be used to declare state variables. The bottom compartment can be used to list transition strings that are internal to the state as well as the following special types of transition. An entry transition is automatically performed whenever the state is entered by any transition. Similarly an exit transition is performed whenever the state is exited by any transition. Entry and exit transitions are shown within the lower state segment with the pseudo event names **entry** and **exit**. This is in effect a useful shorthand that replaces the need to attach the associated event/action block to all transitions either entering or leaving a state. Finally, a "do" transition is used for operations that are ongoing within the state. On exit from the state, the

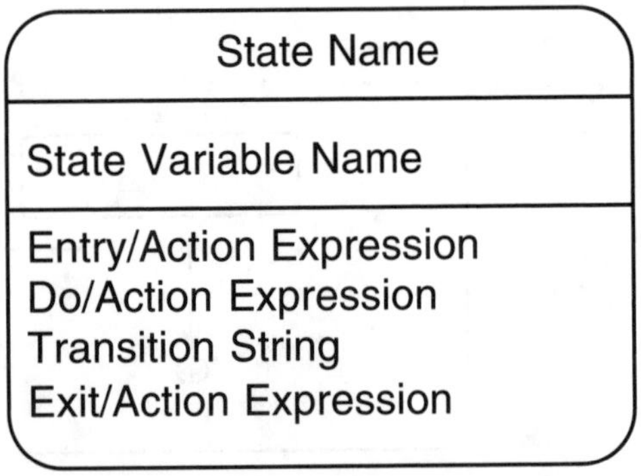

```
┌─────────────────────────────────┐
│           State Name            │
├─────────────────────────────────┤
│   State Variable Name           │
├─────────────────────────────────┤
│   Entry/Action Expression       │
│   Do/Action Expression          │
│   Transition String             │
│   Exit/Action Expression        │
└─────────────────────────────────┘
```

Figure 7.2. State notation compartments.

associated operation is automatically disabled. Do transitions are prefixed with the pseudo event name "**do**."

A state can be partitioned using *and* relationships into concurrent substates or using *or* relationships into mutually exclusive substates. A specific state can only be refined in one of these ways. Substates can be further partitioned using either way. This is extremely useful for dealing with complex diagrams. Special notation is available, as described in the next section. However, in Perspective, nesting of diagrams is considered a much more elegant and readable option.

Nesting of state diagrams is achieved with an operation, which is invoked using the "do" pseudo event name, as indicated in Figure 7.3. Such an operation takes time to complete. Its states are assumed exclusive unless the concurrent notation (next section) is overlaid on the whole subdiagram. Nested state diagrams are particularly useful for managing complexity; for example, hiding sequential series of states that would otherwise clutter the main diagram.

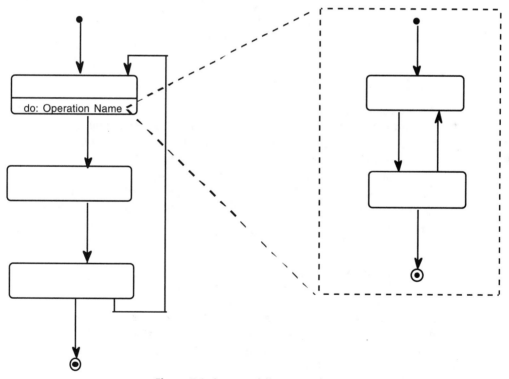

Figure 7.3. State modeling: nested state.

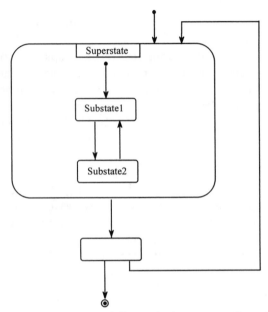

Figure 7.4. State modeling *And* substates notation set.

7.3.2 Further Notation Set

A state can be partitioned using *and* relationships, as shown in Figure 7.4. The substates inherit the transitions of the parent. This is analogous to specialization of classes in an inheritance hierarchy: The different substates inherit the properties of the superstate.

Finally it is possible to model concurrency on a state diagram using concurrent substates shown by partitioning a state into regions with dashed lines. Each region is a concurrent substate. When the enclosing state is entered, there is one thread of control for each substate. Splitting or merging of concurrent threads can be shown by a synchronization bar (see Figure 7.5).

7.3.3 The State Model

State modeling involves building views of classes whose object members exhibit interesting dynamic behavior. Collectively these views together with their underlying definitions are referred to as the "state model." These views are largely diagrammatic with minimal additional textual support.

7.3.3.1 Diagrammatic Views

Diagrammatic views consist of state diagrams, as described previously.

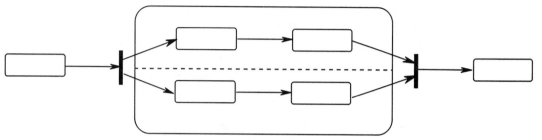

Figure 7.5. State modeling *Or* substates notation set.

7.3.3.2 Textual Views

The only textual views exclusive to the state model are state descriptions and guard conditions in event/action blocks. In design state diagrams it may additionally be useful to include references to particular implementation constraints such as timing constraints.

7.3.6 Integration with Object Interaction Model

An issue that we addressed in chapter 6 was the relationship between state modeling and object interaction modeling. Object-oriented methods often seem to neglect this important area, which often brings consternation not only to the faces of developers, but also experienced consultants! In section 6.2.2.5 we presented some guidelines for addressing this issue. To understand why these are presented as *guidelines* rather than in terms of the rigorous formula that is sometimes sought, we need to understand the wider picture. Each scenario can be pictured as a "slice" of system behavior across different state diagrams from different classes. A use case represents a collective abstraction of such behaviors, which we can picture as a cross-section of typical behaviors across different state diagrams from different classes, as shown in Figure 7.6.

Note how an event transmitted from one object is received by another object causing change of state. Use cases and scenarios are prototypical: They cannot be practically used to give a complete and definitive specification of the entire system's behavior. For a complete picture, it is sometimes argued, we need state diagrams for all classes: Ultimately the set of use cases can be derived from the entire set of state diagrams. Although this is theoretically true in a "white-room" environment, this argument rapidly breaks down in the "pressure cooker" of today's software-development environments. Note that the use case in Figure 7.6 only tracks the state changes indicated by the events itemized; even in this simple example there could be many other possible combinations with corresponding paths through the state diagrams that would not justify modeling in their entirety. Conversely, there are often operation calls made in the object interaction that are not state dependent and do not justify the expense of using state diagrams to model.

Returning to the section 6.2.2 guidelines, the states (and guard conditions) of different objects can govern the possible behaviors in a use case or scenario in terms of preconditions obtaining at the *start* of the use case or scenario. Similarly, on *completion* of a use case or scenario each object should be left in a consistent state that may correspond to the associated postconditions of the use case or scenario. Following the guidelines, with respect to Figure 7.6, yields the results shown in Table 7.1. for the "normal" **scenario**.

We can see even in this simple case that trying to specify the complete set of pre- and postcondition for a **use case** involves multiple optional states that really provide little value. Rather, we may specify a pre- and postcondition pair for each scenario that occurs within a use case.

Also note that the relationship between pre- and postconditions and states is optional. For example, suppose A called an operation on D instead of sending EO3 to D (see Figure 7.6). It may be that the operation can execute in all states of D but has pre- and postconditions associated with attribute values that are simply not worth modeling as states.

7.4 State Modeling Techniques

The key rule is to start simple and gradually introduce complexity.

We start by considering straightforward patterns of events and gradually introduce alternative patterns of events such as errors and exceptions, as understanding of the problem sharpens. As mentioned in section 7.2, there are two broad approaches to state modeling: life-cycles and behavior. Both are event driven: Expect to iterate between state diagrams and events. However, the former concentrates on changes in information state over periods of time that typically span several use cases, whereas the latter focuses on behavioral state

Table 7.1. Results for "Normal" Scenario		
Object	**Precondition**	**Postcondition**
A	start state	a3
B	b1	b2
C	c2	final state
D	d1	d2

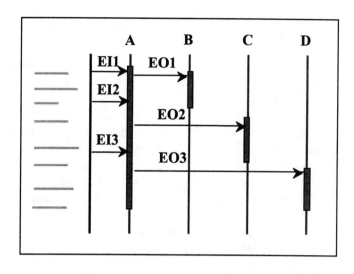

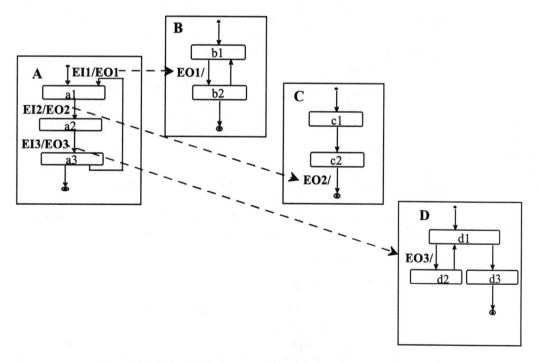

Figure 7.6. Relationship between Object-Interaction Model and State Model.

changes within single use cases or scenarios. For a more detailed treatment of design-state diagrams the reader is referred to Ackley and Stringfield's (1995) article.

Life-cycle analysis concentrates on central business objects.

Life-cycle analysis is performed largely independently of object interaction modeling though it is important to make sure that state diagrams are consistent with collaboration diagrams and sequence diagrams, as described in section 6.2.2. It is best to start with objects that are central to the domain under study; for example, Order in an order-processing domain, Policy in a life-insurance domain. Their states reflect sets of attribute values and links over periods of time, which may span several use cases. For example, a customer account changes from proposed to live to closed. A list of external events, built up from business process modeling can be used to initiate this process as described in section 7.4.1. The initial state diagram is gradually elaborated, as described in section 7.4.2 and 7.4.3.

Behavioral analysis concentrates on control objects.

Behavioral analysis takes the collaboration diagrams and sequence diagrams as its starting point, looking at each scenario or use case and focusing in on particular objects that have a high degree of interaction. Often there are one or two objects in a scenario or use case that are clearly central to the process and handle much of the message traffic. Typically these will be control objects, which are often worth modeling using state diagrams. For example, state diagrams can be used to model control of user interfaces where the system has to process a large number of combinations of events triggered through standard key presses and mouse clicks within a single use case; the behavior changes dynamically over a short space of time (i.e., the duration of the use case). Typical states might be "waiting for input," "displaying a form, " or "searching for data." Sections 7.4.4 and 7.4.5 illustrate the main steps in building a state diagram for a control object.

Further techniques focus on reuse of state diagrams.

Where state-related behavior is potentially reusable across different applications, it is worth considering separating out this behavior to form a new object with its own state diagram; this is covered in section 7.4.6. Such objects are service objects, techniques for which are discussed in chapters 8 and 9. This is particularly important in engineering components that have complex dynamic behavior.

7.4.1 Creating an Initial State Diagram

Initial state diagrams help with scoping issues.

A state diagram can be immensely useful for understanding patterns of required behavior early in a project. Recently, one of the authors was involved in analyzing a dealing system for a bank. In attempting to understand the scope of the system at Feasibility stage, a look at possible use cases proved uninteresting. Deals were simply entered, reviewed, and authorized. However, switching the focus to the central subject of the analysis, the deal, and examining how the deal changed state according to different patterns of events proved much more interesting. Deals could be unauthorized, reviewed, checked, authorized, deferred, and placed: The possible transitions between states yielded lots of interesting business issues that helped with problem understanding. The use of a state diagram enabled communication of business knowledge about objects that would have been difficult to visualize without the assistance of graphical representation.

External system events (see chapter 4) for the Motor Dealership example are listed in Table 7.2. The central subject of this event list is clearly the Job class. Consider the normal pattern of events that affect a Job. There is a clear sequence of events that result in a Job being built up step-by-step from initiation to eventual closure. The Job exhibits a definite life history, from cradle to grave, with respect to the events. Each event causes Job to change its state, forming a precondition for receipt of the next event in the chain. However, the event "Parts requested" is only required if, having established the parts needed for the job, it is found that certain parts are not available. This is an exception that will be addressed shortly. For now a state diagram is constructed for the normal flow of events, as illustrated in Figure 7.7. Notice that the event names are superfluous at this stage for practical purposes of definition within the model.

Start by building an external event list.

7.4.2 Expanding a State Diagram

In the previous section, the event "Parts requested" was recognized as only required if, having established the parts needed for the job, it is found that certain parts are not available. The assumption is that the job will only be scheduled if parts are in stock. This needs to be made explicit on the diagram as it

Table 7.2. Service and Repair Vehicle: Events and EBPs

Event number	External system-event name	Use case
1	Job requested	Book Job for Customer
2	Parts time	Establish Parts for Job
3	Parts requested	Request Parts for Job
4	Schedule time	Schedule Jobs for Day
5	Job completed	Record Job Completion
6	Customer arrives	Close Job with Customer

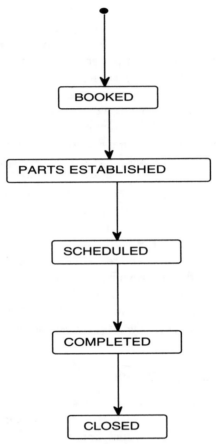

Figure 7.7. Initial state diagram for Job class.

Guard conditions are added where necessary.

reflects important business policy. A guard condition [In Stock] is added to the transition from Parts Established to Scheduled. Another guard condition, [Not in Stock] is introduced to provide transition to a Waiting-for-Parts state. Note this is an example in which a guard condition without an accompanying event can cause a change of state.

Various scenarios are applied in expanding the diagram.

The event "Parts requested" can occur at any time and is an important event with its own use case. However, it does not affect the state of the Job object. **Rather, the Job object is interested in when the required parts are actually received so that it can schedule itself!** On receipt of the required parts control returns to the Established state. "Parts arrive" is in fact a new event that should be added to the event list. It is also important to consider what happens if parts do not arrive before schedule time: It is decided to suspend the job pending action from the customer.

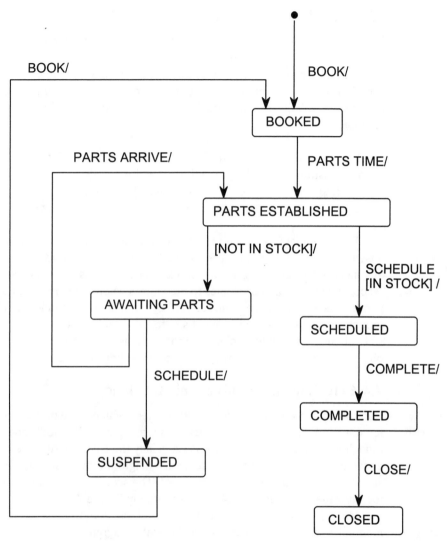

Figure 7.8. Second-cut state diagram for Job class.

Operations on the host class are only used in situations where further logic, other than a simple change of state, is needed. For expediency operations on the host class are shown as event names; for example, Schedule on the host class is invoked in response to Schedule Time [In Stock]. This is abbreviated to Schedule [In Stock] (see Figure 7.8).

Operations are added where necessary on the host class.

7.4.3 Detailing a State Diagram

We need to consider situations not covered by the use cases.

Having established the basic cycle of events, exceptions and other events can be considered and the state diagram expanded accordingly; invoked operations are added and events issued to other objects are included where necessary. This involves thinking about abnormal circumstances and generally testing out the validity of the model in the face of unusual circumstances. For example:

- What happens if the customer decides to cancel the job?
- Can a customer cancel a job without penalty?
- What happens if the mechanic falls ill having already scheduled the job?
- Are jobs to be retained "closed" forever or deleted after a specified time?

Technical neutrality of business objects is retained.

The state diagram is used for raising such questions and documenting the answers, as shown in Figure 7.9. Notice that events outbound to other objects are included where necessary. For example, the Customer object is to be responsible for issuing apologies to customers where jobs have had to be suspended because parts have not arrived or a mechanic has fallen ill. Note that though the state diagram is now at a detailed level, it assumes as little as possible about its possible implementation. This is highly desirable for business objects, such as Job, which must be kept as technically neutral as possible.

7.4.4 Creating an Initial-Control State Diagram

Objects with interesting dynamic behavior are identified.

Control objects such as the Job Control object, which is the user service object for the Book Job for Customer use case, are generally good candidates for modeling as state diagrams. This is especially the case where there is an associated collaboration diagram or sequence diagram that shows significant message traffic gravitating around the object. The sequence diagram for Book Job for Customer (see section 6.4.6), is repeated in Figure 7.10.

Inbound and outbound messages are used to help create a state diagram.

Message flows inbound and outbound on Job Control correspond to inbound and outbound events on the state diagram. Returns on outbound messages may also correspond to inbound events on the state diagram. The "time gap" between inbound messages from the system boundary always corresponds to a state. Such states are imposed by the environment. For example, the time gap between initial creation of the object and receiving customer input corresponds to the "Awaiting Customer Input" state. The time gap between messages inbound from objects will similarly result in corresponding states. Outbound messages to objects may also result in states where there is conditional behavior that depends on the result of the message return. For example, the return from Customer's Find operation results in a transition back to

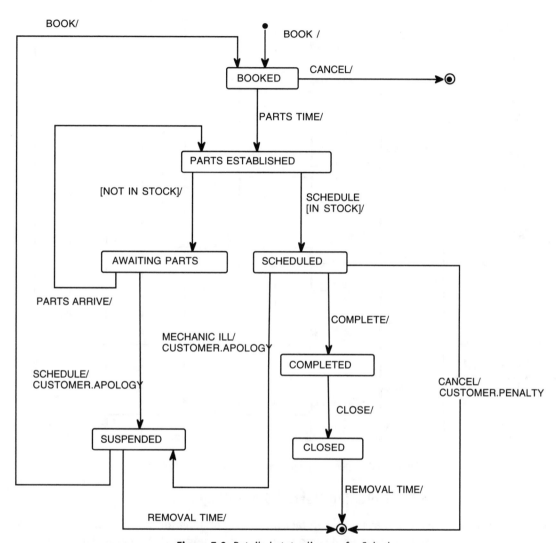

Figure 7.9. Detailed state diagram for Job class.

"Awaiting Customer Input" if the customer is not found, but results in a transition to "Awaiting List Selection" if a customer is found. Therefore a state "Matching Customer" is included to enable this to be conveniently modeled. Note that the state diagram is typically used to include conditional and exception behavior that would clutter the sequence diagram. The resulting state diagram from a first-pass analysis of the sequence diagram is shown in Figure 7.11.

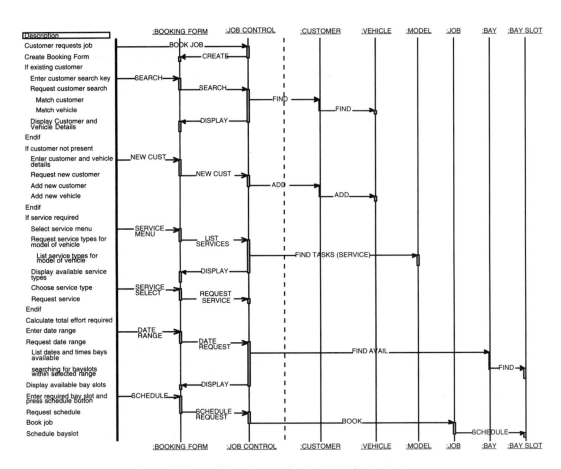

Figure 7.10. Sequence diagram for Book Job for Customer.

7.4.5 Developing Nested State Diagrams

Following UML, state diagrams are also useful for modeling nested behavior.

Suppose that there is in fact more to searching for a customer than a simple match process as described in the preceding text. Suppose that the user is given the facility of entering a search key, say leading characters of surname plus initials, through a search-view form. The search key is used to find a list of matching customers who are then listed on a customer-list view form. The user then selects the required customer from the list. The searching activity can be considered as nested behavior within a "Performing Customer Search" state, as shown in Figures 7.12 and 7.13. Note that the nested diagram corresponds to a search operation on Job Control. This technique is very useful for sequential state-related activities. Finally service selection has been generalized to take advantage of the Find Tasks service on Model.

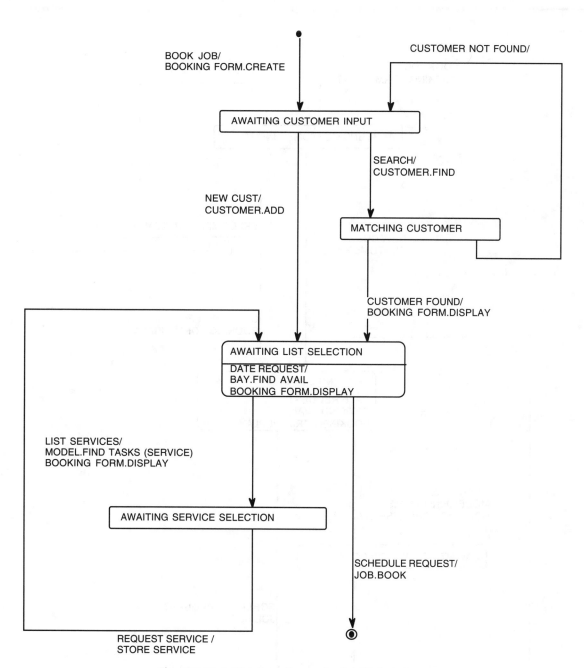

Figure 7.11. Initial state diagram for Job Control class.

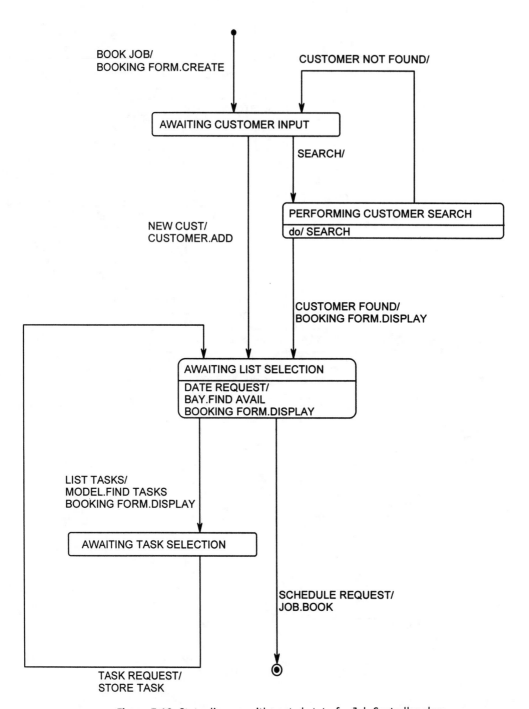

Figure 7.12. State diagram with nested state for Job Controller class.

7.4.6 Reusing Enterprise State Diagrams

Where control behavior is potentially reusable across different applications it is worth considering separating out this behavior to form a new control object with its own state diagram.

Separate out reusable control behavior.

    The customer-search process described previously is a good candidate for abstraction as it might be invocable by lots of different use cases. In fact a Customer Searcher is introduced to manage the matching process as a business service, as described in section 9.3.3. The Customer Searcher object is invoked by sending a triggering message CUSTOMER SEARCHER.SEARCH from Job Control, as shown in Figure 7.14. This causes a transition to the "Performing Customer Search" state as before, except this time responsibility for searching has passed to the Customer Searcher object; the "do:" statement is accordingly removed.

Use the right tool for the job.

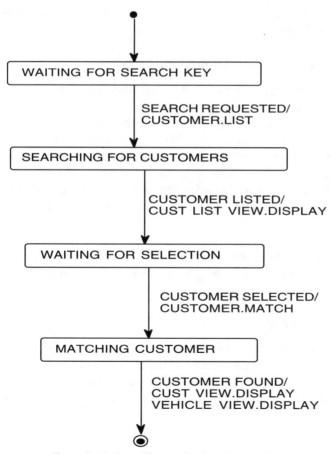

Figure 7.13. State diagram for Search operation.

7.5 Practical Guidelines for State Modeling

Some guidelines follow.

There are certain pragmatic points that we have found to apply in the arena of real-life projects. A summary of these points follows.

7.5.1 State Model or Object Interaction Model?

Try state modeling as an alternative strategy.

A common mistake is to try to cater to too many scenarios using a single use case. This can result in a complicated, large, and messy sequence diagram that is ultimately self-defeating. Collaboration diagrams can be used to model scenarios and are particularly useful for modeling alternative courses. However, it is important to understand that sequence diagrams and collaboration diagrams are both *illustrative* diagrams. Use cases and scenarios should not be employed to cater to every contingency. As we have pointed out to many developers "If your only tool is a hammer, the whole world looks like a nail!" State diagrams provide a complete definition of event-driven behavior for objects of a single class.

7.5.2 Concentrating on Significant Behavior

Examine changes in attribute values.

A state diagram is useful for classes whose objects have an attribute that can take on a small range of values and where the permitted transitions between those values are restricted. In deciding whether or not to create a state diagram for a business class we are often told to "concentrate on classes with significant behavioral patterns." However, there is sometimes a fine line between what may be described as the "significant" behavior amenable to state modeling and other behavior that is not usefully modeled using state diagrams. It is worth examining the attributes of each class and asking the following questions:

1. Does the attribute only take a small range of values (say 7 plus or minus 2) ?
2. Are there business rules which dictate that only certain changes in the attribute's values are allowed?

7.5.3 Consistency

Events should balance.

The different state diagrams should be checked for consistency: An event transmitted by one diagram should either be received by another diagram or sent out of the system. Similarly an event received on a state diagram should either be sent by another diagram or received across the system boundary.

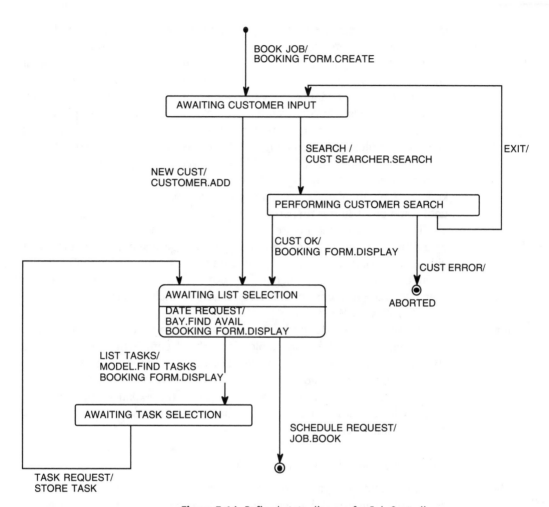

Figure 7.14. Refined state diagram for Job Controller.

7.5.4 Design Structure

State diagrams are a useful tool *in analysis* for a variety of reasons, as we have already seen. However, the applicability of state diagrams *in design* is heavily influenced by the design structure chosen for handling control.

    The procedure-driven structure localizes control within the program code. A procedure issues a call and waits for return; on return of input, control resumes within the calling procedure. This is the traditional way of implement-

Two design structures...

...The procedure-driven structure.

ing control in all major object-oriented languages, such as Smalltalk and C++.

State diagrams are less useful here.

A state diagram can be used to assist in procedure-driven design. However, the designer must convert the state diagram to a master operation and events to statements (or called operations) within the master operation. Asynchronous input cannot easily be handled because inbound and outbound events are always coupled according to call and return. Another problem is that deeply nested control structures within operations can considerably increase complexity. As Rumbaugh (1992) writes, "Each input statement needs to handle any input value that could be received at that point. In highly nested procedural code, low-level procedures must accept inputs that they may know nothing about and pass them up through many levels of procedure calls until some procedure is prepared to handle them."

...The event-driven structure...

The event-driven structure attaches procedures to events that are called by a dispatcher when the corresponding events occur under acceptable conditions. Control is returned by a procedure to the monitor, rather than waiting for input return. This is an increasingly popular structure for building flexible user interfaces and control software; examples include Visual Basic, Visual C++, SunView, X-Windows.

State diagrams are more useful here.

An event-driven design implements a state diagram as a separate class representing a state-transition table. Each object contains its own state variables but calls on the state-transition class to determine the next state and action. If changes are required to the pattern of events they are easily localized within the state-transition class; this approach is expanded by Rumbaugh (1993) who discusses approaches for implementing state diagrams using a state-machine interpreter.

7.5.5 Using State Diagrams for Detailed Design

Implementation affects the value of a detailed design-state diagram.

Behavioral state diagrams are often worth developing further as a detailed design tool. This is certainly worthwhile, if you actually intend to *implement* the state-diagram logic using a state-transition class (with the event-driven structure) or a master operation (with the procedural-driven structure) and are prepared to pay the extra cost of doing so! Life-cycle state diagrams are generally much less useful for modeling detailed design. Often a procedural approach is used to implement such objects and the value of a state diagram to model the design is greatly diminished.

7.5.6 Identifying the Right Events at the Right Time

We follow the principle reinforced throughout this book of keeping interfaces of business objects as technically neutral as possible. In contrast, state diagrams for objects, such as user objects, are closely tied to the requirements of their implementation environment, which is reflected in the appearance of physical events on state diagrams for such objects. As Larry Ackerley and Dawn Stringfield (1995) write, "Events as they are defined during analysis have a fundamentally different character than events as they are specified during design. The former are identified qualitatively. An 'analysis event' represents an occurrence that for business reasons should be communicated to an object at some point in its existence. The means by which the event is sensed, how it is communicated to the interested object, and how the interested object is located will be determined later."

State diagrams for business objects should be technically neutral.

All events are specific stimuli that cause a one-way asynchronous transmission of information. Internal system events are issued by objects and are either directed to other objects or generally broadcast. External system events occur outside the system boundary and require an object to make a response.

Different types of event are important.

External triggering system events are stimuli that trigger complete use cases or scenarios. Some external system events are signaled by the arrival of information from outside the system; for example, Customer submits order or Customer-service clerk requests credit approval. Other external system events may be temporal or conditional. Temporal events are signaled by the arrival of a predefined point in time. Conditional events report the sensing of a particular circumstance, which triggers an elementary process; for example, Credit limit exceeded. External interface system events are implementation-specific mechanisms that typically follow a triggering external system event; examples are mouse clicks and button pushes.

External triggering system events...

In analysis the focus is on external triggering system events; in design the focus is on external interface system events. External interface system events are at a lower level of granularity than external triggering system events. For example, the single triggering event Customer-service clerk requests credit approval might correspond to several interface events at the user interface (security entered, password entered, customer entered, retry button pressed, cancel button pressed, confirm button pressed, and so on). The same external event (triggering or interface) might also correspond to several internal system events communicated between objects (customer found, credit bad, credit good, and so on). Our approach has centered on understanding the external triggering system events first, otherwise you could end up modeling a lot of detail that turns out to be irrelevant.

...and external interface system events.

7.6 Summary

State diagrams are often underused on real-life projects.

In this chapter we have tried to show that state modeling is a valuable activity within Perspective. It is important, however, to apply state modeling selectively and in the appropriate way. A streamlined set of the full UML (1997) notation generally works best. Important features of state modeling are as follows:

- There are two basic approaches: life-cycle analysis, which is best applied to business objects, and behavioral analysis, which is best applied to control objects.
- It is *definitive* of how objects of a single class behave according to events received and object states. This is in contrast to object interaction modeling, which is *illustrative* of how different objects collaborate together to service particular scenarios and use cases. States are often preconditions for successful execution of use cases and scenarios.
- It is essentially an iterative process; therefore it is important to start simple and gradually introduce complexity.

Life-cycle and behavioral state diagrams are importantly different.

Examples were used to illustrate a selection of the more mainstream techniques as follows:

Life-cycle approach:

- Start with a list of business events: Identify the interesting business objects.
- Apply the main business events to each interesting business object to create first-cut state diagrams.
- Expand the state diagram to include further events.
- Consider errors and exceptions and improve the state diagram.
- Try to achieve a technically neutral state diagram.

Behavioral approach:

- Start with sequence diagrams and collaboration diagrams: Identify key objects (usually control objects) with heavy messaging.
- Create an initial state diagram with states to reflect message waits between physical events.
- Expand the state diagram to include further scenarios and exceptions.
- Look for opportunities to reuse state-related behavior.
- Refine the state diagram to cater to all required physical events.

CHAPTER 8

• •

Business-Oriented Component Modeling

8.1 Introduction

Components are a very flexible and powerful means of implementing reusable services through a consistent, published interface that includes an interaction standard. Progress has been made in developing good reusable technical components, such as programming components and document components. However, domain-related *business* components present a set of yet more demanding challenges that the software industry is finding extremely difficult to come to terms with.

Our focus is on business-oriented components.

With the emergence of any new technology there is always a tendency to throw out previous-generation techniques under the illusion that the new technology represents some panacea for all ills. This happened in the early 1990s as many analysts threw out their structured models with the emergence of object-oriented methods. It seems to be happening again today: With the emergence of component technology there is a tendency to dismiss objects as passé. However, experience teaches that effective *architecture* and *process* are keynotes.

Progress in software development is evolutionary.

Perspective includes reuse-oriented techniques.

It is commonly written that reuse is a *management* issue. This is undoubtedly true and requires an effective process, which we describe in chapter 13. However, *techniques* specifically aimed at business-oriented components are often neglected, perhaps for that reason. The scope of this chapter is restricted to a sample of those techniques that are immediately useful for the goal of component engineering in the context of Perspective.

Leveraging legacy assets is an important part of our strategy.

The reality of legacy assets is often ignored by idealistic methods that assume a "clean slate." We discuss approaches to reusing legacy systems, databases, and packages in chapter 9. The present chapter focuses on techniques for helping to ensure that the correct business requirements are addressed before applying wrapping.

8.2 Business-Oriented Component Modeling Principles

8.2.1 Focus of Interest

Business-oriented component modeling seeks to address some key challenges.

We believe the gains to be made from reusing *business* objects are huge compared to potential gains in implementation reuse of class code from libraries. In turn we believe the gains to be made from reusing *business services* outweigh potential gains in reusing business objects. It is *components* that provide the enabling technology for achieving this goal (see Figure 8.1). This is the essence of *business-oriented* component modeling, which seeks to address the following challenges:

Quality: The development of new components, reusable across a range of solutions, requires demanding standards of quality. For example, there is a need for greater degree of rigor and detail; if the resulting components are used in potentially thousands of applications, the effects of mistakes can result in very high accumulated damage. Also our techniques need to help with achieving generality without sacrificing overall maintainability.

Practicality: Potentially reusable but never-used components developed at high cost represent as much of a waste of time as the old tradition of doing the same things over again. There is a need for balance in achieving practical levels of reuse. It is important therefore to maximize harvesting of potential components from local projects and to avoid modeling unnecessary implementation detail.

Focus: The sources of components are potentially extremely diverse: for example, domain knowledge, business process knowledge, frameworks, patterns, legacy assets, and the increasing array of componentware available over the Internet. In setting out to model components it is easy to

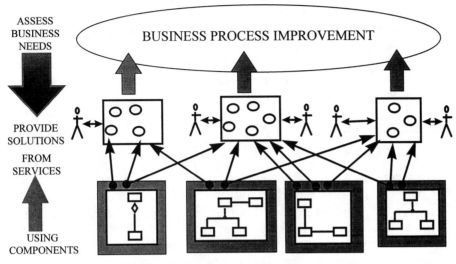

Figure 8.1. Component modeling in context.

"get lost" in this richness of potential material. The techniques described in this chapter are intended to help focus our thinking.

Granularity: Objects are usually at too low a level of useful granularity. Object reuse is implemented in the form of class browsers, which tend to have a very technical implementation focus tuned in to code reuse. At the other extreme objects bundled together into high-level systems tend to perform badly because they inherit unnecessary heavy baggage, are a maintenance nightmare, and are poor in cohesion. The key challenge is to glean an effective level of reuse that can be pitched at business needs. Coding environments are already providing higher level process support. For example, Visual C++ has color syntax editors, wizards for application frameworks, specialized forms of class manipulation, and overviews of systems at the class level. Business-oriented component modeling therefore does not aim for reuse of code (although that is a nice by-product), but aims for reuse of models. Therefore components are not addressed in the sense of "modules" but at the level of "service packages"; see the glossary for clarification.

Legacy Assets: The existence of huge investments in databases and package software as well as bespoke software written in previous-generation languages such as COBOL, PL/1, FORTRAN, and Assembler has to be recognized and dealt with by the brave new world of components. Wrappers hold the promise of migration to object technology while protecting investments in existing databases and code. The temptation is often to wrap legacy assets on the basis that it "seemed like a good idea at the time." Business-oriented component modeling helps ensure that the correct business requirements are addressed, as a foundation for wrapping, which is considered in the next chapter.

8.2.2 Key Concepts

8.2.2.1 Packages

A package is "a general purpose mechanism for organizing elements into groups"(UML, 1997). Such elements can range from model items (classes, use cases, and so on) to legacy assets (for example, compiled code, transaction, or database libraries). A package provides a scope for a set of names of the elements contained within it. The name of a package must be unique. In the component marketplace this name must be unique worldwide in similar fashion to a URL (an Internet address of the form http://ahost/adirectory/afile). The package name must not change once it is published. Importantly, packages are used to declare an interest in reusing legacy assets (see chapter 9) as well as components from external sources, which have been identified using component management facilities.

8.2.2.2 Service Packages and Component Packages

We must be careful to distinguish between two basic stereotypes of package: packages in the sense of collections of executable instances and packages as abstractions that we want to model. In talking packages in implementation we're talking executable components or *component packages*; in talking packages in business-oriented component modeling we're talking about abstractions of components or *service packages*.

Classes that have a high level of interdependency and serve a common purpose should be allocated to the same service package. It is this higher level of granularity that characterizes business-oriented components. By architecting our service packages as early as possible and allocating classes to them we maximize the opportunity to build service reuse. A service package contains a group of classes that should have minimal interfaces with classes outside the service package. A class is included in only one service package.

Packages provide an excellent method for structuring and reusing models. They provide a means of structuring a project in terms of architectural context and allow us to build on and capitalize the very best work of others. A service package is effectively employed to contain a generic model, which can be refined and extended to meet specific needs, in analogous fashion to a framework.

Once a service package is allocated to a node modeled on deployment diagrams (see chapter 10) the package effectively becomes a component package. A component package represents actual code. A deployment diagram represents run-time architecture. Packages on a node represent executable components in contrast to packages unallocated to nodes, which are an abstraction; this corresponds to the difference between instance and type.

8.2.2.3 Dependencies

Dependencies are a Unified Modeling Language (UML, 1997) concept. Where a package uses services from another package, the first package is said to be dependent on the latter. Dependencies can also obtain in the other direction (peer to peer).

8.2.2.4 Services

A service groups one or more operations that bind together to form a contract with consumers of the service. A service is triggered through an operation: *Such operations are stereotyped as services.* There are three service categories (from chapter 2): business service, data service, and user service. User services are always triggered through user objects. Note that both business and data services can be triggered through user objects as well as through objects of the corresponding layer.

8.2.2.5 Service Classes

Classes that are to provide services will need interfaces designed for them. As we want to focus on service-based business-oriented modeling, we don't want to model interfaces. However, we still need a mechanism for identifying and modeling where interfaces are going to be required. This is important for achieving a design that mirrors business needs. This is where *service classes* come in. A service class is a type of class, providing one or more services, which represents an abstraction of a component interface(s). A service class is used to help retain a domain focus in modeling without becoming embroiled in the potential complications of implementation. The fact that a class is a service class *is derived* from the fact that at least one of its operations is stereotyped as a service.

A service class is implemented using one or more component interfaces. Without such a class, all messages from outside a component go directly to its constituent objects, which means that the message senders must have some knowledge of what objects the component contains. A service object delegates by sending each message to the appropriate object. The service class allows the component to wrap its objects and can delegate services to those objects, including resolution of polymorphism.

A service class is typically a control class exclusively designed to provide services through a component's interface. However, services can be allocated to any appropriate class, which then has the role of service class. In either case, the services are implemented through a component interface of the service class. Good design practice indicates that access to the services provided by a component should require knowledge of as few of the component's objects as possible. However, whether or not to use a service class designed exclusively to provide services depends on the circumstances. When building a component for use by third parties, across the Internet, for example, there is much more of a case for using a service class designed exclusively to provide services. On the other hand, there is much less of a case for an exclusive service class with components that are internal to the organization.

8.3 Business-Oriented Component Modeling Notation

8.3.1 Notation Set

The same notations as already described in chapters 4 to 7 are used, with the addition of packages, dependencies, and service classes, as shown in Figure 8.2.

In this book we have adopted the convention that the stereotype name is only shown within the package icon for component packages; if the name is blank you can assume the package is a service package.

Packages can be nested. A class is included in only one package. A lowest level package is the smallest unit used for distribution to different nodes. It is possible to "explode" packages to show contained classes in the form of a class diagram that appears nested within the package; any number of packages can be shown in this way, with package names shown within their "tabs." A class in another package can be shown on a class diagram, by using a path name for the class in the form: PACKAGE-NAME::CLASS-NAME (this can be nested). This is useful where you do not want to view all the detail in projects with lots of classes that have been split into several packages. If such a class is from another package the external class notation may be used; see 8.3.4 for details.

A package dependency is drawn as a dashed arrow from one package to the package that the first package is dependent on. This provides a mechanism for reuse of packages outside of a project; for example, a package that is imported via a component management tool.

NAME	SYMBOL	DESCRIPTION
Package	<<Stereotype>> Package Name Class Name1 Class Name2	Conceptual grouping of model items Service classes may optionally be shown in lower box
Dependency	 - - - - - - - ▶	Source depends on services from target
Service Class	Service Class Name Attribute Name n *Service Name 1* *Service Name 2* .... Operation Name 1	Class name Service names in bold italics

Figure 8.2. Component modeling notation set.

In Perspective we allow service classes to be shown in a drop-down lower box on the package icon. A service class is evident from the notation that those of its operations that are services are italicized in bold text.

8.3.2 Diagrammatic Views

Diagrammatic views are as before with the addition of package dependency diagrams, which show dependencies between packages as arrowed dashed lines pointing from client package to target server package. Packages may also be included on class diagrams. A package dependency diagram provides an architectural view of how we propose to group classes to provide services.

8.3.3 Textual Views

Class browsers have been widely available for some years. However, until recently one of the major obstacles to reuse has been the absence of effective facilities for cataloging and retrieving components in a business-oriented way.

A component management tool holds component information within a repository and provides the ability to browse, install, and register the components in harmony with a model-driven approach. Our approach uses packages as a unit for reuse. Such component management facilities (Allen & Frost, 1996) are important enabling technology for publishing and reusing packages and hence leveraging the approach we describe.

8.3.4 Using Classes from External Projects

A static association can be drawn from any class in a project to a class in another project, simply by declaring the latter as an external class. Such static associations are restricted to *service* classes outside the project for component packages, though any class may be used from a service package. An external class is declared in the consumer project using the "double-lined box" notation; a path name (UML, 1997) is used to indicate the parent package. In Figure 8.3 the object "A" calls the service "d" on the service object "D." Operation "d" has its own sequence diagram. Note that object "A" calling oper-

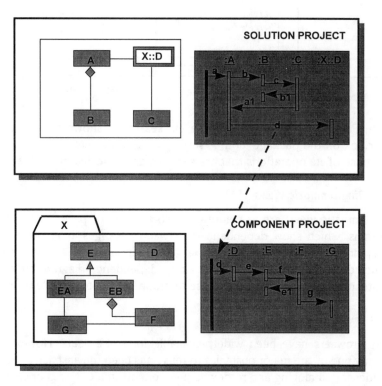

Figure 8.3. Synchronous service provision across projects.

ation "d" does not necessarily require the static association shown on the class diagram; external objects can be declared on a sequence diagram without being shown on a class diagram, provided a dynamic call is possible.

This is fine for synchronous service provision but how about asynchronous communication? State diagrams are used for this. In Figure 8.4 object "A" sends the event "EO3" to external object "D" as a result of receiving event "EI3" in state "a2." If external object "D" is in state "d1" it will respond to event "EO3" by changing state to "d2."

8.4 Business-Oriented Component Modeling Techniques

Business-oriented component modeling draws off a variety of sources, which include the following:

The sources of business-oriented component modeling are potentially diverse.

- domain knowledge,
- business process models, generic processes in particular,

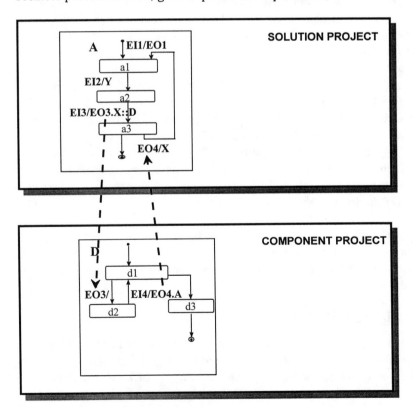

Figure 8.4. Asynchronous service provision across projects.

- solution project feedback,
- generic models and patterns,
- legacy systems and models,
- legacy databases,
- packages.

This chapter focuses on the first four...

Techniques covered in this chapter center on the first four of the above sources as follows:

- Architectural modeling: This is very much a high-level scoping set of activities, which aim to provide a reference map in terms of service packages for the activities that follow. The activity should be kept short (weeks rather than months) and revisited at regular intervals to bring the map into sharper focus, evolving generic models, as project feedback is consolidated. Architectural modeling techniques are covered in sections 8.4.1 to 8.4.3.
- Identification of services: This is a lower level set of scoping activities that aims to analyze generic business requirements in terms of business services. This helps us to understand dependencies between service packages and to develop the overall architecture. Service modeling techniques are covered in sections 8.4.4 to 8.4.5.
- Sowing reuse from solution projects: This is an ongoing assessment activity that aims to pollinate reuse. Candidate fragments of solution models are engineered for reuse in analogous fashion to frameworks and the solution model developed to reflect architectural needs. This is a two-way process that is covered in sections 8.4.6 to 8.4.7.
- Using generic models and patterns: This is a design activity that aims to fashion reusable component structures using various guidelines, including use of generic models and patterns. These techniques are covered in sections 8.4.8 to 8.4.10.

...the last three are covered in chapter 9.

Business-oriented component modeling is a key precursor to considering the final three sources, legacy assets, techniques for which are described in the next chapter. Figure 8.5 illustrates business-oriented component modeling in context.

8.4.1 Domain Modeling

Start by identifying domains, which mirror the semantics of the business.

Domain modeling is typically used in the component process, often by the reuse architect (see section 14.5.2) in order to plan a business-oriented component architecture for the organization in terms of service packages. Each service package represents a domain for which a generic model is evolved. In

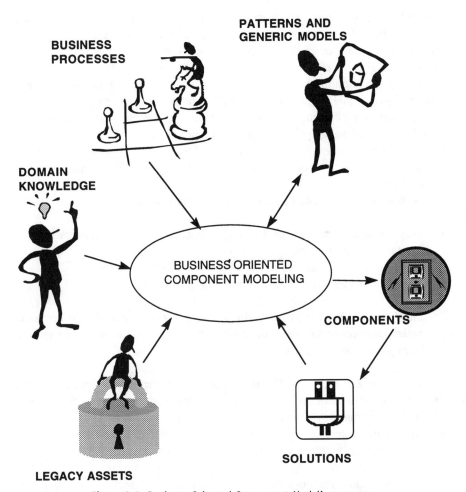

BUSINESS PROCESSES

PATTERNS AND GENERIC MODELS

DOMAIN KNOWLEDGE

BUSINESS ORIENTED COMPONENT MODELING

COMPONENTS

LEGACY ASSETS

SOLUTIONS

Figure 8.5. Business-Oriented Component Modeling sources.

starting out to identify domains it is all too easy to adopt a functional approach grounded in existing departmental boundaries. However, we should be mindful of the fact that it is the assumptions embodied in such structures that we should be challenging.

The focus in this section is on **business** domains, such as missile avionics or life insurance, as opposed to supporting **technology** domains, such as databases, user interfaces, and compilers. The latter are obviously important in architecting the user service (as described in 8.4.10) and data service components (as described in chapter 9). Business domain analysis focuses on like business services, whereas technology domain analysis focuses on the use of

Business domain analysis focuses on similar business services.

similar technology across different business processes. The reader is referred to Booch (1993) for a detailed account of the differences between business and technology domain analysis. The keynote here is that a business domain provides a context for developing business-oriented components.

Aim for domains that are cohesive.

A domain should provide a set of services that contribute to the same business goal. Equally, look for low coupling between domains, encapsulating functionality, and limiting messaging between domains. This echoes well-established good design practice. Structured programmers will be reminded of the need for high cohesion and low coupling (Page-Jones, 1988) and structured analysts too will remember Tom DeMarco's (1978) advice to "partition to minimize interfaces."

Guidelines follow for identifying business domains.

A well-chosen domain has the following characteristics:

• It represents an important part of the infrastructure of the organization.
• It contains key resources.
• It provides common sets of cohesive general business services.
• It encapsulates generic business information or policy.

In short, each business domain is a key service provider to business processes, providing the necessary infrastructure and resources to enable business processes to do their work.

Consider some candidate business domains for the Motor Dealership business.

Parts Inventory, Client, Purchasing, and Payments are candidate domains that represent an important part of the infrastructure of the organization and contain key resources. Each provides common sets of cohesive general business services. For example, stock control, requisition handling, and warehousing within Parts Inventory; supplier management and order monitoring within purchasing; consumer marketing and customer relations within Client; and invoicing within Payments. Parts Inventory centers on parts, which are obviously important resources. The candidate domains also encapsulate generic business information or policy. For example, Parts Inventory provides information about stock levels that is widely used; Customer addresses are used in all correspondence by many different applications; Purchasing covers the generic policy that lead times for any purchased part are defined by the manufacturer's recommendations for that part; Payments covers the policy that all invoices must be paid within 28 days. Each domain forms the potential focus of interest for a component project. This is an iterative process: We expect our early partitioning into domains to mature once we have delved a little deeper, as illustrated later in the chapter as examples are developed.

8.4.2 System Architecture Modeling

System architecture is the overall organization of domains into service packages. We aim to evolve generic models for each domain that can be refined and specialized for use in specific contexts. Typically this is carried out by the component team as part of architectural scoping (see section 13.4).

System architecture is modeled using service packages.

System architecture modeling is also used in the solution process, often by a senior developer in liaison with the reuse architect, in order to scope a solution in terms of proposed service packages. This is important for the following reasons:

- control of complexity, which might otherwise swamp a project,
- achieving an integrated portfolio of solutions,
- allowing later incremental design to focus on specific implementation detail without being overloaded with wider architectural concerns,
- maximizing the potential for reuse.

By architecting service packages in the early phases of development, as a business-oriented activity, the chances of achieving an integrated portfolio of solutions based on a sound reusable infrastructure is increased. This is important in assisting a smooth seamless life cycle. The last thing we want is to have to reorganize our models around a different design architecture midway through a project. A major theme of business-oriented component modeling is the ability to allocate business objects to service packages such that the resulting implementation mirrors the business requirements. A service package should ideally center on related services belonging to a single service category.

The Perspective architecture service categories provide a framework for system architecture.

Let's return to the Maintain Vehicle business process introduced in chapter 3 and consider how to develop a solution for the Service and Repair Vehicle process group. Candidate services are identified for each use case as described in section 4.4.5; normally these are business services as shown in Table 8.1, though it is also possible to identify user services too. Those shown in italics are services that are likely to be provided by service packages outside the context of Service and Repair Vehicles. Component management and browsing tools (Allen & Frost, 1996) are used to assist in the identification of the candidate services. We consider which of the service packages identified above (Parts Inventory, Client Purchasing, and Payments) can be used to provide the business services as shown in Table 8.2.

Candidate services are identified for each use case.

Client and Payment business services are to be provided by legacy system wrappers and Purchasing business services are to be provided by a package wrapper. Parts Inventory and Vehicle Maintenance are both to use wrappers onto existing relational databases. Dependencies are illustrated using a pack-

A package dependency diagram models architectural context.

Table 8.1. Candidate Services for Use Cases

Use case	Use-case step	Candidate business service
Book Job for Customer	Establish customer and vehicle	*Add Customer, Find Customer*
	Agree on service type with customer	Find Services
	Agree on repair estimates	Find Repairs
	Standard Jobs:	
	Find a suitable bay slot	Find Bay Slot
	Book the job	Book job
	Priority Jobs:	
	Check feasibility of priority job	
	Raise Priority Job	Book Job
	Arrange Chauffeur	
Establish Parts for Job	Identify parts needed for job	*Find Parts*
	Create part requests for job	Add Part Request
	Produce part-requests report	Report Part Requests
Request Parts for Job	Reserve parts in stock for jobs	*Reserve Part*
	Order outstanding parts for jobs	*Order Part*
Schedule Jobs for Day	Produce jobs bill of materials	*Report Jobs Bill of Materials*
	Organize parts for each job	
Record Job Completion	Manage job to completion	
	Record job labor	Modify Job
	Record service history	Add Service History
	Produce Highlight report	Report Service Highlights
Close Job with Customer	Establish job	Find Job
	Produce invoice	*Add Invoice*
	Warn customer of highlights	
	Receive payment for the job	*Record Payment*

Table 8.2. Candidate-Service Packages

Business service	Service package
Add Customer Find Customer	Client
Find Parts	Parts Inventory
Reserve Part Raise Purchase Order	Parts Inventory Purchasing
Add Invoice Record Payment	Payments

age dependency diagram as shown in Figure 8.6. (Techniques for wrapping databases, legacy systems, and packages are covered in the chapter 9.)

Package dependencies can be used to gain an early "broad-brush" understanding of likely overall service usage on a use case-by-use case basis and to test out the architectural partitioning, which is then adjusted in line with the use case needs. High-level collaboration diagrams or CRC (class–responsibility–collaborator) cards can be used; however, whiteboard sketches usually suffice; Figure 8.7 shows such a sketch for the use case Book Job for Customer.

Package dependencies can also be explored for each use case.

8.4.3 Modeling Reusable Business Classes

We focus on a domain, which forms a candidate service package, and develop some business classes for it, looking for key abstractions that reflect the vocabulary of the problem domain. Early attempts may often be somewhat intuitive and based on common sense but sufficient to create a first-cut class diagram. The techniques described in chapter 5 are all applicable. Other criteria are described in the text that follows.

A first-cut class diagram is created.

Indirect business processes (see section 8.4.5), from a previous BPM exercise, are an important source of generic requirements. Where a BPM exercise has not been undertaken, the relevant generic requirements are typically available in business policy documents referenced by a project proposal. Examples of generic requirements from the Motor Dealership business include the following:

Generic business requirements are identified.

- Classify parts by type: for example, engine, electrical, interior, or accessory.
- Keep track of demand for parts so that efficient levels can be maintained.

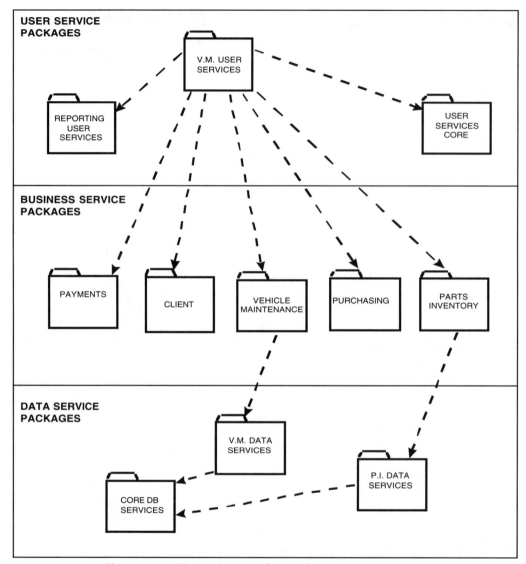

Figure 8.6. Architectural context for Vehicle Servicing and Repairs.

- Enable fast and easy identification of available parts stocked at the various locations so that these can be reserved for different purposes, such as servicing and repairs.

Some guidelines follow...

Generic business requirements provide a rich source of business classes. More generally, it is useful to look for classes that have the following characteristics:

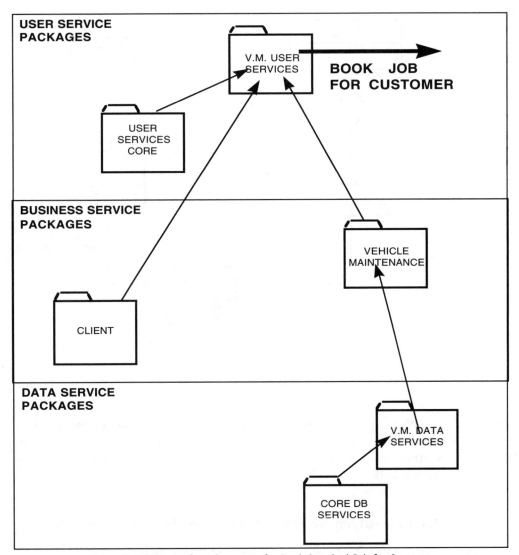

Figure 8.7. Pattern of service usage for Book Standard Job for Customer.

- consistent and cohesive subject matter; parts, holdings, and locations consistently crop up in a Parts Inventory domain,
- independence of subject matter; parts, holdings, and locations as a group do not depend on objects external to the domain,
- provision of communication between business processes; Service and Repair Vehicle raises part requests that require allocation of parts from holdings.

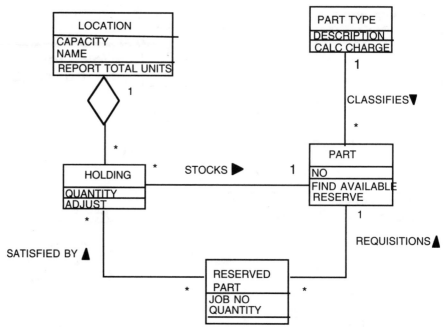

Figure 8.8. Business class diagram for Parts Inventory service package.

...a first-cut
class diagram is
created.

We use the above guidelines to create a first-cut business class diagram, as shown in Figure 8.8. This can evolve as our understanding deepens and sharpens to form a generic model for reuse and refinement, in parallel style to a framework.

8.4.4 Identifying Business Services: Service Types Approach

Guidelines follow for
identifying business
services using
various service
types.

Business services, which operate "behind the scenes," are sometimes less obvious than those gleaned from consideration of use cases, which are usually interactive and always user facing. Some practical guidelines follow for identifying business services from candidate objects using various service types:

• operational services, for example, providing a resource to do a job,
• reference services, for example checking customer credit,
• provision of common business rules, for example, calculation of overtime rates or standard procedures to be followed as part of a task,

Table 8.3. Business Services for Parts Inventory		
Object	**Service Type**	**Business Service**
Part Type	Business Rules	Calc Charge
Location	Summary	Report Total Units
Part	Operational	Reserve Part
Part	Reference	Find Available Parts
Part	Maintenance	Add Part

- summary services; for example, product or sales history,
- maintenance services; for example, adding a customer.

Operational services are often apparent from considering the responsibilities (Wirfs-Brock et al., 1991) of each object. For example, Part is responsible for Order Part and Reserve Part. For reference services and business rules ask the question, "What services or rules can you provide?" Summary services are often found in management information domains where there is a need to aggregate information for management inquiry. This might include "meta objects," which help support monitoring operations across the enterprise; for example, comparison of sales performance by different garages might require a Garage object. Maintenance services are usually fairly obvious and take the form of adding, modifying, and removing objects. Applying these guidelines to Parts Inventory service package yields the examples shown in Table 8.3

We apply the guidelines by example.

8.4.5 Identifying Business Services: Business Process Approach

Indirect processes emerge either from a BPM effort, as described in chapter 3, or from business policy documents typically associated with a project proposal. Such processes do not add measurable business value to the customer but are nevertheless part of the life blood of the enterprise. These may be operational processes, such as Purchasing or Stock Control or key management information processes, such as Analyze Pricing Trends. In analyzing the Service and Repair Vehicle process thread in chapter 3, we identified an EBP Establish Parts for Job. In fact, further analysis reveals that Establish Parts for Job is a generic EBP used by several different process threads, examples of which are Perform Body Repairs and Control Work Breakdown, as illustrated in Figure 8.9.

Other business services can be identified by examining indirect business processes.

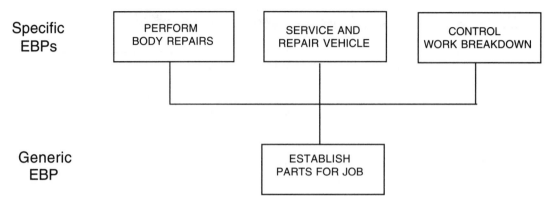

Specific
EBPs

Generic
EBP

Figure 8.9. Generic reuse by other EBPs.

Associated use cases are examined for business services and business rules.

Analysis of associated use cases for generic EBPs reveals correspondingly generic business services. In this example the use case Establish Parts for Job requires the business service Find Parts on Task. We examine this business service in section 8.4.9. Business rules associated with such use cases can often be mapped to invariants. For example, the business rule that each type has a standard surcharge applied for parts of that type might map to an invariant on the Part Type class.

8.4.6 Sowing Reusable Business Components

As class models mature, so they become component candidates.

In chapter 5, as we started to refine the class diagram within the Vehicle Servicing and Repair solution project, we noticed that Model, Task, and Activity were candidates for component engineering, as illustrated in Figure 8.10. They are reference classes potentially reusable across a range of applications that look like good candidates for sowing as business-oriented components. All these classes relate to the overall theme of Work Breakdown. The scoped classes also form a tightly integrated and cohesive group, which makes Work Breakdown a good candidate for modeling within a separate service package, which will be developed into a component(s).

The Work Breakdown domain is examined in more detail.

We ask what is really required here in terms of business process support. For example, it is necessary to know how many of which parts are needed for each activity comprising a task and to be able to locate parts for each activity. Therefore a class Activity-Req is introduced to hold the required quantity and to find the parts. This class is associated with both Activity and Part. It is also found that activities require a description and duration; as the duration is relative to a specific service the multiplicity at the service end of the association is changed to "1."

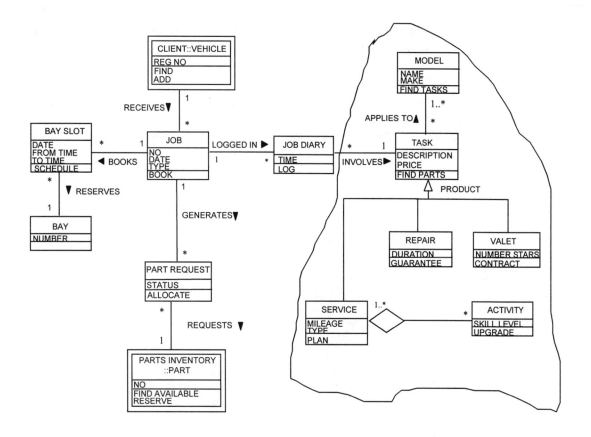

Figure 8.10. Example of a local class diagram showing scoped Work Breakdown classes.

There is a need to track history of demand for tasks for different models. Therefore a class Task Application is introduced to resolve the many-to-many association between Model and Part; note that this could have been modeled as an association class but we prefer to introduce a separate class, as discussed in chapter 5. Task Application allows tasks to be specified for models and for the associated effective date to be recorded. A common requirement, uncovered in the previous section, is to establish parts for jobs; an operation Find Parts is therefore included on each appropriate class to invoke the required Find Part Details service, added to the Parts Inventory service package, which we declare using an external class, as shown in Figure 8. 11.

In real project practice a class model is likely to undergo several iterations before it reaches a sufficient quality to be reused in the manner of a framework as described previously. As Booch (1996) points out: "A framework does not

Examine indirect business processes that use the classes under study.

Reality check: Remember this is an idealized example.

even begin to reach maturity until it has been applied in at least three or more distinct applications."

8.4.7 Revising System Architecture

System architecture is revised to reflect the changes.

Sowing reuse from a solution project affects the system architecture (see Figure 8.12). The Work Breakdown service package is effectively factored out of Vehicle Maintenance to which it provides the service Find Parts. Work Breakdown uses the service Find Part Details from Parts Inventory.

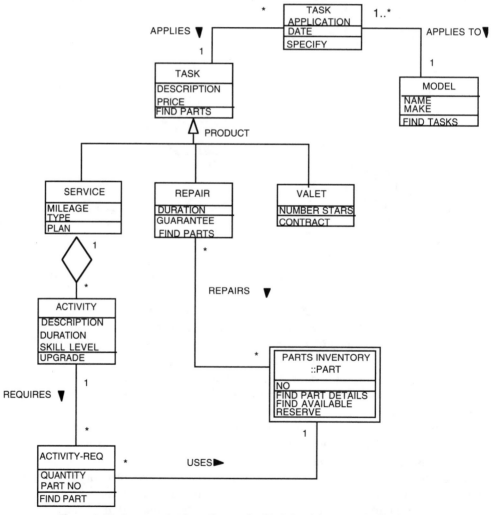

Figure 8.11. An example class diagram for Work Breakdown service package.

8.4.8 Designing Business Components

The Motor Dealership is keen to market Work Breakdown (WB) as a business-oriented component for third parties to use. So there are good political reasons for designing an *exclusive* service class: a separate control class, over and above the existing business classes, used to encapsulate services. Note that in the example we have not created lower level service packages, which would often be the case in real life.

Identify service classes.

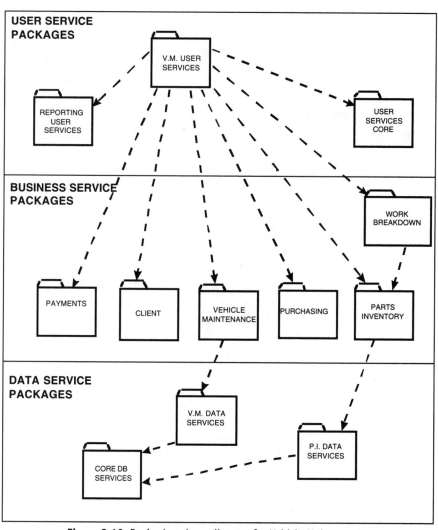

Figure 8.12. Revised package diagram for Vehicle Maintenance.

An exclusive service class may achieve a more reusable design.

If we introduce Find Parts as a service on a WB Control class, instead of a requesting object having to interrogate a specific object with a Find Parts request, it can simply send a Find Parts request to the service class. The service class then resolves polymorphism by delegating to the appropriate object. WB Control, shown in Figure 8.13, is used to group all operations that provide services. Note that Upgrade operation on the Activity class is not invoked as a service; it is invoked by Plan Service.

Prepare to design the services using object interaction modeling.

Use cases make use of the Find Parts business service. For example, the use case Establish Parts For Job requires the service Find Parts (see Figure 8.15). Note the dashed line, which marks the architectural boundary between user and business services. A sequence diagram for Find Parts is shown in Figure 8.16. Effectively, the sequence diagram is nested inside the service Find Parts on the WB Control service class. Notice how the Work Breakdown component collaborates with the Parts Inventory component through the service class Parts Control to get the part details. Having modeled in an abstract business-oriented way, we are now in a good position to begin the detailed design of component interfaces, which effectively implement the service class.

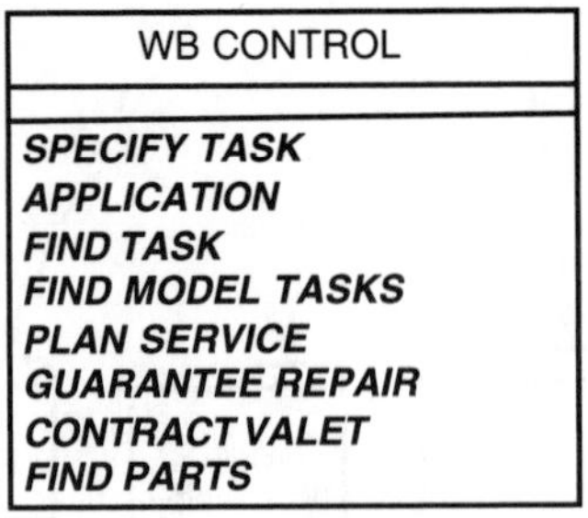

WB CONTROL
SPECIFY TASK   *APPLICATION*   *FIND TASK*   *FIND MODEL TASKS*   *PLAN SERVICE*   *GUARANTEE REPAIR*   *CONTRACT VALET*   *FIND PARTS*

Figure 8.13. Example of a Service Class for Work Breakdown Component.

Figure 8.14. Example of a package showing Service Class.

8.4.9 Using Patterns to Develop Business Components

We have already seen that patterns are useful in helping to develop a class diagram. In chapter 5 we used some *analysis* patterns from Coad (1995) to assist
with the class diagramming. Patterns are even more relevant with respect to
business-oriented components, where the emphasis is on reuse based on
resilient class structures that will stand the test of time. It is here therefore that
design patterns, as opposed to analysis patterns, come into play.

Design patterns are
used to develop the
service packages.

For example, in the Parts Inventory domain there is a need to control
recursive part structures. The company purchases its basic (or leaf) parts from
suppliers. The leaf parts can be assembled together in various ways, accord-

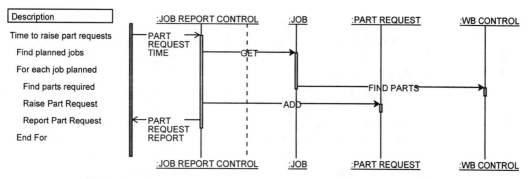

Figure 8.15. An example of a sequence diagram for Establish Parts for Job.

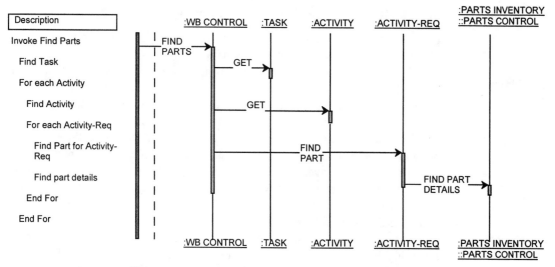

Figure 8.16. An example of a sequence diagram for Find Parts.

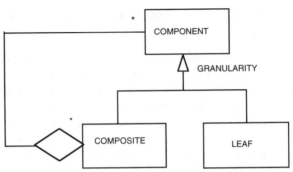

Figure 8.17. Composite pattern.

The composite pattern is applied to the Parts Inventory domain.

ing to different needs, into composite parts. Some composite parts are used in the Servicing and Repair process, others are distributed to garages, which use our services as a distributor. The manufacture of a composite part must be costed in contrast to leaf parts, which are simply bought in. Also, leaf parts have a weight. The weight of a composite part is derivable as the sum of the weights of its constituents. This situation crops up many times in different applications and has been abstracted as a design pattern known as the "composite" by Gamma and his colleagues (1995) as shown in Figure 8.17; other references for design patterns are Buschmann (1996) and Pree (1995). This pattern is now applied within the Parts Inventory service package, as shown in Figure 8.18.

8.4.10 Modeling User-Interface Components

An important part of architectural modeling is identifying HCI components.

User classes are partitioned into user service packages, which focus on particular areas of reuse; for example, Reports, Forms, Communications, and so on. More specifically, we have already seen that aggregation and inheritance can be used to show reuse of user objects; for example, the user class diagram from 5.4.11. In this section we use the same example to show how external classes are used to represent standard components.

The modeling must add value.

Remember, the modeling needs to add value. That means there is little point in modeling known standardized user classes, which are bought in off the shelf or in modeling every last detail of every interface. To do that is not going to tell us anything much that we do not know already. Modeling of reusable user classes becomes important in developing the overall HCI architecture and in setting standards for reuse of user classes.

Use infrastructure classes.

A generic Form is used to provide a standard shell into which all forms must fit. The Form provides ready written operations for common functions and definitions for common attributes. This represents a potentially large sav-

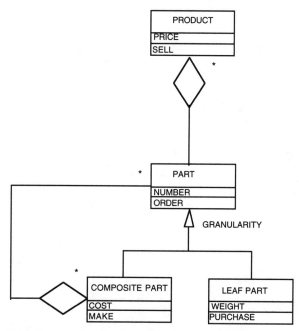

Figure 8.18. An example of a class diagram based on a composite pattern.

ing in time and money over many projects, and provides built-in guaranteed quality. Views and list views are two further types of user class that are introduced to provide root operations for accessing individual business classes and collections of business classes, respectively.

Each business class has a corresponding user class, which specializes the view class and contains information on one business object. Similarly, a business list view specializes the list external class and contains limited information on a collection of objects. For example, Customer View is a specialization of View; Repair List View is a specialization of List View. Business views are used to minimize interaction between user and business objects, to localize maintenance, and provide reuse. For example, customer details are used on countless forms. By introducing a Customer View class, developers do not have to rewrite the interface every time a new form is introduced. The three user classes appear as external classes, as shown in Figure 8.19, in user class diagrams on solution projects. Each is implemented using a component package (as opposed to the business-oriented service package, as discussed previously).

Business classes are mirrored by user classes.

In the Book Job for Customer example, Booking Form inherits common form characteristics using the generic Form component, as shown in Figure 8.20. Inheritance is also used to enable the different view objects to reuse com-

Other infrastructure classes are added.

mon characteristics from the View and List View components. This gives a user class diagram that is properly architected rather than developed "on the fly" as is unfortunately often the case. Note that in chapter 10 we consider how this is modeled in terms of component packages.

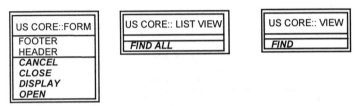

Figure 8.19. Example user classes modeled as external classes.

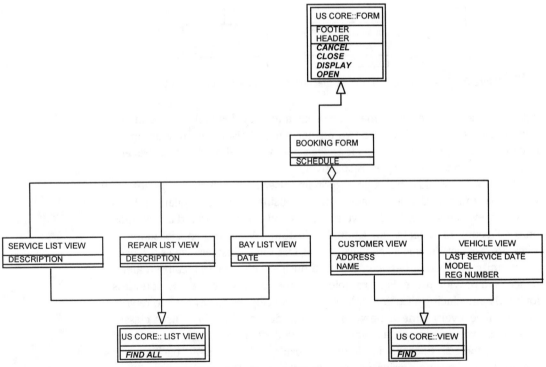

Figure 8.20. User-class diagram showing external classes.

8.5 Practical Guidelines on Business-Oriented Component Modeling

There are certain concerns that we have found to apply in the arena of real-life projects. A summary of these points follows.

Some guidelines follow.

8.5.1 Justification

There is always the question "Why can't everything be an RAD project?" A tempting but flippant answer is "Because of what happened last time!" Another rejoinder is to turn the question on its head and ask what are the consequences of **not** doing a thorough job. A list of the more conventional examples used as justification to management follows:

We are often asked to help with providing a good management case.

- flexibility/extensibility: cohesive units with minimal interfaces help to ensure a robust systems design,
- long-term productivity: through reuse of existing functionality,
- integration with existing technology: by wrapping existing system functionality,
- migration to future technology: identification of units that are potentially distributable across new technologies,
- validation and testing purposes: isolation and management of quality measurement testing,
- partitioning of work: for large systems different components can be allocated to separate teams or projects.

8.5.2 Incremental Development

Business-oriented component modeling is commonly seen as at odds with development of increments to quickly deliver usable functionality. Certainly, development of system increments in isolation to meet tight deadlines will eventually result in fragmented software, which lacks consistency and fails to provide integrated support. Enterprise projects that spend 6 months on analysis and then proceed for 2 years to develop systems where half the functionality is inadequate because early misunderstandings have been cast in stone are incompatible with the philosophy of rapid incremental development. What is called for is an adaptive approach. We have tried to show that this means starting with a general framework and understanding key generic requirements, implementing small portions of local requirements at a time, and then revising the framework in the light of experience. The eventual goal is to "plug in" components as service providers to solutions development. That is true

Business-oriented component modeling fits well with incremental development.

RAAD as described in Gartner (1996). The philosophy underlying this approach is elegantly explained by Tom Gilb (1988).

8.5.3 Component Packaging Metrics

A service package should ideally contain between 5 and 15 units.

Service packages provide a mechanism both for architectural partitioning and for achieving a reasonably high-grained granularity of reuse. Each service package can be subdivided into further service packages or classes. Our experience reflects similar guidelines on subsystems provided by Firesmith (1993) that a service package should ideally contain between 5 and 15 units (service packages or classes), and no more than 20 units.

8.5.4 Flexibility

Imagine what could change.

In JAD sessions it is worth stimulating user discussion as to what could *realistically* change. On recent assignments we have found it useful to invite senior business executives to early JAD sessions to give the team a briefing on relevant strategic directions that could impact the project.

8.5.5 Web and Intranet Usage

Component management facilities are key.

Increasingly, as the availability of reusable software increases, it becomes more and more important to have a good understanding of where to search for suitable components. Connection to the World Wide Web already provides an increasing array of easily accessible product information and high-quality componentware provided first by universities and nonprofit-making organizations and now by commercial software companies. Company intranets also provide an important enabling technology for reuse of business services. Component management tools provide an integrated directory for the reuse of such apparently disparate services (Allen & Frost, 1996).

8.5.6 Balance

The "Grand Design" approach is a nonstarter.

The "Grand Design" approach to developing components attempts to build detailed enterprise-wide object models and abstracts reusable elements into components. Typically a whole range of textbook techniques are employed by a team of enterprise architects. The basic problem with this approach is that by the time the models are complete (which is probably never!), the assumptions on which they are based have changed drastically. It is therefore a nonstarter.

Economics often lead to a piecemeal approach.

The piecemeal approach develops isolated objects for reuse as a means of "dipping the organization's toe" in the object-technology reservoir. For example, various types of implementation objects such as lists and queues are made generally available using class browsers. Although not without merit, this approach takes no account of the long-term issues such as effective business process support and data management. The piecemeal approach is taken by many organizations today partly out of economic necessity and partly because it is perceived as the path of least risk; a good way of cutting one's teeth on the issues of object technology without risking too much. The main problem with this approach is that a higher level of granularity than objects is required for effective reuse.

An important element in our approach is to strive for a level of granularity that is pitched between the two extremes of the grand design and piecemeal reuse, to meet the needs of the individual organization. Service packages, and not objects, are therefore employed as the enabling unit of reuse.

A balanced approach steers a midcourse between these extremes.

8.6 Summary

An analyst once said to one of the authors, "Inside every one of our complex systems is a set of simple systems trying not to get out." This particular analyst saw his job as trying to find the simple systems. In essence we can think of no better way of summarizing business-oriented component modeling. The ultimate promise of component-based development is that software solutions can be composed from reusable components, in an analogous fashion to hardware. Business-oriented component modeling works toward this vision by leveraging reuse at the model rather than the code level. We employ a range of established modeling techniques within our architecture and process to help ensure that the correct business requirements are addressed. Services provide a much more usable level of abstraction at the business level, where the greatest benefits are to be gained. Components, seen in this context, represent enabling technology for servicing business needs in terms of encapsulated families of tightly coupled objects.

Aim for simplicity.

The last thing the beleaguered software manager needs is the promise of some new modeling hype. In this chapter we employ mainly familiar techniques with minimum additional notation. Finally it is worth repeating the old adage that "reuse is not free use." Like a tree planted in the wrong soil these techniques cannot flourish: Management commitment and the right cultural conditions are a precondition of success.

Protect investment in proven techniques.

CHAPTER 9

•••••••••••••••••••••

Component Modeling of Legacy Assets

9.1 Introduction

The issue of "legacy assets" is not currently given adequate treatment by methods and tools vendors. Useful work emerges in isolated areas. Unfortunately, thus far, the attention has been rather piecemeal. The amount of discussion acknowledges the problem, but the absence of clear guidelines reflects the struggle to come to terms with it.

The existence of huge investments in legacy software and models has to be recognized and dealt with by the brave new world of component technology. Years of effort have often been expended developing and maintaining these products and cultivating the required skills. Waste of this effort must be minimized. This chapter addresses three broad areas:

- legacy systems written in previous-generation languages such as COBOL, PL/1, FORTRAN, and Assembler,
- package software,
- legacy databases, particularly relational databases; because of their maturity, and the established skills, relational databases continue to be used for new software development.

The importance of legacy assets is not reflected in today's methods.

Leveraging existing legacy assets is an important part of our strategy.

Business
requirements are
addressed before
applying wrapping.

First we address some general principles for wrapping legacy assets before examining each area in more detail. Examples from previous chapters, where the focus has been on business requirements, are continued in this chapter to illustrate the need for continuity of techniques. As before, we conclude with some pragmatic advice on component modeling of legacy assets gleaned from project experiences.

9.2 Legacy Asset Component Modeling Principles

In this section we consider some generic principles that apply to all types of legacy assets.

9.2.1 Key Concepts

9.2.1.1 Legacy Assets

A legacy asset is a software product, developed on the basis of older technologies, which is past its best but that is so vital to the enterprise that it cannot be replaced or disrupted without a major impact on the enterprise. Note that legacy models (such as data models) are often associated with the legacy asset. Understandably, organizations are keen to preserve the *investment* that has gone into developing such software products; hence the term **legacy asset**. Legacy assets come in various forms: for example, function libraries, programs, program fragments, data structures, database interfaces, data models, etc.

9.2.1.2 Wrappers

In general terms, a wrapper is a component that provides an object-oriented interface to nonobject-oriented software. Wrapping is a technique that takes legacy assets and encapsulates them inside components. Wrappers provide the following three key advantages:

1. They insulate new component-based software from legacy code and from the effects of changes to that code.
2. They reuse that code in a component-based setting.
3. They help ease migration to component technology while protecting investments in existing code and at the same time providing new innovative solutions to business problems.

As with other types of components a higher level of granularity than objects is required for effective reuse. In Perspective a wrapper groups objects that are cohesive to the needs of a particular set of services and provides the required services in black-box fashion through its interface. The service categories of the Perspective architecture provide an ideal basis for wrapping legacy systems, as it is far easier to identify user, business, or data services that are provided by the legacy system than it is to attempt to create "objects" from code that is almost certainly far from being object oriented. Systems are wrapped on the basis of what the business needs, rather than what technology currently offers.

Therefore, as in the previous chapter, service packages are used to model wrappers. The service packages are implemented in terms of component packages, which provide standard interfaces; for example, CORBA IDL interfaces. Methods residing inside the component packages are written in code that interfaces with the legacy product; for example, SQL procedures defined in the logical database schema. Component packages are discussed further in chapter 10. Note that in the case of legacy systems and packages it may well be that the business objects can be packaged and wrapped directly, whereas in the case of legacy databases and models there is a need to design separate wrappers.

9.2.2 A Common Framework

We have found that there are three major preconditions that must be met before wrapper modeling can begin in earnest. These are generic to any type of legacy software product and are reflected in the common framework shown in Figure 9.1. The preconditions are as follows:

Component modeling of legacy assets follows a common framework.

1. The correct business requirements must be addressed.
2. The legacy software product needs to be in a suitable state for wrapping.
3. The architectural context must be clear.

The temptation is often to wrap legacy assets on the basis that it "seemed like a good idea at the time." Business-oriented component modeling helps ensure that the correct business requirements are addressed as a foundation for wrapping. These techniques, described in the previous chapter, are no less important for dealing with legacy assets.

The correct business requirements must be addressed.

Package dependency modeling is used to explore and set the architectural context. This is important in helping establish the technical and financial feasibility of reusing the candidate legacy asset. The architectural scoping phase of the component process (see chapter 13) is where most of the significant decisions on reuse of legacy assets should be taken.

The architectural context must be clear.

The legacy asset
must be in a fit
state for wrapping.

Key abstractions are models, libraries, and specifications that provide a necessary basis for wrapping. The amount of work involved here depends hugely on the quality of associated documentation. This is where legacy models, in particular logical data models, can prove useful. If not available, then it may be worth considering reverse engineering to provide them. In the case of packages and legacy systems, business process models and use case models can prove useful for comparison with target models of business requirements. Also, vendors are moving increasingly to open up their packages to the world of components, in the form of libraries of exposed objects. Function gateways to legacy systems (Tibbetts & Bernstein, 1996) provide similar potential. The

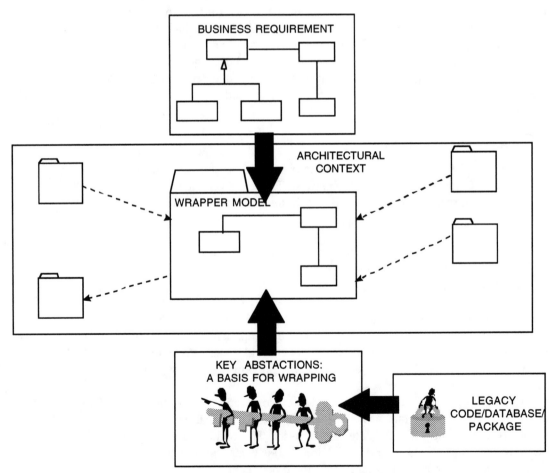

Figure 9.1. A common framework for modeling legacy assets.

assessment phase of the component process (see chapter 13) is where key abstractions are identified.

Component modeling techniques are used to help expose assumptions, highlight differences between business requirements and legacy assets, and make balanced judgments as to when to reuse legacy functionality "as is" and when to make changes. The design challenge is to balance the often conflicting criteria of cohesion, generality, and performance.

Business requirements must be assessed against capabilities of the legacy asset. It is important to establish whether we are wrapping to reuse legacy functionality "as is" or whether we are looking to extend certain features and hide others. We also need to assess whether changes need to be made to the database or legacy system (though this is not usually an option with packages). In well-established and stable applications, like payroll, it is likely that the required business and data services will match closely with the capabilities of the existing software. However, even in the case of relatively stable applications, there is an increasing need to innovate at the user interface. Modeling techniques are therefore also used to explore the required user services and enable effective use of the exposed business and data services.

Other applications may require extended business and data services to meet an organization's specific needs. This is typically the case in applications such as life insurance, where a great deal of functionality is common across organizations but where individual organizations want to leverage their processes. For example, all life-insurance organizations have to make standard underwriting calculations to establish basic risks. A single life-insurance organization might introduce a special policy for higher risks (such as smokers), requiring further special calculations. The wrapper models are therefore developed to take full advantage of standardized features provided by the package objects while ensuring business requirements are satisfied.

Until recently one of the major obstacles to reuse has been the absence of effective facilities for cataloging and retrieving components in a business-oriented way. Component management software holds component information within a repository and provides the ability to browse, install, and register the components in harmony with a model-driven approach. Such component management facilities are important enabling technology for leveraging the approach we describe.

We may need to revise our judgment on the feasibility of reusing the legacy asset. There's no free lunch: It is not worth wrapping code that has poor quality or clashes badly with business requirements. Renovation may be required to bring legacy systems or databases into a fit state for wrapping. There are many established techniques for effectively renovating legacy systems and databases in preparation for wrapping. These include reverse engi-

---

Component modeling techniques are used to build wrapper models.

Business services and data services may be used "as is."

On the other hand, business services and data services may be changed.

Component management tools expedite the process.

Renovation may be required.

neering, repartitioning, data modeling, and event partitioning; the reader is referred to Allen (1991) and Mattison and Sipolt (1995) for a discussion of relevant techniques. Such techniques are aimed at minimizing interfaces between existing systems and reducing data duplication across existing systems.

9.3 Legacy System Wrapping Techniques

Organizations cannot afford to simply scrap their legacy systems.

Many organizations have millions of lines of legacy code running on legacy systems, which represent a $10-trillion investment in the United States alone. Also, years of effort have been expended developing and maintaining these systems and cultivating the required skills. Organizations cannot afford to simply scrap their legacy systems. Even if they could their software staff often lack the skills to exploit component technology in a component-based setting.

Legacy systems were designed for a set of assumptions that no longer holds.

Legacy systems have typically been developed in reactive fashion to meet immediate needs. This results in systems with complex interfaces, duplication of data, and convoluted code. Legacy systems work on the basis of independent data and code that works on the basis of data sharing. This is in sharp contrast to objects that work on the basis of encapsulation of data and function. The code typically consists of a mixture of business logic, which is required regardless of implementation, and implementation logic, which is required solely to support the particular implementation. This presents significant difficulties in migrating to component technology in a component-based setting, the success of which depends on a good design and a clear distinction between business logic and its implementation.

Wrapping can reduce the risk in migrating to component technology.

Reengineering and gradually replacing an entire legacy system is often not practical and is generally risky, especially if you need to respecify the legacy system. Various options are available to the beleaguered IS manager. Wrappers represent an opportunity to reuse legacy systems while taking advantage of component technology to build new solutions that interact with the legacy systems through wrappers. The legacy systems can then be allowed to gradually wither away as pieces are replaced by the new technology.

9.3.1 Assessing the Need for Legacy System Services

Use cases help raise requirements for legacy business services.

In chapter 6, as we started to build a sequence diagram for the Book Job for Customer use case, we noticed that Find Customer looked like a good candidate for development as a business service. Other projects, for example, Marketing and Account Management, have a similar customer-matching requirement, as indicated in Figure 9.2, under the different guises of Retrieve Customer and Match Customer. On closer inspection, the requirement is for a reusable customer-searching facility, as indicated in Figure 9.3.

Customer-searching facilities are in fact already provided by an existing client legacy system, which was pinpointed as a Client service package in the previous chapter. Let's assume this system has been renovated so as to separate its business logic from its presentation logic in the form of a Client Transaction Library, which we model as a package as shown in Figure 9.4. We now consider how to provide a legacy wrapper for this.

A package dependency diagram models the architectural context.

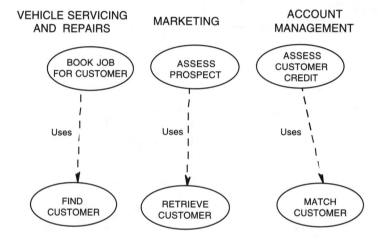

Figure 9.2 Example candidate reusable services.

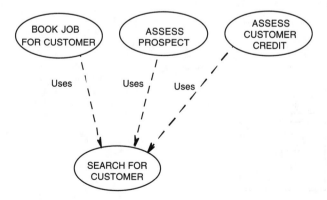

Figure 9.3. Example business service.

9.3.2 Identifying Legacy System Key Abstractions

A business class
model is developed
and compared with
the legacy system.

A business class model is developed for Client, as shown in Figure 9.5. In this example the legacy transaction library provides fairly obvious key abstractions in the form of List and Match transactions. However, even in this simple example, the legacy transaction library differs from the business model in that it is

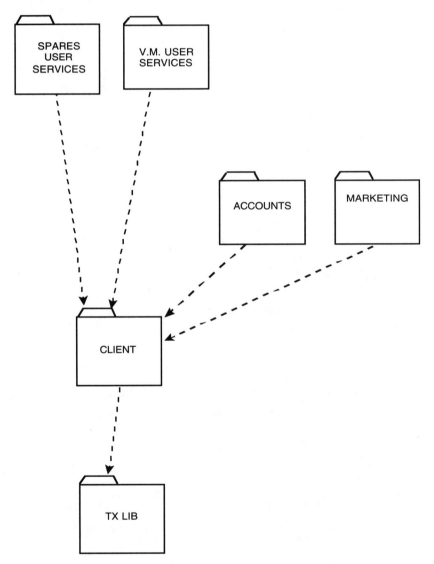

Figure 9.4. Architectural context for Client Wrapper.

built on the premise of a random access Client Master in which vehicle details are held as a repeating group within variable length client records.

9.3.3 Designing a Legacy System Wrapper

We design a business service class, Client Control, which handles the mismatch between the new and old structures. In a simple case such as listing customers by key, the wrapper provides the List Customers business service by issuing a legacy language call to the Report Customer Indices transaction and returning the information to clients, as shown in Figure 9.6. Other situations involve translating the legacy structure to the new object structure. In Figure 9.7 Client Control provides a Match Customer service in which it issues a legacy language call to Report Customer details. Returned information is unpacked, a Customer object created, and separate Vehicle objects created for each occurrence of the Vehicle repeating group.

A business service class is introduced.

9.3.4 Designing the User Interface to a Legacy System Wrapper

Where control behavior is potentially reusable across different applications, it is worth considering separating out this behavior to form a further service package to provide business services at the user interface. This also preserves

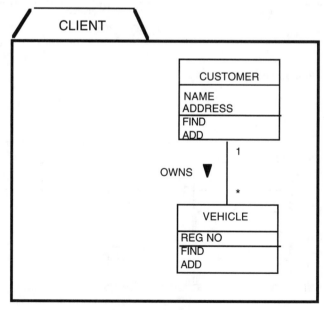

Figure 9.5. Business class diagram for Client Wrapper.

Business services can be "revitalized" at the user interface.

independence of the wrapper from different user interfaces and changes in presentation logic. We introduce a Customer Searcher component that employs a Customer Searcher service class and the user-interface components developed in section 8.4.10 to provide a control layer to coordinate the wrapping services, as shown in Figure 9. 8.

State diagrams help to design in greater rigor.

A service class needs to be developed so as to be as generic as possible while balancing the need for cohesion and performance. A further challenge is the demand for greater rigor of reusable services, such as those demanded by wrapping. A state diagram is useful for this. We use the original state diagram for the Vehicle Servicing and Repairs solution from Figure 7.13 and build in further checks as we seek to engineer to component status, as shown in Figure 9.9.

The state diagram for the service class must be complete.

The operation call Search, which is sent by client objects, is received as an inbound event in the state diagram for Customer Searcher. The diagram also caters to all errors and exceptions. Note that Customer Searcher transmits an

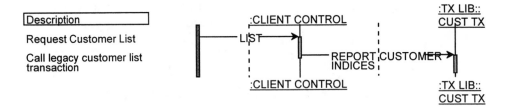

Figure 9.6. Sequence diagram for Client Control::List.

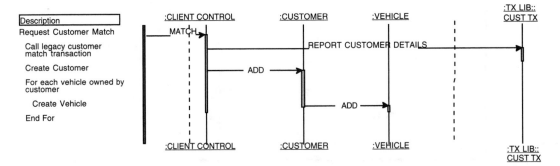

Figure 9.7. Sequence diagram for Client Control::Match.

appropriate event, on transition to its final state, for receipt by a client state diagram. Events outbound to client objects are not targeted to specific objects, but generally broadcast. An event handler would be introduced to route the event to any client object that had registered interest.

On receiving back the Cust OK event a client state diagram continues through its normal path. On receiving a Cust Error event back from the Customer Searcher the client must decide what action to take. The state diagram for a client object, Job Control from chapter 7, is repeated for reference in Figure 9.10. Customer Searcher is invoked by sending a call, Customer Searcher.Search. This causes a transition to the "Performing Customer Search" state, which waits for events returned by Customer Searcher.

The service class is engineered to integrate with its clients.

9.4 Package Wrapping Techniques

A package often contains robust implementations of broad ranges of processes and data that have evolved over the years to meet industry needs. Usually a richness of functionality exists that is reusable across different applications. It is therefore important to leverage this asset within the context of innovative software solutions.

The breadth and maturity of package software cannot be ignored.

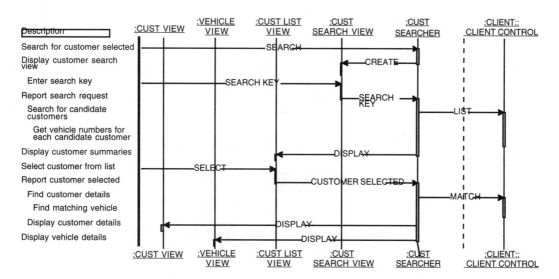

Figure 9.8. Sequence diagram for Cust Searcher::Search.

Software packages are growing more open.

Packages such as SAP's R/3, and Baan's Triton are extremely prevalent in many large organizations. Until recently, these environments were closed to the outside world and were therefore very difficult to integrate with other applications. However, significant moves are being made toward interoperability of packages both within and between enterprises (Hoffman & Killer, 1995). New-generation packages provide libraries of objects, the interfaces of which are exposed using standard interfaces; for example, DCOM or CORBA compliant (Benchmarking Partners, 1996; SAP, 1996). This clearly makes package wrappers a viable proposition.

Wrappers present an important opportunity to reuse package software.

As vendors move to open up their packages to the world of components, there is an increasing need to ensure that developers can easily access the exposed functionality using effective software tools. This requires a balanced approach, in which packages serve the needs of the business and not vice versa! The service categories of the Perspective architecture help distinguish the correct exposed package functionality for mapping to components.

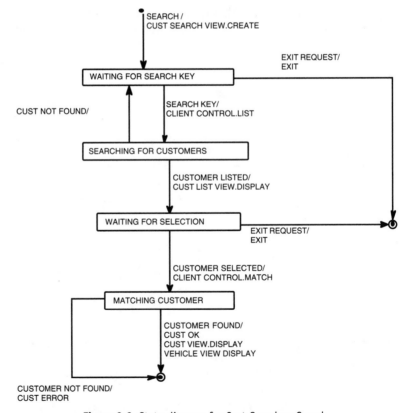

Figure 9.9. State diagram for Cust Searcher::Search.

9.4.1 Assessing the Need for Package Services

In the previous chapter we pinpointed Purchasing as a candidate for package wrapping. A package dependency diagram serves to highlight the architectural context, as shown in Figure 9.11. Spares and Vehicle Maintenance user services raise purchase orders as a result of a user requests; for example, Establish Parts for Job use case in Vehicle Maintenance. Parts Inventory business services raise purchase requisitions as a result of stock levels falling below thresholds.

A package dependency diagram models the architectural context.

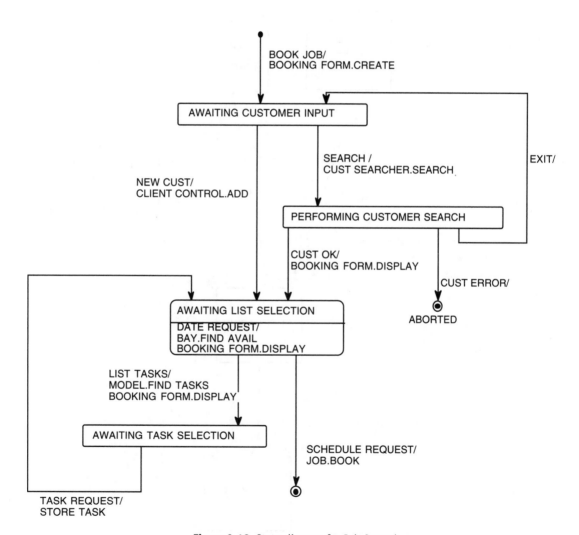

Figure 9.10. State diagram for Job Control.

9.4.2 Identifying Package Key Abstractions

Key abstractions
from the package
are examined.

The proposed XYZ package has an exposed object interface. We use event partitioning (Allen,1991) to identify the event responses required from the package (regardless of technology). This leads us to three XYZ objects that we are particularly interested in using: XYZ Order, XYZ Requisition, and XYZ Supplier. Each exposed object has a clearly defined interface, which provides a reasonable fit with the corresponding business services identified in our business class model, as follows:

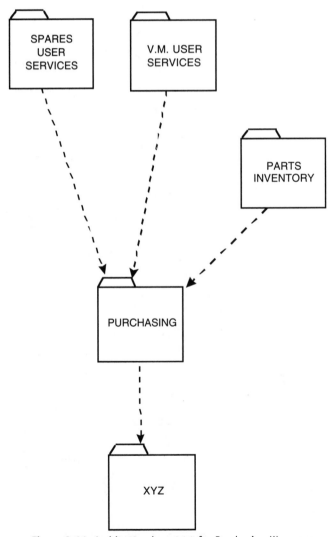

Figure 9.11. Architectural context for Purchasing Wrapper.

• XYZ Order raises and cancels purchase orders. Raising an order takes as input a set of supplier part numbers and amounts, and a supplier name; it returns a purchase order number. There are actually several interface variants available on this object to cater to old parts, as described in 9.4.3.
• XYZ Requisition raises and cancels requisitions. Raising a requisition takes as input a part number and amount and returns a requisition number.

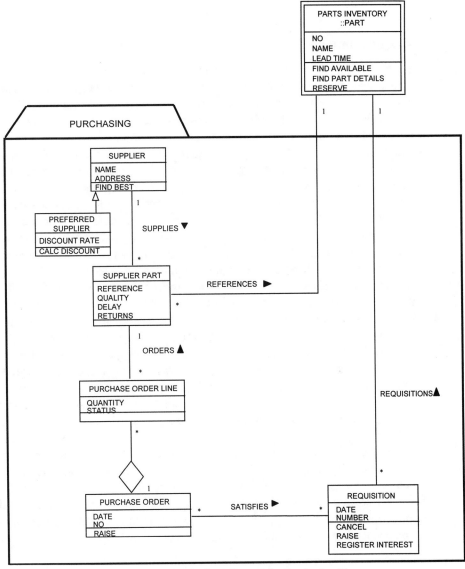

Figure 9.12. Business class diagram for Purchasing Wrapper.

• XYZ Supplier provides maintenance services for supplier details and supplier part numbers.

A business class model is developed.

Again we build a business class model to reflect requirements, as shown in Figure 9.12. Note that the business requirement to raise purchase orders and raise requisitions is satisfied by corresponding operations on the Purchase Order and Requisition business classes.

9.4.3 Designing a Package Wrapper

The business class model is compared with the package.

Designing the package wrapper presents a challenge in matching up what the business wants to do with the constraints of the package. The set of exposed business object definitions are examined to see how closely they match up with our requirement for business services. To assist we can start by developing a use case model for the business requirement and comparing this against event responses supported by the package. This shows a reasonably close match in that the package generates the order and requisition numbers, cancels orders and requisitions, and deals with printing of reports and dispatch of orders to suppliers. A key weakness of the package is that it merely does what it is told to do: It does not work out best suppliers for different orders based on history of supplier performance; this is a capability that is reflected in our business class model. Also notice that preferred suppliers, from whom special discounts are calculable, are not handled by the package.

The package reflects some old business rules, which still need to be recognized.

The package also has different ordering mechanisms for objects for different schemes for older parts made prior to 1993. The scheme number is encrypted within the part number. The package vendor has supplied a separate object to deal with each variant of order, which has its own special rules hard coded into the package. The business has subsequently streamlined its ordering process so that there is one single way of ordering parts. However, we still have the problem of ordering the older parts according to rules previously agreed on. But clearly we do not want to compromise the business object structure by introducing the old package rules.

A collaboration diagram helps with initial design of business services.

Let's consider how to tackle raising of purchase orders. First we introduce a business service class Purchase Control. Collaboration diagrams help to initially develop the design of the business services, as shown in Figure 9.13, for raising a purchase order for a post-1993 part by the Parts Controller; this is actually used by the Establish Parts for Job use case. Note that Find Best Supplier is complex enough to merit its own collaboration or sequence diagrams, which are not shown here for reasons of scope.

9.4.4 Detailing a Package Wrapper

The collaboration diagram gives us a feel for likely objects and required messaging. However, we also need to consider the complete picture, including raising of orders for the old parts. For this we use a sequence diagram, as shown in Figure 9.14. Our solution is to introduce a further business service Raise Old Part Order on Purchase Control. This is called by Raise Purchase Order whenever an old part is detected (by scanning the part number). Raise Old Part Order calls the many different variants of XYZ Order depending on the part number. A purchase order business object is still created once the order number is returned from the package. In this way, once old parts are phased out we can eventually remove the Raise Old Part Order service and we have not compromised the Purchase Order business object.

A sequence diagram is used for detailing the design.

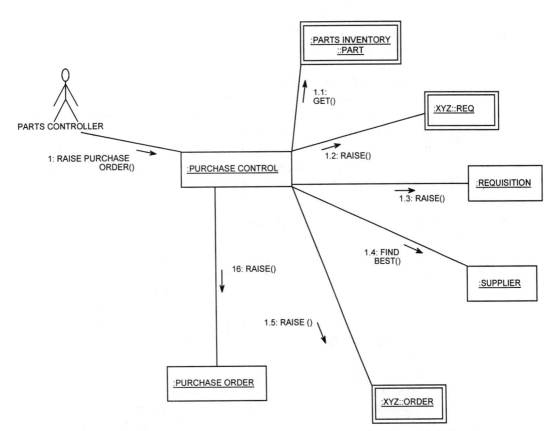

Figure 9.13. Collaboration diagram for raising a purchase order for a post-1993 part.

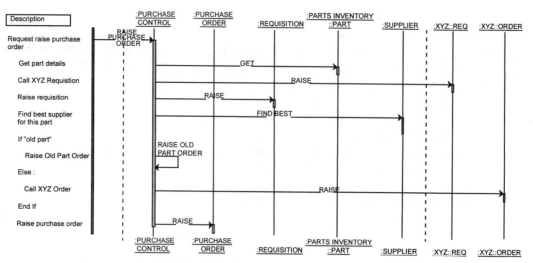

Figure 9.14. Sequence diagram for Purchase Control::Raise Purchase Order.

Additional stored data requirements must also be considered.

Finally we must address the issue of where data additional to that stored within the package database is to be stored; for example, the supplier performance information. In some situations this may require building a separate data services component as described in section 9.5; in this case we assume the additional information is stored in an OODBMS (object-oriented database management system). Either way we need to be careful to consider data integrity across the two data storage structures.

9.5 Data Wrapping Techniques

Data service packages are used to provide data services.

The need for infrastructure for the storage and retrieval of objects in a database must be approached in a way that insulates business objects from the effects of changes. Such changes range from the addition of a new relational table to changes in the database technology itself. Data services are used for the manipulation of data in a way that is independent of the underlying physical storage implementation. Data service packages provide a "buffer" between the relational and object structures, which protects the technical neutrality of business objects.

Two aspects to "impedance mismatch."...

We need basic mechanisms for dealing with the "impedance mismatch" between object structures and data storage structures. There are two aspects to this: structural differences and transaction management differences.

Relational databases are based solely on data structure in terms of tables and foreign keys. In contrast, objects encapsulate function and data. Relational tables use keys and foreign keys, whereas objects have inherent identities and associations by reference or pointer. Less obvious but more important, the two "mind-sets" are very different. For example, an object model should be geared to the semantics of the business domain, whereas a relational database is likely to be based on normalized data models. Such differences are often a challenge in their own right. In contrast the translation process between an object model and an object-oriented database structure is apparently straightforward. However, it should not be underestimated as the object-oriented database structure may be optimized for performance and therefore be markedly different to the object model.

...Structural differences

Transaction management of a relational database is likely to be more complex than with an object-oriented database, such as Versant or Gemstone. This is largely because data integrity checks need to be designed in with the former, whereas with the latter this is handled automatically. Again, however, it should not be underestimated with an object-oriented database; for example, transactions may be under explicit client control, and objects of any kind may participate.

...and transaction management differences should not be underestimated.

Our approach, shown in Figure 9.15, follows the common framework for legacy assets discussed in section 9.2.2. In addition we employ a further stereotype of object known as a "data object." The main aim of data objects is to insulate business objects from the effects of changes in technology by isolating data management system dependencies. Data objects are clustered into data service packages. They provide transaction management and translate persistent business objects into the appropriate storage units and vice versa.

Our approach employs data objects within the common framework.

It is important here to take a brief terminology excursion: The logical data model describes the design of the database according to DBMS architectural constraints (in this case RDBMS), but independently of physical characteristics. This would normally be specified in DDL (data description language) and is diagrammed using an LDSD (logical data structure diagram). The reader should note that despite the "logical" prefix this is not the same as a business data model, which describes pure business data and is diagrammed using an ERD (entity relationship diagram). The logical data model reflects key design decisions such as denormalization as well as aggregating and segmenting records (Dewitz, 1996). The physical data model describes the blocks of consecutive storage locations and exact access methods applying to a particular database (for example, Oracle or DB2). This would normally be expressed in DSDL (data storage description language).

Let's be clear on different types of "data model."

A data service package is used to model data services by grouping data objects that are cohesive to the needs of a particular set of data services. It is implemented using a component package (see chapter 10), which provides the required services in black-box fashion through its interface. There are various approaches to structuring a data service package based on different patterns,

A data service package is structured using an appropriate pattern.

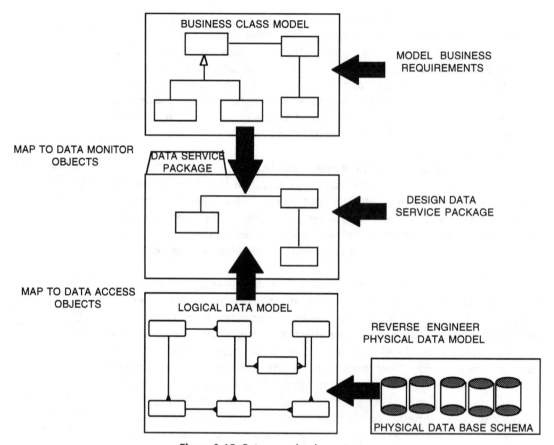

Figure 9.15. Data wrapping in context.

which are outside our current scope. In a simple case a single object might be used to wrap a database table. In most cases, however, life is not so kind. We need a strategy for dealing with more complex situations. Here we use an example pattern based on three stereotypes of data objects (introduced in chapter 2) as follows:

A data monitor object has the following responsibilities:

- It records current database values for the corresponding business object.
- It handles the mapping of object structure (for example, attributes) to relational form (for example, columns).
- It keeps status of how the business object differs with respect to the database; for example, "new," "unchanged," "deleted," "modified."

A data access object has the following responsibilities:

- It handles atomic CRUD(create, read, update, and delete) transactions to the database.
- It encapsulates access and retrieval of data from the database.
- It executes the actual SQL statements on database tables.
- It helps to partition transaction complexity.

Note: Most programming environments provide data access objects; for example, Microsoft SQL Distributed Management Objects for C++ (Microsoft Corporation, 1996).

A data service object has the following responsibilities:

- It acts in the role of service object providing data services; example data services are Get Customer Account, Back-Up Customer Account, Search Customer Account.
- It manages the detailed object interactions between data monitor objects and data access objects in a complex transaction.

The reader should understand that this is a pattern that is tuned to meet particular circumstances. For example, data access responsibilities may be folded into the data service object, especially where there is a close match between the logical data model and the business class model, and where transaction complexity is not an issue.

> The pattern is customized accordingly.

The vast majority of stored data in an enterprise setting is shared across multiple business processes. This raises data management issues such as consistency and integration, which require effective database administration. For example, the database administrator often has concerns regarding security and performance of a database exposed to new object-oriented applications. Data service packages also provide an opportunity to allow database administrators to expose the relevant level of functionality for users and to control access to corporate databases, as shown in Figure 9.16. By specifying user permissions against data services, the database administrator is able to insulate the database schema from "all comers." The database administrator provides the identified users with standardized access and update routines, which are optimized according to their needs.

> Data service packages are also used to leverage database administration.

9.5.1 Assessing the Need for Data Services

Again we start with the business class model. In this example the business service package for Parts Inventory provides a context, as shown in Figure 9.17.

> A business class model is developed.

SOLUTION TEAMS

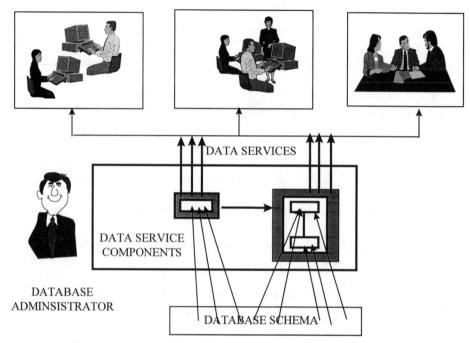

Figure 9.16. Data service components and database administration.

The constraint is that existing relational databases are to be used to provide persistence for these objects.

9.5.2 Mapping Class Model to Logical Data Model

The business class model is mapped to an implied relational structure.

Mapping of business object models to logical data models is a particularly important technique for new developments using a relational database for persistent object storage. We show here that it can also be useful as an initial aid to designing data objects for wrapping an existing relational database in that it provides a view of the relational structure implied by an object model. Database mapping rules are applied to the business class model to create a first-cut logical data structure diagram. The relational mappings are described in Appendix B. Figure 9.18 gives a picture of the implied relational structure against which we can assess the actual legacy database structure.

9.5.3 Establishing the Existing Logical Data Model

A logical data model of the existing database is produced.

Techniques for reverse engineering physical databases to logical SQL database schemas in preparation for renovation and wrapping are commonly supported by many software tools. This exposes the tables, attributes, and procedures associated with each table in the form of CRUD routines and stored proce-

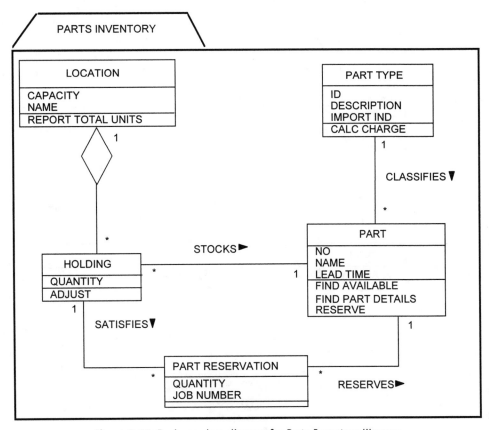

Figure 9.17. Business class diagram for Parts Inventory Wrapper.

dures. Logical data structure diagrams give a graphic view of the logical database schema, as depicted in Figure 9.19. Sometimes these diagrams are available in the form of legacy models, as mentioned in section 9.6. In the example, there are separate relational databases for inventory and parts, as shown in Figure 9.20.

9.5.4 Architecting a Data-Service Component

Let's compare the implied and actual relational structures. The Part_Ref table on the Inventory Database is used to provide a link to Part on the Parts database. The duplication of part number creates an integrity constraint across the databases that the legacy system has been designed to handle. The implied

The implied and actual relational structures are compared.

A skeleton data-service package is produced.

table Part_Reservation is not maintained on either database. In addition the Part Type attribute Import_Ind is not maintained on either database.

Following the design pattern described in 9.5, an initial mapping to a skeleton data-service package (see Figure 9.21) yields the following data objects: The DTX object acts as a data service object; each DM object is a data monitor object that corresponds to a business object; each DB

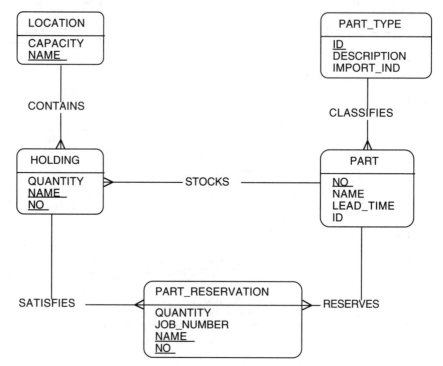

Figure 9.18. First-cut LDSD for Parts Inventory.

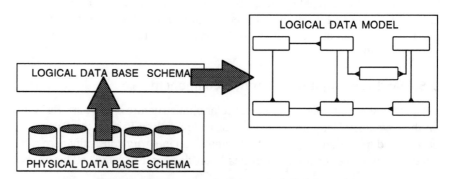

Figure 9.19. Reverse engineering a logical data model.

object is a data access object that corresponds to a database table. Note that this example is deliberately simplified: In a real-life situation available database procedures must be assessed against the overall need for data services and multitable joins handled by a database server. Modeling data objects helps the designer in coming to terms with the structural differences between the business object model and logical data model and with the problem of transaction management alluded to earlier.

9.5.5 Revising the Logical Data Model

We now address the issue of where additional data to that stored within the existing relational databases is to be stored; that is, the Part Reservation object and the Import_Ind attribute. There are two basic choices: Either extend the existing database structure or provide a new storage mechanism, which may

The existing logical data model is modified to reflect requirements.

INVENTORY DB
LOGICAL DATA
STRUCTURE DIAGRAM

PARTS DB
LOGICAL DATA
STRUCTURE DIAGRAM

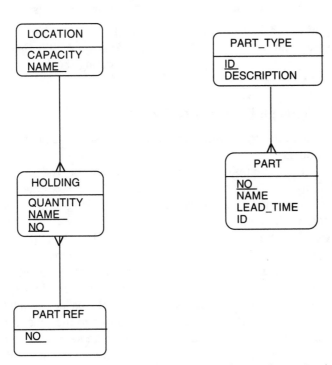

Figure 9.20. First-cut LDSDs for Parts Inventory Database and Parts Database.

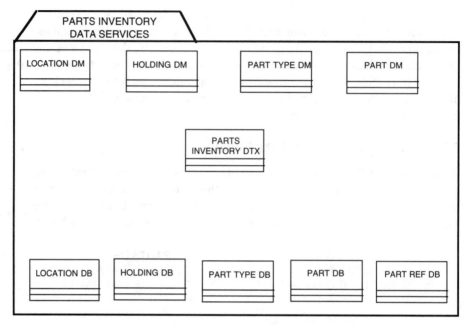

Figure 9.21. Skeleton service package for Parts Inventory.

be OODBMS. Either way we need to be careful and consider the impact on data integrity and to assess the "knock-on effect" on existing legacy applications. In this case we choose to extend the existing databases, as shown in Figure 9.22.

9.5.6 Designing a Data Service Package

Data service classes are designed.

A data service class is identified for each related set of required transactions. A transaction can range from a simple atomic object read or create to a complex set of object creates, which have complex integrity requirements.

Sequence diagrams are used to help design the data services.

CRUD transactions are required for all our business objects. We use a sequence diagram, shown in Figure 9.23 for Read Part, to help design these services based on the pattern described in the previous section. The Read Part data service first attempts to get the part data monitor object (Part DM). If it is found, then it can be returned to the caller to instantiate the Part object. If Part DM is not found, then a call is made to the part data access object (Part DB) to retrieve the required part data from the database. If there is no database record a suitable database error message is returned to the caller and the transaction ends. Otherwise a Part DM is created and returned to the caller for instantiating the Part business objects. The Create Part data service, shown in Figure 9.24, creates data access objects with transaction type "create," for both data-

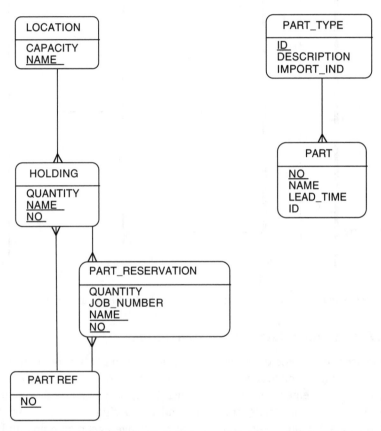

Figure 9.22. Revised LDSDs for Parts Inventory Database and Parts Database.

bases. A call is then issued to the DB Transaction Manager object to commit the object DBs to the databases and a part data monitor object is created.

In this example, we have assumed that a commit occurs for each successful transaction unit. In other cases it may be that saves to the database are better controlled by the user, or are made on a regular temporal basis in order to minimize network traffic. This would require a separate commit transaction on the data service class. For more complex transactions the reader is referred to the case study in chapter 15.

Transaction commits are designed according to requirements.

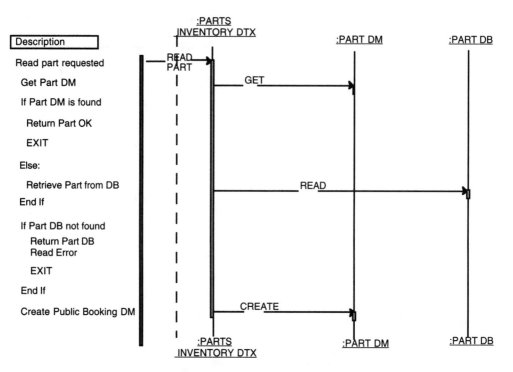

Figure 9.23. Sequence diagram for Parts Inventory DTX::Read Part data service.

9.5.7 Detailing a Data Service Transaction

Further nonfunctional requirements are added.

A data service is a type of transaction in the sense that it is either entirely executed (committed) or totally canceled (aborted or rolled back). Further nonfunctional requirements such as response time, frequency, and volume can also be added as message properties and the design tuned to meet these requirements. Requirements can be captured as average, maximum, and minimum units. This is particularly important for transactions and forms part of the transaction profile. For example Create Part has a required response time of less than 1 second as shown (b − a <1 sec) on the sequence diagram in Figure 9.25, following UML (1997).

Nonfunctional requirements may be further refined.

The fact that Create Part is a transaction is highlighted by the additional notation of a wider elongated control box, as shown in Figure 9.25. Once deployment of the service packages has been considered, as described in chapter 10, we can add further detail to the transaction profiles of the data services. For example, Parts are held current to the last transaction on a local client machine. Data currency is therefore "current" for Part DM. Note that

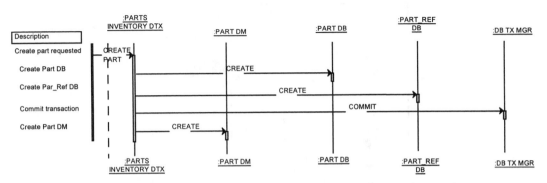

Figure 9.24. Sequence diagram for Parts Inventory DTX::Create Part data service.

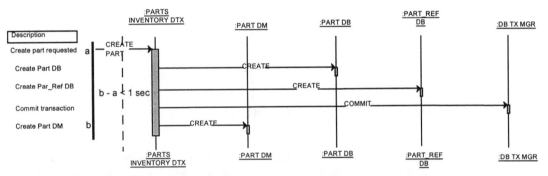

Figure 9.25. Revised Sequence Diagram for Parts Inventory DTX::Create Part data service.

had Parts been maintained on a separate machine and refreshed at 24-hour intervals to the local machine, currency of the Part DM object would have been "up to 24 hours." This information could be further refined to attribute level if necessary; for example, if Part Name was current "up to 24 hours" and Part Name was only current "up to 1 week."

9.6 Practical Guidelines on Component Modeling of Legacy Assets

9.6.1 Legacy Models

Many organizations have significant investments in models produced by traditional structured methods. Such models reflect hard-won business knowledge that organizations are justifiably reluctant to throw away. There is a particular need to capitalize on existing data models as organizations seek to migrate toward the brave new world of component technology and the component

Legacy data models provide a rich source of material.

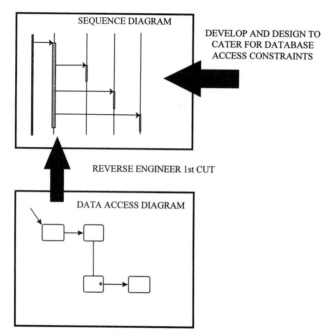

Figure 9.26 Mapping a data access diagram to a sequence diagram.

marketplace. We have seen in the previous section that a logical data model provides a key abstraction on which to build a legacy database wrapper. Such models are also an important vehicle for renovating legacy systems in preparation for wrapping (Mattison & Sipolt, 1995).

Other legacy models also have potential to assist the process.

Other diagrams from structured methods can be used to assist. For example, event lists and context diagrams (Allen, 1991; McMenamin & Palmer, 1984) provide useful scoping information on legacy systems and packages that can assist in reverse engineering and renovation. Entity relationship diagrams and entity life-history diagrams are potentially reverse engineered to first-cut object models. Data access diagrams provide useful information about navigation of databases. The latter is an important issue especially where there is a requirement for complex transactions to be effectively managed by object-oriented solutions that interact with the database. For example, a data access diagram can be mapped to a first-cut sequence diagram as shown in Figure 9.26; examples include enquiry access paths and effect-correspondence diagrams from SSADM (structured systems analysis and design methodology) (CCTA, 1995).

9.6.2 Package Library Object Classifications

The service categories of the Perspective architecture help distinguish the correct exposed package functionality for mapping to components. This is helped further when the package classifies objects into business objects and technical objects, as is, for example, the case with the SAP R/3 Business Object Repository (SAP, 1996), which defines 170 business objects that map to SAP's underlying software. These objects greatly simplify the developer's view of the underlying software and present an opportunity to dovetail package functionality with new object-oriented solutions. Where business objects are provided the advantages are magnified if they can be aligned with the organization's business processes.

Service categories provide a ready route to isolating package functionality.

9.6.3 Wrapping a Heavyweight System with a Lightweight Wrapper

Short term this is always an attractive strategy, based on "blanket wrapping," which is discussed in the text that follows. One of the authors was recently consulting on an object-oriented dealing system. At one point in the deal-input use case, it is necessary to check ability to proceed with the deal. This means checking the client's security holdings. This check is actually a well-established procedure on an existing system, involving some complex logic that has evolved considerably over the years for use by many different applications. To rewrite this in objects would have been a project in its own right. The sheer amount of regression testing alone would have been a huge task. By introducing a wrapper we would kill two birds with one stone: Reuse existing functionality in a legacy system and expedite rapid development of the new dealing system.

This is an apparently attractive strategy.

9.6.4 Wrapping and Incremental Development

On further investigation the holdings wrapper approach described previously was found to incur dependencies that would render our design unwieldy and degrade performance. The legacy system interfaced to several other systems via work files using hidden codes and conventions over which we had no control. Therefore a renovation exercise was initiated to minimize its interfaces to the other systems in parallel with wrapping a limited subset of its functionality, which was free from such dependencies, in a first increment of the new system. Further increments were then evolved in line with the Perspective process, as described in chapter 11.

Use a divide-and-conquer strategy for heavyweight systems.

9.6.5 Blanket vs. Piecemeal Approaches

The blanket approach is to declare that what works should continue to be used "as is."

The legacy asset becomes a single "component" in that its functionality is accessed via some existing or added interface. The idea is to create a layer of software (blanket wrapper) that specifies the legacy system's functions in terms of a clearly defined set of services using a common syntax (for example, CORBA or DCOM). The blanket wrapper translates any messages received as service requests through its interface into calls to the existing software. This solution allows new software to interoperate with the old software. The problem with this approach is that, while it gives the illusion of object orientation, it actually represents a very poor object-oriented design in which data and its related behavior is not kept together. It also begs the question of what are to count as business services, postponing the real work until later. Also, the legacy systems still need to be maintained in their entirety including knock-on effects to wrapper code.

Economics often lead to a piecemeal approach.

Economics often lead to a piecemeal approach, in which isolated small parts of legacy systems are addressed often as a means of "dipping the organization's toe" in the component-technology reservoir. For example, tools are now available for wrapping existing COBOL programs using OO COBOL; for a detailed discussion the reader is referred to Flint (1996) and Gilbert (1996). The existing COBOL code does not change. The methods of wrapper objects are written in OO COBOL, preserving the existing code from the threat of change. This approach promises reduced maintenance and increased reuse of legacy code. Another example of a piecemeal approach is "screen scraping." Screen scraping involves creating a GUI to a legacy application without changing legacy code. For example, it can be used to replace dumb terminals with PCs, whose custom-developed GUI works like a terminal emulator but provides an object-oriented interface for navigating the legacy application. Although this does nothing to distribute functionality among multiple clients, let alone objects, it does nevertheless enable later migration to client–server computing and maintains data and application security. The main problem with these approaches is that because legacy systems are based on the separation of function and data, great care is needed in selecting "the right pieces." It is often extremely difficult to "objectify" small fragments, especially where data sharing across legacy code is high, which it often is!

9.6.6 Setting Out a Strategy

An effective migration strategy steers a balance.

Clearly we need to strive for a level of granularity that is pitched between the two extremes of blanket wrapping and piecemeal wrapping, to meet the needs of the individual organization. That is why we employ service packages and not objects as the enabling unit of reuse. There is a trade-off between components that are rapidly constructed to wrap existing system services and components that are designed to glean the full benefits of an object-oriented approach. "Thin wrappers" have the advantage that they can be developed very quickly at minimum cost, but have the disadvantage that they will usually incur significant rework later on when the organization migrates fully to component technology. "Fat wrappers" have the opposite pros and cons in that it will take longer but is less likely to incur significant rework later on. An effective migration strategy needs to steer a balance between these extremes. This should include clear policy on effective data management, a critical success factor for large organizations; the reader is referred to Graham (1995) for an extensive discussion.

9.7 Summary

A major theme of this chapter is that wrapping is not a panacea for ills. It is a useful technique but it is one that is easily abused. The effectiveness of wrapping depends on how it is used in context with many other techniques. In addition, there are important related areas such as renovation of legacy systems and databases and the use of legacy structured models that, for reasons of scope, we have only been able to touch on in this chapter.

Wrapping is not a "cure-all."

Too often wrappers are constructed on the basis that it seemed like a "good idea" at the time. In Britain a tradition is to wrap "fish and chips" in newspaper to keep them warm. At first there is a strong smell of hot newspaper. However, this is soon replaced by the smell of fish. Likewise a legacy wrapper can soon start to smell of the COBOL or PL1 it was designed to reuse, if it is poorly designed! The modeling techniques described in this chapter are aimed at helping to avoid this situation.

Effective wrappers are based on sound models.

CHAPTER 10

••••••••••••••••••••••

Deployment
Modeling

10.1 Introduction

In Perspective we take a minimalist approach to modeling and want to avoid the type of detailed design modeling that runs counter to the principles of RAAD. Up to now we have focused on business-oriented component modeling as independently as possible of implementation concerns. In an ideal world with "perfect technology" it would be great if we could stop there! However, we need to build a sound component infrastructure with respect to the technology architecture. Deployment modeling directly addresses these concerns by exploring and defining the configuration of run-time processing elements and the component packages that live on them. This short chapter introduces some minimal additional notation and outlines some deployment-modeling techniques.

Deployment modeling explores and defines run-time architecture.

10.2 Deployment-Modeling Principles

So why is deployment modeling important in taking a business-oriented approach? Decisions made in deployment modeling clearly affect the user of the system in terms of such basics as cost, response time, convenience of access to the system, business efficiency, and usability of the system. For example, choice of a central mainframe, rather than a distributed network of

Decisions made in deployment modeling affect the user of the system.

workstations, could mean the difference between a user traveling 2 hours to the central office or invoking the system in 2 seconds at his or her desk. Once deployment modeling is complete you should know all of the things that affect the user: What the system will do, how it will look and perform at least in outline, how much it will cost, and how long it will take to build.

The focus is on which components may be run on which platforms.

A package dependency diagram has only a type form. A deployment diagram has an instance form: It is used to model the structure of the run-time system in terms of the configuration of run-time processing units (nodes). We use deployment diagrams simply to show which components may be run on which nodes. However, we do not model dependencies between component instances that live on the nodes.

The scope of deployment modeling can vary enormously.

Clearly, the criteria and scope of deployment modeling vary enormously depending on whether the developer is designing a solution (as part of the solution process) or designing reusable components (as part of the component process). For example, the solution developer has choice over run-time architecture for a component that he or she is designing, but no choice over the run-time architectures required for components that are being reused. In contrast, the component developer has a much wider potential choice of potential run-time architectures in designing for components that are capable of running on a number of potentially different hardware hosts. In this case it may well not be appropriate to choose particular nodes: Simply define a set of characteristics (including capacity and capability) that will be provided by all the foreseen hosts and allocate to a single node.

10.3 Deployment-Modeling Notation

10.3.1 Notation Set

Deployment diagrams provide a graphic view of the use of a particular technical architecture for implementation of components (see Figure 10.1). Deployment diagrams (UML, 1997) show nodes (as 3-D boxes) and connections between nodes (as lines between boxes). A connection is an association that indicates a communication path between nodes; for example, a physical link such as ethernet or fiber-optic link. The latter are stereotypes of connection, which may optionally be shown on the diagram. Where there is more than one occurrence of a node the multiplicity is indicated in the top right corner of the box (* = any number). Component packages allocated to a node are optionally viewable on the deployment diagram, displayed in the lower section of a node box (analogous to attributes in a class box).

NAME	SYMBOL	DESCRIPTION
Node	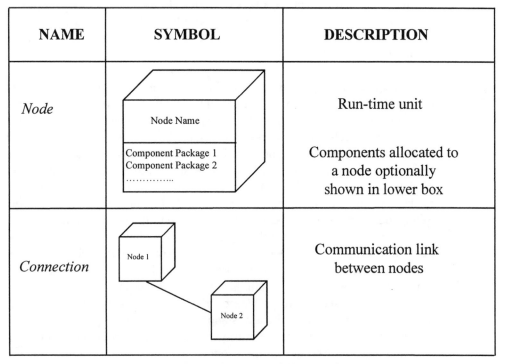	Run-time unit Components allocated to a node optionally shown in lower box
Connection		Communication link between nodes

Figure 10.1. Deployment modeling notation set.

A node has a technology type (for example, Windows NT or UNIX). A component package is indicated by stereotype (<<component package>>). A component package allocated to a node has a run-time architecture (for example, NETSCAPE).

10.4 Deployment-Modeling Techniques

Deployment modeling covers the following closely related iterative activities:

A family of related activities is involved in deployment modeling.

- It creates component packages through which service packages are to be implemented. A service package is promoted to the status of component package once its classes have stabilized and we can anticipate which classes are to require interfaces.
- It partitions a component package into a number of smaller component packages to meet nonfunctional requirements.
- It chooses nodes on which to implement the component packages. This entails considering all nonfunctional requirements, particularly physical constraints that might directly drive choice of nodes.

- It allocates component packages to nodes. This entails considering which component packages are to be deployed on which nodes.
- It evaluates alternative deployment architectures in terms of capabilities and capacities of the chosen nodes.

The modeling notation must add value to the overall process.

A service package is implemented in terms of one or more component packages. Each service class is implemented through one or more interfaces. An interface may be used to implement several service classes. The potential many-to-many relationship between interfaces and service classes can result in top-heavy complexity, especially if further notations are used to model these relationships. In fact we have witnessed some horrendous "spaghetti models" during the course of our work. In Perspective, which is based on minimalist modeling, we have therefore deliberately striven to avoid this situation: Remember, a modeling notation must add value to the overall process.

Our goal is a sound component infrastructure.

Coding environments are already providing detailed design-modeling support. For example, Visual C++ has color syntax editors, wizards for application frameworks, specialized forms of class manipulation, and overviews of systems at the class level. Such features are rapidly emerging in code-generation tools, which are seeking to provide ever-more sophisticated wizard support using technology frameworks and standardized mapping options. Therefore our design modeling is pitched at the goal of providing a sound component infrastructure with respect to the technology architecture. We model dependencies between component packages, which can be partitioned into smaller packages, as a means of setting the architectural context.

10.4.1 Creating Component Packages

Package dependency diagrams model component architecture.

The Vehicle Maintenance business service package and its associated user service packages are allocated to the same node (a Reception Desktop) as described in the next section. Each service package is implemented in terms of a component package, as shown in Figure 10.2. Service classes on these packages will require interfaces to be designed. Note that the User Service Core component package has three service classes, which were introduced back in section 8.4.10. We might consider partitioning each into a separate component package to meet nonfunctional requirements.

10.4.2 Allocating Component Packages to Nodes

Service packages are implemented using component packages.

Allocating component packages to nodes is a technique that assigns various component packages to different nodes of the technical architecture. The service package dependency diagrams are business oriented: That is, they are partitioned according to service type. The decision as to where component

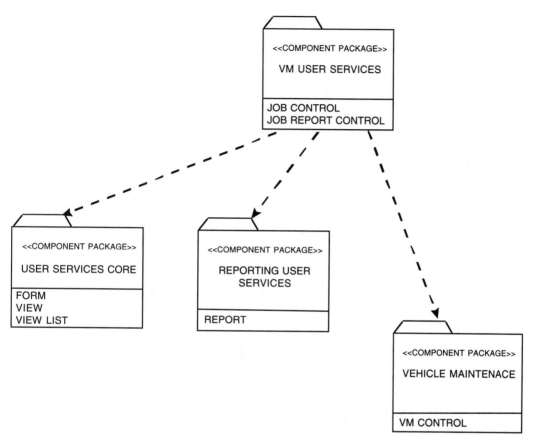

Figure 10.2. Component package dependency diagram.

packages will actually run and how they will be partitioned is made once a good understanding of service packages has been achieved.

Implementation constraints are a major factor in deciding how to partition service packages across nodes and components. However, the service-type partitioning gives an ideal picture and a key method guideline is to try to minimize distortion of this. Deployment modeling is used to visually portray the different design trade-offs and to stimulate discussion as to how best to design an effective physical architecture.

Figure 10.3 shows a set of nodes for the Vehicle Maintenance solution comprising a central server, a set of dealership servers, and a set of reception desktops; notice that nodes are named according to generic technology type and according to their business role. Each service package is to be implemented using a single component package.

Service packages are weighed against implementation constraints.

A deployment diagram helps allocate component packages to nodes.

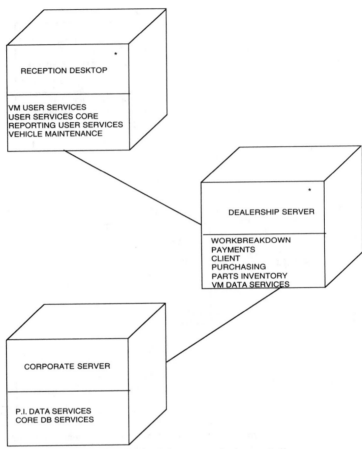

Figure 10.3. Vehicle Maintenance deployment diagram.

Service categories guide the allocation.

Vehicle Maintenance user and business services are to run in Visual C++ on a number of Windows NT desktops situated in the reception area of each dealership. The remaining business services are reused C++ components running on local servers. Vehicle Maintenance data services are to run using Oracle SQL, also on the local servers, one of which is located in each dealership. The remaining data services are to run using Oracle SQL on a corporate server. All run-time architectures are to use NETSCAPE.

10.5 Practical Guidelines on Deployment Modeling

10.5.1 Application Partitioning

Ultimately we would like the ability to move deployed components around from one node to another to facilitate better processing and network management; for example, significantly increase network performance by reducing traffic or improve control by moving processing off desktops and onto a server where it can be more easily managed. Any reassignment of components to nodes usually involves rewriting or adding new code. Our experience is that an application partitioning tool greatly facilitates the process by providing "capabilities for building and running applications across multiple platforms without re-conversion of the code for the target platforms—including the respective operating and GUI windowing systems, as well as any communications mechanisms necessary for the application to function" (Harmon, 1995a).

A flexible deployment architecture is clearly advantageous.

10.5.2 Using Imagination in Deployment Architectures

We need to use some imagination and ask "how well" the deployment architecture meets requirements in terms of quality attributes (Gilb, 1988); for example, efficiency and usability. Some of these may be general (for example, "In the event of loss of service from the application the System Manager will be responsible for the restoration of these services within 1 working day"); others may be specific to a model item (for example, "It shall be possible to obtain a print of any archived Job Instruction Sheet within 1 working day").

Evaluate alternative deployment architectures.

10.5.3 Guarding Against Assumptions in Deployment Architectures

It may be that specific platforms are mandated in some form of physical constraints document. The designer may apparently have no choice in the matter of which nodes to use. However, this is a dangerous assumption. It is important to ensure that nodes stipulated in the physical constraints document are suitable for what you want to do. Many of the problems encountered in systems design are caused by people without the necessary technical knowledge picking technology that is totally unsuitable for what has to be done on it. The people who make these unsuitable choices may not realize that the money they save on the hardware will shrink in comparison to the money spent on trying to develop suitable software to run on it. (These comments also apply to prestipulated software architecture, such as operating systems and communications packages.) It is important therefore to evaluate prestipulated nodes and feed back your findings for resolution. This may lead to

Evaluate prestipulated nodes and feed back your findings for resolution.

reassessment of the original choice of nodes or modifications to requirements to make the chosen nodes more viable. The irony is that if you start off with the wrong nodes, a badly structured system may have to be designed, simply to cope with the inadequacies of the nodes.

10.6 Summary

This is neither
a simple nor
mechanical activity.

Deployment modeling explores and defines the configuration of run-time processing elements and the component packages that live on them. The five interrelated activities are as follows:

1. Create component packages.
2. Partition component packages (optional).
3. Choose nodes.
4. Allocate component packages to nodes.
5. Evaluate alternative deployment architectures.

CHAPTER 11

• • • • • • • • • • • • • • • • • • • •

The Perspective Process

11.1 Introduction

This chapter provides an overview of the Perspective process in preparation for the remaining chapters in this part of the book, which deal with specific details. General ground rules for the use of processes are introduced, including the use of process templates. This provides a context for discussion of specific themes of the Perspective process, which are as follows:

The Perspective process provides a flexible "how-to-do-it" framework.

- RAAD (rapid architected application development),
- iteration,
- product-focused development,
- incremental development,
- evolutionary development,
- constant validation,
- positive politics,
- process refinement.

There are two "subprocesses": the solution process and the component process, which are aimed at the development of solutions and components, respectively. Guidelines are presented for assessing the type of process that is appropriate for the needs of specific projects in preparation for the detailed

The Perspective process is a two-tier process.

descriptions of the solution process in chapter 12 and the component process in chapter 13. It is important to understand that solution and component processes are ideals: Commonly you will need to use elements of both processes adapted to your own specific needs.

BPM is integrated into the process.

The chapter includes a process framework for employing the BPM techniques that were presented in chapter 3. This shows how to drive the solution and component processes from a previous BPM effort.

Teams reflect the needs of the process.

Teams should be multidisciplinary with a range of skills represented in one team. This is in sharp contrast to the traditional approach of an analysis team throwing requirements "over the wall" to a design team that in turn throws specifications over the wall to coders and then to testers and so on. Techniques such as JAD are used to facilitate the process. These important related subjects are addressed in chapter 14.

11.2 Process Fundamentals

11.2.1 What Is a Process?

This section explains basic ground rules for an effective process.

The term "process" as used in the present context is in fact an abbreviation of the term "process model." All models are abstractions that are designed to view the real world from a particular viewpoint and thereby provide a useful level of definition and understanding. Our present viewpoint is that of software development. Thus, the process described in this chapter is an abstract description of the software development activities within the Perspective approach.

11.2.2 Why Is a Process Useful?

A process should bring structure to complexity.

The development of a significant software system presents substantial project management and technical challenges. The use of a process by a software development team is one of the mechanisms for meeting such challenges by providing overall guidance from both management and technical viewpoints.

For example, a process should assist managers in the following tasks:

- identification and partitioning of work,
- identification of progress achieved,
- planning the staff resource profile,
- planning the requirement for physical resources, for example, test rigs,
- provision of cost and time scale estimates for the work yet to be performed.

From a technical viewpoint a process should assist in the following areas:

- identification of preconditions required before each activity is started,
- specification of the products and deliverables required from each activity,
- techniques that may be used during each activity,
- experience gained from earlier work.

11.2.3 The Perspective Process Template

Software development is a highly skilled, creative, and adaptive process. Too often processes are produced for projects that ignore this fact and attempt to rigidly prescribe the development process to an extreme level of detail. If the process is too rigidly prescriptive and described at too low a level of detail a number of problems will arise, these are as follows:

The Perspective process is not rigidly prescriptive...

- the cost of maintaining the process will be prohibitive,
- the project managers will be swamped with requests for waivers because of numerous "special cases,"
- the development team will be swamped with noncompliance reports by the project's auditors because the more detailed the process description the more easy it is to be noncompliant,
- a culture of "malicious compliance" may result where developers do what the process specifies rather than what they know to be correct.

It is a flexible and open process described in terms of stages that employ the following template:

...it provides a framework for development.

- **Purpose**: a brief summary of the objectives of the stage.
- **Inputs:** a list of models and deliverables that are preconditions of beginning the stage.
- **Outputs:** a list of models and deliverables that are postconditions of completing the stage.
- **Task Catalog:** a list of procedures with short descriptions that are usefully employed to carry out the work involved in the stage. Modeling techniques (contained in section 4 of chapters 3 to 10) are referenced for appropriate tasks.
- **Keynotes**: important general points to be aware of in carrying out the work.

Suggested lists of inputs, outputs, and tasks are included in chapters 12 and 13 in order to provide the reader with a starting point. The items included are based on the authors' practical experience of employing Perspective to real-life projects. However, no one organization is the same as another and the templates are designed to be customized to suit individuals' needs.

The templates are customizable.

11.2.4 A Model-Based Process

Model reuse represents the greatest potential to increase productivity.

Clearly, building and refining generic models is an important aspect of component-based development where we want to leverage model reuse rather than code reuse. Most of the time involved in software development is consumed in analysis and design and relatively little time (10%–20%) (Harmon, 1995b) is involved in actually writing the code. Even if class libraries are extensively employed to increase coding productivity, they only reduce effort by a corresponding amount (10%–20%). A model-based approach facilitates reuse at the high end of the process before any code is even attempted, with correspondingly greater opportunities to save effort.

Generic models are refined to meet solution needs.

Service packages provide a means of structuring a project in terms of architectural context and allow us to build on and capitalize on the very best work of others. A service package can be effectively employed by a component project to contain a generic model, which can be refined and extended to meet the specific needs of a solution project, in analogous fashion to a framework.

Models evolve to code.

The model solution space evolves to contain more detail as a project moves through the iterations of the Perspective process. Eventually portions of the model are mature enough to be transformed into code, preferably through a code generator to smooth the process and maximize productivity. The tested code represents the model at its most detailed level of abstraction. Note that this is in contrast to deliverables, which are created as evidence of productivity at various points in the process. Deliverables are simply views of a maturing model. This may seem a very obvious point but we think it is worth emphasizing here as many processes do not work on this basis, relying instead on reworking and elaboration of deliverables and not models, which is clearly time-consuming and not practical for RAAD.

11.3 Themes in the Perspective Process

This section describes a number of key themes that underpin the Perspective process.

11.3.1 RAAD

All software processes can be considered to be somewhere on a spectrum of rigor.

Processes with no method (i.e., "hacking") sit at one extreme of a spectrum of rigor and processes based on the use of formal mathematical specifications sit at the other, as illustrated in Figure 11.1. Those processes toward the "no method" end of the spectrum tend, broadly, to have the advantage that results are produced fast but incur the disadvantage that the resultant software systems may be unreliable, impossible to reuse, and difficult to maintain and

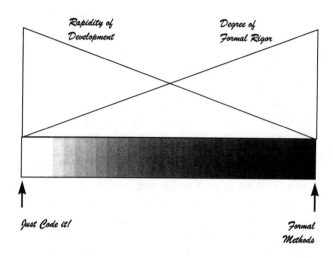

Figure 11.1. The spectrum of process rigor.

extend. Those software processes toward the other end of the spectrum tend, broadly, to have the advantage that the resultant software systems are reusable, reliable, maintainable, and flexible but incur the disadvantage that results are produced very slowly or not at all.

An ultra-RAD approach will result in software that will have so many bugs as to render it unusable. The long-term consequences of ultra-RAD approaches are in fact self-defeating. Because solutions are always geared to immediate needs, software never gets reused. This means that in the long term applications become increasingly inconsistent. The same code has to be replicated in an increasing number of places. Changes to that code are an increasing maintenance drain on valuable resources. Conversely, the ultraconservative approach will never actually deliver anything as management "pulls the plug" in frustration at development inertia or "analysis paralysis." Attempts at software reuse will be "theoretical."

Perspective addresses this dilemma by the use of models within an architecture that is designed to provide both early value through solution increments and a long-term investment for software reuse in terms of component services. How exactly though do we "position" a process along this spectrum? The level of rigor appropriate for a particular development is dependent on perceived value of the software to be produced. For instance, if the main value driver is speed of delivery of a simple data-capture or inquiry system with a short life span, then a development process with little rigor may be appropriate. If, however, the software is for a safety-critical flight-management system then maximum reliability, accuracy, and maintainability are required from the

The extreme points in the spectrum are in fact "no-hopers."

Risks must be assessed against quality features.

development process. Positioning of a suitable process along the spectrum of rigor is of course much more complicated than described in the above simplistic scenario. For example, perceived value is a function of many different software and process quality features, which are traded off against acceptable risk. Software features include quality attributes such as performance, security, and usability (Gilb, 1988). Process features include speed of delivery and effort involved (Fenton, 1991). Risks include user computer literacy and system volatility. A full discussion of trading off risks and quality features is outside our scope; the reader is referred to Folkes and Stubenvoll (1992).

The means must justify the end.

The salient point is that the appropriate degree of rigor in the development process should balance the risk-accounted value drivers. For example, acceptable degree of rigor will be a function both of the speed with which early results are required and the level of reliability and maintainability required for those results. Often we find that processes are applied blindly without sufficient thought concerning perceived value. For example, much unreliable and unmaintainable software has resulted from first-generation client-server developments working exclusively to speed of development and look and feel of user interface as their only criteria. Conversely other systems are overengineered to the dictates of elaborate standards, resulting in systems that are never actually delivered because of very justified user frustration.

The Perspective process can be varied in its degree of rigor.

Perspective uses the term "RAAD" from Gartner (1996) to highlight the fact that modern businesses require solutions that confer early user benefits at minimum cost, leveraging existing legacy systems where possible but not at the cost of sacrificing maintainability, flexibility, and reusability. This requires trading off short-term and long-term objectives. As a rough guide solution projects tend toward the left side of the spectrum in contrast to component projects, which tend toward the right side of the spectrum; solution and component projects are characterized in section 11.4.3.

11.3.2 Iteration

The waterfall model fails the "reality test."

The process most used, historically, during software development is often referred to as the waterfall model (Royce, 1970). In this model a number of stages are defined (typically the stages are requirements analysis, design, coding, testing) and the development consists of a single sequential pass through these stages. In addition, a stage is not allowed to begin until its predecessor has finished. The waterfall model is predicated on the assumption that it is possible to completely and unambiguously define a set of requirements at the outset of a project. The experience of many software projects has shown this assumption to be fallacious. "Build one to throw one away. You will anyway" (Brooks, 1975) is a lesson that Fred Brooks learned in the 1960s during the development of the OS operating system. It seems to have taken considerably longer to permeate through to the system-building community as a whole!

Various life cycles have been proposed and tried in order to address the iterative nature of software development, while retaining the original framework of the waterfall model. The most popular of these seem to be spiral models deriving from the work of Barry Boehm (1986) at TRW. This recognizes that the specification of *all* the requirements at the outset of a project is an impossibility and allows *detailed* requirements to "emerge" during the development according to acceptable risk.

Spiral models are designed to cope with reality.

The spiral model has a series of repetitive steps whose iterations are intended to converge toward an operational prototype through four quadrants of activity (Plan - Determine Objectives - Evaluate Alternatives - Develop). Areas of greatest risk can be revisited through the spiral, whereas areas that have stabilized can be developed through to implementation. The spiral is thus aimed very clearly at addressing the iterative nature of systems development. More recently, the spiral model has been adapted, tailored, and extended in various ways to come to terms with the reality of software development. Examples include the following:

Areas of greatest risk are revisited.

- recursive/parallel model (Berard, 1993),
- fountain model (Henderson-Sellers & Edwards, 1994),
- cluster emphasis (Meyer, 1990),
- round-trip gestalt engineering (Booch, 1994).

Booch (1994) expresses the maxims underlying each of these approaches by quoting from Heinlein (1966): "When faced with a problem you do not understand, do any part of it you do understand, then look at it again." Perspective also recognizes that this is the natural way that we humans work, not only in software development, but in tackling any complex problem.

The Perspective process is iterative...

11.3.3 Product-Focused Development

Activity-based processes are geared to the measuring of activities as an indication of progress. The problem with this is that activities are not tangible enough to be measured. The question, "How much of the analysis is complete?" begs the more significant question of "How much of the analysis product is complete?" The second problem with an activity-based approach is that it is too rigidly prescriptive. Software development is not naturally like following a cooking recipe. By focusing development on specified products to be produced in agreed periods of time, a product-based approach enables the team

...and product focused as opposed to activity focused.

to select the most appropriate activities for the type of product. It is the end that is significant, not the means chosen to achieve it. Perspective includes catalogs of suggested activities that can be used at each stage of development. However, the sequence and timing of the activities are open.

11.3.4 Incremental Delivery

The Perspective process is incremental.

An incremental approach delivers software in a number of additive phases. In Perspective increments are delivered in terms of services. The principal reasons for the use of an incremental delivery strategy are as follows:

1. to reduce the project management risks associated with the "big bang" approach of delivering all the software at the same time;

2. to gain "buy in" from the business owners through the early availability of some functionality; delivery of "the juicy bits first" (Gilb, 1988) inspires user confidence and encourages their collaboration.

The philosophy underlying the incremental approach is embodied in the "80:20" rule.

It should be possible to deliver 80% of system functionality in 20% of the overall time. As software developers we tend to spend 80% of our time "gilding the lily," in elaborating and polishing the design to accommodate detailed user changes and introducing cosmetic niceties. This is evidenced by the time-honored reply of "95% done" by the developer in response to the manager's question of "How far to go?" Under these circumstances critical business functionality can be delivered much earlier than if a "big bang" approach is adopted and the remaining functionality, of lesser business value, can be delivered in a less pressured environment.

Use case modeling lends itself well to this approach.

An incremental delivery strategy is only possible if a mechanism exists to split the required, total functionality into discrete pieces. Each incremental delivery is then made up of a number of these discrete pieces. Use cases form a natural business-oriented basis on which to identify increments that are delivered in terms of services.

11.3.5 Evolutionary Development

The Perspective process is evolutionary.

Waterfall approaches assume that it is possible to state requirements entirely and in detail before delivering any software. This assumption has been challenged by drawing an analogy with the Heizenberg Uncertainty Principle: "Any systems development activity inevitably changes the environment out of which the need for the system arose" (Jackson & McCracken, 1982). One of the strengths of an incremental approach is that the effects of implementing requirements are demonstrated early. An evolutionary approach takes this a step further by driving development from users' actual experiences in using the evolving software. The Perspective process accommodates the need to evolve software solutions in the form of a feedback loop after rolling out increments. What makes the Perspective process unique, however, is that it is based on the *evolution of models:* ***Only by evolving the underlying models is a truly seamless approach to software development possible.***

11.3.6 Constant Validation

One serious problem with the waterfall process is that the business owner of the software system may have no contact with the developers between signing of the statement of requirements document and witnessing acceptance testing. Such an approach is inherently risky. The Perspective process minimizes the above risk through the use of validation practices at every stage of the development. In addition to the normal validation activity of testing, Perspective encourages the participation of business owners through all stages of the development, thereby providing many opportunities for identifying errors and omissions. For example, business owners may review prototypes that are produced through iterative design, take part in JAD sessions, or use functionality that is delivered as early increments.

The Perspective process encourages validation through participation.

11.3.7 Positive Politics

Our experience shows that a key enabler of successful projects has nothing to do with types of system or with technology. A major condition for success is in fact a political one:

Politics is a key factor in successful projects.

- As a rookie systems analyst, one of the authors remembers being baffled by a phrase that more senior colleagues would often use in the aftermath of long discussion meetings with users: "X was just playing politics" they would say with a unique combination of exasperation and resignation. It soon transpired that what users were doing was protecting their own interests against changes implied by a new system by putting up obstacles to its development. This was an early example of negative politics.
- In another example of negative politics, a large and detailed "statement of requirements" document was produced at the start of a waterfall development and used as a battleground over which arguments between the user and development communities raged concerning acceptance testing, ambiguity, completeness, and so on. This resulted in an adversarial and blame-ridden culture.
- A third example of negative politics arose when users were reluctant to accept the disruption to existing working practices that a newly introduced

iterative incremental approach required. Despite paying lip service to the principles of such an approach, emancipation from the "get-it-all-right-first-time" mind-set was difficult for the users.

Ground rules need to be agreed on and positive measures taken at the outset.

There are various things that can be done to help with this situation, including education and expert mentoring. For example:

1. There has to be an acceptance by senior user management that you are not going to "get it totally right the first time." User management must accept this philosophy as the price of proactive development. Equally, developers must respect users as "part of the team."

2. Users must accept that solutions will be delivered in small pieces, each of which will do a basic functional job. Developers must resist the temptation to aim for perfection: Refinements to the small pieces can be added later, in the light of the user actually using the system in the business environment.

Users and developers are "in this together."

Fostering positive attitudes through a proactive workforce is a keynote of our approach. Perspective's adoption of an iterative model allows a cooperative relationship—rather than an adversarial one—to function between the developers of the software and the business owners of that software. For a useful discussion of the effects of politics the reader is referred to Block (1983).

11.3.8 Process Refinement

Process improvement does not happen overnight.

Perspective is very much an adaptive process that can be tuned and customized to specific organizational needs. However, to get the most out of any process, the process itself must be refined in the light of actual usage. Checkpoints are built into the Perspective process to help evolve it. This includes documenting the lessons learned so that others can avoid making the same mistakes. In particular, estimation techniques should be refined based on experience with the aim of building a metrics database (DeMarco, 1982).

It is particularly important to refine estimates.

For example, in the Feasibility Phase, it is possible to base an estimate on the complexity of the use cases, using a modified form of Function Point Analysis (FPA). It is important to note that we cannot expect a high level of accuracy. However, over time, analysts will build up sufficient experience in the techniques to at least give us something better than the usual "finger-in-the-air" approach. Estimates are then refined as we work through the development of the project. Once the Analysis Phase is complete, we will have a much greater understanding of the complexity of use cases. We can therefore revise our estimates using a similar, modified form of FPA to that discussed in the Feasibility section. As each increment is completed, we have an opportunity to revise the estimates for the remaining increments based on actual results. The data can also be used for other projects, so that future estimates should be more reliable.

11.4 Solution and Component Processes

11.4.1 Basic Concepts

Perspective recognizes that there are two broad process types with respect to the spectrum discussed in 11.3.1.

The more potentially reusable the software, the more rigorous the process.

1. The **solution process** is aimed at development of solutions, typically in terms of user services, to provide maximum early user value; chapter 12 describes this process in detail.

2. The **component process** is aimed at development of components providing commonly used business and/or data services across different departmental systems or for use by third parties; chapter 13 describes this process in detail.

The relationship between the two processes involves a dynamic that is as much cultural as technical; the specific features shown are discussed later in this section. Solution projects are driven by specific business requirements targeted to specific business areas or departments; the aim is to harvest reusable services in the manner of component assemblers. Component projects are driven by generic business requirements, legacy reuse requirements, and feedback from solution projects; the aim is to sow reusable services in the manner of component builders. This is illustrated in Figure 11.2. We have summarized the typical product features for each process. It is important to note that *both processes are incremental*.

The two processes work in an interleaved fashion.

The dual-process approach reflects the movement toward hybrid organizational models of software development reported by the Gartner Group: "Application development (AD) is done by the business units to achieve the benefits of decentralization, but some advantages of centralization are retained. This is accomplished by maintaining centralized control of such IT elements as the technology and applications architectures and the infrastructure. The main advantages (of the approach) are that economies can still be achieved by centrally controlling the cross-component IT elements. There are also advantages to having a centralized AD organization responsible for archi-

This approach reflects industry needs.

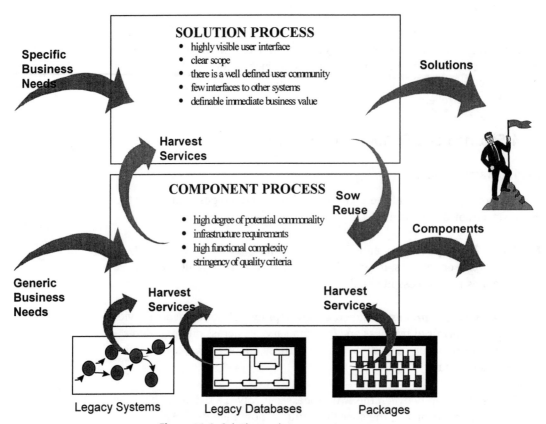

SOLUTION PROCESS
- highly visible user interface
- clear scope
- there is a well defined user community
- few interfaces to other systems
- definable immediate business value

Specific Business Needs

Solutions

Harvest Services

COMPONENT PROCESS
- high degree of potential commonality
- infrastructure requirements
- high functional complexity
- stringency of quality criteria

Sow Reuse

Components

Generic Business Needs

Harvest Services

Harvest Services

Legacy Systems   Legacy Databases   Packages

Figure 11.2. Solution and component processes.

tectural control, which gives the business unit developers an architectural framework within which to develop their applications." (Gartner, 1995)

11.4.2 Reuse of Services

Services are delivered in an evolutionary incremental fashion.

The Perspective process, like the Perspective architecture, operates at the level of services rather than classes (see Figure 11.3). Services provide a very usable level of granularity in that services are geared directly to meeting requirements. This is in contrast to classes that are at a lower structural level. A service employs a family of collaborating objects to meet its objectives. We can think of each increment as a successive release of a set of services provided by evolving components. The process is particularly geared to maximizing reuse of business services and data services, where the greatest gains are to be achieved. Service-based component management tools provide the ability to browse, install, and register the components in a repository. The repository includes definitions of component interfaces and the services supplied through

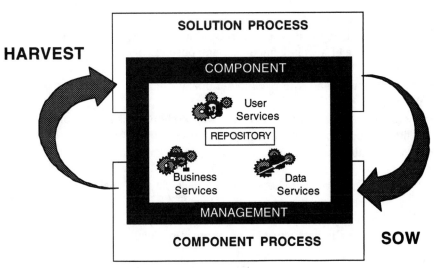

Figure 11.3. A service-based process.

those interfaces. The repository should also enable identification of models that are associated with the components and that we compose, extend, and adapt through the modeling process. Also, in practice, reuse is not a binary concept: There is a need to control and administer levels of reuse. Such component management facilities are important enabling technology for leveraging the approach we describe; these are described in Allen and Frost (1996).

11.4.3 Characteristics of Solution Projects and Component Projects

It is necessary to have some basic criteria for assessing whether a project should follow a solution or a component process (see Figure 11.4). Basic criteria are included in this section; further details are supplied in chapters 12 (solution process) and 13 (component process). Sometimes a project may contain elements of both processes and you will need to customize. The processes should be *adapted* to meet your own needs and not rigorously *adopted*.

Perhaps the most important system characteristic of a solution project is that it can be divided into small increments that can be delivered in weeks rather than months, with a low cost and short pay-back period. Our experience shows that the following system characteristics are also very important:

Remember: The processes, shown in Figure 11.4, are ideals.

Solution projects address the need for early user value.

• A highly visible user interface is needed: Much of the functionality can be exposed through the user interface; note that this does not necessarily mean that the system is implemented that way.

• A clear scope is desirable: The project proposal or vision statement is reasonably stable and addresses clearly defined business requirements.
• The existence of a well-defined user and business owner community is beneficial.
• An application that is not computationally complex benefits the solution project.
• A system that has few interfaces to other systems; it is also helpful if there is little "knock-on effect" requiring changes to other systems.
• Business value that is immediately identifiable and definable.

Component projects address the need for high-quality reusable software.

A component project should also be divisible into small increments that can be delivered as quickly as possible. However, it is recognized that costs will be higher and pay-back periods longer. Our experience shows that there are two key system characteristics for component projects:

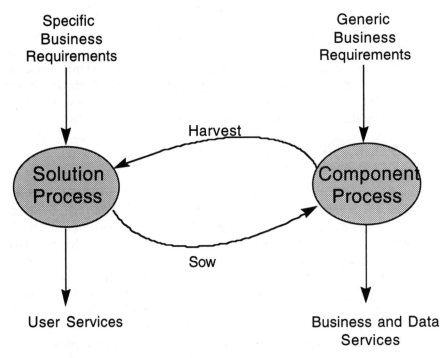

Figure 11.4. High-level view of solution-and-component processes.

- a high degree of potential commonality (for example, infrastructure requirements),

- stringency of quality criteria (for example, performance and reliability) that
  accompanies shared requirements.

Projects with further characteristics not covered previously can also benefit from the modeling techniques covered in this book. Such projects are likely to require further extension and tailoring. Examples of such projects include
the following:

Other types of projects can also use the Perspective process.

- systems needing the stringency of a fully detailed requirements definition
  before design can begin,
- real-time embedded systems with little user interface,
- systems with very complex algorithmic logic,
- safety-critical applications with highly stringent nonfunctional requirements.

11.5 BPM and the Perspective Process

In this section we outline how to use business process modeling to drive the
process, with respect to the BPM techniques presented in chapter 3.

11.5.1 BPM and the Perspective Process

Solution and component processes can be driven in different ways according to organizational culture. However, like any good component, the
Perspective process, shown in Figure 11.5, is open. Providing its interfaces
are used consistently it does not matter which context it is used in! For
example, requirements may emerge as a result of a forerunning project
proposal, business strategy, business survey, preliminary investigation, or
many other routes, including BPM. The advantage of using a BPM
approach is twofold:

The BPM process "plugs onto" the Perspective process.

1. The starting point is readily amenable to a componet-based approach:
   Business processes produced using the Perspective guidelines in chapter 3
   lend themselves very well to a component-based approach.

2. The resultant component-based models should be a formal reflection of
   needs that are rooted firmly in business processes.

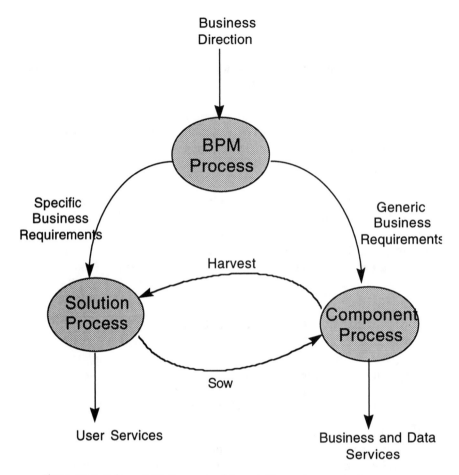

Figure 11.5. Using a BPM Process to drive solution and component processes.

11.5.2 Outline Process for Business Process Modeling

The BPM process is iterative and incremental.

The overall process for BPM is depicted in Figure 11.6. Once the initial scoping is completed, the remaining stages work as an iterative and incremental loop. Business processes can be analyzed in isolation or in related groups as appropriate. Stage outlines are also included in sections 11.5.2.1 to 11.5.2.7. The positions of the modeling techniques, from chapter 3, are indicated using tabularized references.

11.5.2.1 Scoping

Clarify objectives and identify the current set of business events and processes. Scoping requires the identification of the purpose of the business process

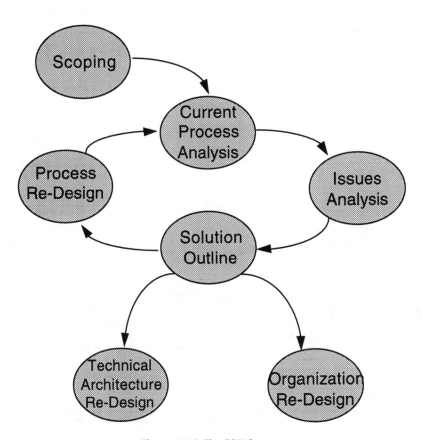

Figure 11.6. The BPM Process.

and the work done to achieve it. Once the set of business processes are identified the four stages of the BPR loop, shown in Figure 11.6, can be performed for each process in turn.

3.4.1	"As Is" Process Hierarchy Diagramming

11.5.2.2 Current Process Analysis

Produce a model of the current implementation of the selected business process. Note that identification of indirect processes may be left until "To Be" modeling.

3.4.1	"As Is" Process Hierarchy Diagramming
3.4.2	"As Is" Process Thread Diagramming
3.4.7	Identifying Indirect Processes

11.5.2.3 Issues Analysis

Analyze the current business process, which was modeled during the previous stage, in order to identify a set of issues and associated impacts on the business process. In some circumstances simulation of the process using relevant volumes may be useful in order to highlight bottlenecks, peaks and troughs, and other problems.

| 3.4.2 | "As Is" Process Thread Diagramming |

11.5.2.4 Solution Outline

Consider the possible options that will move the organization toward achieving its goals. A model of the required process is produced for a selected option. The level of detail of this model will depend on the extent of the required change to the current business process. However, the model produced is most likely to be at an outline or concept level.Once a solution outline has been produced the three redesign activities associated with the process, the architecture, and the organization can be performed.

3.4.3	"To Be" Process-Hierarchy Diagramming
3.4.4	"To Be" Process-Thread Diagramming
3.4.5	Process Thread Storyboarding
3.4.7	Identifying Indirect Processes

11.5.2.5 Process Redesign

Produce a more detailed model of the required process; this should include descriptions, including business rules, of indirect processes previously identified. As a result of the redesign, a software solution development using Perspective may be required. Typically specific requirements emerging in the form of EBPs help to drive the solution process; generic requirements for indirect processes help to drive the component processes.

| 3.4.5 | Process Thread Storyboarding |
| 3.4.6 | Analyzing EBPs. |

11.5.2.6 Technical Architecture Redesign

Redesign the technical architecture that will be used to support new IT systems. Infrastructure redesign covers the work associated with, for example, technology principles, object partitioning, server distribution, use of standards such as DCOM, CORBA, and DCE, and so on. Any development work that is required will be performed by a Perspective infrastructure team (see chapter 14).

11.5.2.7 Organizational Redesign

Describe the roles and responsibilities of the people implementing the new processes. A model of the organizational structure is built, showing how the roles in the process team fit together across functions or departments.

11.5.3 Business Domain Modeling

In Perspective, business domain modeling (as described in chapter 8) is treated as part of the component process. However it may well be expedient to carry this out in parallel with BPM, if your terms of reference allow it. One advantage is that early business domain modeling can help avoid the tendency toward function decomposition that sometimes accompanies BPM employed in isolation.

CHAPTER 12

•••••••••••••••••••••

The Solution Process

12.1 Introduction

A common reaction to the pressure of immediate business needs is to virtually abandon planning and control in the name of producing fast results under the misnomer of RAD (Rapid Application Development). RAD brings useful techniques, such as prototyping, timeboxing, and JAD (Joint Application Development) to the table. However, it fails to exploit the value of established modeling techniques to align solutions with business needs. This requires a special process: a solution process.

Producing quality software to tight schedules is a challenging goal.

The literature contains a proliferation of advice in the area of the software process. Since Barry Boehm's (1986) work on the spiral life cycle, a seemingly countless number of software life cycles have been postulated to cater to an often conflicting set of requirements, including iterative and incremental development and software reuse. It is not our purpose to discuss these here. We simply note, based on repeated experience, that most project managers seek simple and pragmatic guidelines for planning their projects.

Most methods and tools do not provide a clearly defined software process.

In this chapter, guidelines are presented for assessing the type of process that is appropriate for the needs of specific projects. The solution process is described in terms of stages that employ a common template. A task catalog provides the project manager with a practical list of suggested contents. References to the techniques sections of this book show specifically where

We present a template for the solution process.

modeling techniques fit in. The project manager is able to configure the template and adapt the contents to suit individual project needs.

12.2 Applicability of the Solution Process

12.2.1 Solution Projects

Solution projects typically deliver user services.

A solution project works at a business unit or departmental level to deliver a set of increments, typically in the form of user services, which provide maximum early user value. Where BPM (business process modeling) has been performed such requirements will be reflected in a business process or part of a business process. The aim is to provide usable functionality quickly and to gain early user feedback into the process.

Use cases provide the driver for incremental design.

Use cases are identified early in the project, in the Feasibility stage. They provide an excellent basis for scoping increments rooted in business requirements. However, it is services, specifically user services, that are typically delivered by incremental design. The differences between use cases and services are summarized in Table 12.1

Solution projects actively seek to reuse services.

It is vital to be aware of the possibilities for reuse. The emphasis is on producing solutions by assembly, in contrast to producing solutions by starting from scratch every time. Solution projects are reuse consumers and need to regularly look for opportunities to reuse services. An important part of the process is to build on generic models by specialization and refinement, in the manner of frameworks. Checkpoints are included in the process to encourage solution teams to ask key questions as they seek to harvest reuse. Such reuse may be provided by existing databases, packages, or legacy systems as well as by components developed "in house."

A solution project is contrasted with a component project.

A component project provides a set of software services that potentially support one or more solution projects. Whereas a solution project is devel-

Table 12.1. Use Cases vs. Services

Use Case	Service
Modeling technique	Computing capability
Incomplete: set of scenarios	Complete: working code
Partially outside system boundary	Inside system boundary
Supported by set of services	Provided through component interface
Drives incremental design	Delivered through incremental design
User focus	Design focus
Reuses services	Reuses services

oped at a departmental level, a component project develops commonly used services across different departmental systems.

12.2.2 Key Characteristics of Solution Projects

Perhaps the most important system characteristic of a solution project is that it is partitionable into small increments that can be delivered in weeks rather than months, with a low cost and short pay-back period. Our experience shows that the following system characteristics are also very important:

Solution projects address the need for early user value.

- a highly visible user interface is needed; much of the functionality can be exposed through the user interface (note this does not necessarily mean that the system is implemented that way).
- a clear scope is desirable; the project proposal is reasonably stable and addresses clearly defined business requirements.
- the existence of a well-defined user and business-owner community is necessary.
- an application that is not computationally complex is beneficial.
- a system that has few interfaces to other systems; it is also helpful if there is little "knock-on effect" requiring changes to other systems.
- business value that is immediately identifiable and definable.

A further tier of important characteristics follows. For a detailed list the reader is referred to the Dynamic Systems Development Method (DSDM) suitability filter documented in appendix A of DSDM (1997):

- clear routes for scaling up initial deliveries,
- few operational user types,
- few external supplier issues,
- available reusable components,
- few "learning curves"; that is, there are not new technologies, methods, and tools to master.

12.2.3 Key Principles of the Solution Process

The dynamic approach to development reflects the nine principles of the Dynamic Systems Development Method (DSDM, 1997; Stapleton, 1997). These are summarized below:

Projects following the solution process take a dynamic approach to development.

1. Active user involvement is imperative.
2. DSDM teams must be empowered to make decisions.
3. The focus is on frequent delivery of products.

4. Fitness for business purpose is the essential criterion for acceptance of deliverables.
5. Iterative and incremental development is necessary to converge on an accurate business solution.
6. All changes during development are reversible.
7. Requirements are baselined at a high level.
8. Testing is integrated throughout the life cycle.
9. A collaborative and cooperative approach among all stakeholders is essential.

12.2.4 Timeboxing

Timeboxing is a useful planning philosophy during a solution project.

"Timeboxing" has its roots in RIPP (Rapid Iterative Production Prototyping), an approach developed by El du Pont de Nemours and sold later under the slogan "Your system in 128 days or your money back. " A timebox sets a rigid limit to prototype iterations to ensure management control. A small team develops a tested prototype that is both end-point and deliverable. RIPP spawned a host of approaches under the infamous RAD label, which are characterized in the James Martin (1991) book of the same name.

Target dates are not allowed to slip.

During a traditional planning regime the focus of the plan is to deliver a certain set of functionality. If the planned date is reached before the functionality is available, then the delivery date slips. Under a timeboxing regime it is the functionality that slips, not the time: that is, the delivery date is always held even if the contents of a particular delivery are scaled down. The timeboxing philosophy recognizes the business pressure to have functionality available by an agreed date. Our experience reflects that of others in that we find around 90-day timeboxes to commonly work best; for example Yourdon (1995).

12.3 Solution Process Overview

The solution process is driven by specific requirements.

The key driver of the solution process is a set of specific requirements to meet the needs of a business process; where BPM has been performed such requirements will be reflected in a business process or part of a business process, typically a set of EBPs, as described in chapter 3.

The solution process delivers a set of software increments.

Various models are produced throughout the process, which evolve in detail as the process unfolds. Opportunities are continually sought to extend and refine existing generic models. Parts of the model are selected on a use case-by-use case basis for incremental development of user services. Section 12.3.2 includes recommended levels of detail for each stage. There are several deliverables that are produced at various points including feasibility, analysis, and design reports.

An overview of the solution process is presented in Figure 12.1 . Feasibility is essentially a scoping exercise that is expected to be completed once for a set of requirements. This may result in several "subprojects" for sets of use cases depending on the scale and complexity of the proposed solution. Analysis and prototyping are pursued iteratively to bring requirements into sharper focus. This results in identification of a number of use cases for which increments are to be designed in terms of user services. Each increment undergoes a design, acceptance, and roll-out loop, with feedback iterating back to the planning of the next increment and to adjustment of analysis where necessary. Prototypes produced in analysis may be used to help drive the design, and may be evolved into the working increment. The delivery loop is repeated in iterative fashion so as to evolve the system in line with actual use.

One-off scoping is followed by an iterative incremental delivery loop.

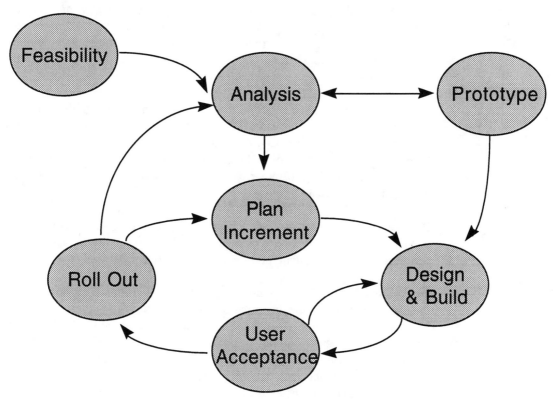

Figure 12.1. The solution process.

12.3.1 Solution-Process Stage Overviews

The following paragraphs provide a brief overview of the purpose of each of the stages in the solution process.

Feasibility: *Scope the development* in terms of proposed solutions and produce both a business case and first-cut project plan. Use cases provide the major scoping technique. This stage seeks to harvest reuse by looking to see if the problem has been solved before. Generic models, produced by the component process, are used to leverage such reuse opportunities.

Analysis: *Explore the requirements* for the software to such a degree that the scope is confirmed and that sufficient information is provided to allow an incremental delivery plan to be produced. Analysis is driven by the use cases identified in Feasibility. This stage seeks to harvest reuse by looking to see if existing services can be used to solve the problem. This may involve refining generic models to help provide the services. A closed iterative loop with the prototype stage exists as a means of eliciting requirements.

Prototype: *Elicit requirements* from the business owners through the construction of screens. The stage should form a tight iterative loop with analysis. Prototypes may also be used to help drive the design and build stage. Increasingly, with the use of GUI(graphical user interface) builders such as Visual Basic and PowerBuilder, prototypes produced during analysis are evolved to a working increment.

Plan Increment: *Develop a plan* for producing user services in terms of a set of incremental deliveries. The plan should indicate the order of delivery, the contents of each increment, and the estimated time scales and costs.

Design and Build: *Construct, assemble, and test the software* that is specified for the user service(s) comprising a particular increment. This stage seeks to harvest reuse by looking to see if existing components can be used to solve the problem. Refinement of generic models may be used to assist in the manner of frameworks. Dependent on the level of user involvement an iterative loop with User Acceptance may exist. Regression testing of previous increments must also be taken into account.

User Acceptance: *Ensure acceptance of an increment* prior to its roll out in the live environment. Dependent on the level of user involvement, an iterative loop with Design and Build an Increment may exist.

Roll out: *Install an increment* successfully in the live user environment.

Our main aim is to give the reader a flavor of how to apply the process, but we want to do this in some detail. Each section is a template that you can customize to your own specific needs. References to the Perspective modeling techniques are included at appropriate points to demonstrate how they fit in. Deliverable definitions are included in Appendix A.

Each stage is presented in more detail in the sections that follow.

12.3.2 Solution Process: Evolution of Models

A question often asked is, "What level of detail should we aim for in our models at each stage in the process?" The three stages that affect the models are feasibility, analysis, and design. Table 12.2 summarizes model evolution in terms of the expected level of detail at the conclusion of feasibility, analysis, and design.

Models are evolved to a state in which they can be readily generated to code.

12.4 Feasibility Study

12.4.1 Purpose

- Explore the business problem and propose a number of IT solutions.
- Establish the scope of each of the solutions.
- Recommend one of the solutions for development.
- Produce a business justification for the recommended solution that provides a cost/benefit analysis.
- Produce first-cut project and test plans.

12.4.2 Inputs

- A vision statement input by the business sponsor that provides a high-level set of requirements.
- Terms of reference for the team undertaking the feasibility study; this may reference some form of project proposal or a set of business process models as appropriate.

12.4.3 Outputs

- *Models as shown in Table 12.3.*
- Feasibility study report (definition is included in Appendix A).
- First-cut project plan and test plan.

Table 12.2. Model-Stage Detail for the Solution Process			
Model	**Feasibility Level of Detail**	**Analysis Level of Detail**	**Design Level of Detail**
use case model	high-level descriptions, use case diagrams	detailed formatted descriptions	
object interaction model		collaboration and sequence diagrams for key scenarios and use cases; business objects only	collaboration and sequence diagrams for key scenarios and use cases; user objects, data objects included
class model	high-level class diagram	includes all attributes with data types; and operations with responsibilities defined; may include user classes and service classes	includes all attributes with definitions; operations with signatures defined; must include service classes; may include user and data classes
state model	high-level; states and events only	high-level; outbound events and operations may be included	transition strings fully detailed
component model	high-level service package dependency diagrams	lower-level service package dependency diagrams	component package dependency diagrams; interfaces defined and classes allocated
deployment model			shows technical architecture; allocation of component packages
logical data model			used to model supporting non-OO database structure

Table 12.3. Model-Stage Details for the Feasibility Stage	
Model	**Level of Detail**
use case model	high-level descriptions, use case diagrams
class model	high-level class diagram
state model	high-level; states and events only
component model	high-level service package dependency diagrams

12.4.4 Task Catalog

• *Explore the business problem.*

Express the business problem to be addressed in terms of a concise statement of purpose.

4.4.1	Determining the Statement of Purpose

Summarize the business processes or business areas to be supported, the major areas of risks, and broad costs and benefits.

The volume and complexity of the work within this step will vary enormously among different projects. In some cases, for example, if a detailed BPM activity has already taken place or if a detailed set of terms of reference has been provided by the project sponsor, the work will be minimized, as only one solution is possible. In other circumstances a number of possible solutions will exist with each one of them either satisfying a subset of the overall business requirements or realizing different benefits for associated costs. In this case a set of possible solutions, each with its own statement of purpose, is presented from which a recommended solution will be selected.

• *For each possible solution:*

   • Understand nonfunctional requirements.

   Document the physical constraints (such as platforms, operating systems, and databases) and quality attributes (such as overall performance and reliability criteria).

   • Explore possible division into service packages.

Scout ahead to gain an early indication of possible partitioning of the solution into service packages. Search for possible reuse of service packages. Package dependency diagrams can be used for this. This activity needs to be marshaled with respect to the component process, as detailed in chapter 13.

8.4.2	System Architecture Modeling

- Scope the solution in terms of actors and use cases.

  Identify actors and use cases.
  Create a use case diagram or set of use case diagrams; in the case of complex solutions, which are to be partitioned into separate analysis projects, a separate use case diagram can be used to depict each solution partition. Describe actors and use cases in business language. At this stage it is only necessary to specify the intent of a use case and include a summary description for the basic course.

4.4.2	Identifying Actors
4.4.3	Identifying Use Cases
4.4.4	Creating a Use Case Diagram
4.4.5	Describing a Use Case

- Scope the solution in terms of business classes.

  Identify high-level business classes and create a business class diagram giving a broad-brush indication of potential subject areas.

5.4.1	Discovering Classes
5.4.2	Examining Use Cases for Classes
5.4.3	Examining Events for Classes
5.4.4	Creating a First-Cut Class Diagram

- Examine key business event cycles.

  Where there are regular patterns of business events that affect specific business subject areas, construct an initial state diagram for each associated business class.

7.4.1	Creating an Initial State Diagram

- Search for possible areas of reuse.

  Ask whether the problem has been solved before and reassess candidate service packages, list possible services and external classes. Examine generic models for possible reuse opportunities. This activity needs to be marshaled with respect to the component process as in chapter 13.

4.4.6	Identifying User Services and Business Services
5.4.10	Harvesting Business Services

- Iterate as above.

• *Recommend a solution.*

Analyze the cost/benefit of each of the possible solutions to find which one of them is most optimum. In order to perform this step, a standard method must be adopted for assessing the costs of the development and for quantifying the benefits. The following issues need to be considered

- business goals that are covered by each possible solution given that each solution is likely to cover a different subset of these overall business goals,
- business benefits both tangible (e.g., avoiding costs or increasing revenue) or intangible (e.g., improving service or increasing job satisfaction),
- organizational, procedural and physical impact of each solution,
- development costs associated with hardware, staff, external consultants, training, documentation,
- operational costs associated with financial depreciation, maintenance, training, staff,
- risks in terms of business and technology.

• *Ensure requirements traceability.*

Ensure all requirements are referenced as appropriate.

• *Produce a first-cut project plan.*

- Create an estimate for each use case based on its perceived complexity. This may use a standard method based on a simple, medium, or complex basis, or may use a mathematically based system, such as Function Point Analysis.

- Create a high-level plan for the entire project focused on the delivery of business functionality rather than on the low-level development activities that are concerned more with software construction issues.
- Embed control points into the plan where senior management can review progress and authorize progression.

• *Produce a first-cut test plan.*

• *Approve the feasibility report.*

Gain approval from the project sponsor for the development to progress. This approval would normally be sought at a meeting during which the feasibility report and the project plan would be reviewed.

12.4.5 Keynotes

- Keep it short: weeks and not months; a 2-week feasibility is typical.
- JAD techniques are used to facilitate the modeling and maximize user involvement.
- Estimates of complexity of use cases and classes are produced and converted into cost and duration through the use of company cost-drivers. From the estimates a schedule for the project can be derived.
- It should be noted that if a BPM activity has been performed prior to the feasibility stage of Perspective, then a number of the steps below may be considerably simplified. Under such circumstances the input set of documents will probably provide considerably more detail than that usually found in a vision statement and the terms of reference.
- The high-level business focus of the project plan allows the business sponsor to identify the dates when identifiable pieces of functionality will be made available to the business. A lower-level plan, detailing software development tasks, is produced later, after analysis.

12.5 Analysis

12.5.1 Purpose

- Understand and define business requirements in terms of a set of models.
- Provide a sound basis for an incremental delivery plan.
- Refine the first-cut estimates and test plans that were produced during the feasibility stage.

Table 12.4. Model-Stage Details for the Analysis Stage	
Model	**Level of detail**
use case model	detailed formatted descriptions
object interaction model	collaboration and sequence diagrams for key scenarios and use cases; business objects only
class model	includes all attributes with data types; operations with responsibilities defined; may include user classes and service classes
state model	high-level; outbound events and operations may be included
component model	lower-level service package dependency diagrams

12.5.2 Inputs

• Models from feasibility stage.
• Feasibility study report.
• First-cut project plan and test plan from feasibility stage.

12.5.3 Outputs

• *Models as shown in Table 12.4.*
• Analysis report (definition is included in Appendix A).
• Refined estimates.

12.5.4 Task Catalog

• *Develop business class model.*

Apply discovery techniques to develop the business class model.

5.4.1	Discovering Classes
5.4.2	Examining Use Cases for Classes
5.4.3	Examining Events for Classes
5.4.4	Creating a First-Cut Class Diagram

• *Develop use case model.*

Expand use case description details to cover steps for basic courses by identifying user services and business services. Identify alternative courses and develop required user services and business services by refining the use case model in terms of uses and extends relationships.

4.4.5	Describing a Use Case
4.4.6	Identifying User Services and Business Services
4.4.7	Developing User Services
4.4.8	Developing Business Services

• *Develop initial object interaction model.*

Understand broad-brush interactions between business objects to support use cases and scenarios.

6.4.1	Creating a First-Cut Business Sequence Diagram
6.4.2	Creating a First-Cut Collaboration Diagram

• *Perform prototyping.*

Iterate to prototyping as described in section 12.6: Repeat as necessary!

• *Develop the initial state model.*

Create state diagrams for classes with interesting life cycles.

7.4.1	Creating an Initial State Diagram

• *Understand user classes.*

Include user class diagrams where appropriate.

5.4.12	Modeling User Classes

• *Improve business class model.*

Apply knowledge of detail and structural techniques to develop the business class model.

5.4.5	Developing a First-Cut Class Diagram using Attributes and Operations
5.4.6	Applying Patterns to Develop the Class Diagram
5.4.7	Using Association Classes
5.4.8	Using Inheritance
5.4.9	Using Aggregation

- *Complete use case model.*

Fill out details of formatted use case descriptions, such as pre- and post-conditions.

4.4.8	Completing the Use Case Descriptions

- *Enhance object interaction model.*

Understand detailed interactions between business objects to support use cases and scenarios, scouting ahead to examine alternative overall interaction designs and playing specific scenarios through the model. It is also possible to nominate service classes, although this is often best left until the first tier of increment design.

6.4.3	Examining the Initial Collaboration Diagram
6.4.4	Developing a Sequence Diagram
6.4.5	Developing an Example Scenario

- *Enhance the state model.*

Improve state diagrams to include further patterns of behavior and outbound events.

- *Search for possible areas of reuse.*

7.4.2	Expanding a State Diagram
7.4.3	Detailing a State Diagram

Ask whether existing generic models can be used to solve the problem and reference proposed reusable model items. Search for reuse of all types of services. Consider refining generic models to help provide the services. This activity needs to be marshaled with respect to the component process, as described in chapter 13.

5.4.10	Harvesting Business Services

• *Iterate as above.*

• *Revise feasibility details.*

Details that might have been somewhat tentative in the feasibility study are revised in the light of further information unearthed by the analysis. Examples include the following:

- Nonfunctional requirements,
- Risks,
- Proposed environment.

• *Refine estimates.*

Update the estimates that were developed during the previous stage, given the more detailed level of knowledge available for each use case.

• *Ensure requirements traceability.*

Update requirement references developed during the previous stage, given the more detailed level of modeling.

12.5.5 Keynotes

- Keep it short: weeks and not months; a 2-week analysis is typical.
- It is expected, for some developments, that a tight iterative loop will exist between this stage and the subsequently described prototype stage. Many solution projects will have a significant user interface and therefore requirements for these projects can be elicited and validated through the development of appropriate prototypes.
- The distinction between prototyping as a requirements capture tool and prototyping as a user interface design tool is becoming more blurred because of the increasing flexibility and power of today's GUI builders. We recommend not to construct detailed sequence diagrams until after at least some prototyping has been done. We also recommend using collaboration diagram for playing individual cases through the model, independent of prototyping, to assess technical feasibility before prototyping.

- Use case modeling and class modeling are continued at greater depth to help understand the problem in more detail. Use case descriptions are refined and further details, such as pre- and postconditions added. A greater emphasis is placed on class modeling than in the feasibility stage where the class modeling is essentially high level.
- Most effort is concentrated on business classes, though some user class modeling may also be useful, especially in the latter stages of analysis as a forerunner to user interface design.
- Object interaction modeling is applied to gain an understanding of scenarios in terms of collaboration diagrams and of use cases using sequence diagrams. It is best to restrict the focus of sequence diagrams to business classes in analysis to avoid becoming bogged down in excessive design detail.
- State modeling is particularly useful for examining business classes with interesting dynamic behavior associated with different patterns of business events.
- Given Perspective's theme of constant validation the above steps should involve the business users[1] of the software under development as much as possible. This involvement can be fostered through a number of strategies, as follows:

  - JAD sessions should be used to involve the business users in the requirements specification process.
  - A technique for allowing the business users to understand the models, such as animation, should be made available.
  - The tight, iterative loop with the prototype stage, in which business users are centrally involved.

12.6 Prototype

12.6.1 Purpose

- Validate and refine the understanding of the use cases.
- Agree on the business requirements.
- Involve business users in order to validate the models developed during the analysis stage and generate their support for the project.
- Pass any suitable prototypes into the design and build an increment stage of Perspective, if possible.

---

[1] The term "business user" is used as an abbreviation for various possible user roles described in chapter 14: adviser user, ambassador user, visionary, and executive sponsor.

12.6.2 Inputs

• Models developed during previous stages.
• User interface design standards.

12.6.3 Outputs

• Functional prototypes (see section 12.6.5) agreed by executive sponsor.

12.6.4 Task Catalog

The following steps are recommended for this stage of Perspective:

• *Establish an overall approach to prototyping.*

Before work begins on any prototypes, a strategy must be specified for their construction and evaluation. A dynamic strategy is to build screen-based prototypes and to significantly involve the business users during the construction through the use of JAD sessions. A more conservative strategy is to use paper-based prototypes that are reviewed "off line" by the business users. There are also "midway" strategies that involve initial white-board storyboarding followed by the use of software prototypes to focus in on particular areas; the reader is referred to Allen (1991) and Connell and Shafer (1996) for more detailed treatment of this subject.

• *Conduct storyboarding sessions.*

Initial storyboards in the form of white-board sketches built interactively with users are an excellent mechanism for building a navigational high-level model of required screens. Use cases are used to drive this process. The essence of the exercise is to identify required screens without being sidetracked into details, such as specific fields, command buttons, and screen cosmetics. A screen image is represented on each storyboard with a short series of bulleted points describing the interaction.

During this activity a "mental" model of the computer system is developed. The purpose of this model is to identify how the users "see" the computer system so that this model can be replicated at the user interface. An example of a mental model is a map of a city's underground railway. Such a map represents how passengers visualize the railway rather than the actual layout of the lines.

• *Create Prototypes.*

The purpose of this step is to produce a number of prototypes that enable validation of the requirements that are modeled during the feasibility and analysis stages of Perspective. Use a GUI builder to create a working model to support selected use cases. Initial creation is confined to a basic course through the use case or perhaps a key scenario. Preexisting user objects and business objects should be used wherever possible to facilitate the process.

• *Evaluate Prototypes.*

The business user "test drives" the prototypes that are developed in the previous step and compiles resultant comments for feedback to the development team. It is here that the business user has real influence in shaping the solution.

The evaluation strategy that is adopted will vary depending on the level of involvement of the business users during the previous step. Given Perspective's emphasis on constant validation it is likely that the prototypes will have been developed during a number of JAD sessions and therefore that a significant degree of evaluation will have taken place already. If JAD sessions have been used, then the evaluation during this step is likely to be relatively simple, perhaps through the demonstration of the prototypes to members of the business community who were not present during the JADs. If, for some reason, JAD sessions were not used during the development of the prototypes, then this step will require a much more lengthy evaluation process.

Any evaluation comments should be captured and fed back to the development team. Comments may require the analysis stage models to be updated if they are unable to support the user interfaces that are developed during prototyping. In addition, nonfunctional requirements (such as usability, reliability and performance) are collated for the design and build an increment stage.

• *Modify Prototypes.*

Perform agreed changes to the prototypes. Decisions have to be made as to when and how often to modify: iteration must be controlled to prevent the prototype being in a continual state of flux. As the prototypes mature, so further scenarios through the use cases can be addressed, eventually culminating in alternative courses.

• *Complete Prototypes.*

Once the prototypes are satisfactory to all parties, agreement is reached on conclusion of the cycle. Up to three passes around this loop are common characterized by:

- first loop: skeletal prototypes (little information retrieval and no updating) for key scenarios and basic courses, reflecting desired "look and feel" of user interface, but avoiding detailed user interface design,
- second loop: partially functional prototypes for key scenarios and basic courses,
- third loop: fully functional prototypes for some major use cases and key basic courses.

12.6.5 Keynotes

It is important to understand that Perspective recognizes that the purpose of prototyping depends on the context in which it is used, as discussed in the following text. The prototyping *stage* in Perspective focuses on prototyping functional requirements. However, prototyping *as a technique* continues throughout the increment design phase to help with implementation issues such as details of user interface design and performance. Perspective recognizes four different types of prototypes:

1. Business functionality. A business functionality prototype is designed to demonstrate the business functionality fulfilled by the software system. The purpose of such a prototype is not to look and feel similar to the production quality software but to demonstrate that the development team understands the business requirements.

2. User interface. A user interface prototype is designed to pilot the look and feel of the required system. These prototypes may have already been developed, at a high-level, during the prototype stage. If no prototypes have been forwarded from the analysis stage then the work associated with overall user interface design that is described in the prototype stage would need to be performed during design and build an increment, along with the more detailed user interface design.

3. Performance. A performance prototype is developed in order to demonstrate that the final software system will exhibit the required performance and capacity attributes. Although the business users of the system may be involved during the development and assessment of this type of prototype, its principal use is as an aid to the software development staff.

4. Technique. A technique prototype may be used by the software development team in order to assess the applicability of a particular design strategy. This type of prototype will seldom be viewed by the business users of the system and may be "throwaway."

12.7 Plan Increments to Deliver

12.7.1 Purpose

- To develop a plan that indicates the increments to be delivered, the use cases to be supported, and the services that comprise each increment.

12.7.2 Inputs

- Feasibility and analysis reports.
- Models developed during previous stages.
- Project plan and test plan output from feasibility stage.
- Refined estimates output from the analysis stage.

12.7.3 Outputs

- Overall incremental plan.
- Detailed project plan and test plan for the next increment.

12.7.4 Task Catalog

• *Recalibrate Estimates.*

The purpose of this step is to use the information concerning the actual time spent and time scale of the previous increment in order to recalibrate the estimates for all the subsequent increments.

The ability to perform such recalibration is one of the benefits of an incremental delivery approach because the estimating and planning for later increments should be more accurate given the experience gained during the early increments.

• *Identify and Order Increments.*

The purpose of this step is to identify and scope use cases for which increments are to be designed and then to order those increments for delivery. In a solution project an increment typically comprises one or more user services, each of which is designed to support one or more of the scoped use cases.

As part of the cost/benefit analysis during the feasibility stage some measure of business benefit will have been allocated to each use case. The business benefit may be concerned with the reduction of errors, or the increased business throughput, or the reduction in staff costs, or some other benefit.

Planning involves assessing the use cases against a number of drivers, the most important of which is likely to be business benefit. Other drivers include quality factors, development complexity, and logistical priority. These need to be traded off and weighted in order to work out the overall priorities of the use cases; see section 15.6.1 for an example.

• *Produce Incremental Plan.*

The purpose of this step is to schedule the delivery of the increments based on the relative values calculated in the previous step. An incremental plan should be specified that can be agreed on by all parties and that demonstrates exactly what will be delivered, when, and in what order.

• *Produce a Detailed Plan of the Next Increment.*

The purpose of this step is to produce a more detailed plan for the development of the next increment. This should be developed collaboratively by IT staff and business staff, and will be specified in terms of the delivery of business functionality rather than in terms of the low-level constructional tasks associated with software development. This approach to planning is to maintain the project focus on functional (i.e., business) issues rather than constructional (i.e., design) issues.

12.7.5 Keynotes

- A timeboxing philosophy is particularly appropriate during the production of the lower level plans to maintain the focus of the development team on the primary importance of the delivery date for the increment. In a timeboxed plan it is the functionality that is allowed to slip, not the delivery date, if the plan cannot be successfully completed in the scheduled time. This means that the least important item of the planned activities, in terms of delivering business functionality, should be scheduled last in the timebox. A timebox should produce more than one deliverable otherwise it is not possible to "drop"deliverables from the timebox if all the deliverables cannot be produced by the delivery date.
- This stage forms part of the incremental loop within Perspective; that is, the stage is performed once for each increment. The following steps describe the production of the various outputs, *or their update*, dependent on whether the stage is entered for the first, or subsequent increments. For example, the contents of subsequent increments may be amended as a result of the experience gained during the production of a particular increment.

12.8 Design and Build an Increment

12.8.1 Purpose

- Develop an increment as quickly as possible.
- Satisfy management that business needs are effectively met.
- Refine estimate for remaining increments.

12.8.2 Inputs

- Models produced during the Analysis stage.
- Prototypes developed during prototyping stage that are considered to be useful during this stage.
- Detailed plan for this increment produced during the plan increments to deliver stage.

12.8.3 Outputs

• *Models as shown in Table 12.5.*

- Increment Design Specification (definition is included in appendix A).
- Code.
- Test documentation.
- Refined estimates.

Table *12.5*. Model-Stage Details for the Design and Build an Increment Stage

Model	Level of detail
class model	includes all attributes with definitions; operations with signatures defined; must include service classes; may include user and data classes
object interaction model	collaboration and sequence diagrams for key scenarios and use cases; user objects, data objects included
state model	transition strings fully detailed
component model	component package dependency diagrams; interfaces defined and classes allocated
deployment model	shows technical architecture; allocation of component packages
logical data model	used to model supporting non-OO database structure

12.8.4 Task Catalog

Design and build tasks work in three iterative tiers, gradually addressing more detail through each iteration. Tier 1 assesses overall technical feasibility and deployment of the increment in its wider architectural context, in a way that maximizes reuse of existing components. Tier 2 adds implementation details to the models and searches for reuse for this particular increment. Tier 3 codes and tests the increment.

12.8.4.1 Task Catalog Tier 1

• *Model technical architecture.*

Use deployment diagrams, described in chapter 10, to explore technical architecture in terms of processor and device configurations.

• *Map classes to component packages.*

Allocate classes to component packages, using package diagrams. Adjust deployment where necessary. Firm up on service classes.

10.4.1	Creating Component Packages

• *Model deployment of component packages.*

Use deployment modeling to explore overall distribution of component packages across processors. Adjust mapping of classes to components where necessary.

10.4.2	Allocating Component Packages to Nodes

• *Understand increment objectives.*

Clarify the objective of each increment in a couple of sentences to make sure the goal is really understood.

12.8.4.2 Task Catalog Tier 2:

• *Explore required object interaction.*

Use object interaction modeling to establish overall design in terms of user services.

6.4.6	Developing a User Service using a Sequence Diagram

• *Refine prototypes.*

Where appropriate, evolve prototypes developed during the prototype stage of Perspective to meet usability criteria and design constraints. During this activity the usability requirements that are critical for success should be identified, for example, what is the allowable learning period for new users, what are the required performance characteristics of the user interface.

• *Develop object interaction model.*

Expand object interaction model to cover user objects and to cater to design constraints.

6.4.7	Identifying Further Services

• *Detail user class model*

Where appropriate, develop user class model to reflect both user needs and design constraints.

5.4.12	Modeling User Classes

• *Optimize structure of business class model.*

Apply patterns and structural techniques to optimize the model for implementation.

5.4.6	Apply patterns to develop the class diagram
5.4.8	Using inheritance
5.4.9	Using aggregation

• *Refine object interaction model.*

Optimize object interaction model usage of services.

6.4.8	Reusing Business Services

• *Develop state model.*

Where appropriate apply state modeling to specify complete behavior of key business objects and control objects.

7.4.3	Detailing a State Diagram
7.4.4	Creating an initial Control State Diagram
7.4.5	Developing Nested State Diagrams

• *Detail business class model.*

Supply specifications of operations and attributes in the business class model.

5.4.13	Documenting operations and attributes

• *Search for possible areas of reuse.*

Ask whether existing components and services can be reused. In particular consider generic models and look for opportunities to specialize or refine in the manner of frameworks. This activity needs to be marshaled with respect to the component process as described in chapter 13. It is a "two-way" process: It may be that on inspection there are services developed specifically for the solution that are good candidates for component engineering.

5.4.10	Harvesting Business Services
5.4.11	Sowing Business Services
6.4.7	Identifying Further Services
6.4.8	Reusing Business Services
7.4.6	Reusing Enterprise State Diagrams

• *Assess the need for data services.*

If an object-oriented database system is used, then the mapping of the class model to the database is relatively simple because there is no paradigm shift. If a nonobject-oriented database is to be used, then it is necessary to develop data service components. This is very common with the continued use of relational technology to support object persistence.

9.5.1	Assess the Need for Data Services

Note: This task (and the following two tasks) is more usually carried out as part of a component project. Here it is applied where the data storage requirement is local to a particular business unit, as opposed to shared across different business units.

• *Develop logical data model.*

Given that a data service component is required, the purpose of this step is to map the business class model onto appropriate storage technology and to assess the suitability of existing databases for wrapping. If a relational database is to be used as the implementation technology, then it is necessary to map the object model to an appropriate set of tables, columns, rows and keys; this is discussed at some length in appendix B.

| 9.5.2 | Mapping Class Model to Logical Data Model |
| 9.5.3 | Establishing the Existing Logical Data Model |

• *Develop data class model.*

Depending on the degree of impedance mismatch between object and relational structures it may be necessary to model the interface between the application and the database in terms of required data objects, revising the existing logical data model where appropriate, and addressing transaction design.

9.5.4	Architecting a Data Service Component
9.5.5	Revising the Logical Data Model
9.5.6	Designing a Data Service Package
9.5.7	Detailing a Data Service Transaction

12.8.4.3 Task Catalog Tier 3:

• *Code the increment.*

The purpose of this step is to code the services that comprise the increment. Objects and/or components need to be mapped to appropriate implementation technology and coded up accordingly. If the system is to be physically distributed, consideration of the distribution technology will be necessary.

• *Test the increment.*

The purpose of this step is to test the increment and ensure that it meets its requirements. A testing strategy is required that determines issues such as the use of automatic test tools, the level of code coverage, and so on. Use cases provide a basis for construction of test plans. In addition, a regression test strategy is also required that specifies the testing required when each increment is added into the existing system.

- *Refine estimates.*

Reassess estimates of the effort required for the development of each remaining use case (for delivery as an increment or part of an increment). The estimates are refined using data from the development of previous use cases. After the final user service is delivered, metrics and records, for use on future projects, are published in the design specification (see A.1.3).

- *Refine risks and nonfunctional requirements.*

Analyze major risk areas for the remaining use cases (e.g., complex use cases, usage of new technology (e.g. new hardware and software). Similarly, reassess nonfunctional requirements (e.g., performance, reliability) in the light of lessons learned from development of the current increment. After the final user service is delivered, critical areas and an analysis of those use cases most likely to change, for use on future projects, are published in the design specification (see A.1.3).

- *Ensure requirements traceability.*

Update requirement references developed during the previous stage given the more detailed level of modeling.

12.8.5 Keynotes

- Use cases provide the driver for incremental design. Use cases have been identified early in the project, in the feasibility stage. Therefore gathering metrics for use cases is immensely useful for assisting the estimation process, which is especially difficult in the early stages of a project. However, remember it is services, specifically user services, that are delivered by incremental design.

- It is likely that the effort required to complete this stage of Perspective is significantly larger than the effort required for the previous stages. This is principally because the work required during this stage involves the software development activities of coding and testing. In order to reduce the two risks of budget overrun and the construction of a system that does not meet all the business requirements, two of Perspective's key themes need to be woven into the steps of this stage:

- Constant validation: The business owners should maintain a constant involvement with the development even though the tasks being undertaken are principally those of software construction.

- Timeboxing: Under a timeboxing regime it is the functionality that slips, not the time, that is, the delivery date is always held even if the contents of a particular delivery are scaled down. The timeboxing philosophy recognizes the business pressure to have functionality available by an agreed date.

- An iterative prototyping strategy may be adopted for this stage of Perspective. Be aware of the different prototyping strategies mentioned in section 12.6. It may well be that a requirements prototype, provides input to this stage. However, it is important to avoid the deliberate use of requirements prototyping in iteration with increment design, as the functional requirements for the increment should have stabilized by the time increment design begins.

12.9 User Acceptance of an Increment

12.9.1 Purpose

- To enable the executive sponsor to approve the increment prior to roll out.

12.9.2 Inputs

- The tested increment from the design and build an increment stage.

12.9.3 Outputs
- Beta-testing comments.
- Beta-testing strategy.
- The increment for roll out to the entire user population.

12.9.4 Task Catalog

• *Agree on Beta Testing Criteria.*

Discuss and agree on the beta-testing program for the increment. The following issues should be considered:

- length of beta-testing program,
- impact on normal work load,
- recovery procedures should the increment fail,
- reporting mechanisms so that both regular feedback and errors and omissions are fed back to the development team,
- which users should have access to the beta version,
- criteria for determining that the software is good enough to be rolled out to all users at all sites.

• *Produce a Training Plan, Create Materials, and Carry Out Training.*

Draw up a training plan and create any training materials that will be required for the beta-testing program. The training plan should cover both users and system administrators. The time scales of the training plan should reflect both users' availability and the users' needs for operating the increment.

Once a training plan has been agreed on the necessary training should be performed so that the set of users who will perform the beta-testing are appropriately skilled.

• *Perform the Beta-Testing and Necessary Rework.*

Perform the beta-testing to the level determined in the beta-testing strategy and to rework the increment as necessary so that it can be rolled out to the entire user population during the next stage.

12.9.5 Keynotes

- It should be noted that the amount of effort expended during this stage may vary enormously among different projects. For example, in a small project that makes good use of JAD sessions and that is implemented only at a single site the stage may be missed completely. Conversely, a significant effort may be required for a complex software system that is to be implemented across many sites.

12.10 Roll Out of Increment

12.10.1 Purpose

- To install an increment in the user environment.

12.10.2 Inputs

• A beta-tested increment.
• The feasibility report.

12.10.3 Outputs

• Implementation plan.
• An increment functioning in the business environment.

12.10.4 Task Catalog

• *Produce an Implementation Plan.*

Create a plan for the deployment of the increment within the business organization. This should indicate the mode of deployment (e.g., one enterprise
might deploy the increment by geographical region, another might deploy in
all locations simultaneously) and how the change is to be effected from the
old system to the new application.

• *Installation and Handover.*

Install the increment and perform the necessary data migration.

A final production test is carried out before authorization for live running is
given. There is a formal handover of control to the operations group and
then the live running of the new increment is initiated and the old system
phased out, where necessary.

• *Monitor and Support.*

Monitor the rolled-out increment in the period immediately following
deployment, in order to ensure that the success criteria that were documented during feasibility have been realized. It is important therefore to
monitor performance against these criteria after deployment.

• *Product and Process Improvement.*

Analyze the performance of the development process and feed this information back in order that future increments or projects can benefit. It should
be viewed as a formal final step for each increment and for the project as a
whole, to ensure that process improvement becomes "habitual."

CHAPTER 13

• •

The Component
Process

13.1 Introduction

Creating reusable components is an important goal that changes the view of software from a liability to an asset. The need for high quality and generality is increased by an order of magnitude. Producing quality assets that are trusted by multiple consumers not only requires special design skills it also requires a special process: Hence the need for the *component process*.

A component project develops potentially reusable software.

Whereas a solution project may be developed at a departmental level, component projects develop commonly used services across different departmental systems. In practice the component and solution processes work in an interleaved fashion. Reuse producers need to see what consumers have achieved in order to identify what could be engineered for general use. Conversely, reuse consumers need to use components to decide whether these products are really general purpose and valuable enough to be deemed assets. A key characteristic of Perspective's component process is that it, no less than the solution process, is iterative and incremental. This is in contrast to waterfall approaches that do not reflect the realities of today's needs for rapid delivery of solutions.

The production of components and the delivery of solutions are linked processes.

Guidelines are presented for assessing the type of process that is appropriate for the needs of specific projects. The component process is described in terms of stages that employ a common template. A task catalog provides

A template and task catalog are presented for the component process.

the project manager with a practical list of suggested contents. References to the techniques sections of this book show specifically where modeling techniques fit in. The project manager is able to configure the template and adapt the contents to suit individual project needs. For reasons of scope we have only touched on other significant tasks, for which references are provided for further detail. In particular, traceability, testing, and quality assurance are vital areas; the reader is referred to Goldberg and Rubin (1995) for a detailed account of process implications for these subjects.

13.2 Applicability of the Component Process

13.2.1 Component Projects

Component projects typically deliver business services and data services.

A component project is aimed at development of components providing commonly used business and/or data services across different departmental systems or for use by third parties. The aim is to sow reusable services in the manner of component builders. An important part of the process is to develop generic models, which can be specialized and refined by solution builders, in the manner of frameworks. Component projects are driven by generic business requirements. Such requirements may emerge directly from BPM projects, from the need to reuse existing legacy assets, and from feedback from solution projects.

New component projects require separate feasibility and analysis stages.

There is a difference between a component project that delivers a new set of services and one that delivers upgraded services. New component projects often work to confer direct early user value, which is highly visible; for example, providing new generic stock management services with GUIs to a variety of users. The required set of business services and/or data services should be scoped and analyzed using the feasibility and analysis stages of the solution process in order to provide more detail to the component process.

Upgrade component projects do not usually require separate feasibility and analysis stages.

Upgrade component projects center on enhancing existing services so that they are more generally available to a wider set of solutions or perform more efficiently; for example, streamlining premium calculation facilities for use by a set of existing insurance solutions. Such projects usually result in a set of black-box business services or data services for use in different solution contexts. In this case it is usually unnecessary to perform separate feasibility and analysis stages providing the requirements are clear.

13.2.2 Key Characteristics of Component Projects

High-quality reusable software is the keynote.

It is important to apply the component process to appropriate project types. The main indicators are degree of potential commonality (for example, generic requirements) and the stringency of quality criteria (for example, performance and reliability) that accompanies shared requirements.

A key characteristic of Perspective's component process is that it, no less than the solution process, is iterative and incremental. This is in contrast to waterfall approaches that do not reflect the realities of today's needs for rapid delivery of software. Typically, service packages are allocated to different teams. Project management is facilitated by architecting service packages in early phases of development. An additional advantage is that incremental design can focus on specific implementation detail without being overloaded with wider architectural concerns. Services are released in incremental fashion through a set of evolving components.

Organizations are increasingly looking to find an effective way to reuse their investments in existing packages, databases, and legacy systems within the context of component technology. Unfortunately most processes offer little advice in this area, making the implicit assumption that the component builder always starts afresh. The component process must bring existing software into the process as an asset, rather than ignoring it as a liability.

> Note that this not the same as a "non-RAD" process.

> Component projects seek to reuse legacy assets.

13.2.3 Quality Attributes

Component development is unique in that it is specifically aimed at creating **reusable** software. This requires a high level of quality that inspires trust in consumer bases, which have the potential for huge growth with the Internet. The need to satisfy potentially diverse users while aiming for high performance can result in trade-offs and compromises, which conflict with quality criteria. For example, it is important to engineer maximum generality into components without sacrificing cohesion; maximum maintainability without sacrificing performance. This in itself is often a considerable challenge requiring skilled and thorough design. The documentation has to indicate in clear terms how the software interfaces to other software and the design needs to be general enough to be usable in as yet unforeseen circumstances. In view of such complexity the temptation is to retreat to the far right end of the process spectrum discussed in chapter 11.

> Component development presents demanding technical challenges.

We have emphasized the importance of metrics in the previous chapter, mainly with regard to development costs and time scales. In the component process *quality* metrics assume a particular significance. *Quality attributes* are statements about *how well* the system is expected to function; examples include reliability, efficiency, usability, maintainability, testability, portability, as well as the central concern of the component process: reusability. A full discussion of quality attributes is outside our current scope; the reader is referred to Fenton (1991) for a useful discussion on quality models and to Meyer (1995)

> "You can't control what you can't measure" (DeMarco, 1982).

for the significance of quality with regard to object orientation. The salient point here is that the component process must not be based on a rigid water-fall, which is a no-hoper in today's demanding environments. However, it must explicitly address quality attributes.

Quality templates provide a mechanism for defining quality attributes.

Quality templates (Gilb, 1988) provide a consistent means of capturing the information required to measure a quality attribute. A quality template includes the unit of measurement, and upper and lower acceptable limits. For example, average response time is measured in seconds and has an acceptable range of between 1 and 5 seconds. Quality templates are applied at the high end of the component process to define overall measurable quality objectives for a set of services to be delivered by a project. They are also applied at a more detailed level to provide essential input to the design process, allowing the designer to make well-grounded trade-offs and providing criteria by which system success can be measured.

13.2.4 Organizational Factors

A piecemeal approach is taken by many companies today.

Working at reuse from the "bottom up" involves driving the process from solution projects, gradually promoting locally used objects to the status of components. This can put excessive pressure on teams usually working with tight deadlines to deliver increments. Often project-specific objects are recognized as having reuse potential. However, it takes time to modify the object, as well as additional time for testing, quality assurance, and the documentation effort that goes well beyond the effort needed for local development. The project manager then says "no" to reuse because this would blow the time and budget of his or her project. Another problem with reuse from the bottom-up perspective is that it tends to be ad hoc. Someone has a "good idea" for reuse on one project, someone else has a "good idea" for reuse on another separate project. The larger the organization, the more difficult it becomes to manage the "good ideas." This leads to a piecemeal approach to reuse, which, it is often argued, is "better than nothing." In fact it is a situation common throughout many companies today, where management is reluctant to release funding for reuse initiatives that are perceived as an academic waste of time.

The "Grand Design" seeks components on the basis of an abstract plan.

Conversely, working at reuse from a purely top-down perspective drives reuse from a grand design. The problem with this approach is that it is nice theory but lousy in practice! It is very difficult to produce software of practical value on the basis of an abstract plan. Often, by the time anything useful is delivered the original business assumptions on which it is based have changed dramatically. Many organizations tried this approach with data modeling in the 1980s and most (certainly the ones known to the authors) failed. Faced with short-term deadlines and an aggressive approach to exploiting new technolo-

gy, the grand plans are soon abandoned and reactive development of simulta-
neous applications is soon the order of the day.

It is important to understand that organizations that adopt component-
based development techniques do not automatically gain the benefits of reuse.
In fact, reuse can be achieved using traditional techniques. The underlying critical success factors are less technical than organizational and cultural. The
management challenges of reuse are well documented (Goldberg & Rubin,
1995; Griss, 1995). To fully exploit the reuse potential of the component
process requires instituting the right cultural conditions:

Software reuse does not happen in a vacuum.

- Compensation systems that reward developers for reusing classes and services created by others and for providing reusable classes and services.
- Provision of easy access to reusable components in the form of catalogs,
  browsers, and other tools.
- Procedures that encourage and support reuse; for example, effective team
  structures as discussed below.
- Training and education in the theory and practice of reuse.

We agree that effective management is imperative for success. An effective component process requires a fundamental shift in an organization's culture. This takes time: for example, many organizations find they have to iterate through several versions of a repository before they have one that is solid.
Although we can only do cursory justice to such organizational issues within
our current scope, we do nevertheless feel that team organization is so important that it merits an integral place within the Perspective process. This important topic is therefore addressed in chapter 14. Teams should be multidisciplinary, with a range of skills represented in one team. This is in sharp contrast
to the traditional approach of an analysis team throwing requirements "over
the wall" to a design team that in turn throws specifications over the wall to
coders and then to testers and so on.

The right culture does not "happen overnight."

We recognize that reusable components need to be based on actual usage
in the business environment. That means waiting until components have been
produced before evaluating the candidates and reworking to the status of
component. However, we also recognize the need for an architectural base to
channel reuse in a common direction. That is the only way to avoid piecemeal
development and achieve a fully integrated portfolio of services. This involves
two particularly key gear shifts:

There are two particularly critical team roles.

1. The architectural base must be allowed to evolve in terms of generic models. This means driving the component projects from generic business

requirements and requires a *reuse architect* (see chapter 14) to plan and evolve the generic models.

2. Solution projects must be continually assessed for cross-project reuse opportunities. This requires a *reuse assessor* (see chapter 14) to cross-fertilize potential software assets from different projects.

13.3 Component Process Overview

Generic business
requirements drive
the process.

The generic business requirements that drive component projects may emerge in different ways, as follows:

• directly from BPM projects,
• the need to reuse existing legacy assets,
• feedback from solution projects.

A migration strategy
provides steer.

A migration strategy should provide steer on issues such as data management and policy with regard to reuse of legacy applications, packages, and databases. Similarly a technical architecture should provide steer on infrastructure hardware and software.

Generic models are
produced.

Various models are produced throughout the process that evolve in detail as the process unfolds. An important part of the process is to evolve the models so that they can be specialized and refined by solution builders, in analogous fashion to frameworks.

A set of reusable
components is
delivered.

Parts of the model are selected for incremental development, typically as business and/or data services, to form an evolving set of components. Section 13.3.2 includes recommended levels of detail for each stage. There are several deliverables that are produced at various points, including component design specifications and updated service catalogs.

Separate control and
delivery cycles are
used.

An overview of the component process is shown in Figure 13.1. The assessment and scoping stages are in essence ongoing and proactive, although they are also deployable as stages in a component project. For example, scoping and assessment may comprise a business requirement evaluation project. The remainder of the diagram depicts stages that are delivery focused. The techniques used vary according to specific project needs.

Assessment may
result in separate
feasibility and
analysis stages.

For new component requirements feasibility and analysis stages, as described in the previous chapter, are required prior to service planning, as indicated by the "New Path" in Figure 13.1. In contrast and depending on the results of assessment, component upgrades can usually proceed direct to service planning as indicated by the "Upgrade Path."

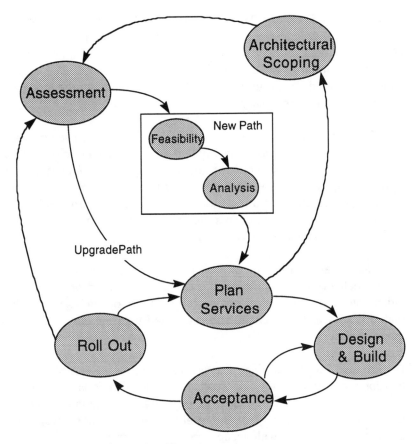

Figure 13.1. The component process.

There is a greater emphasis on quality attributes than on a solution project, with checkpoints built in throughout the process. A wider variety of interested parties are involved in the process (for example, end-users, solution project staff, and quality assurance staff) and a wider spectrum of activities is involved; for example, quality certification (Folkes & Stubenvoll, 1992) and variant analysis (Barnes & Bollinger, 1991).

Quality is not bolted on: it runs through the process.

13.3.1 Component Process Stage Overviews

The following paragraphs provide a brief overview of the purpose of each of the stages in the component process.

Architectural Scoping: *Provide an overall context* for component projects. Sets of generic business requirements are analyzed in terms of business services and/or data services and generic models. Nonfunctional requirements are analyzed in terms of an overall quality plan. Proposed plans for services (emerging from the plan services stage) are gauged against the models, which are adjusted where necessary.

Assessment: *Assess needs for reusable services against the available resources.* Assessment is a coordination activity that aims to pollinate reuse across solution projects. It involves identifying and weighing up requirements for services against the generic models. Potentially reusable services may arise from analyzing legacy assets or as a result of analyzing feedback from either solution projects or rolled-out components. Assessment also determines whether separate feasibility and analysis stages are required.

Plan Services: *Develop a plan for a component project* in terms of incremental delivery of reusable services. The plan should provide an overall indication of the order of delivery, the contents of each service, the estimated time scales and costs, and a detailed plan for development of the next set of services.

Design and Build: *Construct, assemble, and test the components* that are specified for a particular enterprise service. Additional time is often required to rework the design so that it is general enough to be used in a variety of solutions. Therefore, dependent on the level of user and solution project involvement, an iterative loop with acceptance may well exist.

Acceptance: *Ensure acceptance and certification of a set of components* prior to their roll out in the live environment. Dependent on the level of user, quality assurance, and solution project involvement, an iterative loop with design and build an increment may exist.

Roll out: *Install a set of components* successfully in the repository supporting the live user environment. This involves marshaling effective reuse of components and services by solution projects.

Each stage is presented in more detail in the sections that follow.

Our main aim is to give the reader a flavor of how to apply the process, but to do this in some detail. Each section is a template that you should customize to your own specific needs. References to the Perspective modeling techniques are included at appropriate points to demonstrate how they fit in. Deliverable definitions are included in appendix A.

13.3.2 Component Process: Evolution of Models

Generic models are evolved from first-cut skeletal models on first iterations of scoping through to fully detailed specifications at design. Table 13.1 summarizes model evolution in terms of the expected level of detail at these two extremes. Note that a new component project may also involve feasibility and analysis (see section 13.2.1); the associated level of detail for these stages is shown in the previous chapter (see Table 12.2).

Models are evolved to a state in which they can be readily generated to code.

Table 13.1. Model-Stage Detail Table for the Component Process		
Model	**Scoping Level of Detail**	**Design Level of Detail**
use case model	(list of candidate services only)	
class model	high-level class diagram	includes all attributes with definitions; operations with detailed specifications and signatures defined; relevant nonfunctional requirements and constraints; must include service classes; may include user and data classes
object interaction model		collaboration diagrams and sequence diagrams for key scenarios and use cases; user objects and data objects included; also include relevant nonfunctional requirements and constraints
state model		transition strings fully detailed also include relevant nonfunctional requirements and constraints
component model	high-level service package dependency diagrams	Component package dependency diagrams; interfaces defined and classes allocated
deployment model		shows technical architecture; allocation of component packages
logical data model		used to model supporting non-OO database structure

13.4 Architectural Scoping

13.4.1 Purpose

- Provide an architectural context for component projects required to meet business needs.
- Overall evolution of generic models.

13.4.2 Inputs

- Vision statement.[1]
- Migration strategy and technical architecture.
- Legacy asset documentation.
- Terms of reference.[2]
- Feedback from planning to adjust generic models.

13.4.3 Outputs

- *Models as shown in Table 13.2.*
- Lists of candidate services.
- Quality plan.
- Terms of reference for feasibility studies for component projects.

13.4.4 Task Catalog

- *Develop generic models.*

The volume and complexity of work will vary according to the amount of preparatory work that has taken place. For example, where a set of generic business requirements is available, as in the form of indirect processes (see section 3.4.7), this greatly facilitates the work.

Use domain knowledge to partition generic requirements into a high-level set of service packages. Develop an overall architecture using high-level service package dependency diagrams.

---

[1] A vision statement is input by the executive sponsor and provides a set of overall business goals.

[2] Terms of reference are provided by the executive sponsor and include a set of generic business requirements that may reference a project proposal, a set of business process models (typically indirect processes) and/or candidate legacy systems, packages, and databases as appropriate.

Table 13.2. Model-Stage Details for the Architectural Scoping Stage

Model	Level of Detail
component model	high-level service package dependency diagrams
class model	high-level class diagram

Develop first-cut generic models within one or more of the service packages. It is important to stay away from of detail: The main purpose of the exercise is to provide an architectural base that can be evolved to reflect subsequent work. The architecture will almost certainly require adjustment as a result of the assessment activity.

8.4.1	Domain Modeling
8.4.2	System Architecture Modeling
8.4.3	Modeling Reusable Business Classes

• *Perform horizontal prototyping.*

Investigate the overall end-to-end feasibility of envisaged services using horizontal prototypes. This is important where use of services stretches across several interworking users and is especially relevant where visualization of these services is difficult. A horizontal prototype provides a shallow pass across families of interdependent services that require high user interaction. Often this can be achieved using screen "mock-ups" with little underlying functionality but with sufficient navigation to enable some key scenarios to be fed through by users.

• *Confirm technical design architecture.*

Identify corporate policy with regard to resources required to implement the generic models in line with total business requirements. This involves verifying and confirming the technical architecture in terms of hardware, communications infrastructure, and software infrastructure (for example, operating systems, databases, programming languages). Deployment diagrams, as described in chapter 10, can be used to assist in gaining a picture of overall processor configuration.

The volume and complexity of work will vary according to the amount of preparatory work that has taken place.

• *Confirm migration strategy.*

Establish overall policy with regard to reuse of legacy systems, packages, and databases. There is a trade-off here between components that are rapidly constructed to wrap existing system services and components that are designed to glean the full benefits of an object-oriented approach. The former have the advantage that they can be developed very quickly at minimum cost, but have the disadvantage that they will usually incur significant rework later on when the organization migrates fully to object technology. The latter approach has the opposite pros and cons in that it will take longer but is less likely to incur significant rework later on. An effective migration strategy needs to steer a balance between these extremes. A migration strategy also covers areas such as data management policy; the reader is referred to Graham (1995) for an extensive discussion.

• *Develop an overall quality plan.*

Set overall expectations on quality attributes using quality templates, as described in section 13.2.3. This can involve developing generic interface models to establish commonly used interface structures. Also a set of "look and feel" standards is produced in order to ensure consistency across all parts of the interface. However, it is important to stay away from detail: The main purpose of the exercise is to develop a framework for subsequent work.

8.4.10	Modeling Enterprise User Interface Classes

As with the previous task, the volume and complexity of work will vary according to the amount of preparatory work that has taken place. For example, where a set of infrastructure nonfunctional requirements is available, as a result of a prior computing strategy or BPM recommendation, much of the necessary work may have been done already.

• *Identify business services.*

Analyze generic requirements into a set of candidate business services. Do not attempt to model in any detail. Simply list the identified business services.

8.4.4	Identifying Business Services: Service Types Approach
8.4.5	Identifying Business Services: Business Process Approach

• *Identify candidate legacy assets.*

Make an early stab at identifying candidate legacy systems, packages, and databases that look capable of meeting service requirements. The identified legacy assets will be examined in more detail (in the assessment stage) to see if they are suitable for wrapping or reverse engineering.

9.3.1	Assessing the need for Legacy System Services
9.4.1	Assessing the need for Package Services
9.5.1	Assessing the need for Data Services

• *Raise terms of reference for feasibility studies.*

Assess component projects that will result in services that can be delivered in increments that confer early value. Where appropriate raise terms of reference for commissioning a feasibility study (and possible analysis) for these projects, as described in chapter 12. Documents and models produced as a result of such feasibility and analysis stages provide input to the plan services activity described in section 13.6.

13.4.5 Keynotes

- Initial scoping involves building an outline set of generic models to provide an architectural framework for the business as a whole. This should be done quickly, in weeks rather than months.
- Subsequent scoping addresses key sets of generic business requirements that can be met with services that provide early user value, using principles of incremental delivery.
- Scoping is not an activity that is done once and then forgotten. It requires iterative revisiting to reflect results from solution projects and feedback from the use of services.

13.5 Assessment

13.5.1 Purpose

Essentially this is a coordination activity that aims to pollinate reuse across solution projects.

- Assess needs for reusable services.
- Make recommendations for upgrading or developing business services and data services.
- Analyze impact of proposed changes.

13.5.2 Inputs

- Vision statement.[3]
- Migration strategy and architecture.
- Legacy asset documentation.
- Generic models from architectural scoping.
- A set of requirements emerging from solution projects.

13.5.3 Outputs

- A set of proposed upgrades that need planning.
- Terms of reference for feasibility studies for component projects.
- Revised quality plan.
- Summary of recommendations.

13.5.4 Task Catalog

• *Perform vertical prototyping.*

Investigate integration of new technologies using vertical prototypes. This is important where components are to be implemented using different technologies that have not been used in combination before. A vertical prototype provides a thin cut downward through elements of the different technologies to investigate interoperability.

• *Search for opportunities to sow reuse.*

This is essentially a proactive task involving active collaboration with solution project teams with a view to sowing reuse from solution projects. Conduct comparative studies of solution project models that appear to overlap. Identify opportunities to generalize common features and sow services.

• *Search for opportunities to harvest reuse.*

Again this is a proactive activity aimed at pollinating reuse across solution projects. The aim is to service common local requirements by refining generic models. Assess requirements for reusable model items. Identify existing generic models that could be further refined to meet requirements.

Identify existing business services and/or data services that could be further refined to meet requirements.

---

[3] A vision statement is input by the executive sponsor and provides a set of overall business goals.

• *Revise overall quality plan.*

Revisit and revise each quality attribute captured in the quality plan.

• *Assess candidate legacy systems and packages.*

Assess candidate legacy systems and packages against the requirements for business services and/or data services. Identify key abstractions from the legacy systems or packages. Determine the need for renovation and the viability of wrapping. Develop outline wrapper models if appropriate.

| 9.3.2 | Identifying Legacy System Key Abstractions |
| 9.4.2 | Identifying Package Key Abstractions |

• *Assess candidate legacy databases.*

Assess candidate legacy databases against the requirements for data services. Determine the need for renovation and the viability of wrapping. Develop an outline architectural model for the wrapper if appropriate.

9.5.2	Mapping Class Model to Logical Data Model
9.5.3	Establishing the Existing Logical Data Model
9.5.4	Architecting a Data Service Component

• *Analyze impact.*

Analyze impact of the proposed development of generic models as a basis for business services and/or data services. Explore various routes to developing the services and assess the resulting impact.

• *Recommend upgrades to services.*

Summarize recommended improvements with overall cost–benefit justification.

Itemize and model proposed upgrades to services.

• *Raise terms of reference for feasibility studies for new component projects.*

Where more investigation is needed it may be necessary to raise terms of reference for feasibility studies and subsequent analyses in order to clarify and understand requirements for services.

13.5.5 Keynotes

- Candidate solution classes require reengineering before they can be delivered in the form of components. This includes abstracting a class out of its context to remove dependencies.
- Recommendations for upgrade should cover a range of issues such as the following:

  - Documentation. Standards for documentation for components that are entered into the repository will be different from those in use on solution projects. For example, documentation is required to provide an additional level of detail concerning design and interfaces.
  - Testing. Testing standards for components entered in the repository will be more demanding than those in use on solution projects. For example, testing coverage criteria may be more severe in order to ensure their reliability.
  - Quality attributes specified in the quality plan need to be considered; for example performance, security and reliability.

13.6 Plan Services

13.6.1 Purpose

- Review and prioritize needs arising from the assessment stage.
- Develop a plan for incremental delivery of reusable services. The plan should provide an overall indication of the order of delivery, the contents of each service, the estimated time scales and costs, and a detailed plan for development of the next set of services; quality and test plans are also included for development of new components or for a set of upgrades to existing components.

13.6.2 Inputs

- Set of scoped generic models, typically a service package.
- Set of proposed upgrades identified by the assessment stage.
- Optionally, for a new component project, a feasibility study and analysis document.

13.6.3 Outputs

- Overall incremental plan.
- Set of detailed component project plans including test and quality plans.

13.6.4 Task Catalog

Most of the tasks involved in planning delivery of business and/or data services are analogous to those involved in planning increments, which are detailed in chapter 12. These are summarized below for convenience. An overall plan is held for each component project. Detailed plans are held for the next services to be delivered.

- Recalibrate estimates.
- Identify and order increments.
- Produce an incremental plan.
- Produce a detailed plan of the next increment.

However, the planning context for this activity is much wider than that for developing solution project increments and involves coordination of activities across different consumer solution projects.

Quality planning of specific increments is much more stringent and involves additional tasks:

• *Recalibrate quality attributes.*

The purpose of this step is to use the information concerning the measurement of quality attributes of previously delivered working components in order to recalibrate the quality attributes for all the subsequent increments. The overall quality plan produced in the scoping and assessment stages may be adjusted to reflect the feedback.

• *Specify quality attributes.*

The purpose of this step is to specify the quality attributes that apply to the next increments in more detail.

13.6.5 Keynotes

- Do not underestimate the planning issues involved, which are considerably more complex than with a solution project. For example, it will be necessary to trade off priorities between different services and plan for the coordination of the roll out of the services.
- Remember that planning a new component project (see 13.2.1) may well involve initiating separate feasibility and analysis stages in analogous fashion to a solution project.

- It is important to also consider means for acquiring legacy services as well as developing your own services for wrapping legacy assets. The reader is referred to Goldberg and Rubin (1995) for a useful account. Options include:
  - contract for development with vendor,
  - purchase existing product,
  - purchase industry standard framework for customization.

13.7 Design and Build Components

13.7.1 Purpose

- Develop business services and/or data services.
- Refine estimates and quality attributes for remaining increments.

13.7.2 Inputs

- Models produced during the scoping stage.
- Proposed upgrades identified during assessment.
- Optionally, for a new component project, a feasibility study and analysis document.
- Detailed plan produced during the plan services stage.

13.7.3 Outputs

- *Models as shown in Table 13.3.*
- Component internal design specification (definition is included in Appendix A).
- Coded components.
- Test documentation.
- Refined estimates and quality attributes.

13.7.4 Task Catalog

The design and build tasks work in three iterative tiers, gradually addressing more detail through each iteration. The emphasis is on providing reusable components to multiple solutions. Tier 1 maps the models developed thus far to implementation units, in a way that maximizes potential for reuse and assesses overall technical feasibility. Tier 2 adds details to the models and seeks to engineer reuse in a trade-off with other quality attributes. Tier 3 codes and tests the components.

Table 13.3. Model-Stage Details for the Design and Build Components Stage	
Model	**Level of Detail**
class model	includes all attributes with definitions; operations with detailed specifications and signatures defined; relevant nonfunctional requirements and constraints; must include service classes; may include user and data classes
object interaction model	collaboration diagrams and sequence diagrams for key scenarios and use cases; user objects and data objects included; also include relevant nonfunctional requirements and constraints
state model	transition strings fully detailed also include relevant nonfunctional requirements and constraints
component model	component package dependency diagrams; interfaces defined and classes allocated
deployment model	shows technical architecture; allocation of component packages
logical data model	used to model supporting non-OO database structure

13.7.4.1 Task Catalog Tier 1

• ***Map classes to component packages.***

Allocate classes to component packages, keeping the components as reusable as possible across different implementations. Firm up on service classes.

10.4.1	Creating Component Packages

• ***Assess potential deployment of component packages.***

Explore overall distribution of component packages across technical architecture. Adjust mapping of classes to components where necessary.

10.4.2	Allocating Component Packages to Nodes

13.7.4.2 Task Catalog Tier 2

• *Develop design structure.*

Improve structure of components using established techniques and capitalizing on use of appropriate patterns.

5.4.6	Applying Patterns to Develop the Class Diagram
5.4.8	Using Inheritance
5.4.9	Using Aggregation
5.4.11	Sowing Business Services

• *Develop design collaborations.*

Improve interaction both between and within components, using established techniques and capitalizing on use of appropriate patterns.

5.4.11	Sowing Business Services
6.4.5	Develop Example Scenario using OCD
6.4.7	Identifying Further Services
6.4.8	Reusing Business Services

• *Develop design dynamics.*

Improve class dynamics within components, using established techniques and capitalizing on use of appropriate patterns.

7.4.3	Developing a State Diagram
7.4.5	Developing Nested State Diagrams

• *Design business components.*

Design components to supply business services. Evolve generic models within service packages. Recommend revisions to the architecture, identified in the scoping stage, where necessary. Engineer model items from solution projects to generic model status. Use patterns to assist and guide the design process.

8.4.6	Sowing Reusable Business Components
8.4.7	Revising System Architecture
8.4.8	Designing Business Components
8.4.9	Using Patterns to Develop Business Components

• *Design legacy system wrappers.*

Design components encapsulating services supplied by existing legacy systems.

9.3.3	Designing a Legacy System Wrapper
9.3.4	Detailing a Legacy System Wrapper

• *Design package wrappers.*

Design components encapsulating services supplied by existing packages.

9.4.3	Designing a Package Wrapper
9.4.4	Detailing a Package Wrapper

• *Design database wrappers.*

Design components encapsulating data services supplied by existing non-OO databases, typically relational databases. It may be necessary to revise the existing logical data model where appropriate.

9.5.5	Revising the Logical Data Model
9.5.6	Designing a Data Service Package
9.5.7	Detailing a Data Service Transaction

• *Detail user interface components.*

Where appropriate, develop user interface components to reflect both user needs and design constraints.

8.4.10	Modeling User Interface Components

• *Rework the design.*

Ensure that the design is general enough to be used in a variety of solutions in the light of feedback from acceptance. Aim for components that can be extended or refined for anticipated consumer use. A useful technique to assist with this task is variant analysis (Barnes & Bollinger, 1991), which helps designers identify and prioritize likely variations of an artifact.

• *Specify internal design details.*

Specify internal design details for components, including nonfunctional requirements such as operating constraints and quality attributes such as security and reliability.

• *Specify services.*

Define component interface descriptions to include services. Specify services using external specification techniques such as preconditions and postconditions. This information will be published in the service catalog as part of the roll-out stage.

5.4.13	Documenting Classes, Operations and Attributes

13.7.4.3 Task Catalog Tier 3

• *Code the components.*

The purpose of this step is to code components in line with internal design specification and interface descriptions. Code should be written to standards specified in the technical architecture. Code by assembly from other components providing this does not conflict with quality attributes.

• *Test the components.*

The purpose of this step is to test the components and ensure that they meet requirements. A testing strategy is required that determines issues, such as the use of automatic test tools, the level of code coverage, and so on. The tasks involved in this activity are performed to greater depth and rigor than those for designing and building solution project increments.

Regression testing is a key activity. This needs to be performed across different consumer applications to ensure that the components are fit for consumption by all users.

The relevant quality attributes (such as performance and reliability) and constraints (such as communications protocols) assume a much greater importance than in a solution project. Components must be tested to ensure they meet such nonfunctional requirements.

• *Refine estimates.*

Reassess estimates of the effort required for the development of each remaining component. The estimates are refined using data from the development of previous components.

• *Refine risks and quality requirements.*

Analyze major risk areas for the remaining components (e.g., complex components, usage of new technology like new hardware and software). Similarly, reassess quality attributes (e.g., performance, reliability) in the light of lessons learned from development of the current components. After the final component is completed, detail any areas that may prove critical or difficult to maintain in the future, together with an analysis of those components most likely to change.

• *Ensure requirements traceability.*

Update requirement references developed during the previous stage given the more detailed level of modeling.

13.7.5 Keynotes

• Component information is captured at two levels.

  1. At the external or public level, component interface descriptions are captured, which should be viewable within an evolving catalog of services, published in the roll-out stage.

  2. At the internal or technical implementation level, detailed constraints and quality attributes relating to each component are viewable within a detailed internal design document.

• Traceability is more stringent than is the case with the solution process. Generic requirement references must be included at as detailed a level of modeling as possible. It is also worth tracking which solution projects are making use of which enterprise services.

13.8 Acceptance of Components

13.8.1 Purpose

• Ensure acceptance of a set of components prior to their roll out in the live environment.

13.8.2 Inputs

• Tested components.

13.8.3 Outputs

• Accepted components.
• Acceptance testing comments.

13.8.4 Task Catalog

The tasks involved in this activity are performed to greater depth and rigor than those for accepting solution project increments. Typically a component project will require greater levels of regression testing and a cross-section of acceptance testers from software development, quality assurance, and the user community. This naturally puts greater demands on the activity, as several types of test may need to be run. The tasks are as follows. First, tasks are performed as for a solution but in greater quantity and to a greater level of detail:

• Agree on beta testing criteria.
• Produce a training plan and materials and carry out training.
• Perform the beta testing and necessary rework.

Second, there are tasks that are unique to component acceptance:

• Certify the design.

    This involves measuring the design against nonfunctional requirements constraints and quality attributes.

13.8.5 Keynotes

• Acceptance test personnel will vary according to project requirements. For example, if the services are transparent to the users, the acceptance testers will be technical development staff and project leaders of the affected solution projects. On the other hand, if the services are user facing, as in a component project delivering user-value infrastructure services, the acceptance testers will be interested users. Finally, certification should be carried out by quality assurance personnel. Typically a component project will involve both elements and therefore a cross-section of acceptance testers will participate in this stage.

13.9 Roll Out Components

13.9.1 Purpose

- Install a set of components successfully in the repository supporting the live user environment.
- Marshal effective reuse of components by solution projects.

13.9.2 Inputs

- Accepted components

13.9.3 Outputs

- Components available in the repository.
- Updated service catalog (definition is included in Appendix A).

13.9.4 Task Catalog

A key task is to ensure clear and unambiguous service specifications:

- Publish services.

  Verify the service specifications included on component interface descriptions for publishing in the service catalog.

5.4.13	Documenting Classes, Operations and Attributes

Other tasks are analogous to the tasks for rolling out a solution increment, which are repeated below for convenience. However, both the level of detail and extent of work are likely to be much greater where the service is being rolled out across many solution projects and users. All components are implemented within some form of repository.

- Produce an implementation plan.
- Installation and handover.
- Monitor and support.
- Product and process improvement.

Further key tasks associated with roll-out components are as follows:

- Publicize available services.
- Communicate with solution projects to assist in the roll-out of components as they are needed.

CHAPTER 14

••••••••••••••••••••

Perspective
Teams

14.1 Introduction

The right organizational, cultural, and political conditions are prerequisites for successful adoption of the Perspective process. This is a key message that has repeatedly emerged from our experiences of component-based development projects in a variety of organizations. In particular, effective structuring of teams is important. Perspective therefore includes a set of guidelines for effective teams, which are presented in this chapter. The chapter begins by summarizing some of the key team attributes that are particularly important for successful deployment of Perspective. We also include a brief account of JAD, which has proven to be a particularly important communication technique in our use of Perspective on many projects.

Broadly, roles correspond to either the solution process or the component process but can be mixed and matched according to the needs of specific projects. This reflects the move toward hybrid organizational models of software development reported by the Gartner Group (1995), which we discussed in chapter 11. We show how the Perspective process described in the previous three chapters is realized in terms of teams. This involves a discussion of the different team types in preparation for understanding team roles: Team roles are key enablers of the Perspective process. The roles presented are an abstract set that can be mixed and matched according to the needs of your

Guidelines for effective teams are a key part of the process.

This chapter explains how to employ team roles within Perspective.

own organization and projects. In effect the roles form a library that can be customized to the needs of the process. We conclude with some illustrations of how the roles might be employed to service the needs of a set of different example projects.

14.2 Team Attributes

This section describes a number of positive attributes that Perspective teams should exhibit.

14.2.1 Self-Managed Teams

Self-managed teams are responsible for their own actions.

Traditional software development teams receive orders from the project managers and then execute those orders. Within a Perspective project the team should not be a passive receiver of instructions, but a dynamic entity that takes responsibility for the delivery of a specific piece of business functionality. Table 14.1 (DSDM, 1995) provides a comparison between traditional teams and self-managed teams.

14.2.2 Empowered Teams

Self-managed teams carry the authority that goes with responsibility.

The attribute of empowerment complements the self-managed attribute that was previously discussed. One of the key themes of Perspective is the idea of RAAD, described in section 11.3.1. In order for any development to be rapid the development team must not be encumbered by the constant necessity of having to refer to higher management for authority to proceed. This concept of empowerment does not mean that each Perspective team is a "free radical" that can do anything that it wants, nor does it mean that the Perspective team

Table 14.1. Traditional versus Self-Managed Teams

Traditional teams	Self-managed teams
Take directions	Take initiative
Seek individual reward	Focus on team contributions
Focus on low-level objectives	Concentrate on solutions
Compete	Cooperate
Stop at preset goals	Continually improve
React to emergencies	Take steps to prevent emergencies
Spend money on quality improvement	Save money by improving quality

need never talk to anybody else. The concept of empowerment should result in the appropriate level of delegation of authority down to the lowest possible level.

Given that a Perspective team will be made up of staff both from the IT and business communities, the empowerment that is granted must cover both technical and business issues. The technical staff on the team must be able to make decisions regarding design, testing, configuration management, and so on without referring to higher technical authorities. The business staff on the team must be able to make decisions regarding the business requirements of the software.

Empowerment covers both technical and business issues.

The purpose of integrating the business and IT staff is to avoid the traditional problems over the production of, and subsequent arguments concerning, the "statement of requirements" document. Given that the business staff in a Perspective team are authorized to make decisions concerning the functionality of the software, the staff should be chosen with care. If sufficient care is not exercised, then a company may find it moves from a position in which software systems are "gold plated" by the IT staff to one where they are "gold plated" by the business community. It is usual for the degree of empowerment to be recorded in a "terms of reference" document for each Perspective team.

Business and IT staff must be practically focused.

14.2.3 Compact Teams

The maximum number of members in a Perspective team is six. There are two principal reasons for a Perspective team to be compact. First, a large team is much more likely to be skewed toward the IT staff than the business staff. If a team is heavily biased toward the IT staff, then the business staff on the team will be overwhelmed and will have a reduced influence over the direction of the development. This is potentially catastrophic given the reliance of Perspective on the elicitation of the low-level requirements through the collaboration of the IT and business staff. Second, large teams tend to have lower productivity than smaller teams. The reason for the reduced productivity of larger teams is that the number of communication paths among team members grows more than linearly as the number of team members grows. If there are x number of staff in a team, then the number of possible communications on a person-to-person basis is $x(x-1)/2$. Thus if the team has 6 members, then the number of paths is 15; if the team equals 10 then, the number of paths is 45.

Perspective teams should be small.

When teams get large the usual method of overcoming misunderstandings is for the project manager to insist on more and more detailed documentation. This strategy increases the average workload for a member of a large team, compared to a small team, and therefore only exacerbates the produc-

The larger the team, the greater the misunderstandings.

tivity differential. A number of studies (Martin, 1991) have measured the relative productivity between large and small teams showing a differential of up to an order of magnitude.

14.2.4 Collaborative Teams

Collaboration of staff from the IT and business communities is essential.

The collaboration that Perspective requires is not only that the team should gel but also that the team should consist of staff from both the IT and business communities. The purpose of this collaboration is to

- encourage a feeling of joint ownership of the software under development,
- ensure that the correct set of low-level requirements is elicited and implemented,
- maintain a business focus on the development,
- remove the adversarial environment that historically existed between the two communities,
- allow an iterative software process model.

Effective collaboration is "egoless."

In order for the team to gel and the above advantages be realized, the team members must exhibit a certain set of personal attributes. Team members must be good communicators without overpowering personalities.

14.2.5 Business-Aware Teams

Team members must be aware of the overall goals of the business.

Perspective teams are empowered to make decisions concerning not only the technology of the resultant software systems but also the business requirements for those systems. In order for such empowerment to result in useful systems the team members must be aware of the overall goals of the business and how the software system that they are building helps to meet those goals. The presence of business staff in Perspective teams helps ensure that the team is correctly focused. However, this focus can be greatly enhanced if the IT staff on the team has a good understanding of how the business functions and what its goals are. Most IT staff relish the idea of escaping from the "back room" so that they can apply their skills with more precision and be justly proud of knowing that their efforts have ensured that the business has moved toward its goals.

14.2.6 Modeling-Literate Teams

The value of good modeling skills should not be underestimated.

In order for the progress in a project to be as rapid as possible, the IT staff on the project team needs to be skilled in the methods and tools that are to be used for the development. This is particularly important as regards modeling skills. Chapters 3 to 10 of this book described a set of modeling techniques that form a core part of Perspective. Certain techniques may be more useful than others depending on the organizational context. Techniques may be added or expanded to the organization's portfolio. It is useful to allocate responsibility for knowledge and development of the techniques to one or two individuals who will work with skilled consultants to acquire the necessary skills over a period of time. Often this can be done as part of an initial pilot project. Indeed, much of the authors' own time is spent mentoring to help with the necessary skills transfer on such projects.

A SWAT (skilled with advanced tools) team is a small group, typically no more than six, of experienced and well-trained developers who can work together efficiently and effectively. Ideally this team should include individuals who have worked together on many projects, thereby developing an understanding of each other's work styles and skills.

SWAT teams take this idea to its logical conclusion.

Proficiency in modeling depends on the team member's role, as will be discussed in section 14.5. For example, at one end of the spectrum users should at least understand the concepts of use cases; at the other end of the spectrum, designers should understand the semantics of sequence diagrams.

Proficiency in modeling skills can vary.

14.2.7 Comfortable Teams

In recent years IT staff and other office workers are increasingly likely to find themselves working in cramped, open-plan office environments. The justification for the move to this environment is one of cost, that is, overhead costs per employee are reduced if an increased number of employees are placed in a given area. Such a strategy represents a cost–benefit analysis that ignores the lack of benefits arising in such environments.

Planning of IT environments is often shortsighted.

A number of studies have demonstrated the effect of environment on productivity (DeMarco & Lister, 1987). Psychologists describe as "flow," the state of deep, almost meditative thought that intellectual workers require in order to develop ideas and solutions. The state should be familiar to all intellectual workers and is characterized by a sense of euphoria and an unawareness of the passage of time. Unfortunately, a worker cannot enter a state of flow on request; a slow descent, known as the immersion period, is required. The immersion period may take 10 to 20 minutes. If the worker is interrupted, the state is destroyed and a further immersion period will be required.

A good environment helps focus the mind.

In order to measure the ability of a given environment to produce the state of flow DeMarco and Lister (1987) propose an Environment, or E Factor:

An "E Factor" can be used to measure flow.

$$E = \frac{\text{Number of Hours at Work with no Interruption}}{\text{Number of Hours Present at Work}}$$

For example, if an individual works for 40 hours in a week and during that week there are 10 hours when work can be uninterrupted, then E = 0.25.

A number of
environmental
issues need to be
considered.

Very few organizations consider the affect on productivity caused by a particular office configuration. Yet, as the above studies indicate, significant gains, or losses, in productivity can result from thoughtless office design. If an organization wishes to maximize productivity by ensuring that its employees are able to enter the flow state for long periods of time, then certain issues need to be considered; for example

- the amount of dedicated work space per individual,
- the use of meeting rooms,
- the use of e-mail, so that an individual receives a message when it is convenient,
- the use of telephones.

14.3 Joint Application Development

Traditional
communication
makes no use of
group dynamics.

Traditionally, communication among participants in software development is conducted at two levels. First, there is the interview level where analysts elicit requirements from users in 1:1 sessions and then retire to write up notes for formal agreement. Developers use the requirements notes to drive the system specification, which is agreed using the second level of working, which involves a group meeting of all relevant users and senior developers. Typically the specification is "walked through" on a page-by-page basis, with change requests noted. A further meeting resolves the change requests.

This results in large
communication
gaps.

There is normally a lot of discussion in the early stages of the project, at the kick-off meeting and in early interviews, and there is also a lot of debate in the late stages of the project at acceptance meetings. However, there is very little genuine communication during the intervening period.

JAD cultivates
positive team
attributes...

The traditional approach does not foster any of the positive team attributes previously outlined. Perspective recognizes that a far more effective approach is to use workshop environments alongside traditional techniques. Joint application development is an approach for effective employment of workshop environments that can be used at certain points during a project in order to foster good communication and accelerate the development process.

...fosters
communication

JAD derives from a technique developed by IBM in the 1970s that was originally named Joint Application Design. The IBM user organization GUIDE has in fact published several papers on the subject (GUIDE, 1986). Historically, the practical use of group dynamics embodied in JAD has its roots in the following four key principles, as listed in (Allen, 1991):

1. Traditional meetings with the most senior individual as chairperson do not lend themselves very well to problem solving. Rather such sessions need to be facilitated; hence the need for a facilitator role, described below.

2. Decisions agreed on should be consensus decisions with which all participants can identify. There are no losers. The documentation produced is a group product, in which we all have a stake.

3. The agenda itself is produced by the group as part of the documentation; this avoids negative feeling that the meeting might be biased before it is even started.

4. Documentation should be produced on the spot and not as minutes after the session. It is openly displayable as "group memory" preferably using an electronic whiteboard; hence the need for a scribe role, described below.

JAD is applied to develop the models described in this book as a group product. All project participants are assembled in one place at various times to establish objectives, to agree on what is needed, and how it will look. Participants work toward an agreed objective and agenda in order to focus the session. Modeling sessions are often timeboxed to further assist in keeping participants geared to tight objectives.

...and leverages the modeling techniques.

Each participant performs a specified role, as described in section 14.5, within the JAD session. There are two additional roles that apply specifically to JAD sessions:

Roles are an important element of JAD.

Facilitator: The facilitator structures and prepares the sessions. He or she encourages the participation of all the attendees, ensuring that the session moves forward (particularly if it is timeboxed). The facilitator should be a skilled moderator, acting as an independent arbiter and working to stimulate an egoless environment.

Scribe: The scribe is responsible for the production and maintenance of all the documentation resulting from the session. It is important that this role not be considered suitable for a clerical secretary, as the ability to capture business rules or technical information during, or after, the session is paramount. The scribe role becomes particularly important if the session makes use of computer tools. For example, screen-building tools can be used by the scribe to capture the design of prototypes, or the scribe may use an analysis and design tool set to capture business requirements in a modeling notation as they emerge during the session.

There is a lot more to JAD than in the above account!

Because of the scope of this book, we have in fact only touched on the subject of JAD here. For a practical step-by-step guide to the use of JAD the reader is referred to Judy August's (1991) book.

14.4 Team Types

Team members perform various roles.

A Perspective team consists of a number of individuals working together in a coordinated fashion to meet a defined set of objectives. A role is a related set of activities that may be performed by more than one person; also one person may fulfill more than one role.

Management structures are required to organize large projects.

A Perspective project is undertaken by one or more small cohesive teams. Ideally, the number in a Perspective team should not exceed six. If teams are to remain compact, then a management structure must be introduced for a project that requires considerably more than six staff members. Figure 14.1 indicates such a structure. Significant Perspective developments may require additional management structure in order to ensure both that each team is compact and that each project manager has a realistic number of direct reporting lines. Figure 14.2 indicates such a structure.

Solution teams are contrasted with component teams.

Solution teams work on projects whose mission is delivery of increments and follow the solution process, as discussed in chapter 12. Component teams work on projects with the aim of delivering reuse and follow the component process, as discussed in chapter 13. Note that component teams, no less than solution teams, work on projects: However, they have longer term goals that include ongoing maintenance and administration of generic models and components. As with the two processes, the two types of team are ideals that serve to channel our thinking: In practice a team may often include elements of both. Finally, a technical infrastructure team works to ensure the necessary technical capability, in terms of hardware, communications, operating systems, and so on, monitoring performance and capacity.

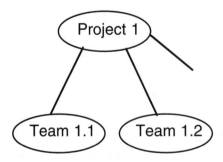

Figure 14.1. Project and team relationship.

14.5 Team Roles

In this section team roles are discussed with respect to solution, component, and technical infrastructure teams. It is important to understand that the roles presented are abstract and to remember that an individual could play several roles on different teams at any one time and that conversely several individuals could be playing the same role on a single team.

Team roles are abstract.

Permanent roles are integral to the day-to-day functioning of the team and take responsibilities for meeting the immediate objectives of the team. Part-time roles are involved on a more occasional basis but take wider responsibilities for ensuring that the team produces results that are in line with the organization's business and technical objectives. In situations where projects are large and complex enough to require splitting into subprojects, the part-time roles assume an increasing importance in ensuring consistency of results across the various subprojects, each of which is staffed by a separate team.

Team roles may be permanent or part time.

14.5.1 Solution Team Roles

The following team roles are based on roles from the Dynamic Systems Development Method (DSDM). We have provided a short summary of each; the reader is referred to DSDM (1997) for a full discussion.

Solution team roles follow...

Project Manager: The project manager reports to senior management, plans and estimates, motivates the team, and coordinates projects involving several

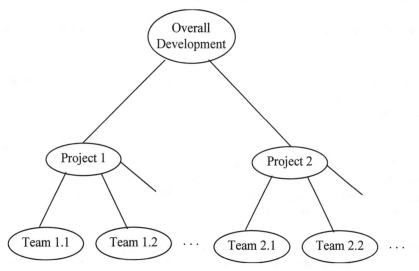

Figure 14.2. Projects and teams in a large development.

teams. The responsibility is to ensure that the solution as a whole is delivered as agreed.

Technical Coordinator: The technical coordinator sets the technical standards and controls configuration management procedures. The role ensures technical coherence and consistency across different teams. It can incorporate that of "database administrator" and will normally be provided by Technical Infrastructure Team, as described in section 14.5.3.

Executive Sponsor: The executive sponsor owns the solution and is ultimately responsible for it. The role must hold a sufficiently high position to resolve business issues and make financial decisions.

Visionary: The visionary acts as the driving force behind the project and ensures business objectives are met. The visionary will probably be from the business community and have originally identified the need for a solution.

Developer/Senior Developer: This role models and interprets user requirements and uses a range of skills (for example, analysis, design, coding, and testing) to develop the models through to effective solutions.

Ambassador User: The ambassador user drives the business requirements and provides a key focus for bringing in input from end-users, user management, and the business community in general.

Adviser User: The adviser user provides advice to the ambassador user on the business requirements.

Team Leader: The team leader runs the team on a day-to-day basis and ensures the part of the solution for which the team is responsible is delivered as agreed.

The above-mentioned roles are presented as a minimum "key set." However, almost all developments have particular problems that require the project manager to recruit specialist staff to fulfill specialist roles. Additional staff may, for example, fulfill the following roles, which may also be provided by the component team as described in section 14.5.2.

Reuse Identifier: The reuse identifier monitors development in order to identify potentially reusable services and conversely to identify opportunities to reuse existing services.

Testing Specialist: This role requires an expert on testing tools and techniques; provides independent advice on testing strategy, planning, and practice.

Human Factors Specialist: This role advises on design and ergonomics of the user interface. The role may also provide specific expertise, such as graphic design skills for Web pages.

Business Consultant: This role advises on specific business policy and procedures in specialist areas; for example, compliance or legal issues.

14.5.2 Component Team Roles

The component team roles are as follows:

Component team roles follow...

Reuse Manager: The reuse manager plans and controls the activities of the component team, makes policy decisions concerning reuse, and monitors component projects.

Reuse Librarian: The reuse librarian has a combination of administration and technical skills. The role controls the generic models and repository and also publicizes capabilities of the generic models and repository. It is responsible for checking in and checking out model items or components. Component management tools as described in Allen and Frost (1996) are used to assist.

Reuse Assessor: The reuse assessor has good working knowledge of existing systems, packages, databases, generic models, and available components. This knowledge is used to assess reuse opportunities (for example, legacy systems and local models) and to evaluate reuse requirements. The role identifies areas for reuse improvement and pollinates reuse across solution projects.

Reuse Architect: The reuse architect has overall vision, carries out architectural scoping, identifies and acquires reusable components, and carries out architectural modeling. The role promotes the value of reuse, acting as a "reuse promoter."

Component Developer: This role codes and tests components and calls for highly developed program-design skills.

The component team supports the entire component process and can also make a call on solution team roles, in particular the user roles, as described in section 14.5.1. There are two modes of working. First, the team works at the

There are two modes of working for component projects.

ongoing level: It is responsible for scoping and maintaining an architecture to provide a corporate context for reuse and for continuous assessment of reuse opportunities through communication with local and component projects. Second, the component team members work to upgrade existing components or deliver new components in incremental fashion.

Component team roles are increasingly important.

Whether a separate component team physically exists and the numbers of individuals comprising the team depends on the size of the organization. However, at the very least a single individual should be responsible for each of the component team roles.

14.5.3 Technical Infrastructure Team Roles

Technical infrastructure roles follow...

The technical infrastructure team roles areas follow:

Technical Facilitator: The technical facilitator works with the solution and component teams to ensure that the technical architecture is correct and consistent with standards. The role also controls and directs the technical infrastructure team.

Network Expert: The network expert has a good working knowledge of object request broker software and has the networking and PC skills to ensure that the network runs smoothly. The role also provides advice on interoperability issues including legacy wrapping.

Web Expert: The Web expert has a specific knowledge of Internet and intranet software. The role is responsible for operational control of a Web site and also provides advice on related issues, such as sizing, performance, and security.

Capacity and Performance Manager: The capacity and performance manager ensures that the network capacity and performance are adequate to meet enterprise needs.

The technical infrastructure team maintains the communications infrastructure.

This team ensures that solution and component teams have the necessary technical infrastructure to meet their needs. Again, whether a separate technical infrastructure team physically exists and the number of individuals comprising that team depends on the size of the organization. However, at the very least a single individual should be responsible for each of the technical infrastructure team roles.

14.6 Dynamics of Solution and Component Projects

The positive team attributes discussed earlier are particularly relevant in encouraging interplay between solution and component projects. This is very important in cross-fertilizing good practice across solution projects and in pollinating reuse from component projects, as illustrated in Figure 14.3. Solution teams should ask key questions at the right points in the process as they seek to harvest reuse, as illustrated in Figure 14.3. For example, at feasibility stage, " Have we solved this problem before?"; at analysis stage, "Can existing models be used to solve the problem?"; at design and build stage, " Can existing software components be used to solve the problem?" This requires open discussion with the component team, which in turn will bring its own set of questions to the table in its mission to sow reuse.

A certain dynamic between solution and component projects is needed.

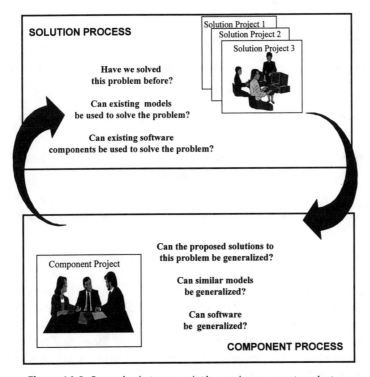

Figure 14.3. Dynamics between solution and component projects.

14.7 Examples of Team Configurations

Let's look at some typical examples of team roles.

Up until now we have focused on the mapping of Perspective roles to teams in the abstract, without specifically considering the effect of the type of work each team may be required to perform. Tables 14.2 and 14.3 provide a number of sample configurations that may be applicable to a six-person team. Table 14.2 describes three possible configurations for a six-person solution project team and Table 14.3 provides the same for a six-person component project team. The team configurations are detailed after the Tables.

Table 14.2. Examples of Solution Project Configurations		
Solution Project Teams		
Configuration 1	**Configuration 2**	**Configuration 3**
senior developer and team leader	ambassador user and team leader	senior developer and team leader
developer	adviser user	ambassador user
developer	adviser user	developer
developer and reuse identifier	senior developer	developer
ambassador user	developer and reuse identifier	human factors expert
adviser user	developer	business consultant

The above team configurations can be interpreted as follows:

• **Configuration 1.** This represents a team that is driven by members of the IT department. A full-time member of the business community fulfills the ambassador user role. A part-time adviser user provides additional business input to ensure that the ambassador user does not forget any of the business drivers. A reuse identifier role is included because the reuse potential of the project is high.

• **Configuration 2.** This represents a team that is more driven by the business community than the first configuration. The project is responsible for developing flexible and highly visible user services with maximum reuse of business and data services from existing components. A reuse identifier role is included because the need to harvest reuse is high. The team is heavily weighted toward the business community with the team leader having business knowledge and with the use of two adviser users.

- **Configuration 3.** This represents a team that requires a number of specialist skills in order to fulfill its goals.

Table 14.3. Examples of Component Project Configurations

Component Project Teams

Configuration 1	Configuration 2	Configuration 3
reuse manager and team leader	reuse architect and team leader	reuse manager and team leader
component developer	component developer	senior developer
developer	reuse librarian	business consultant
object wrapper	reuse assessor	reuse architect
reuse librarian	ambassador user	reuse assessor
reuse assessor	adviser user	ambassador user

The above team configurations can be interpreted as follows:

- **Configuration 1.** This represents a team that is required to wrap legacy systems in order to make their functionality available to a number of new component-based solution projects. The user-based roles are being fulfilled by the reuse assessor and reuse librarian, acting as brokers between the component team and the solution teams, who wish to use the services of the wrapped legacy systems.

- **Configuration 2.** This represents a team that is producing a number of business and data services that will be visible at the user interface; a user-value component project (see section 13.2.1). The project is driven by generic business requirements. This requires reuse architect and reuse assessor roles. Given the visibility and importance to the end-user, the roles of ambassador user and adviser user have been included in the team.

- **Configuration 3.** This represents a team that is performing generic architecture modeling. This involves the tasks of architectural scoping and assessment described in chapter 11. The roles of reuse architect and reuse assessor are therefore included. Given the importance of alignment with strategic business requirements ambassador user and business consultant roles are included.

Further roles may be needed in larger projects.

The introduction of additional management structure, as shown in Figure 14.2, may require that additional roles, or additional types of teams, be created. For example, if a number of component project teams exist then a reuse manager team role will be required in order to manage the overall reuse strategy for an enterprise. In addition, a project director role may be required for a number of project managers.

14.8 Summary

Certain critical success factors apply.

Teams should possess the right attributes: Teams should be self-managed, empowered, compact, collaborative, business aware, literate, and comfortable. Second, teams should communicate well: Traditional interviewing and meetings have their place, but interactive and dynamic communication techniques such as JAD greatly assist the process.

There are two types of teams: solution teams and component teams.

Solution teams work on projects whose mission is delivery of software solutions to agreed project objectives. Component teams also work on projects, but also have longer term architectural goals. The different types of teams have roles, which can be mixed and matched to suit your own needs. The team types are ideals: In reality a team may well exhibit a mix of characteristics, as we saw in the examples in section 14.7.

Positive interplay needs to be encouraged.

A certain dynamic between solution and component projects is needed to cross-fertilize good practice across solution projects and to pollinate reuse from component projects. Solution teams should ask key questions at the right points in the process as they seek to harvest reuse. This requires open discussion with the component team, which in turn will bring their own set of questions to the table in their mission to sow reuse.

CHAPTER 15

• •

Case Study: VWX Software Inc.

15.1 Introduction

In this chapter we illustrate the use of Perspective modeling concepts in an enterprise setting. Of course it is not possible to illustrate the entire process within these few pages but we do aim to give an overall feel for the use of Perspective. Elements of both solution and component processes are illustrated. Certain areas, including those most frequently misunderstood on real projects, are treated in some depth. Other areas are skimmed over; these are the areas that, are better understood in our experience and that are not particularly illustrative of the modeling problems encountered on real projects. Modeling illustrations are maximized. Narrative commentary is minimized.

15.2 Business Process Modeling

VWX Software Inc. specializes in supplying visual modeling tools and training to the software engineering marketplace. A brief business strategy has identified a need to take a more customer-based approach both in bringing its products to market and in working with its customers to help them achieve their goals. First, there is a need to address the growing demand for consultancy services in the use of its products. Second, it has long been recognized that there are many inefficiencies in the current processes that often result in loss of business.

Charles Vawex, the CEO of VWX, wants demonstrable results quickly. He understands that the software industry is moving toward component-based development. Object-oriented wrappers have already been prepared for the company's aging but indispensable Payments and Stock systems. Developers have also built an object-oriented GUI onto the customer database.

This situation has been fine for well-established infrastructure operations. However, the CEO also recognizes that any technical solution is only as good as the understanding of the business problem the solution is designed to address. And, as we are about to see, currently VWX's business processes are in something of a mess! Streamlining the existing processes is therefore a key priority. VWX Software Inc. anticipates a need to both partially reengineer and to improve its business processes. Charles Vawex is mindful of a business study carried out 3 years ago that took lots of time and money, but actually had to be abandoned through lack of results. So we need to take a pragmatic approach to modeling business processes quickly as a basis for building effective component-based solutions.

15.2.1 Scoping and Current Process Analysis

The first step is to gain an overall understanding of the existing business processes, to scope the areas to be addressed, and to understand those areas in more detail. A brief study reveals a hierarchy of processes organized along departmental lines as shown in Figure 15.1. Documentation of the top-level processes turns out to be shelf-ware. Apparently the team of consultants came in 3 years ago, spent months talking to management and producing the documentation, but then the budget ran out. The reality is that the top-level processes are carried out in a reactive and ad hoc fashion.

Rather than try to analyze the whole business in detail, which was one of the mistakes previously made, we take a closer look at Supply Training, which turns out to be a priority area. In particular, the supply of public courses is giving lots of cause for concern so we need to explore this area in more detail using process thread diagrams. Processes within our scope are highlighted on the "As-Is" process hierarchy diagram.

15.2.2 Issues Analysis

We first notice that there actually is no process as such for Schedule Public Courses. This is done on a "gut-feel" basis by the Training Manager. Deliver

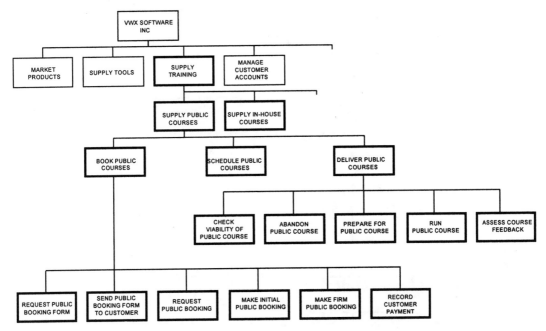

Figure 15.1. "As-Is" process hierarchy diagram: VWX Software Inc.

Public Courses and Book Public Courses are better understood and we produce "As-Is" process thread diagrams for them, as shown in Figure 15.2 and Figure 15.3, respectively. We also take a look at Supply In-house Courses but exclude the results for reasons of scope.

Having analyzed the processes within our scope we can now start to document some of the issues:

1. Booking process is too convoluted and takes too long.

2. Scheduling of courses is ad hoc and needs greater support in assessing best times to run courses according to seasonal demands and historical factors, as well as getting the most suitable and available consultant.

3. Difficulties in responding effectively to changes in course schedule, such as switch of consultant or problems with venue.

4. Manual raising of requisitions for courseware and reservation of equipment is subject to error and neglect causing "double booking" of classrooms and incorrect and/or late delivery of course materials for scheduled courses.

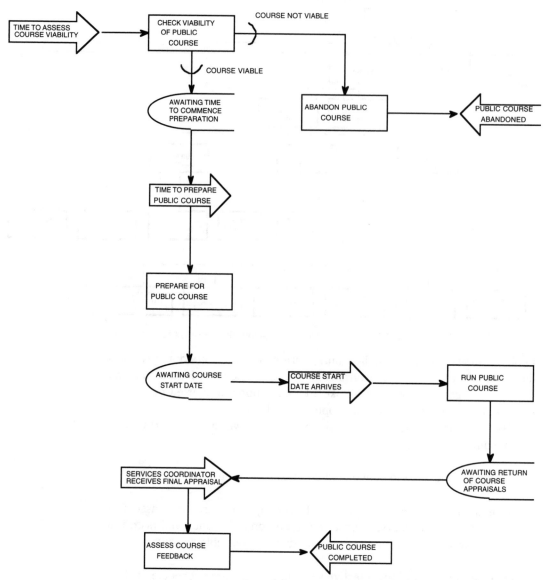

Figure 15.2. "As-Is" process thread diagram Deliver Public Courses.

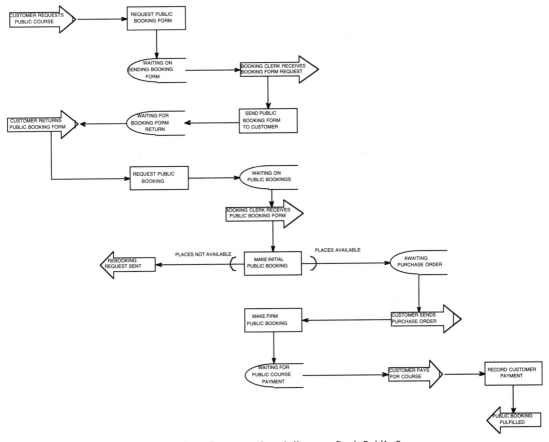

Figure 15.3. "As-Is" process thread diagram: Book Public Courses.

5. Manual checking of course viability is error prone, resulting in running of courses that have too few attendees to justify cost. Attempts to rectify this have resulted in courses being abandoned very late, causing annoyance to customers.

6. No control over the design of new courses, which are not produced according to market needs but more on the basis of "good ideas."

On a typical project there would be many more, but we have enough for our current purposes.

15.2.3 Solution Outline

The solution should address fundamental changes, such as the move to a service-based approach including consultancy, as illustrated in the "To-Be" hierarchy diagrams shown in Figures 15.4 through 15.8. At a more detailed level the solution should address the issues identified in the previous section.

We address each of the issues in turn in identifying the need for "To-Be" processes and modeling on a "To-Be" process hierarchy diagram:

1. The process is still "Book Public Courses." We can use a "To-Be" process thread diagram to streamline the internals.

2. A Plan Public Courses process is introduced to address the scheduling issue.

3. Exception processing needs proper management: Manage Course Exceptions is introduced.

4. Plan Public Courses needs to include a scheduling process that automates requisitioning.

5. The process is still "Deliver Public Courses." We can use a "To-Be" process thread diagram to address viability checking.

6. A Design Courses process is introduced to address the need for well-conceived courses.

Note Abandon Public Course and Reallocate Public Course are not worth modeling on process threads as they sit independently in single response to exceptional events such as "VWX invaded by contagious virus" or "Consultant notifies absence through illness." The reason we have chosen to show them on the diagram is that it is important to highlight processes that deal with key business exceptions.

Indirect processes are not shown on the diagram but are cataloged for reference and reuse by other business processes. Examples include Stock Management, Service Provider Management, and Equipment Management.

15.2.4 Process Redesign

Process redesign (and design in the case of the new processes) involves first modeling process threads to the elementary business process level. To model all possible threads in their entirety would take a possibly infinite amount of

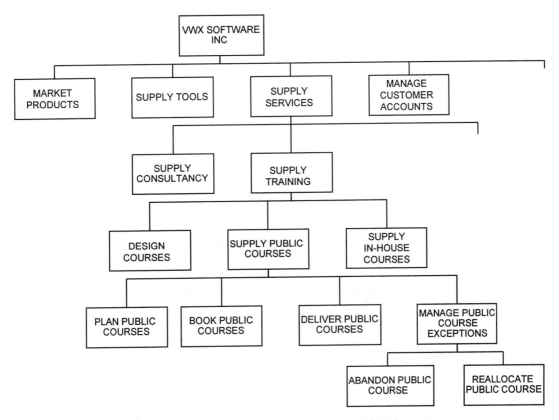

Figure 15.4. "To-Be" process hierarchy diagram: VWX Software Inc.

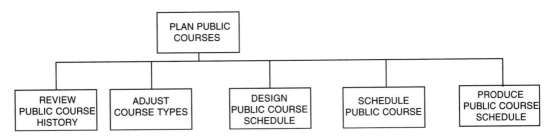

Figure 15.5 . "To-Be" process hierarchy diagram: Plan Public Courses.

time and add little value. We therefore concentrate on the threads representing the major paths through the process and also on the more important exceptions (see Figures 15.9–15.12).

Each EBP is described in terms of the responsible business actor and the series of steps needed to accomplish it. We try to keep the EBPs as technically neutral as possible but when it is clear whether a step is to be manual or

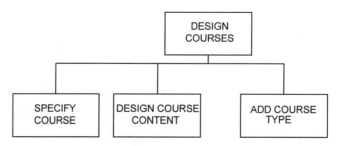

Figure 15.6. "To-Be" process hierarchy diagram: Design Courses.

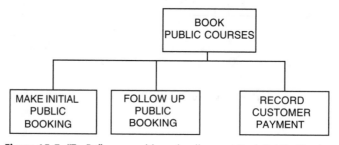

Figure 15.7. "To-Be" process hierarchy diagram: Book Public Courses.

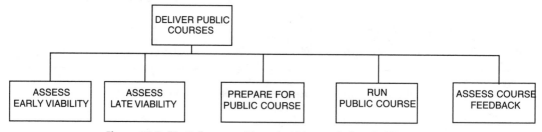

Figure 15.8. "To-Be" process hierarchy diagram: Deliver Public Courses.

automated then this can be indicated. Otherwise we can leave the decision open at this stage. Some of these EBPs, like Prepare for Public Course and Design Course Content, are totally manual. Included in Table 15.1 are EBPs requiring at least some involvement of an automated system.

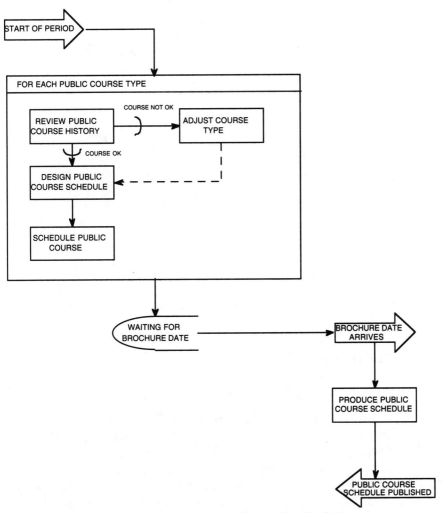

Figure 15.9. "To-Be" process thread diagram: Plan Public Courses.

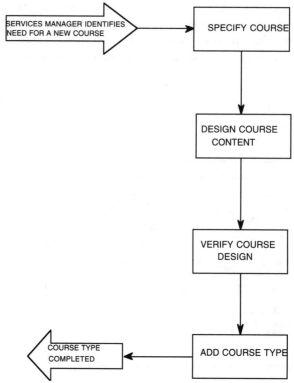

Figure 15.10. "To-Be" process thread diagram: Design Courses.

15.3. Feasibility Study

15.3.1 Scoping and Assessment

The EBPs identified within the scope of our "To-Be" BPM provide a business context for our project. First we establish the scope of the project in relation to overall system architecture. We sketch out proposed service packages and identify constraints affecting our system boundary, represented by the Course-Booking service package. This is particularly important for maximizing reuse and is carried out in consultation with the reuse architect. Our experience indicates that because this is a "technical" activity it is often left until design time. This is usually a mistake as it can turn earlier assumptions upside-down. Therefore we do it now, no matter how tentatively; it can be revised as our understanding develops. The package diagram shown in Figure 15.13 indi-

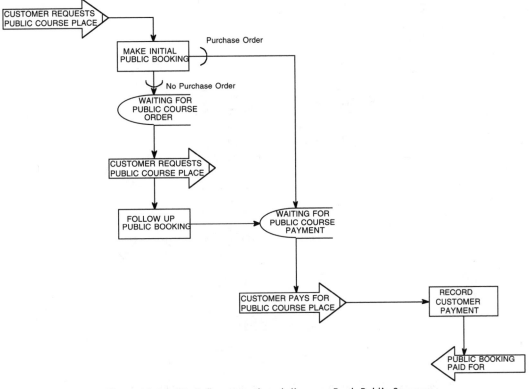

Figure 15.11. "To-Be" process thread diagram: Book Public Courses.

cates that Course-Booking uses services provided by four service packages: Payments, Stock, Client, and Service Provider.

Payments: Payments is a group of business service components that have been designed to provide an object-oriented wrapper onto legacy accounts systems, written in COBOL. We anticipate using invoicing business services in order to bill customers for public course bookings.

Stock: Stock is a group of user service and business service components that have been designed to provide an object-oriented wrapper onto a stock control package, which has an exposed objects repository. We anticipate requisitioning user services and business services to order course materials.

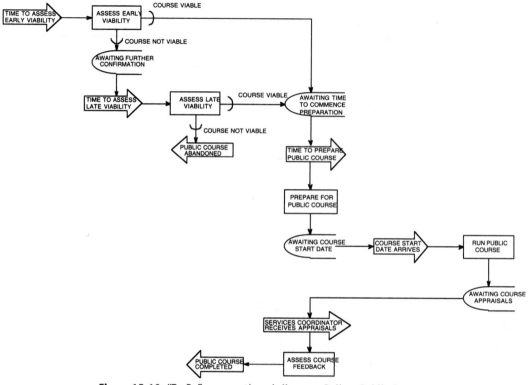

Figure 15.12. "To-Be" process thread diagram: Deliver Public Courses.

Client: Client is a group of components that have been built to provide a range of services using a GUI interface onto the existing Client RDBMS. Visual Basic Forms provide searching and maintenance services as illustrated in Figure 15.14. We anticipate using these services in order to support the booking process.

Service Provider: Service Provider is a group of new components that are being developed to provide consultant resourcing and skills-development services. This is part of a separate component project. We anticipate using these services in scheduling public courses (in order to identify and allocate consultants). The reuse team obviously needs to keep a close eye on coordination of activities between our team and the team developing Service Provider components.

Table 15.1. EBP–Business Actor Mapping	
EBP	**Business Actor**
Add Course Type	Services Manager
Adjust Course Type	Services Manager
Review Public Course History	Services Manager
Design Public Course Schedule	Services Manager
Schedule Public Course	Services Manager
Reallocate Public Course	Services Coordinator
Abandon Public Course	Services Manager
Produce Public Course Schedule	Service Coordinator
Make Initial Public Booking	Booking Clerk
Follow up Public Booking	Booking Clerk
Record Customer Payment	Booking Clerk
Assess Early Viability	Service Coordinator
Assess Late Viability	Service Coordinator
Assess Course Feedback	Services Coordinator

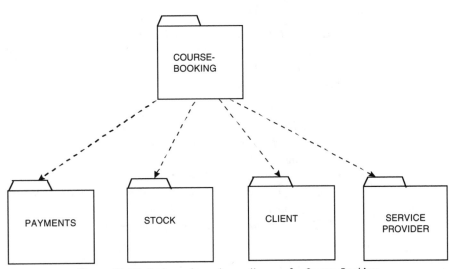

Figure 15.13. Package dependency diagram for Course-Booking.

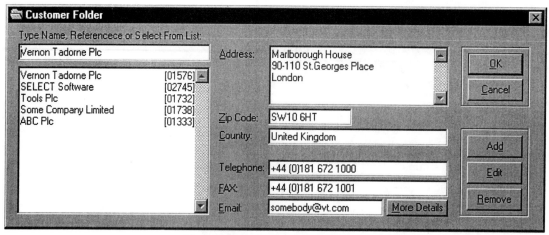

Figure 15.14. Customer folder form.

15.3.2 Nonfunctional Requirements:

We note the key constraints, which are as follows. Course-Booking is to use Visual Basic for user services, C++ for business services, and existing ORACLE databases for data services. An existing Customer-Booking relational database is to be used to provide data storage. It is anticipated that this database will need to be extended and improved to deal with new storage requirements that are likely to emerge from this project.

15.3.3 Statement of Purpose

The purpose of the Course-Booking System is to enable effective support for the basic design of all types of course and for streamlining the planning and delivery cycle of public courses. The system must provide the following facilities:

- *recording the design details for all types of course,*
- *planning and scheduling of public courses, including automatic requisition of materials and reservation of venue,*
- *booking of public courses,*
- *reallocation and abandonment of public courses,*
- *maintenance of all course-type requirements and scheduled public course details,*
- *ad hoc reporting and inquiries for the above.*

The system needs to be flexible enough for future extension to other types
of training requirements, including in-house courses.
BPM Reference: Supply Public Courses, Design Courses.
Exclusions: Record Customer Payment, Supply In-house Courses.

15.3.4 Actors

To identify actors we begin by considering each business actor in relation to
the envisaged system boundary. Notice in the example detailed in Table 15.2
that the business actors correspond to system actors. This need not always
be the case. For example, if bookings took place in different ways depending
on whether a sales agent took the booking using a laptop on client site or a
booking administrator at head office using a desktop, the single business actor
"booking clerk" could correspond to two different system actors, "sales
agent" and "booking administrator." System actors are listed as in Table 15.2.

Table 15.2. Actor Catalog

Actor	Description
Services Manager	Overall responsibility for course planning and design, according to corporate strategy, and for key operational decisions, such as whether to abandon a public course.
Service Coordinator	Responsible for maintaining and monitoring scheduled courses, including viability of scheduled courses and dealing with emergencies such as reallocation of consultants. Also accountable for day-to-day booking of both in-house and public courses.
Booking Clerk	Responsible for day-to-day booking of public courses.

15.3.5 Use Cases

Each EBP description is examined for required user–system interaction using
the use case criteria explained in chapter 4. The use case must be a *self-con-*
tained unit performed by a *single actor in a single place*, achieve some *business*
capability, and leave the system in a *stable state*. Most of our EBPs correspond
to single use cases, as shown in Table 15.3

Table 15.3. EBP–Use Case Mapping

EBP	Use Case	System Actor	System Event(s)
Add Course Type Adjust Course Type	Maintain Course Types	Services Manager	Services Manager submits new course type. Services Manager submits course-type adjustment.
Design Public Course Schedule Add Scheduled Public Course	Schedule Public Course	Services Manager	Services Manager requests to schedule public course.
Reallocate Public Course	Reallocate Public Course	Service Coordinator	Service Coordinator notified of public course problem.
Example: Assess Course Feedback.	Maintain Course and Venues	Service Coordinator	Example: Service Coordinator assesses course appraisals.
Abandon Public Course	Abandon Public Course	Services Manager	Services Manager decides it is not possible to run public course.
Make Initial Public Booking	Make Public Booking	Booking Clerk	Booking Clerk submits new public booking.
Follow Up Public Booking	Follow Up Public Booking	Booking Clerk	Booking Clerk submits follow up public booking.
Assess Early Viability of Public Course	Assess Early Viability of Public Course	System Output to Service Coordinator	Time: Daily.
Assess Late Viability of Public Course	Assess Late Viability of Public Course	System Output to Service Coordinator	Time: Daily.
Examples: Review Public Course History, Produce Public Course Schedule	Produce Public Course Reports	System Output to Service Coordinator	Ad Hoc and Time: Example Brochure date arrives.

Exceptions to this are as follows. Add Course Type and Adjust Course Type are different ways of applying the same maintenance activity. Use cases must add value to our modeling. If we do not apply some restrictions it is easy to end up with hundreds of separate maintenance use cases, all of which share the same basic simple structure. It also makes sense to combine Design Public Course Schedule and Add Scheduled Public Course because in practical system use the two processes work in synergy: The Service Manager needs the ability to be able to schedule the course *immediately* having determined when to run it. This is not to say that the schedule can be designed in its entirety before doing the scheduling; we can still construct the use case to allow that.

Finally there are certain use cases (for example, Maintain Courses and Venues and Produce Public Course Reports), which correspond to single EBPs (for example, Assess Course Feedback and Produce Public Course Schedule) but that are usable more generically. These are usually maintenance or reporting use cases. In such cases the EBP and triggering system event are usefully annotated to show these are examples among many potential ones.

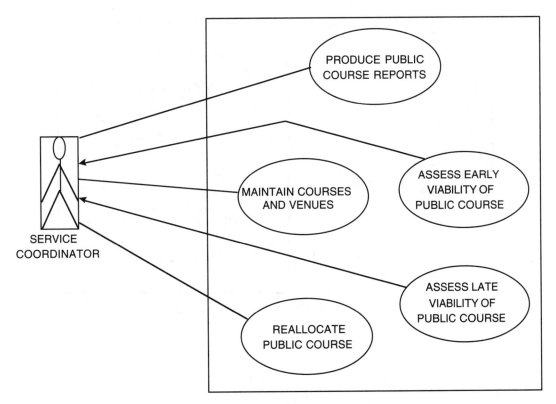

Figure 15.15. Service Coordinator use case diagram.

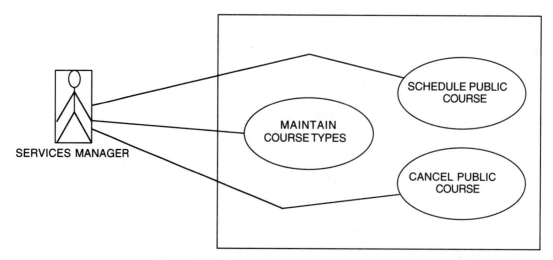

Figure 15.16. Service Manager use case diagram.

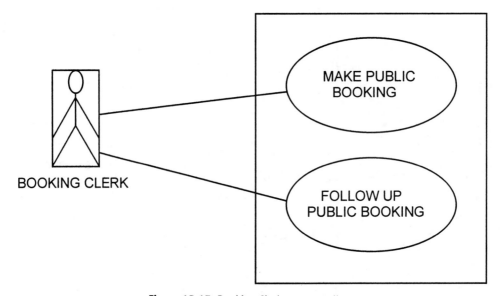

Figure 15.17. Booking Clerk use case diagram.

Use case diagrams as shown in Figures 15.15 through 15.17 are also use-ful as part of the use case identification process. Note how the diagrams are organized around responsible actors.

On a previous project someone had read what a good idea use cases were and the team spent 6 months creating a complex 300-page use case document that the users could not even begin to understand. We therefore provide a *simple* description of each use case. The users actually put these together with a little help from ourselves at a JAD session. At this stage we need to ensure the intent of each use case is clearly described and agreed on. The use case descriptions need to be as simple as possible to avoid getting bogged down in detail, which is always a danger with this technique early in a project. We elab-orate the conversational details of the use cases in analysis.

Use Case Name	**Maintain Course Types**
Use Case Intent	To record a new course type with its requirements and changes in course type details, including skills, equipment, and courseware requirements.

Use Case Description

For new course types: Establish required skills, courseware, and equip-ment from system-produced lists, confirm course type details and requirements.

For existing course type: Make any required course type detail changes, make any required changes/additions/removals to skill, equipment, or courseware requirements.

Use Case Name	**Schedule Public Course**
Use Case Intent	To verify feasibility of running a public course, to schedule a suitable consultant, reserve a classroom, and requisition required equipment and courseware

Use Case Description

Establish required course type and start dates using system search facilities. Identify venue and available consultants qualified to teach this course type from system-produced lists. Submit the scheduled public course details. The system reserves selected venue, books consultant, reserves equipment, and requisitions courseware.

Use Case Name	Reallocate Public Course
Use Case Intent	To record changes in scheduled public course allocation of consultant and venue.

Use Case Description

Establish required scheduled public course. For change of venue identify venue from system-produced list: System reserves selected classroom and removes reservation of the previously selected classroom. For change of consultant identify available consultant qualified to teach this course type from system-produced list: System schedules selected new consultant and removes course from the schedule of any previously scheduled consultant.

Use Case Name	Maintain Courses and Venues
Use Case Intent	To maintain venue name and capacity, course rating, and number attended.

Use Case Description

Enter course or venue changes. Venues may be added, modified, or deleted. Courses may be modified or deleted. (Note: Schedule Public Course adds courses.)

Use Case Name	Abandon Public Course
Use Case Intent	To record abandonment of scheduled public course including cancellation of all resources.

Use Case Description

Establish required scheduled public course and check booking details. Confirm the abandonment: System cancels reservation of classroom, cancels course from the schedule of scheduled consultant, cancels reservations of equipment and requisitions of materials; system also cancels bookings and sends letters of apology to the customers with bookings.

Use Case Name	**Make Public Booking**
Use Case Intent	To verify and record initial public bookings.
Use Case Description	

Establish customer details using system search/add facilities. Identify required scheduled public course using system search facilities. Enter booking details, including delegates (if known): System records booking.

Use Case Name	**Follow Up Public Booking**
Use Case Intent	To verify and record follow-ups to public bookings, including removals.
Use Case Description	

Establish booking details using booking id. Where booking id not available: Identify customer using system search and identify required scheduled public course using system search facilities. Select booking from system-provided list of existing bookings for customer for selected course. Where booking to be changed enter booking detail changes. Where booking to be removed enter "remove" request.

Use Case Name	**Assess Early Viability of Public Course**
Use Case Intent	To provide advance indication of whether there are sufficient numbers to justify running a public course.
Use Case Description	

The system assesses bookings for each scheduled public course due in 14 days. Where number of firm bookings is > or = minimum required number of places, letters of confirmation are sent to customers with firm bookings, and invoices raised. A summary report is produced.

Use Case Name	Assess Late Viability of Public Course
Use Case Intent	To provide a final decision on whether there are sufficient numbers to justify running a public course.

Use Case Description

The system assesses bookings for each scheduled public course due in 7 days. Where number of firm bookings is > or = minimum required number of places, letters of confirmation are sent to customers with firm bookings, and invoices raised. Otherwise the course is canceled, letters of apology are sent to customers with firm bookings, and any invoices previously raised for confirmed bookings are canceled. A summary report is produced.

Use Case Name	Produce Public Course Reports
Use Case Intent	To produce flexible reports ranging from individual public course bookings to full public course schedule report.

Use Case Description

Example reports include bookings by course code and public courses by course type.

Selection criteria include date range, public course status.

Options include: Sort sequence; screen or hard copy, summary or full details.

15.3.6 High-Level Business Classes

We sketch out an initial class diagram based on the architectural context and the use cases. This is based on a scan through of the use case descriptions for candidate objects and associations. Notice that we are deliberately staying out of detail here; no attributes, operations, or association multiplicities have been included. The objective is to sketch out the structural scope of the system, represented by the Course-Booking service package, just as we sketched out the

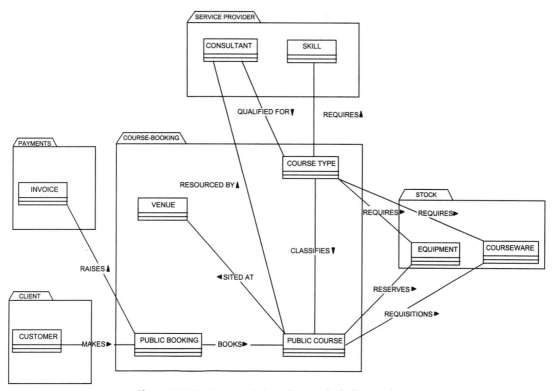

Figure 15.18. High-level class diagram including packages.

behavioral scope with use case diagrams. We use the high-level diagram (see Figure 15.18) to help drive the analysis and develop the detailed view of classes, for our system, as our understanding deepens.

15.3.7 Candidate Reusable Services

Finally we make a stab at identifying possible areas of reuse. We run through the use cases and pick out likely services, which are as follows. This information can be added to the use case catalog and used in the analysis phase.

Maintain Course Types:
- Search for Courseware.
- Search for Equipment.
- Search for Skills.

Schedule Public Course:
• Search for Capable Consultants.
• Book Consultant.
• Reserve Equipment.
• Requisition Materials.

Reallocate Public Course:
• Rebook Consultants.

Abandon Public Course:
• Cancel Consultant Booking.
• Cancel Equipment Reservation.
• Cancel Materials Requisition.

Make Public Booking:
• Search for Customer.
• Add Customer.

Assess Early/Late Viability of Public Course:
• Raise Invoice.

Assess Late Viability of Public Course:
• Cancel Invoice.

15.4 Analysis

15.4.1 Class Model

Let's start by looking at the class model for Course-Booking in a little more detail. The maintenance use cases are a good place to start because although usually uninteresting from a system-behavior viewpoint, such use cases reveal a lot about required attributes and static structure. We do not describe the maintenance use cases in detail because that would add little value to the modeling. Instead we focus mainly on the attributes required and ask questions about them.

Maintain Course Types records a new course type with its requirements and changes in course type details, including skills, equipment, and course-ware requirements. Course Type has a number of attributes, which emerge from this use case, shown in the class diagram shown in Figure 15.19. In looking at the requirements in more detail we find that it is important to record the date the requirement becomes effective. Different skills have different weightings for different course types. There are different numbers of equipment items and courseware materials that are ordered by default for different types of course. There are several ways of modeling this situation. One way would be to introduce separate association classes between Course Type and Skill/Courseware/Equipment. Although technically correct, this leaves very little flexibility for other possible future types of course requirement, and also introduces some complex static dependencies to external classes.

Perspective encourages us to look for reuse rather than get bogged down in modeling detail. Using VWX's component management tool we find that the following business services are available.

From the Stock service package:
• Search for Courseware.
• Search for Equipment.

From the Service Provider service package:
• Search for Skills.

We therefore choose to introduce a Course Requirement class and subclass, on the basis of Hard or Soft requirements, to Skill Requirement and Material Requirement. Skill code and Stock Id provide the required parameters used in invoking the appropriate services.

Analysis of maintenance use cases always reveals lots of Get/Add/Modify/Remove operations on host classes, which we choose not to show in the interests of clarity. However, responsibility for the course requirements is allocated to the Course Type class as the natural point of ownership; Add Req, Modify Req, and Remove Req are therefore shown.

A closer look at Maintain Courses and Venues results in the attributes Venue Name and Capacity being allocated to Venue. Course Rating and Number Attended look initially like attributes of Public Course. Our statement of purpose states that our system needs to be flexible enough to cater to other types of training requirement. It therefore makes sense to prepare a class structure that will stand us in good stead for dealing with in-house courses. A Course is added to generalize common features of courses and provide flexibility for dealing with all potential types of scheduled courses. In JAD sessions with our users there are in fact several attributes, unique to In-House Courses, that emerge as shown in Figure 15.19. We also find that course rating and number attended are to be recorded on completion of both in-house and public courses.

The JAD sessions also reveal that public courses have a unique life cycle, which we address using a state diagram in the next section (hence the status attribute), and that it is important to track available places on a public course.

15.4.2 Initial State Model

Now we sketch out some initial state diagrams (see Figure 15.20). In the previous section we noted that Public Course has a definite life cycle that it goes through in the build up from initial scheduling to final completion. JAD sessions reveal that a public course is initially set up in a scheduled state from

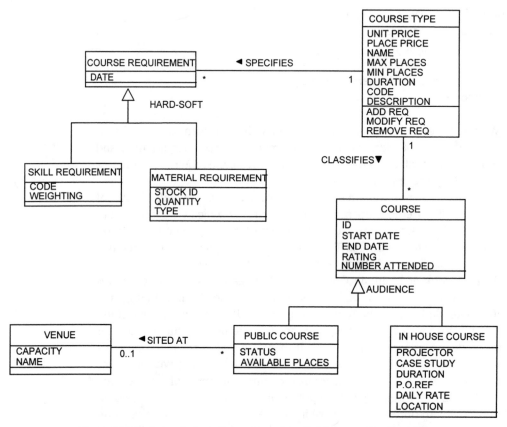

Figure 15.19. First-cut class diagram based on Maintenance Requirements.

which it is possible to cancel or delete altogether. Once the Public Course has been deemed viable (either a week or 2 weeks before the course start date) it is not possible to cancel it; the company is committed to running the course.

Sketching out the state model in this way helps give a better focus to the use case analysis. In particular the states provide pre and postconditions for use cases and scenarios.

A state diagram for Public Booking (see Figure 15.21) illustrates the policy that though the company can cancel a booking regardless, a booking can

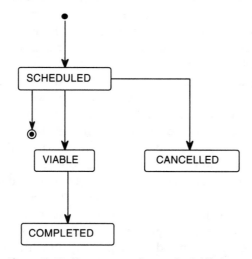

Figure 15.20. First-cut state diagram for Public Course.

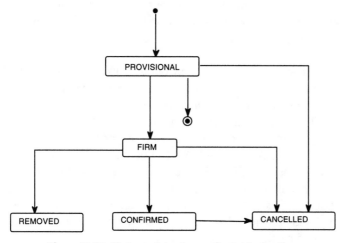

Figure 15.21. First-cut state diagram for Public Booking.

only be deleted by the client if it is still provisional. A firm booking canceled by the client goes into a Removed state; confirmed bookings cannot be canceled by the client. This allows penalties to be charged where appropriate.

15.4.3 Use Cases and Object Collaboration

We now run some JAD sessions with key users to detail the use cases to show human and system responsibilities. We use a slightly different format to that used earlier in the book, which separates the user and system responsibilities into separate columns. This helps address some of the ambiguity that is inherent in ordinary language descriptions by forcing clear separation of user and system responsibilities.

For convenience of presentation and readability we have presented each use case together with a sample (for brevity) of accompanying sequence diagrams and collaboration diagrams. Prototypes are shown separately in section 15.5. In fact this is how the models are likely to be presented in the documentation. However, the reader should bear in mind that this does not reflect the *process*.

Once we've done our first pass on the use cases, sequence diagrams and collaboration diagrams are used to explore object interaction required to fulfill the system responsibilities for each use case. The class model is refined, use cases adjusted, and prototypes developed to sharpen our understanding. Typically this requires several "passes" of the use cases. It is important to start simple and gradually introduce complexity. In particular we resist the temptation to begin prototyping too early. Prototyping can be used, in controlled conditions, as a pure requirements-capture technique. However, previous experience of using prototyping at VWX has resulted in some "clever" designs that were never in fact used because they were solutions to the wrong problems!

Let's start with Schedule Public Course. This use case is actually a single scenario, so a single collaboration diagram is sufficient for now: Adding a sequence diagram at this stage probably adds little value.

A collaboration diagram is constructed for the normal scenario and reveals the possibility to make extensive reuse of business services external to the project: Book Consultant, Reserve Equipment, Requisition Materials and List Capable Consultants (see Figure 15.22). We use the state models to help determine pre and postconditions. The precondition is valid Course Type and Venue exist. The postcondition is Public Course Status = Scheduled. Note how this corresponds to the Scheduled state shown in the state model for Public Course back in section 15.4.2.

Use Case Name	Schedule Public Course
Use Case Intent	To verify feasibility of running a public course, to schedule a suitable consultant, reserve a classroom, and requisition required equipment and courseware

Use Case Description

Establish required course type:	
Enter course type search request.	Show list of available course types.
Select course type.	Show details of selected course type.
Request scheduled public courses.	Show list of scheduled public courses for course type.
Assess potential start dates.	
For each start date, compile scheduled public course details:	
Enter start date.	Show list of available venues (names and capacities). Show list of available consultants qualified to teach this course type.
Select venue and consultant.	
Confirm course to be scheduled.	Record scheduled public course details and generate course id. Reserve selected venue. Book selected consultant. Reserve equipment. Requisition courseware. Show course id.

The operations, shown in Figure 15.22, are added to the class model (shown in Figure 15.18). A response-time requirement of under 5 seconds is documented for the use case. Finally a business rule and alternative courses are added as shown in the items that follow.

Use Case Feature	Feature Description
Nonfunctional Requirements	Response time less than 5 seconds.
Business Rules	Consultant may be unknown: schedule consultant is optional.
Alternative Courses	View public course schedule if required. Retry alternative date when consultant not available. Raise query report where no skilled consultant is available

Now we progress to the related use case, Reallocate Public Course.

Use Case Name	Reallocate Public Course
Use Case Intent	To record changes in scheduled public course allocation of consultant and venue.

Use Case Description	
Establish required scheduled public course: Enter course id.	Show scheduled public course details, including consultant and venue.
For consultant change: Enter consultant search request.	Show consultants, qualified to teach this course type, who are available on required date.
Select consultant from list of available qualified consultants.	
For venue change: Enter venue search request.	Show venues available on date.
Select venue from list of available venues.	
Confirm the changes: Enter confirmation	Schedule new consultant and removes course from schedule of any previously scheduled consultant. Reserve classroom and remove reservation of previously selected classroom.

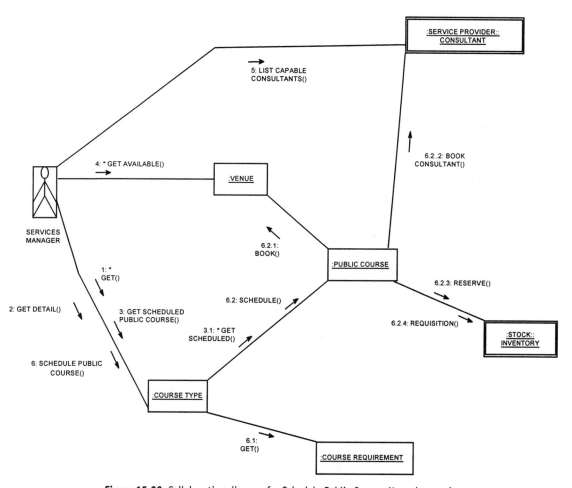

Figure 15.22. Collaboration diagram for Schedule Public Course: Normal scenario.

A sequence diagram is created as shown in Figure 15.23. Reuse is made of List Capable Consultants, Get Consultant, and Rebook Consultant business services from the Service Provider service package. The precondition is Public Course Status = Scheduled or Viable; this corresponds to the Scheduled and Viable states shown in the state model for Public Course back in section 15.4.2. There are no special postconditions. A collaboration diagram is created for the replacement of consultant scenario (see Figure 15.24); the same precondition applies. Note that two different service classes from the Service Provider package are used.

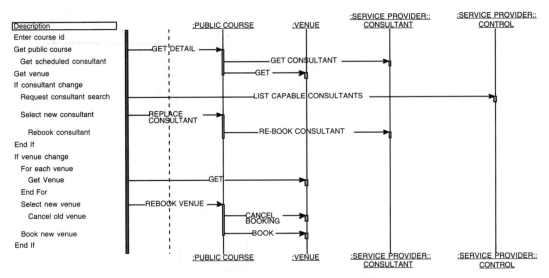

Figure 15.23. Sequence diagram for Reallocate Public Course.

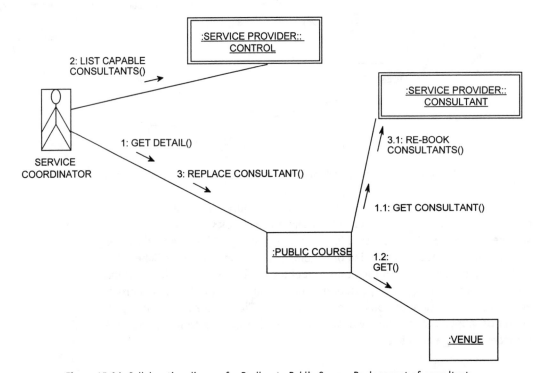

Figure 15.24. Collaboration diagram for Reallocate Public Course: Replacement of consultant.

Further details are added to the use case as follows:

Use Case Feature	Feature Description
Nonfunctional Requirements	Response time less than 5 seconds.
Business Rules	If course status = "completed" then cannot change consultant, venue, or public course detail.
Alternative Courses	Allow allocation of consultant/venue where no existing consultant/venue allocated.
	Allow selection of scheduled public course from list using course type search request.

Now let's consider Abandon Public Course.

Use Case Name	**Abandon Public Course**
Use Case Intent	To record abandonment of scheduled public course including cancellation of all resources.

Use Case Description	
Establish scheduled public course details: Enter course id. Request booking details	Show scheduled public course details. Show all existing bookings for course.
Verify and confirm the abandonment: Enter confirmation.	Cancel reservation of venue. Cancel course from the schedule of scheduled consultant. Cancel reservations of equipment. Cancel requisitions of materials. Cancel bookings and send letters of apology to the customers with bookings with status not = "canceled." Cancel any invoices previously raised for confirmed bookings.

Let's consider the main scenario, where there are no previous invoices to cancel, as shown in Figure 15.25. Again we use the state models to help determine pre-and postconditions. The precondition is Public Course Status = Scheduled, the postcondition is Public Course Status = Canceled. This shows reuse of further business services external to the project: Cancel Consultant Booking, Cancel Reservation, and Cancel Requisition.

From a first pass of the use cases we notice that both Abandon Public Course and Assess Late Viability involve cancellation of a course. We can model this as a uses relationship, as shown in Figure 15.26. Cancel Public Course is a candidate business service. The logic for Cancel Public Course business service is abstracted out for later detailing in its operation specification.

We use a sequence diagram to model the business service, as shown in Figure 15.27. The pre- and postconditions actually correspond to the ones described previously: The precondition is Public Course Status = Scheduled,

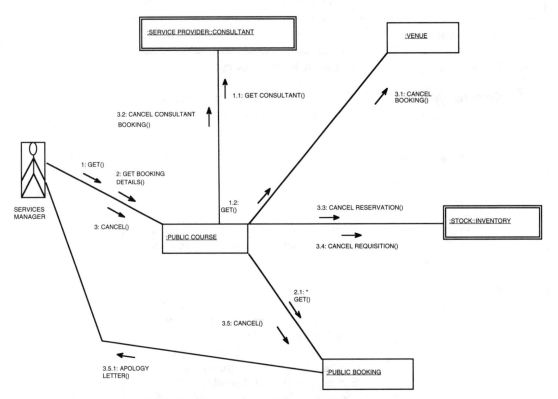

Figure 15.25. Collaboration diagram for Abandon Public Course: Normal scenario.

the postcondition is Public Course Status = Canceled. Public Booking recognizes the need for an apology and transmits the event "Apology Letter." Later we can add a Course Report user object to recognize the event and deal with producing the letter; this preserves the technical neutrality of the Public Course object, which simply transmits an event requesting the apology letter, without knowledge of its target.

The class model should reflect the details added during the use case and interaction modeling. For example, the Rebook Venue operation is allocated to Public Course, and Get Available, Book, and Cancel Booking operations allocated to Venue (see Figure 15.28).

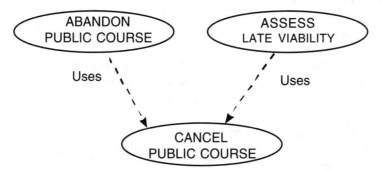

Figure 15.26. Cancel Public Course uses relationships.

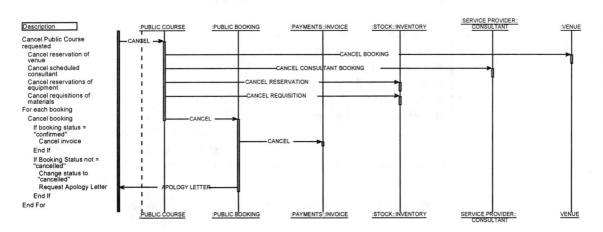

Figure 15.27. Sequence Diagram for Cancel Public Course.

Now we move on to the two booking use cases; first, Make Public Booking:

Use Case Name	**Make Public Booking**
Use Case Intent	To verify and record initial public bookings.
Use Case Description	
Establish customer using customer search:	
For an existing customer enter search key.	Match and show customer details.
For a new customer enter new details.	Record new customer details. Customer Ref and customer name are returned.
Establish booking requirement:	
Enter course type search request.	Show list of available course types.
Select course type.	Show details of selected course type.
Request scheduled public courses.	Show list of scheduled public courses for course type.
Set up the booking: Enter number of places required, delegate names (if present), and purchase order number (if present).	Calculate cost.
If cost is acceptable confirm booking.	Record booking and delegate details; generate and show booking date, cost, status and booking id.

We sketch out a collaboration diagram as shown in Figure 15.29.

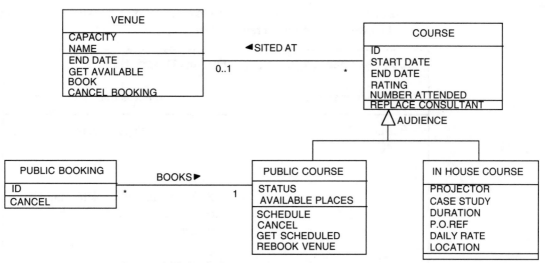

Figure 15.28. Partial class diagram reflecting the previous use cases (Schedule, Reallocate, and Abandon Public Course).

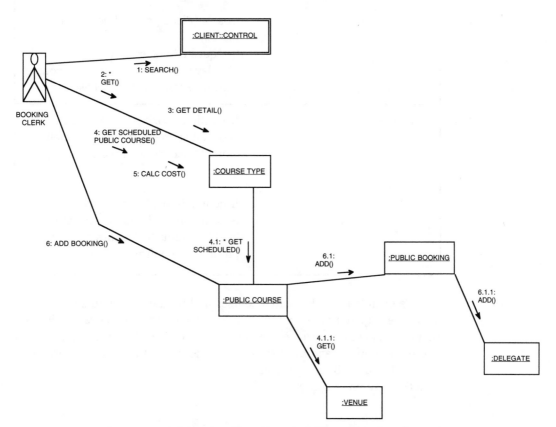

Figure 15.29. Collaboration diagram for Make Public Booking: Normal scenario.

Further details are added to the use case as follows. These are addressed later when we come to the increment design.

Use Case Feature	Feature Description
Nonfunctional Requirements	Response time less than 5 seconds.
Business Rules	Anonymous Delegates allowed. If P. O. present, the booking status = "firm," otherwise booking status = "provisional." Requested places < or = available places. Cost = (Place price x Requested places)- [(Requested places-1) x 20] If today's date within 6 days of course start date must have purchase order.
Alternative Courses	If existing booking found for customer, allow adjustment of booking details, amend/delete/insert required delegates. If course is viable and purchase order is newly entered, the system sets booking status to "confirmed" and produces a confirmation letter.

We examine the alternative courses and business rules to see how they affect the required object interaction, sketching out some collaboration and sequence diagrams (excluded here for brevity) on a whiteboard. Looking at the alternative courses and business rules we notice that these also apply to the Follow Up Public Booking use case, with which there is quite a bit of overlap. So let's move on to that one.

Use Case Name	Follow Up Public Booking
Use Case Intent	To verify and record follow-ups to public bookings, including removals.

Use Case Description	
Establish booking details. Enter booking id.	Find booking using booking id and show booking details.
Where booking id not known: Search for customer details.	Match and show customer details. Customer Ref and customer name are returned.
Enter course type search request. Select course type. Request scheduled public courses. Select required scheduled public course from list.	Show list of available course types. Show details of selected course type. Show list of scheduled public courses for course type. Find and show list of existing bookings for customer for selected scheduled public course. Show booking details.
Select booking from list.	
Where booking details to be changed: Enter changes to number of places, delegate names, and enter purchase-order number (if present). If cost is acceptable confirm booking.	Calculate cost. Record changes to booking and delegate details.
Where booking to be removed: Enter removal request.	Delete booking from system (if status is "provisional"). Mark booking "removed" (if status is "firm") and show warning to reconcile account.

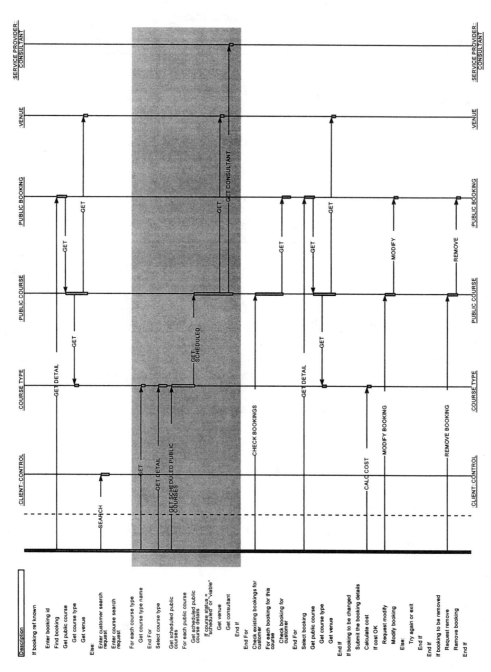

Description

If booking ref known
- Enter booking id
- Find booking
- Get public course
  - Get course type
  - Get venue
Else:
- Enter customer search request
- Enter course search request
- For each course type
  - Get course type name
- End For
- Select course type
- Get scheduled public courses
- For each public course
  - Get scheduled public course details
  - If course status = "scheduled" or "viable"
    - Get venue
    - Get consultant
  - End If
- End For
- Check existing bookings for customer
- For each booking for this course
  - Check booking for customer
- End For
- Select booking
- Get public course
  - Get course type
  - Get venue
- End If
- Submit the booking details
- Calculate cost
- If cost OK
  - Request modify
  - Modify booking
- Else:
  - Try again or exit
- End If
- End If
- If booking to be removed
  - Request remove
  - Remove booking
- End If

Figure 15.30. Sequence diagram for Follow Up Public Booking.

This time we'll start with a sequence diagram for the whole use case (see Figure 15.30). The precondition is Public Course = Scheduled or Viable and Public Booking = Provisional or Firm. Postconditions are not specified as these are much more variable depending on specific scenario; these depend on the state model as described in section 15.4.2.

This use case involves searching for courses (Course Type and Scheduled Course), which is highlighted in Figure 15.30. This requirement has already surfaced several times, in the make public booking, schedule, and reallocate public course use cases. We don't need to draw uses relationships to work this out! We simply note the need for a potential Search Courses service. A sequence diagram is used to model this, as shown in section 15.7.6; note how the invocations of the business objects remain intact.

Both Modify and Remove Booking are candidate business services that require further analysis. In Figure 15.31 we include the sequence diagram for the former.

We also draw a collaboration diagram for a scenario that brings out some different characteristics (see Figure 15.32). We try the scenario where the booking id is known and a delegate is added. The precondition is Public Course = Scheduled or Viable and Public Booking = Provisional or Firm. Postconditions are actually the same (adding a delegate does not affect the state of either object). The operations Modify Booking, Remove Booking, and Add Booking are added to the Public Course class (see Figure 15.33). Further details are added to the Class Model. A Delegate class is introduced. Finally,

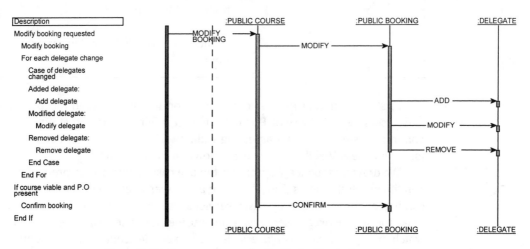

Figure 15.31. Sequence diagram for Modify Booking business service.

we address Assess Early Viability of Public Course and Assess Late Viability of Public Course.

Use-Case Name	**Assess Early Viability of Public Course**
Use Case Intent	To provide advance indication of whether there are sufficient numbers to justify running a public course.
Use Case Description	
	Assess bookings for each scheduled public course due in 14 days.
	Where number of firm bookings is > or =minimum required number of places: Set public course status to "viable." Send letters of confirmation to customers with firm bookings and raise invoices.
	Send reminder letters to customers with provisional bookings.
	Produce an Early Viability Summary Report.

First we note that there is much common ground between this use case and Assess Late Viability of Public Course: It is fairly obvious that both need common business rules for assessing viability. These can be abstracted out to form an Assess Viability service, as shown in Figure 15.34.

We draw a sequence diagram for the use case. There are no pre-and post-conditions. Both Assess Early Viability and Assess Late Viability are obvious candidates for modeling as user services (see Figure 15.35). Therefore we make the split between user service and business service now rather than later, which may be the case with a less clear-cut example. Course Report Control is introduced to supply the service and can also conveniently act as service class for other reporting user services.

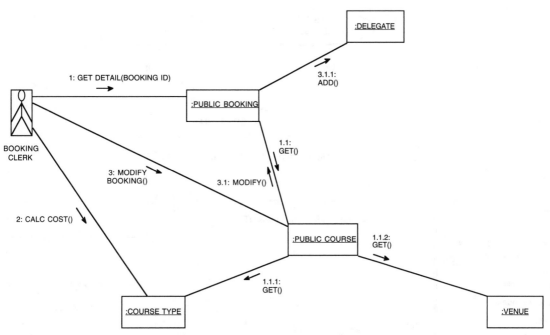

Figure 15.32. Collaboration diagram for Follow Up Public Booking: Add Delegate, Booking Id Known.

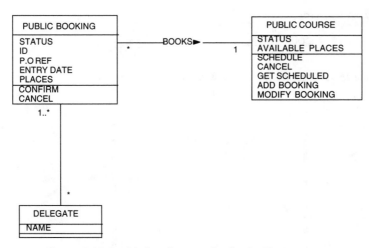

Figure 15.33. Partial class diagram reflecting Booking use cases.

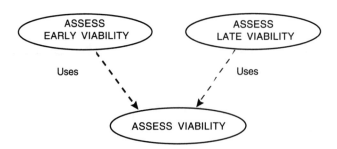

Figure 15.34. Assess Viability uses relationships.

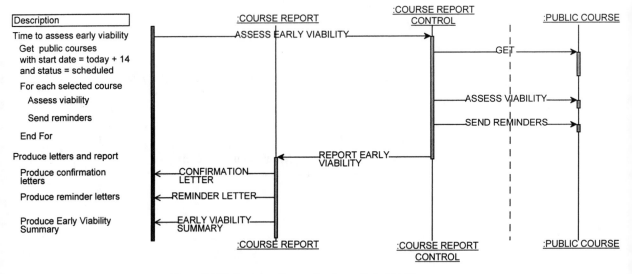

Description
Time to assess early viability
Get public courses with start date = today + 14 and status = scheduled
For each selected course
Assess viability
Send reminders
End For
Produce letters and report
Produce confirmation letters
Produce reminder letters
Produce Early Viability Summary

Figure 15.35. Sequence diagram for Assess Early Viability use case.

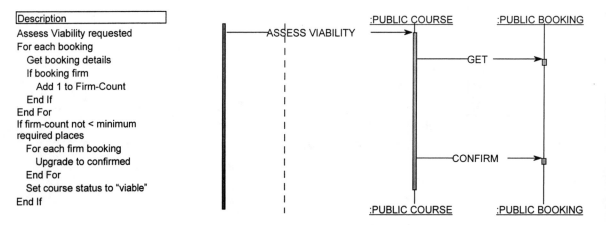

Description
Assess Viability requested
For each booking
Get booking details
If booking firm
Add 1 to Firm-Count
End If
End For
If firm-count not < minimum required places
For each firm booking
Upgrade to confirmed
End For
Set course status to "viable"
End If

Figure 15.36. Sequence diagram for Assess Viability service.

Assess Viability is modeled separately as a business service (see Figure 15.36). The precondition is Public Course Status = Scheduled; the postcondition is Public Course Status = Scheduled or Viable.

Use Case Name	Assess Late Viability of Public Course
Use Case Intent	To provide a final decision on whether there are sufficient numbers to justify running a public course.
Use Case Description	
	Assess bookings for each scheduled public course due in 7 days.
	Where number of firm bookings is > or = required number of places: Set public course status to "viable." Send letters of confirmation to customers with firm bookings and raise invoices.
	Where number of firm bookings is < minimum required number of places: Cancel Public Course.
	Produce a Late Viability Summary Report.

Again we draw a sequence diagram (see Figure 15.37).

15.4.6 State Model Revisited

We revisit the Public Booking state diagram, sketched out earlier, to include events, guards, and actions resulting from analysis of the use cases (see Figure 15.38).

15.4.7 Consolidated Class Model

We review and consolidate the class model. Although all required operations are captured, it is only those operations that are candidate business services that we show on Figure 15.39, to avoid clutter. Sometimes it is necessary to introduce separate control classes to handle business services. Our candi-

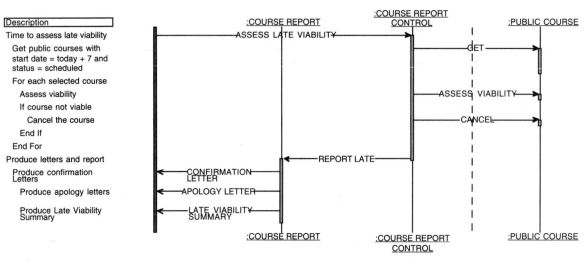

Description
Time to assess late viability
Get public courses with start date = today + 7 and status = scheduled
For each selected course
Assess viability
If course not viable
Cancel the course
End If
End For
Produce letters and report
Produce confirmation Letters
Produce apology letters
Produce Late Viability Summary

Figure 15.37. Sequence diagram for Assess Late Viability use case.

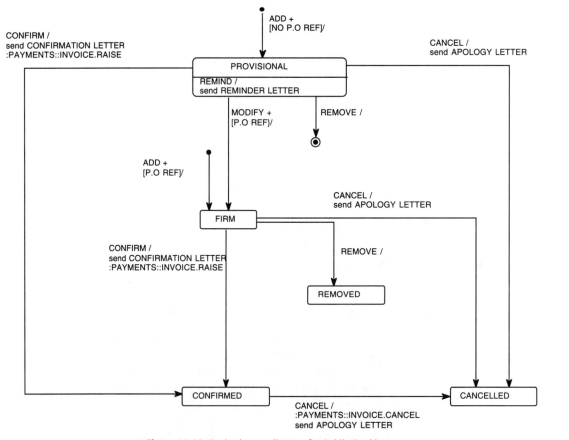

Figure 15.38. Revised state diagram for Public Booking.

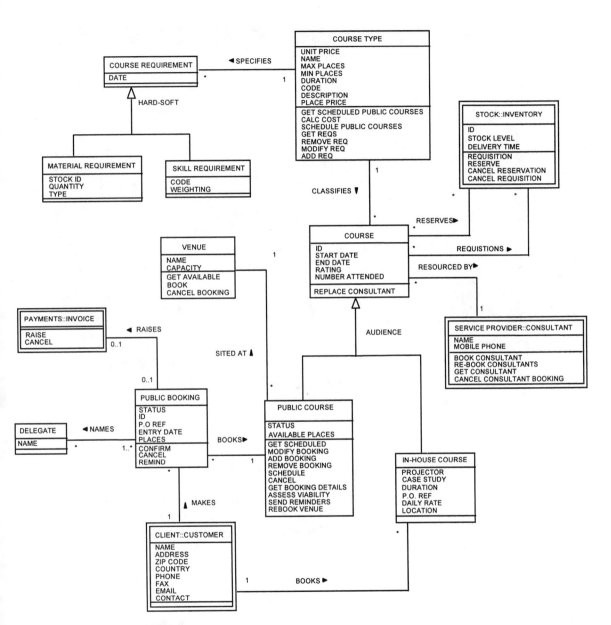

Figure 15.39. Consolidated class diagram for Course-Booking.

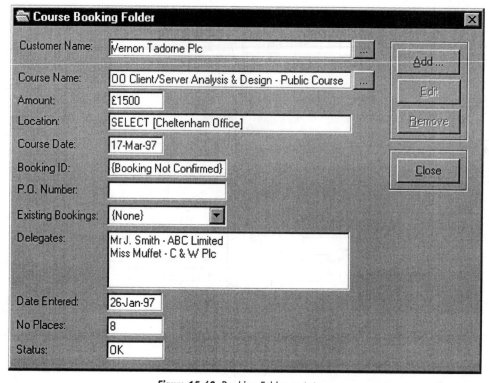

Figure 15.40. Booking Folder prototype.

date business services have been allocated directly to business objects, in line with the principle of allocating responsibility for an operation to its natural owner. In any case we do not firm-up on business services until design, which is the appropriate time to decide on whether entirely separate business service classes are needed or whether existing business classes can perform this role.

15.5 Prototyping

As we worked through our analysis we iteratively built prototypes of the Course-Booking Folder and Course Folder, which are shown in Figures 15.40 and 15.41. The prototypes gives us an early feel for the correctness of the use cases before we commit to the design details. More significantly, the proto-

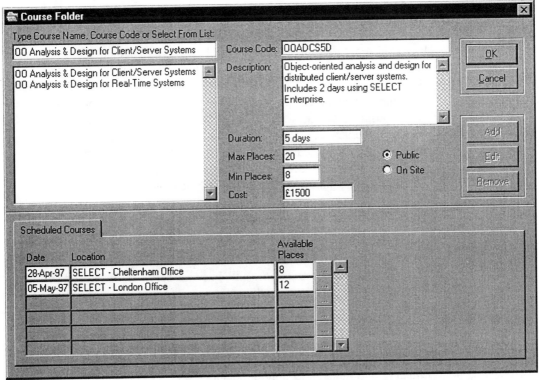

Figure 15.41. Course Folder Prototype.

types also form a basis from which to evolve our design. This was less important in the days when rapid prototypes were used as a means of exploring
requirements and then "thrown away." However, today the chances are that if
you begin building a prototype in Visual Basic or Smalltalk, that prototype will
evolve through optimization into the implementation environment. The distinction between prototyping as a requirements capture tool and prototyping
as an interface design tool is becoming more blurred because of the flexibility and power of today's GUI builders.

Course-Booking Folder is used in the two booking use cases. We need to
design a user service for this and nominate a Booking Control class as a user
service class.

The Course Folder is used for the course search business service (see
Figure 15.41). It also provides the basis for course scheduling, reallocation, and
abandonment use cases, though it requires some further extensions. For now
it can be used as a precursor to designing the course search business service.

15.6 Increment Planning

Increments are identified and planned based on a balance between business priority and logistics. The key business priority is to deliver user services that streamline the booking process based on the bookings use cases and the Bookings Folder prototype. Logistics dictate that this can only be achieved once business services are in place for identifying courses, based on the Course Folder prototype. More fundamentally, bookings need to be stored and retrieved from a database and courses need to be retrieved from a database. Data services are required for guaranteeing object persistence based on the underlying constraint of existing RDBMS technology.

15.6.1 Identifying Increments

Related use cases are packaged into candidate increments so that an increment design plan can be constructed. Each increment effectively forms a group of potential user services and business services. Business priorities are supplied by Charles Vawex, the executive sponsor. Business priorities and logistic priorities are usefully weighted and multiplied together to give an overall priority, as shown in Table 15.4; the lower the number the higher the priority. The reader should note that these figures are simply intended to illustrate the principle; on a real-life project, other factors such as degree of technical difficulty and innovation may be included and a more sophisticated formula applied to derive the overall priority.

Remember we also identified the need for a separate interactive business service Search for Courses (back in the Make Public Booking use case), which is used by many different use cases. Finally a set of data services are required based on an enhanced Customer Bookings Database. These are therefore added to our list of increments, as listed in Table 15.5. A first-cut increment plan is shown in Figure 15.42.

15.7 Increment Design

In sections 15.7.1–15.7.2 we consider architectural design for the system as a whole. In the remaining sections we focus on design of the following three increments:

1. Public Course Bookings (a user service)
2. Course Search (a business service)
3. Course-Booking Data Services

15.7.1 Class Model Architectural Design

We now consider overall design decisions affecting the class model. For example, a one-way static association is required from Course to Consultant. Other associations to classes contained in external packages are handled dynamically through service invocations. The associations from Booking to Delegate and Course Type to Course Requirement are single-direction associations.

We choose to keep Customer Ref and Customer Name, returned by Client::Control, as attributes of Public Booking. This is because we need to

Table 15.4. Increment Priorities

Use Case	Increment	Business Priority	Logistic Priority	Overall Priority
Maintain Course Types	Course Maintenance	2	1	2
Schedule Public Course	Public Course Scheduling	3	3	9
Reallocate Public Course	Public Course Scheduling	3	3	9
Maintain Courses and Venues	Course Maintenance	2	1	2
Abandon Public Course	Public Course Scheduling	3	3	9
Make Public Booking	Public Course Bookings	1	3	3
Follow Up Public Booking	Public Course Bookings	1	3	3
Assess Early Viability of Public Course	Viability Reporting	4	5	20
Assess Late Viability of Public Course	Viability Reporting	4	5	20
Produce Public Course Reports	Course Reporting	3	5	15

Table 15.5. Increments Priorities for Business and Data Services

Increment	Business Priority	Logistic Priority	Overall Priority
Course Search	1	3	3
Course-Booking Data Services	5	1	5

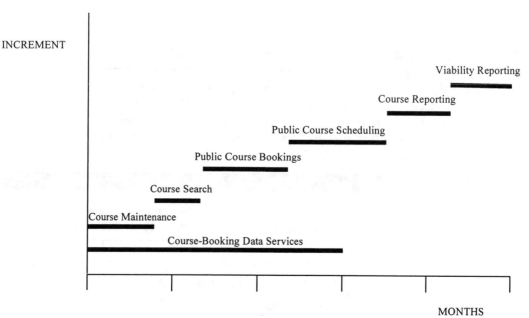

INCREMENT

Viability Reporting

Course Reporting

Public Course Scheduling

Public Course Bookings

Course Search

Course Maintenance

Course-Booking Data Services

MONTHS

Figure 15.42. Course-Bookings: Increment Plan.

store references to customers (in the Course-Booking database) for fast access of bookings and delegates by customer. Also Customer Name is often the only piece of customer data used in the bookings use cases. The alternative would be to include booking and delegate references in the Client database, which would be much slower to access and compromise a heavily shared database with local data. Customer Ref and Customer Name are also added to In-House Course. An updated class diagram is shown in Figure 15.43. .

With the help of collaboration diagrams and sequence diagrams developed earlier we review the class model in order to identify business services, which are "first-port-of-call" operations called directly by use cases and scenarios. However, in the course of our design work we also need to look for other operations, which though nested within the identified business services, nevertheless look as though they might be reusable themselves. We declare business services, on the class diagram illustrated in Figure 15.43, the importance of which we highlight as italicized operations.

15.7.2 High-Level Component Design

15.7.2.1 Reusing Services

High-level component design involves identifying component packages and modeling dependencies between component packages, including those exter-

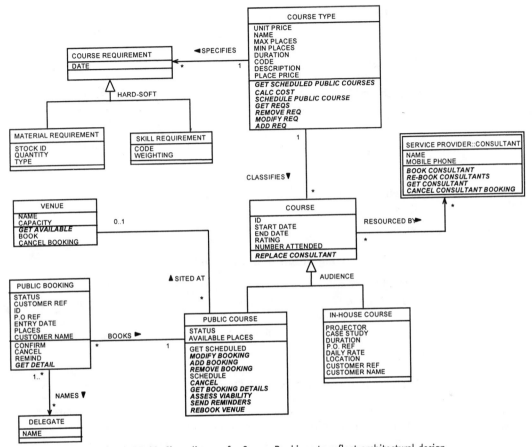

Figure 15.43. Class diagram for Course-Bookings to reflect architectural design.

nal to the system. During analysis we have identified many high-level component design services, external to the system, that can be reused. These are
firmed-up by service class, as follows:

Service Provider::Control
• Search for Skills
• Search for Capable Consultants

Service Provider::Consultant
• Book Consultant.
• Rebook Consultants
• Cancel Consultant Booking
• Get Consultant

Stock::Inventory
- Reserve
- Requisition
- Cancel Reservation
- Cancel Requisition
- Search for Courseware
- Search for Equipment

Client::Control
- Search

Payments::Invoice
- Raise
- Cancel

15.7.2.2 Identifying Business Service Classes

We need to identify the component packages that are to be designed for our system. A good place to start is by identifying service classes. As far as business services are concerned we have largely already done so, as we have allocated most of them to business classes. The one exception is Search for Courses. We need a control class for that: Course Searcher.

15.7.2.3 Identifying User Service Classes

Reporting and updating user services are likely to require separate service classes to cater to different needs. Reporting user services generally need to be very flexible. A useful strategy is to introduce a generic reporting user service. In fact we already introduced a service class, Course Report Control, to cater to course reports back in the Assess Early Viability use case.

As far as update user services are concerned, we partition service classes by actor where possible, as each actor is likely to have different operational requirements, but we'll also need to look for common subject matter in order to aim for cohesion. Most user services correspond to use cases but this does not have to be so. For example, the two booking use cases are sufficiently similar to be handled by a single user service, Book Public Course. These are exclusive to the Booking Clerk actor and center on a common subject matter: bookings. Therefore we allocate Book Public Course to a Booking Control class.

The remaining use cases look sufficiently different (at this point) to warrant separate user services for each. We can always combine (or split) them later on in any case. Most are used by the Services Manager actor and center on the subject matter of courses. We therefore allocate these user services to a Course Control class (Figure 15.44).

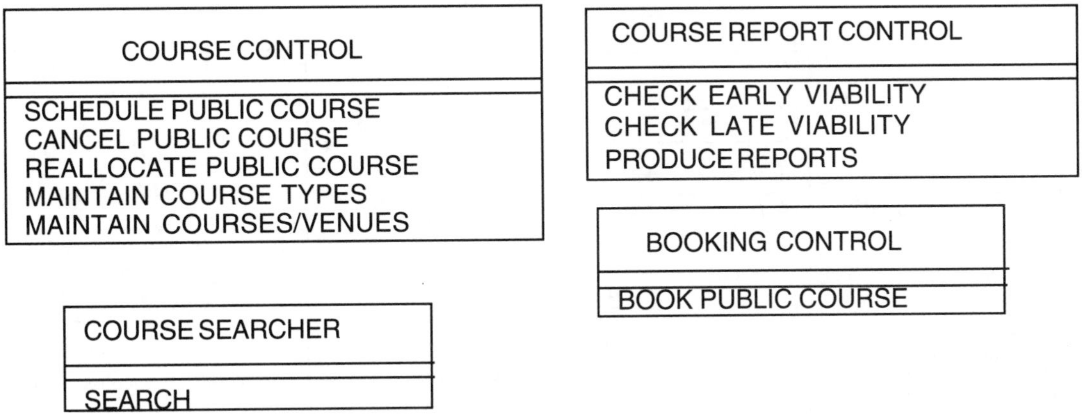

Figure 15.44. Service classes.

15.7.2.4 Identifying Data Service Classes

Finally we need three data services classes, one for each major business class: Public Booking DTX, Public Course DTX, Course Type DTX. We need a clear and consistent data management strategy concerning database access and update. It is decided that business objects can access the database directly via data services but that, to preserve implementation independence, business objects shall not issue database update requests to data services; commits and rollbacks of database transactions are to be done via user objects.

15.7.2.5 Modeling Component Package Dependencies

The system is divided into component packages based on service categories and domain partitioning, as shown in Figure 15.45. Component packages evolve from service packages, developed in analysis. Importantly, the bulk of our analysis has centered on business classes within the service package Course-Booking, which fall within the component package Course-Booking Business Services. We note that each service class allocated to a component package needs one or more component interfaces designing for it.

15.7.3 Increment Objectives

Before embarking on detailed design we need to get our objectives clarified. We provide examples of increment design for three different types of increment, which will be described in the text that follows.. A full project would include objectives for all increments. For brevity we restrict the discussion here on a representative cross-section.

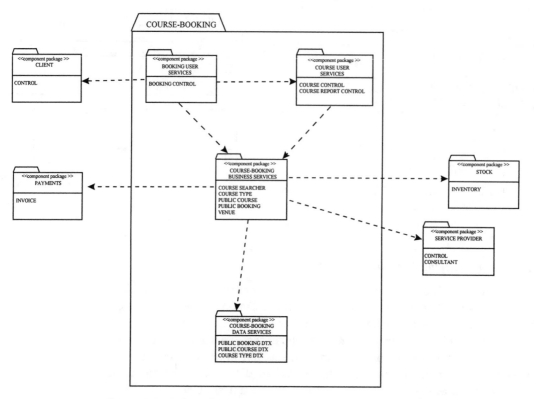

Figure 15.45. Package-dependency diagram showing component packages.

15.7.3.1 Course-Booking Data Services

Objective: Provide data services based on existing Customer Bookings Database and extend the database structure to cover Course Type, In-House Course, Course Requirement, and Venue classes not currently supported.

Data Services: Public Booking DTX: "CRUD," Course Type DTX: "R," Public Course DTX: "R."

15.7.3.2 Course Search Business Service

Objective: Provide effective searching facilities for identifying course type and for showing scheduled public courses for course type.

Use Cases: Required by Make Public Booking, Follow Up Public Booking, Schedule Public Course, Reallocate Public Course.

Business Services: On Course Searcher: Search. On Course Type: Get Detail, Get Scheduled Public Course.

15.7.3.3 Public Course Bookings User Services

Objective: Provide user services to streamline the public booking process.

Use Cases: Make Public Booking, Follow Up Public Booking.

User Services: On Booking Control: Make Bookings.

Business Services: On Public Course: Modify Booking, Add Booking, Remove Booking. On Public Booking: Get Detail.

15.7.4 Deployment Model

A deployment diagram for the system is shown in Figure 15.46.

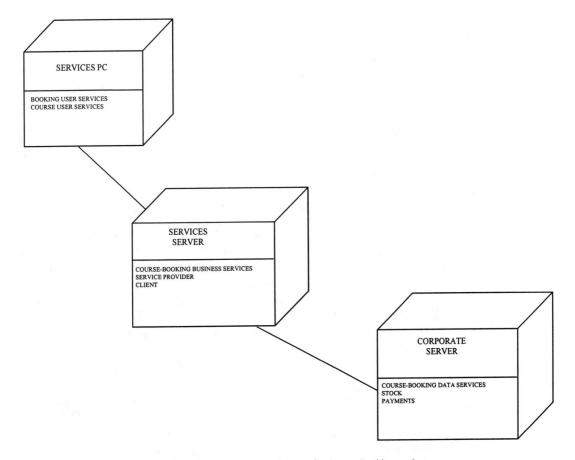

Figure 15.46. Deployment diagram for Course-Booking project.

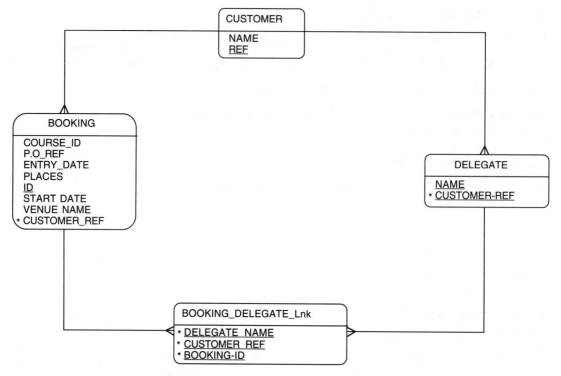

Figure 15.47. Existing logical data structure diagram.

15.7.5 Increment 1: Course-Booking Data Services

First we need a logical data structure diagram for the existing Customer-Bookings database (see Figure 15.47). The consolidated class model is mapped to a new initial logical data-structure diagram (see Figure 15.48).

A separate project handles database conversion and upgrade of existing database routines to use the new structure. This project is tasked with building a data services component to wrap the new structure.

The next step is to design data monitor classes to reflect the business diagram; one is identified for each business class: Public Booking DM, Delegate DM, Public Course DM, In-House Course DM, Venue DM, Course Type DM, Course Requirement DM.

The second step is to design database access classes; one is identified for each database table: Public Booking DB, Delegate DB, Course DB, Public Course DB, In-House Course DB, Venue DB, Course Type DB, Course Requirement DB, Material Requirement DB, Skill Requirement DB, Customer DB, Book-Delg DB.

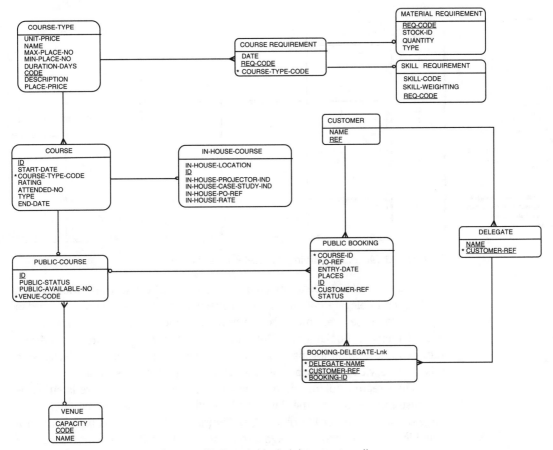

Figure 15.48. Extended logical data-structure diagram.

We design data service classes on the basis of identified data services. A data service class is identified for each related set of required transactions. A transaction can range from a simple atomic object read or create to a complex set of object creates, which have complex integrity requirements. In the context of the other two increments CRUD transactions are required for Public Booking and read-only transactions for Course Type and Course. A good start is therefore to try three data service classes: Booking DTX, Course Type DTX, Course DTX.

The Read Booking data service first attempts to get the Public Booking Data Monitor (see Figure 15.49). If it is found, then it can be returned to the caller to instantiate the Public Booking object. If the Public Booking data monitor is not

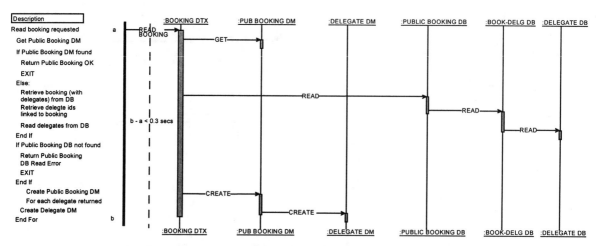

Figure 15.49. Sequence diagram for Read Booking data service.

found, then a call is made to the database access objects to retrieve the required booking and delegate data from the database. If there is no database record, a suitable database error message is returned to the caller and the transaction ends. Otherwise Booking and Delegate data monitor objects are created and returned to the caller for instantiating the corresponding business objects. Note this data service has a response time requirement of < 0.3 seconds.

The Create Booking data service first checks to see if there is an existing customer record on the database by calling a Read using customer reference on the Customer DB object (see Figure 15.50). If there is no customer a suitable database error message is returned to the caller and the transaction ends. If there is an existing customer database record, then a Create is invoked on the Booking DB object. Each new delegate is added to the database having checked that the delegate is not already on the database using the Delegate DB object. Book-Delg DBs are created for each delegate booked. The course-available places are decreased by invoking an Update on the Public Course DB. Having successfully made the various database creates and updates a call is issued to the DB transaction manager object to commit the object DBs to the database and appropriate data monitor objects are created. Note this data service has a response-time requirement of < 1.0 second.

15.7.6 Increment 2: Course Search Business Services

Note that although Search Courses is a business service it is actually triggered using a user object, Course Searcher. First we construct a sequence diagram

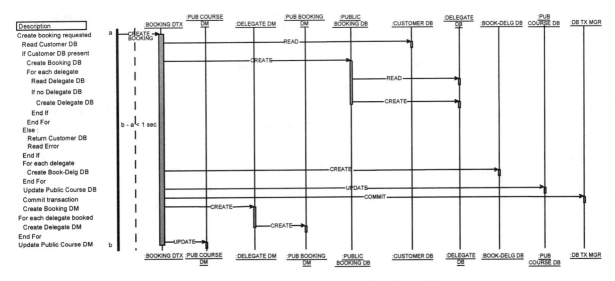

Figure 15.50. Sequence diagram for Create Booking data service.

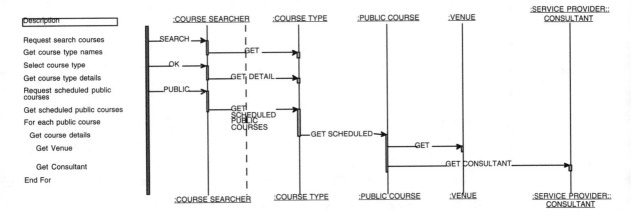

Figure 15.51. First-Cut sequence diagram for Search Courses business service.

to identify required business objects (see Figure 15.51). Now we can consider the user interface design itself. Implementing in Visual Basic requires a "control structure" in which forms communicate with business objects via a control object; in this case this is the Course Searcher object (see Figure 15.52). Course Type View is designed to provide a mirror image of the Course Type business object; Course Type List View provides a list of all course type names. Note the use of the business service Get Scheduled Public Course (see Figure 15.53).

15.7.7 Increment 3: Booking User Services

We investigate Make Public Booking and Follow Up Public Booking and after some discussion realize that the two are in fact remarkably similar. The resulting sequence diagrams, as shown in Figures 15.54 and 15.55, based on the

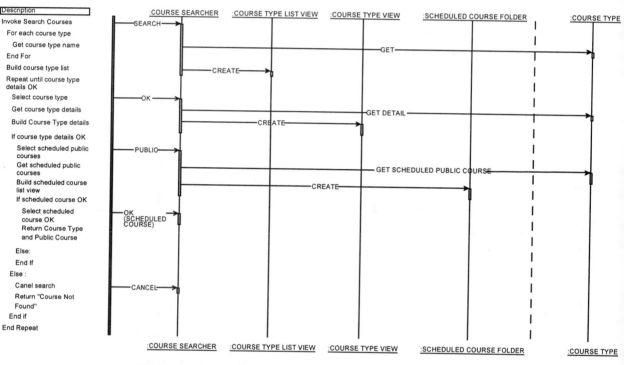

Figure 15.52. Detailed sequence diagram for Search Courses business service.

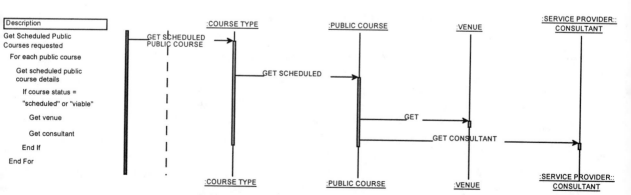

Figure 15.53. Sequence diagram for Get Scheduled Public Courses business service.

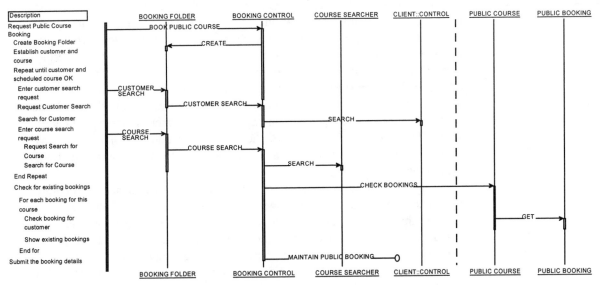

Figure 15.54. Sequence diagram for Make Public Booking use case.

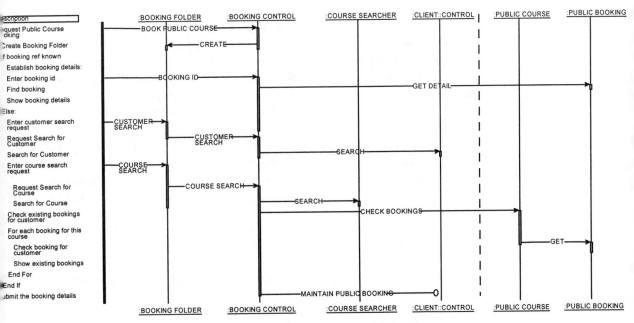

Figure 15.55. Sequence diagram for Follow Up Public Booking use case.

Booking Folder prototype. Both use cases invoke the Customer Search and Course Search business services and both share the same basic features. Both use cases now include a conditional check on existing bookings, which we have introduced to cater to an alternative course identified earlier. This results in a Check Bookings business service added to Public Course. The only real difference between the two use cases is that follow-ups need to access bookings directly using booking id. We have therefore abstracted out the common core of the use case as a probe, Maintain Bookings, which is modeled in Figure 15.56. The user service, Book Public Course, introduced on the Booking Control object handles both use cases and can be extended to other situations if required.

Calc Cost and Add Booking are invoked as business services; a separate sequence diagram for Add Booking is included in Figure 15.58. The three data services that deal with committing details to the database are invoked from the Booking Folder user object, which acts as a direct user interface to the data services. This reflects our strategy of not involving business objects with issuing update requests. However, the user service itself, implemented through the Booking Control user service object, only accesses the database via business services, not directly. Note also that displays from Booking Control are not explicit on the earlier diagrams to avoid clutter. We can use a state diagram for a more rigorous and detailed view, as shown in Figure 15.57. (Note: NEXT/ from any user wait state always returns to WAITING FOR INPUT.)

Having worked out the basic structure of the required object interaction we return to consideration of business services. We identified lots of potential business services when analyzing the system; for example, we developed a sequence diagram for Modify Booking. These can now be "slotted in" to our design and further business services detailed using sequence diagrams. We include an example for the Add Booking business service shown in Figure 15.58. A conditional check on late bookings, from an alternative course, is added, with a message to confirm booking. Note how Public Booking issues an event "Confirmation Requested," which is picked up by our Course Report Control service class. The integrity of this business object is still maintained because it merely broadcasts the event without knowledge of its target. Course Report Control is designed with an event-handling mechanism to recognize such requests for reports.

Finally we need to ensure all operations are clearly specified; examples are included in Tables 15.6–15.8.

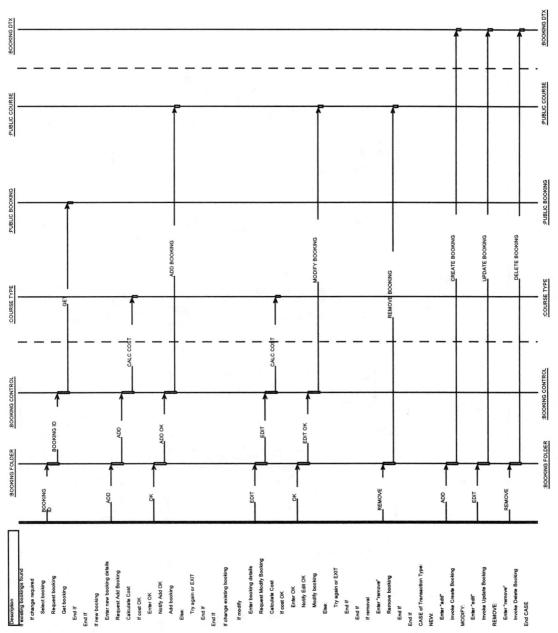

Figure 15.56. Sequence diagram for Maintain Bookings probe.

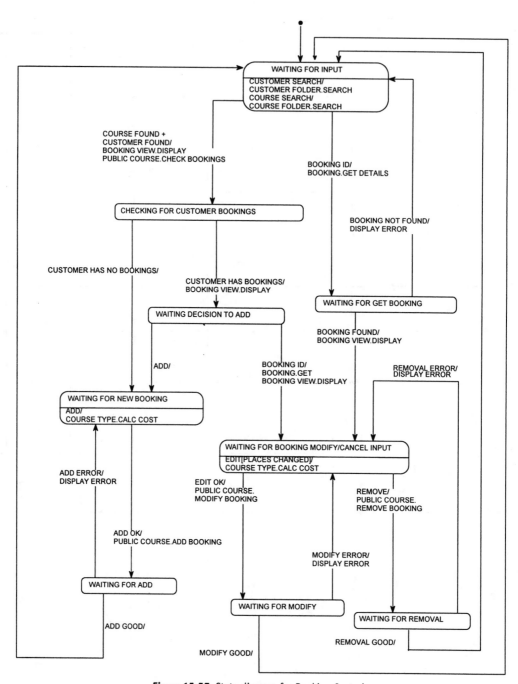

Figure 15.57. State diagram for Booking Control.

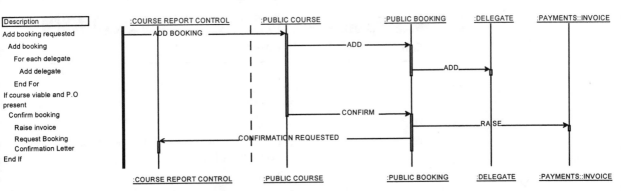

Figure 15.58. Sequence Diagram for Add Booking business service.

Table 15.6. Operation Specification for Public Course::Add Booking	
Operation Name	**Public Course::Add Booking**
Intent	To verify and control addition of new booking
Stereotype	Business Service
Signature	(Public Booking: Class, Delegate*: Char, Requested Places: Int): (Booking.Id: Int, Bool)
Precondition 1	Requested places < or = available places and [Today + 6 < or = Start Date or Today + 6 > Start Date and P.O. present]
Postcondition 1	Public Booking::Add is called
Precondition 2	Precondition 1 Public Course::Status = Viable and P. O. Ref present
Postcondition 2	Public Booking::Add is called Public Booking::Confirm is called
Called Operations	Booking::Add Booking::Confirm
Transmitted Events	None
Attributes (Get)	Start Date
Attributes (Set)	Available Places
Nonfunctional Requirements	Response time less than 0.5 seconds.

Table 15.7. Operation Specification for Public Booking::Add

Operation Name	Public Booking::Add
Intent	To set up booking details; generates Booking::Id
Stereotype	
Signature	(Public Booking: Class, Delegate*: Char): (Booking::Id: Int, Bool)
Precondition 1	P. O. Ref present
Postcondition1	Public Booking added with Public Booking::Status = Firm
Precondition 2	P. O. Ref not present
Postcondition 2	Public Booking added with Public Booking::Status = Provisional
Called Operations	Delegate::Add
Transmitted Events	
Attributes (Set)	Status
	Id
	P.O Ref
	Entry Date
	Places
Non-functional Requirements	Response time less than 0.5 second

Table 15.8. Operation for Public Booking::Confirm

Operation Name	Public Booking::Confirm
Intent	Changes Booking::Status to "confirmed," transmit requests for confirmation letter and invoice
Stereotype	
Signature	(): bool
Precondition	Public Booking::Status = Provisional or Firm
Postcondition	Public Booking::Status = Confirmed
Called Operations	Payments::Invoice::Raise
Transmitted Events	Add Confirmation
Attributes (Set)	Status
Non-functional Requirements	Response time less than 0.5 second

APPENDIX A

. . . .

Deliverables

This appendix outlines the deliverables that are produced during the Perspective process. It has two main sections: deliverables for a solution project and deliverables for a component project.

The solution project deliverables consist of a single document to which more detail is added as baselines are passed.

For component projects, there are two levels of deliverables: a scoping and assessment document, which provides an architectural context for component development, and specification documents, which provide the component details.

Our approach to deliverables is easy on form but hard on content: Detailed presentation formats for the various models are left open to provide maximum flexibility. However, recommended levels of model detail are included for each stage to provide the necessary guidance.

A.1 Deliverables for Solution Projects

During the development of a solution project a single document is produced. More detail is added to the document as the project progresses through the various baselines in the life cycle. This approach eases version control and management of the document, thereby encouraging developers to keep the documentation up to date. The baselines are as follows:

- end of feasibility study,
- end of analysis,
- end of each increment.

The documentation is also intended to be relatively brief and to read more like a business plan than a requirements specification.

A.1.1 Feasibility Study

A.1.1.1 Overall Sections

• **Executive summary.**
This section gives an overview of the project. In particular, it addresses the following subjects:

- business areas/processes to be supported,
- statement of purpose,
- major areas of risk,
- cost-benefit summary,
- feasibility of the project given time and cost constraints.

• **Proposed environment.**
This section covers the hardware and software environment for the project and should highlight any major new requirements for capital expenditure.

• **Nonfunctional requirements.**
Constraints and quality attributes against which the final solution is judged.

• **Summary of Recommended Solution.**
A summary of reasons for selecting the recommended solution, including a detailed cost-benefit analysis.

A.1.1.2 Solution-Specific Sections

Where there is more than one possible solution separate sections are included for each solution. It is likely that more detail is supplied for the recommended solution with only outlines provided for the other candidate solutions. Also it may be the case that there is only a single solution.

• **Models.**
This section contains models shown in Table A.1,

• **Proposed usage of services.**
References to proposed services (from Service Catalog, described in A.2.2.1) to be used.

Table A.1. Model-Stage Detail for the Feasibility Document	
Model	**Level of Detail**
use case model	high-level descriptions in the form of actor and use case catalogs, use case diagrams
class model	high-level class diagram
state model	high-level; states and events only
component model	high-level service package dependency diagram

Note: state models and class models are optional.

• **Estimates.**
An estimate of the effort required for the development of each use case is provided. The estimates are based on their complexity.

• **Risk analysis.**
The major risk areas are analyzed in this section. Some examples follow:

• complex use cases,
• usage of new technology,
• business case,
• organization,
• external dependencies.

A.1.2 Analysis Document

The following sections are as for the feasibility study baseline, but with added detail because of the greater understanding of the project requirements:

• **Executive summary.**

• **Proposed environment.**

• **Nonfunctional requirements.**

• **Models.**
This section contains models shown in Table A.2.

Table A.2. Model-Stage Detail for the Analysis Document	
Model	**Level of Detail**
use case model	detailed formatted descriptions
object interaction model	collaboration and sequence diagrams for key scenarios and use cases; business objects only
class model	includes all attributes with data types and operations with responsibilities defined; may include user classes and service classes
state model	high level; outbound events and operations may be included
component model	lower-level service package dependency diagrams

• *Proposed usage of services.*
References to proposed services (from Service Catalog, described in A.2.2.1) to be used.

• *Estimates.*
The estimate of the effort required for the development of each use case is . revised in the light of the greater detail provided by analysis.

• *Risk analysis.*

A.1.3 Increment Design Specification

As each increment is developed, the document is refined. The document contains the following sections, which are the same as for the analysis baseline, but with added detail because of the greater understanding of the project requirements:

• *Executive summary.*

• *Proposed environment.*

• *Nonfunctional requirements.*

Model	Level of Detail
class model	includes all attributes with definitions; operations with signatures defined; must include service classes; may include user and data classes
object interaction model	collaboration and sequence diagrams for key scenarios and use cases; user objects, data objects included
state model	transition strings fully detailed
component model	component package dependency diagrams; interfaces defined and classes allocated
deployment model	shows technical architecture; allocation of component packages
logical data model	used to model supporting non-OO database structure

Table A.3. Model-Stage Detail for the Increment Design Specification

• *Models.*
This section contains models shown in Table A.3.

• *Proposed usage of services.*
References to proposed services (from Service Catalog, described in A.2.2.1) to be used.

• *Estimates.*
An estimate of the effort required for the development of each remaining use case (increment) is provided. The estimates are refined using data from the development of previous use cases. After the final use case is completed, this section contains metrics and records for use on future projects. The complexity estimates grow more reliable as more increments are delivered.

• *Risk analysis.*
The major risk areas for the remaining use cases (e.g., complex use cases, usage of new technology (hardware and software, etc.) are analyzed in this section. After the final use case is completed, this section details any areas that may prove difficult to maintain in the future, together with an analysis of those use cases most likely to change.

A.2 Deliverables for Component Projects

Component projects operate on two levels, each of which provides different deliverables. The scoping and assessment stages, which are in essence ongoing and proactive, produce evolving high-level documentation, which provides a framework for detailed component development. The component delivery stages, which are focused on designing and building components, produce specification documents.

A.2.1 Component Scoping and Assessment Document

A.2.1.1 Overall Sections

• *Executive summary.*
This section gives a context for component development as a whole. References are provided to key drivers such as the following:

- vision statement,
- migration strategy,
- legacy asset documentation,
- technical design architecture.

• *Models.*
This section contains models shown in Table A.4.

• *Quality plan.*
This section contains overall guidelines on quality factors such as flexibility and performance.

A.2.1.2 Component-Specific Sections

• *Terms of reference.*
Terms of reference may be for feasibility studies (as described in the solution process) or for component delivery. Feasibility studies are typically carried out for component projects that produce increments to provide early user value in their own right or where more detailed information is required before proceeding to component delivery. At minimum this should include the following:

- indirect business processes,
- vision statement,
- scoped component models (as above),
- list of candidate services,
- list of service upgrades.

A.2.2 Component Specification Documents

The component delivery stages produce two types of specification: a service catalog and an internal design document. Each of these documents serves a different audience as described in A2.2.1 and A2.2.2. The level of detail of the models is shown in Table A.5. Again presentation formats of the various models are left open.

Table A.4. Model-Stage Detail for the Scoping Document	
Model	**Level of Detail**
component model	high level service package dependency diagrams
class model	high level class diagram

Table A.5. Model-Stage Detail for Component Specification Documents	
Model	**Level of Detail**
class model	includes all attributes with definitions; operations with detailed specifications and signatures defined; relevant nonfunctional requirements and constraints must include service classes; may include user and data classes
object interaction model	collaboration diagrams and sequence diagrams for key scenarios and use cases; user objects and data objects included; also include relevant nonfunctional requirements and constraints
state model	transition strings fully detailed also include relevant nonfunctional requirements and constraints
component model	component package dependency diagrams; interfaces defined and classes allocated
deployment model	shows technical architecture; allocation of component packages
logical data model	used to model supporting non-OO database structure

A.2.2.1 Service Catalog

This defines services from an external user's viewpoint. Suggested sections are included in the list that follows. At a lower level the catalog should be viewable in terms of component interface descriptions. This might be in the form of an explorer-like tree structure, giving graduated levels of service description down to components at the lowest level.

- *Component definition.*
A clear definition of the objective of the component is provided.

- *Service category.*
User Service, Business Service, or Data Service.

- *Service definition.*
A clear definition of the objective of the service is provided.

- *Service interface definition.*
A formal description of the component's interface in terms of the parameters expected and returned, together with any relevant pre- and postconditions.

- *Requirement references.*
Cross-references back to original requirements to ensure traceability.

- *Models.*
A sub-set of models (see Table A.5) relating to the service

A.2.2.2 Component Internal Design Specification

This is for the private use of the developers of the component and contains all information gained during development of the component. This includes the following:

- *Observations.*
This contains an indication of areas that may prove critical or difficult to maintain in the future and an indication of likelihood of change.

- *Implementation-specific information.*
This information relates to the specific implementation of the component. For instance, legacy application wrapper objects may contain additional information that specifies internal operating constraints imposed by its native operating environment.

• *Requirement references.*
Cross-references back to originating requirements to ensure traceability.

• *Certification criteria.*
This includes specification of constraints (such as operating constraints) and quality attributes (such as security and reliability). Further information on certification criteria is contained in Goldberg and Rubin (1995).

• *Model views.*
This section contains models shown in Table A.5.

APPENDIX B

· ·

Relational Mappings

This appendix describes the rules that govern mapping a class model to a first-cut logical data model for a relational database.

B.1 Basic Concepts

B.1.1 Relational Concepts

A relational database stores data in tables. Each table has a specific number of columns, or fields, and an arbitrary number of rows. Tables correspond to classes, fields correspond to attributes, and rows correspond to objects or links. Each field must be assigned to a domain (a set of allowed values) such as date or number. A field value is stored in each cell in a table. The value must either belong to the applicable domain or be null.

A primary key is used to identify a specific row; a primary key is a combination of one or more fields whose value unambiguously locates each row in a table. Foreign keys are used to implement associations between tables; a foreign key is a primary key of one table that is embedded in another (or the same) table.

Note that in contrast each object has inherent identity. However, it may be that certain attributes can be used to uniquely identify an object; these are known as candidate keys. A candidate key must not take null values.

B.1.2 Logical Data Structure Diagrams

A logical data model documents the organization of data into tables according to relational principles independent of physical characteristics. A logical data structure diagram is a graphic tool for diagramming the logical data model. The reader should note that despite the "logical" prefix this is not the same as an ERD (Entity Relationship Diagram), which describes pure business data. The logical data model is developed to reflect key design decisions such as denormalization as well as aggregating and segmenting records (Dewitz, 1996). We use a notation adapted and simplified from CCTA (1995) as shown in Figure B.1.

Full field names always start with their parent table name, but this is suppressed on the diagram. The last part of a field name indicates its domain. For example PERSON_BIRTH_DATE belongs to the PERSON table and has a domain of DATE. It appears on the diagram as BIRTH_DATE.

B.1.3 Scope

The mapping rules describe how to create a first-cut logical data model from a class model. The first-cut logical data model is deliberately "naive" in the sense that it models the relational structure implied by the class model regard-

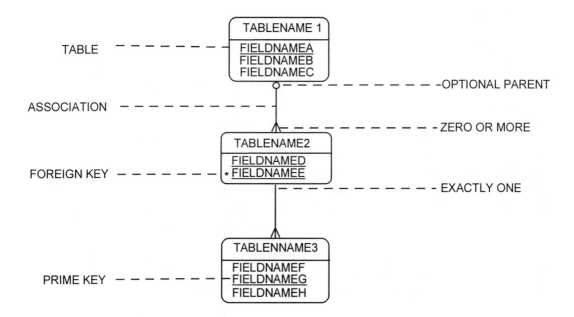

Figure B.1. Logical data modeling notation set.

less of implementation constraints and quality attributes, such as flexibility and performance.

The database designer can proceed to adjust and develop the naïve model according to well-thought-through trade-offs, such as flexibility versus performance. Key logical database design decisions such as denormalization and aggregating and segmenting records may be applied to the logical data model in order to create a better design.

After the logical data model has been specified using DDL (data definition language) it is tuned to meet the needs of its specific target environment in terms of physical file organization and performance tuning, including the use of indexes. This results in a physical data model expressed in DSDL (data storage description language). For relational databases, SQL (structured query language) is used for both DDL and, with physical extensions, for DSDL.

B.2 Mapping Rules

B.2.1 Classes

A class maps to a table of the same name. We need to specify a primary key for the table. If there is a candidate key that can be used to uniquely identify objects, then this can be nominated as primary key, as in the example given in Figure B.2, where Course Type Code is used. Otherwise we need to create a field to act as primary key.

B.2.2 One-to-Many Associations

A one-to-many association is mapped by posting the primary key on the "one" table as a foreign key in the "many" table as shown in Figure B.3.

Figure B.2. Class to table mapping example.

B.2.3 One-to-One Associations

A fully mandatory one-to-one association is mapped by joining the two tables, as shown in Figure B.4.

If the association is partially (or fully) optional, merging the two tables results in some fields with null values. An alternative mapping in the case of a partially optional association is illustrated in Figure B.5. The primary key of the mandatory table is posted as a foreign key in the optional table. In the case of fully optional one-to-one associations, we might introduce a new table with the primary key from each table embedded (similarly to a many-to-many association, described in section B.2.4).

B.2.4 Many-to-Many Associations

A many-to-many association is mapped by introducing a new table. The primary key of the new table is the concatenation of the primary keys from the

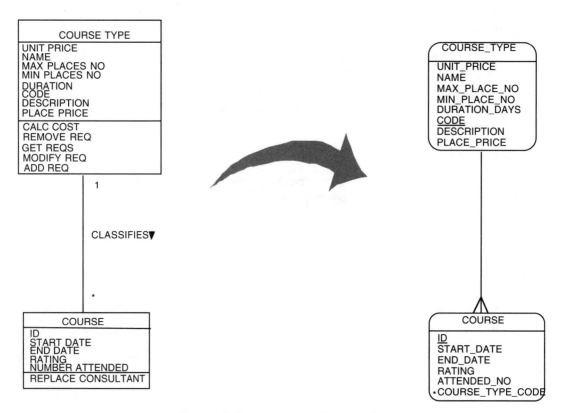

Figure B.3. One-to-many mapping example.

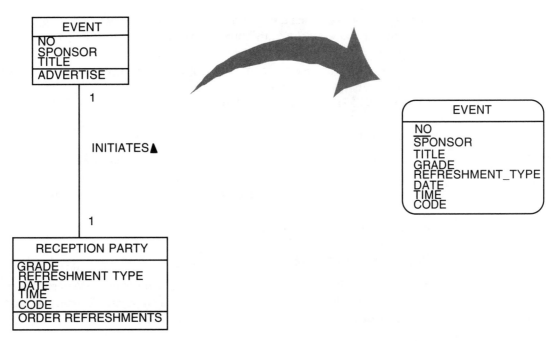

Figure B.4. One-to-one (fully mandatory) mapping example.

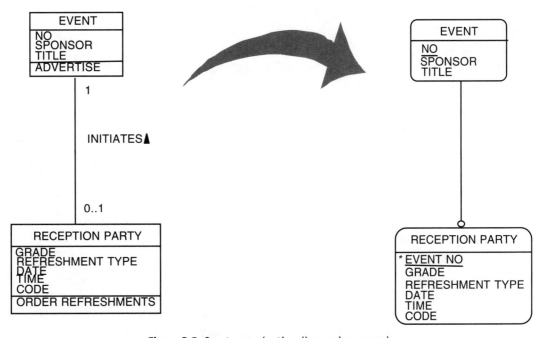

Figure B.5. One-to-one (optional) mapping example.

two tables, each of which also acts as a foreign key, as shown in the Figure B.6. Note that if there are link attributes specified on the association these are mapped to fields in the intersection table.

Also note in this example that the mapped EVENT_NO acts as primary key of the Event table. The Venue class does not have a candidate key. Therefore VENUE_CODE is added to act as primary key of the Venue table.

B.2.5 Association Classes

An association class is mapped to a new table in a similar fashion to a many-to-many association, with attributes mapped to fields of the new table. We also need to consider whether one of these attributes can act as primary key. If it can, then the embedded primary keys from the two associated classes still act as foreign keys, as shown in Figure B.7.

B.2.6 Ternary Associations

Ternary associations are dealt with in the same fashion as many-to-many associations. A new table is introduced with primary key composed of the primary keys of each participating table. Each embedded primary key also acts as a foreign key.

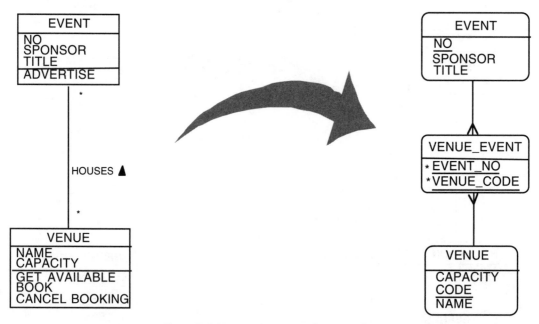

Figure B.6. Many-to-Many mapping example.

B.2.7 Aggregations

Aggregations are dealt with in the same way as associations.

B.2.8 Inheritance Hierarchies

There are three possible mapping types for inheritance hierarchies: one to one, roll-down, and roll-up. The one-to-one mapping is the preferred approach, as it represents very cleanly the implied relational structure regardless of implementation constraints. The other two approaches are motivated by a desire to improve performance, which is much better addressed as part of database design once the first-cut mapping has taken place. However, all three are presented here to give maximum choice according to the reader's practical needs.

B.2.8.1 One to One

The superclass and subclasses each map to a table. Each table has the same primary key. In the example given in Figure B.8. Id is used as primary key of all three tables. The attraction of the one-to-one mapping is that it represents

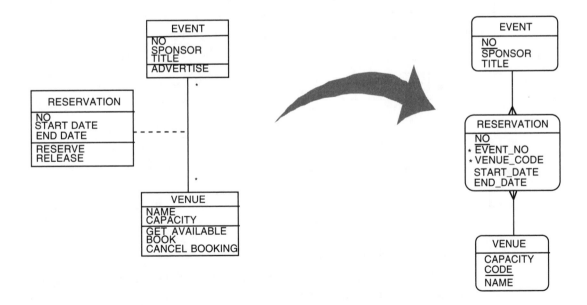

Figure B.7. Association class mapping example.

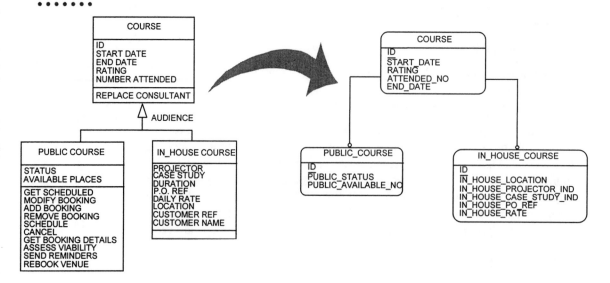

Figure B.8. Inheritance one-to-one mapping example.

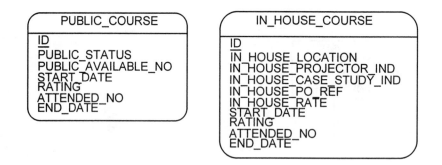

Figure B.9. Inheritance roll-down mapping example.

minimal distortion of the class model. The price paid is that navigation between tables may be slow.

B.2.8.2 Roll-Down

Each subclass maps to a table. The superclass is "rolled down" and the generalized attributes from the superclass are replicated in each of the tables. Each table has the same primary key. In the example given in Figure B.9, ID is used as primary key of both tables. This may be a useful approach if the superclass has few attributes and there are many subclasses, or if the subclasses have many attributes themselves. The price paid is duplication of field names.

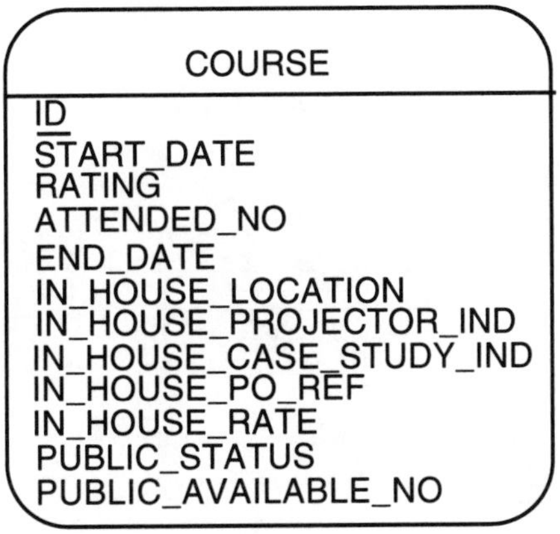

```
COURSE
ID
START_DATE
RATING
ATTENDED_NO
END_DATE
IN_HOUSE_LOCATION
IN_HOUSE_PROJECTOR_IND
IN_HOUSE_CASE_STUDY_IND
IN_HOUSE_PO_REF
IN_HOUSE_RATE
PUBLIC_STATUS
PUBLIC_AVAILABLE_NO
```

Figure B.10. Inheritance roll-up mapping example.

B.2.8.3 Roll-Up

The entire inheritance structure maps to a single table. The subclasses are "rolled up" and the attributes from the subclasses are merged into the single table (see Figure B.10). Each row takes field values that are pertinent to the subclasses that apply to that row. The remaining sets of fields mapped from the subclasses take null values. This option is useful if there are relatively few subclasses with few attributes. The price paid is that certain fields can take null values.

Glossary

Abstract class: A class without objects; intended so that behavior common to a variety of classes can be factored out in one place, where it can be defined once and reused repeatedly.

Activity: A generic term used to describe a process group, process thread, or elementary business.

Actor (Business): A role (or set of roles) that is played in relation to the business. Examples are as for system actor; one of the practical differences is that a business actor is usually more abstract and can be realized by several system actors, depending on choice of system interface. However, it is possible for several business actors to be realized by the same system actor.

Actor (System): A role (or set of roles) that is played in relation to a system; it could be a person, a group of persons, an organization, another system, or a piece of equipment. An actor can be external or internal to the business; for example, Customer or Credit Controller. An actor can be considered a role that has a specific set of responsibilities relating to a set of system use cases.

Actual Parameter: *See* **Argument.**

Aggregation: A whole/part relationship where the whole or aggregate is composed of one or more objects, each of which is considered a part of the aggregate.

Architecture (Perspective): The structure used to guide the modeling process in terms of service categories and object stereotypes. It defines how software is put together independent of implementation.

Argument (Actual Parameter): The actual value of a parameter.

433

Association: A relationship between any number (including one) of classes that abstracts a set of links between object members of those classes.

Association Class: An association that also has class properties.

Attribute: A named property of a class.

BPI: Business Process Improvement

BPM: Business Process Modeling.

BPR: Business Process Reengineering.

Business Event: A stimulus that triggers an elementary process; it may be input or output driven. Input-driven business events are signalled by the arrival of an input information flow; they can be external or internal; for example, Customer submits order (external) or Customer-service clerk requests credit approval. Output-driven business events may be temporal or conditional. Temporal events are signalled by the arrival of a predefined point in time. Conditional events report the sensing of a particular circumstance, which triggers an elementary process; for example, Credit limit exceeded.

Business Object (Class): Business objects are sometimes referred to as *conceptual* objects because they are geared to meet business requirements, regardless of technology. A business object interacts with user objects, data objects, and other business objects. Business objects are used to provide business services in collaboration with data objects and user objects. A business object transforms data into *information*. The data may be acquired from data services or user services.

Business Process: A collection of process groups.

Business Process Improvement (BPI): Under some circumstances the radical nature of the changes envisaged with a BPR exercise are unacceptable, resulting in a drive for improvement of the current processes, however defined, rather than reengineering. The term "BPI" is used to indicate where improvements are sought within the current business constraints.

Business Process Reengineering (BPR): The radical reorganization of an enterprise along the flow of work that generates the value sought by the customer.

Business Service: "A collection of business rules and business function that generate and operate on information. The information is based on data provided by data or user services. When data is requested from data services, business services are responsible for building those requests" (Microsoft, 1996).

Business Step: Part of an elementary business process consisting of a definable piece of work. Business steps provide a mechanism for identifying service requirements of an elementary business process, and can be reused both within and across elementary business processes.

Class: A set of objects that share a common structure and a common behavior.

Class Diagram: A graphic tool for modeling the existence of classes and their associations.

Collaboration Diagram: A graphic tool for modeling and documenting object interactions with respect to links between objects. The collaboration diagram is particularly suited to providing a network view of the object interaction required to service a scenario.

Component: A component is an executable unit of code that provides a physical black-box encapsulation of related services. A component's services can only be accessed through a consistent, published interface that includes an interaction standard. A component must be capable of being connected to other components (through a communications interface) to form a larger group.

Component Package: A package that groups together one or more closely related components. A component package implements a service package that has been allocated to a node. A component package represents an executable set of one or more components.

Component Process: The component process is a key element of Perspective. It is described in terms of stages that employ a common template. A process library provides the project manager with a practical list of suggested contents and references to clearly defined techniques. The component process develops reusable components with the objective of providing commonly used services across different departmental systems or for use by third parties (contrast: **solution process**).

Contract: The list of requests, with associated operation signatures, that a client object can make of a server object.

Control Object (Class): An object that models functionality not naturally tied to any other object. Typically such behavior involves coordinating several different objects.

Data Object (Class): Data objects provide infrastructure for the storage and retrieval of objects in a data management system (for example, a DBMS or file system). The main aim of data objects is to insulate business objects from the effects of changes in technology by isolating data management system dependencies. Data objects therefore need to be able to handle database transactions, translate persistent business objects into the appropriate storage units, and vice versa. To provide data services a data object usually works in collaboration with other data objects but can also collaborate with business objects and user objects.

Data Service: "Data services support the lowest visible level of abstraction used for the manipulation of data within an application. This support implies the ability to define, maintain, access, and update data. Data services manage and satisfy requests for data generated by business services" (Microsoft, 1996).

Dependency (Package): Used in package diagrams to indicate that a package uses the services of another package. A package dependency is drawn as a dashed arrow from one package to the package that the first package is dependent on.

Dependency (Process): Used in process thread diagrams to indicate the postcondition of one activity that is a precondition for a following activity to be successfully triggered by a business event.

Deployment Diagram: A graphic tool for modeling and documenting the configuration of run-time processing nodes and the components that are allocated to them.

Domain: A domain provides a set of services with a common subject matter. Business domains focus on like business services, whereas technology domains focus on the use of similar technology across different business processes. A business domain provides a context for developing business-oriented components. User interface domains and database domains are examples of technology domains.

Elementary Business Process (EBP): A task that is performed, in response to a business event, by one person in one place at one time, which adds measurable business value to the customer and leaves the data in a consistent state; for example, Approve Credit or Price Order. Elementary business processes can be reused both within and across different process threads.

Event: Events fall into two categories: *system events*, which assume the existence of a human–computer boundary and *business events*, which obtain regardless of the choice of human–computer boundary. A business event may give rise to a number of system events. Conversely, a system event may result from a number of different business events. *See* **Business Event** and **System Event** for more detail.

Parameter: A variable used for transmitting data to or receiving data from an operation or for transmitting data with an event. A name and type may be specified for the parameter.

Pattern: Reusable analysis or design knowledge that describes a problem and its recommended solution in terms of arrangements of model items. Patterns should be recognizable and concise (i.e., small but packing a heavy punch) so that an experienced practitioner can look at a pattern and recognize it, including its core concepts, the benefits of using it, and so on.

Polymorphism: The ability of two or more classes of object to respond to the same message, each in its own way.

Postcondition: An assertion that must be true immediately, on successful completion of an operation, use case, or scenario, given a certain precondition.

Precondition: An assertion that must be true for an operation, use case, or scenario to execute successfully.

Primary Key: A combination of one or more fields whose value unambiguously locates each row in a table.

Process (Business): *See* **Business Process**.

Process (Perspective): A RAAD software process consisting of integrated solution and component processes.

Process (Software): The overall shape to the phasing of software development activity from inception to delivery; examples include waterfall, spiral, V-Model, and X-Model.

Process Group: A process group may be *direct* or *indirect*. Both types of process groups can be nested within process groups to manage complexity.

- A direct-process group is a grouping of activities performed in response to a set of related business events; that is, a grouping of one or more related process threads.

- An indirect-process group is not associated with predefinable events; it denotes an "indirect-value" process, such as a management information process. Indirect-process groups do not have process threads.

Process Hierarchy Diagram: A graphic tool for modeling decomposition of business processes (or more generally activities).

Process Thread: A value chain of EBPs. It is used to model the flow of EBPs, initiated by a single business event, in terms of sequence dependency, iteration, parallelism, and process breaks. A process thread normally produces

Extends: A relationship between use cases in which one use case (the extending use case) is said to extend the behavior of the other use case. The extending use case provides behavior outside of the basic course, such as error and exception handling.

External Object (Class): An external object provides a reference to an object in a separate work space. Static associations may be drawn from a class within a project to the external class (shown as a double-lined box on a class diagram). Messages can similarly be sent to the external object using a collaboration diagram, sequence diagram, or state diagram.

Foreign Key: A primary key of one table that is embedded in another (or the same) table.

Framework: A generic reusable model, specification, or set of classes that normally requires refinement/extension. If we consider a component to be a black box that we can only address through its interface, then the framework is a white box—we can tinker inside it until it is just right. The framework may well be based on patterns (see below), which have been used to guide its creation.

Functional Requirement: A statement of what the system is expected to do, irrespective of nonfunctional requirements.

Guard Condition: An assertion used on a state diagram that must be satisfied in order to cause an associated transition to be triggered.

HCI: Human–Computer Interface.

Human–Computer Interface (HCI): The interface between users of a system and the system itself.

Implementation Constraint: A nonfunctional requirement that specifies **how** the system is to be implemented; for example, use of a specified operating system and DBMS.

Infrastructure: The basic structural foundations of a system; includes operating system, communications software, database management software, and HCI software.

Inheritance: An association among classes, wherein one class shares the structure or behavior defined in one (single inheritance) or more (multiple inheritance) other classes. Inheritance defines a "kind-of" hierarchy in which a subclass inherits from one or more superclasses; a subclass typically augments or redefines the existing structure and behavior of its superclasses.

Interface: An interface documents what a component does, not how it does it, in terms of a set of externally visible operation signatures. An interface must conform to an established communication mechanism and interaction standard.

Invariant: An assertion that must be true for all objects of a class both prior to and after the execution of any operation on that class.

Joint Application Design (JAD): A structured approach for the use of group dynamics in systems development that is particularly useful in modeling system requirements and user interface modeling. For a detailed account the reader is referred to August (1991).

Legacy Asset: A software product, developed on the basis of older technologies, which is past its best but that is so vital to the enterprise that it cannot be replaced or disrupted without a major impact on the enterprise. Note that legacy models (such as data models) are often associated with the legacy asset. Understandably, organizations are keen to preserve the *investment* that has gone into developing such software products; hence the term **"legacy asset."** Legacy assets come in various forms: for example, function libraries, programs, program fragments, data structures, database interfaces, data models, and so on.

Link: A semantic connection between objects; a link is normally a pair of object references. A link may be static where it is an instance of an association between classes, or dynamic where there is no such association.

Logical Data Model: The organization of data into records or tables according to DBMS architectural constraints but independent of physical characteristics. The logical data model reflects key design decisions such as denormalization as well as aggregating and segmenting records (Dewitz, 1996).

Logical Data Structure Diagram: A graphic tool for diagramming the logical data model. The reader should note that despite the "logical" prefix this is not the same as an ERD (Entity Relationship Diagram), which describes pure business data.

Message: A request for an operation or notification of an event that is sent to an object or class; a message may be used to invoke an operation or send an event. A message may have associated parameters. For an operation these may be both input arguments and return values; an event may have input arguments but not associated return values. In Perspective, messages can also be used to transmit events out of the system, for example, to denote production of outputs.

Method: The implementation of an operation.

Model: An abstract representation with a defined structure containin mation with the following characteristics:

- nonredundancy: there is no repeated information in the model,

- formal rigor: the structure provides rules for completeness and cons

- "runnability": a complete model should be realizable in some cond architecture; in less abstract terms, a complete model should be tes

Model Item: An elementary model building block that has a defined s and relationship to other model items.

Module: "A software unit of storage and manipulation. Modules source code modules, binary code modules, and executable code m (UML, 1997).

Multiplicity: A rule regarding the potential numbers of objects that mitted to participate in links of an association, from the point of view gle object at the opposite end of the links. Multiplicity is expressed as of possible values.

Nonfunctional Requirement: A statement of how the system is to b mented or how well the system is expected to function. Examples c include proposed hardware configurations and software infras Examples of "how well" include: reliability, efficiency, usability, main ty, testability, portability, and reusability.

Node: A run-time computational resource, representing a particular l platform that plays a particular role in deployment. Nodes are name ing to role (e.g., Payroll Workstation) and not a specific item (wo 4563Z), and may refer to groups of computers.

Object: Something you can do things to. An object has state, beha identity; the structure and behavior of similar objects are defined in tl mon class. The terms "instance" and "object" are interchangeable.

Object Orientation (OO): The principle of organizing systems i tions of objects that interact together via messages.

Operation: A unit of work that can be requested from an object to specific function. An operation must have a signature.

Package: "A general purpose mechanism for organizing elem groups" (UML, 1997). Packages can be nested.

some result that represents business value. A result from one process thread is often a business event relative to another process thread. Note that process threads can be diagrammed at a higher level of granularity by clustering EBPs into process groups.

Process Thread Diagram: A graphic tool for modeling process threads; *see* **Process Thread**.

Project: A set of activities that organizes and employs resources to create or maintain a product (or part of a product).

Qualifier: An attribute(s) of a role that distinguishes among the set of objects at the "many" end of an association. An object and a qualifier value identify a unique object across the association.

Quality Attribute: A nonfunctional requirement that specifies **how well** the system is expected to function; for example, performance, reliability, and usability.

Rapid Architected Application Development (RAAD): Perspective uses the term RAAD (Gartner Group, 1996) to highlight the fact that modern businesses require solutions that confer early user benefits at minimum cost, leveraging existing packages, databases, and legacy systems where possible but not at the cost of sacrificing maintainability, flexibility, and reusability. Solution and component processes work in harmony to achieve these aims.

Result: An outcome from a process thread that generally represents some added value; for example, Credit approved. Note that a result from one process thread may be a business event relative to another process thread.

Role Association(): One end of an association; always attached to a participating class. Most association properties are attached to a role. For example, each role indicates the multiplicity of its class. A role may or may not have a name.

Role (Team): A related set of responsibilities and skills that may be performed by more than one person in a team; also one person may fulfill more than one role.

Scenario: A single sequence of object interactions and interactions between objects and actors. A scenario is usefully employed to illustrate a particular *instance* of a use case.

Sequence Diagram: A graphic tool for modeling and documenting object interactions with respect to time sequence. The sequence diagram is particularly suited to providing a view of the object interaction required to service a use case.

Service: "A set of functionality that supports activities and/or yields information. A service is accessed through a consistent, published interface. A service represents some computing capability. A description of this capability can be used to represent a contract between the provider of the capability and the potential consumers. Using the description, an arms-length deal can be struck that allows the consumer to access the capability" (Microsoft, 1996). In modeling terms, a service groups one or more operations that bind together to form a contract with consumers of the service. A service is triggered through and manifests itself as an operation: Operations can be stereotyped as services. *See also* **Business Service, Data Service, User Service.**

Service Object (Class): A type of class, providing one or more services, which represents an abstraction of a component interface(s). A service class is used to help retain a domain focus in modeling without becoming embroiled in the potential complications of implementation. A service class is typically a control class exclusively designed to provide services through one or more interfaces. However, services can be allocated to any appropriate object, which then has the role of a service class. In either case, the services are implemented through a component interface(s) of the service class. The fact that a class is a service class is derived from the fact that at least one of its operations is a service.

Service Package: A package that groups together closely related services. At a high level service packages correspond to service categories (e.g., user service package). At a low level service packages are used to represent an abstraction of component groupings that are used in business-oriented component modeling.

Signature: The formal specification of the inputs to and outputs from an operation, in terms of operation name and parameter names and types.

Solution Process: The solution process is a key element of Perspective. It is described in terms of stages that employ a common template. A process library provides the project manager with a practical list of suggested contents and references to clearly defined techniques. The solution process works at a business unit or departmental level to deliver software solutions in terms of increments that provide maximum early user value. The emphasis is on producing solutions by assembly in contrast to producing solutions by starting from scratch every time (contrast: **component process**).

State: A time window that represents a condition or situation, obtained during the life of an object, which helps govern the behavior of an object. A state is often associated with waiting for a stimulus to occur, which may cause tran-

Extends: A relationship between use cases in which one use case (the extending use case) is said to extend the behavior of the other use case. The extending use case provides behavior outside of the basic course, such as error and exception handling.

External Object (Class): An external object provides a reference to an object in a separate work space. Static associations may be drawn from a class within a project to the external class (shown as a double-lined box on a class diagram). Messages can similarly be sent to the external object using a collaboration diagram, sequence diagram, or state diagram.

Foreign Key: A primary key of one table that is embedded in another (or the same) table.

Framework: A generic reusable model, specification, or set of classes that normally requires refinement/extension. If we consider a component to be a black box that we can only address through its interface, then the framework is a white box—we can tinker inside it until it is just right. The framework may well be based on patterns (see below), which have been used to guide its creation.

Functional Requirement: A statement of what the system is expected to do, irrespective of nonfunctional requirements.

Guard Condition: An assertion used on a state diagram that must be satisfied in order to cause an associated transition to be triggered.

HCI: Human–Computer Interface.

Human–Computer Interface (HCI): The interface between users of a system and the system itself.

Implementation Constraint: A nonfunctional requirement that specifies **how** the system is to be implemented; for example, use of a specified operating system and DBMS.

Infrastructure: The basic structural foundations of a system; includes operating system, communications software, database management software, and HCI software.

Inheritance: An association among classes, wherein one class shares the structure or behavior defined in one (single inheritance) or more (multiple inheritance) other classes. Inheritance defines a "kind-of" hierarchy in which a subclass inherits from one or more superclasses; a subclass typically augments or redefines the existing structure and behavior of its superclasses.

Interface: An interface documents what a component does, not how it does it, in terms of a set of externally visible operation signatures. An interface must conform to an established communication mechanism and interaction standard.

Invariant: An assertion that must be true for all objects of a class both prior to and after the execution of any operation on that class.

Joint Application Design (JAD): A structured approach for the use of group dynamics in systems development that is particularly useful in modeling system requirements and user interface modeling. For a detailed account the reader is referred to August (1991).

Legacy Asset: A software product, developed on the basis of older technologies, which is past its best but that is so vital to the enterprise that it cannot be replaced or disrupted without a major impact on the enterprise. Note that legacy models (such as data models) are often associated with the legacy asset. Understandably, organizations are keen to preserve the *investment* that has gone into developing such software products; hence the term **"legacy asset."** Legacy assets come in various forms: for example, function libraries, programs, program fragments, data structures, database interfaces, data models, and so on.

Link: A semantic connection between objects; a link is normally a pair of object references. A link may be static where it is an instance of an association between classes, or dynamic where there is no such association.

Logical Data Model: The organization of data into records or tables according to DBMS architectural constraints but independent of physical characteristics. The logical data model reflects key design decisions such as denormalization as well as aggregating and segmenting records (Dewitz, 1996).

Logical Data Structure Diagram: A graphic tool for diagramming the logical data model. The reader should note that despite the "logical" prefix this is not the same as an ERD (Entity Relationship Diagram), which describes pure business data.

Message: A request for an operation or notification of an event that is sent to an object or class; a message may be used to invoke an operation or send an event. A message may have associated parameters. For an operation these may be both input arguments and return values; an event may have input arguments but not associated return values. In Perspective, messages can also be used to transmit events out of the system, for example, to denote production of outputs.

Method: The implementation of an operation.

Model: An abstract representation with a defined structure containing information with the following characteristics:

- nonredundancy: there is no repeated information in the model,

- formal rigor: the structure provides rules for completeness and consistency,

- "runnability": a complete model should be realizable in some conceivable architecture; in less abstract terms, a complete model should be testable.

Model Item: An elementary model building block that has a defined structure and relationship to other model items.

Module: "A software unit of storage and manipulation. Modules include source code modules, binary code modules, and executable code modules" (UML, 1997).

Multiplicity: A rule regarding the potential numbers of objects that are permitted to participate in links of an association, from the point of view of a single object at the opposite end of the links. Multiplicity is expressed as a range of possible values.

Nonfunctional Requirement: A statement of how the system is to be implemented or how well the system is expected to function. Examples of "how" include proposed hardware configurations and software infrastructure. Examples of "how well" include: reliability, efficiency, usability, maintainability, testability, portability, and reusability.

Node: A run-time computational resource, representing a particular hardware platform that plays a particular role in deployment. Nodes are named according to role (e.g., Payroll Workstation) and not a specific item (workstation 4563Z), and may refer to groups of computers.

Object: Something you can do things to. An object has state, behavior, and identity; the structure and behavior of similar objects are defined in their common class. The terms "instance" and "object" are interchangeable.

Object Orientation (OO): The principle of organizing systems as collections of objects that interact together via messages.

Operation: A unit of work that can be requested from an object to perform a specific function. An operation must have a signature.

Package: "A general purpose mechanism for organizing elements into groups" (UML, 1997). Packages can be nested.

Parameter: A variable used for transmitting data to or receiving data from an operation or for transmitting data with an event. A name and type may be specified for the parameter.

Pattern: Reusable analysis or design knowledge that describes a problem and its recommended solution in terms of arrangements of model items. Patterns should be recognizable and concise (i.e., small but packing a heavy punch) so that an experienced practitioner can look at a pattern and recognize it, including its core concepts, the benefits of using it, and so on.

Polymorphism: The ability of two or more classes of object to respond to the same message, each in its own way.

Postcondition: An assertion that must be true immediately, on successful completion of an operation, use case, or scenario, given a certain precondition.

Precondition: An assertion that must be true for an operation, use case, or scenario to execute successfully.

Primary Key: A combination of one or more fields whose value unambiguously locates each row in a table.

Process (Business): *See* **Business Process**.

Process (Perspective): A RAAD software process consisting of integrated solution and component processes.

Process (Software): The overall shape to the phasing of software development activity from inception to delivery; examples include waterfall, spiral, V-Model, and X-Model.

Process Group: A process group may be *direct* or *indirect*. Both types of process groups can be nested within process groups to manage complexity.

- A direct-process group is a grouping of activities performed in response to a set of related business events; that is, a grouping of one or more related process threads.

- An indirect-process group is not associated with predefinable events; it denotes an "indirect-value" process, such as a management information process. Indirect-process groups do not have process threads.

Process Hierarchy Diagram: A graphic tool for modeling decomposition of business processes (or more generally activities).

Process Thread: A value chain of EBPs. It is used to model the flow of EBPs, initiated by a single business event, in terms of sequence dependency, iteration, parallelism, and process breaks. A process thread normally produces some result that represents business value. A result from one process thread is often a business event relative to another process thread. Note that process threads can be diagrammed at a higher level of granularity by clustering EBPs into process groups.

Process Thread Diagram: A graphic tool for modeling process threads; *see* **Process Thread**.

Project: A set of activities that organizes and employs resources to create or maintain a product (or part of a product).

Qualifier: An attribute(s) of a role that distinguishes among the set of objects at the "many" end of an association. An object and a qualifier value identify a unique object across the association.

Quality Attribute: A nonfunctional requirement that specifies **how well** the system is expected to function; for example, performance, reliability, and usability.

Rapid Architected Application Development (RAAD): Perspective uses the term RAAD (Gartner Group, 1996) to highlight the fact that modern businesses require solutions that confer early user benefits at minimum cost, leveraging existing packages, databases, and legacy systems where possible but not at the cost of sacrificing maintainability, flexibility, and reusability. Solution and component processes work in harmony to achieve these aims.

Result: An outcome from a process thread that generally represents some added value; for example, Credit approved. Note that a result from one process thread may be a business event relative to another process thread.

Role Association(): One end of an association; always attached to a participating class. Most association properties are attached to a role. For example, each role indicates the multiplicity of its class. A role may or may not have a name.

Role (Team): A related set of responsibilities and skills that may be performed by more than one person in a team; also one person may fulfill more than one role.

Scenario: A single sequence of object interactions and interactions between objects and actors. A scenario is usefully employed to illustrate a particular *instance* of a use case.

Sequence Diagram: A graphic tool for modeling and documenting object interactions with respect to time sequence. The sequence diagram is particularly suited to providing a view of the object interaction required to service a use case.

Service: "A set of functionality that supports activities and/or yields information. A service is accessed through a consistent, published interface. A service represents some computing capability. A description of this capability can be used to represent a contract between the provider of the capability and the potential consumers. Using the description, an arms-length deal can be struck that allows the consumer to access the capability" (Microsoft, 1996). In modeling terms, a service groups one or more operations that bind together to form a contract with consumers of the service. A service is triggered through and manifests itself as an operation: Operations can be stereotyped as services. *See also* **Business Service, Data Service, User Service.**

Service Object (Class): A type of class, providing one or more services, which represents an abstraction of a component interface(s). A service class is used to help retain a domain focus in modeling without becoming embroiled in the potential complications of implementation. A service class is typically a control class exclusively designed to provide services through one or more interfaces. However, services can be allocated to any appropriate object, which then has the role of a service class. In either case, the services are implemented through a component interface(s) of the service class. The fact that a class is a service class is derived from the fact that at least one of its operations is a service.

Service Package: A package that groups together closely related services. At a high level service packages correspond to service categories (e.g., user service package). At a low level service packages are used to represent an abstraction of component groupings that are used in business-oriented component modeling.

Signature: The formal specification of the inputs to and outputs from an operation, in terms of operation name and parameter names and types.

Solution Process: The solution process is a key element of Perspective. It is described in terms of stages that employ a common template. A process library provides the project manager with a practical list of suggested contents and references to clearly defined techniques. The solution process works at a business unit or departmental level to deliver software solutions in terms of increments that provide maximum early user value. The emphasis is on producing solutions by assembly in contrast to producing solutions by starting from scratch every time (contrast: **component process**).

State: A time window that represents a condition or situation, obtained during the life of an object, which helps govern the behavior of an object. A state is often associated with waiting for a stimulus to occur, which may cause transition to another state. The stimulus is often an event but can be an operation request or a guard condition.

State Diagram: A graphic tool for modeling an object's allowable state-related behavior with respect to its parent class. Changes of state are triggered by conditions or events, which can cause operations to be activated and events to be issued.

Stereotype: "The classification of an element. A stereotype has semantic impact. Certain stereotypes are predefined in UML others may be user defined" (UML, 1997).

Stimulus: A message or probe.

Subclass: A class that inherits operations and/or attributes from another class.

Superclass: A class from which specific operations and/or attributes are inherited.

System Event: An occurrence of a point in time causing a one-way asynchronous transmission of information that can have parameters with names and types. System events may be *external* or *internal:*

- *External System Event:* An event that occurs in the system's environment and requires the system to make a response. Such an event is either *Triggering* (e.g., triggers a use case or scenario) or *Interface* (e.g., mouse click).

- *Internal System Event:* An event issued by an object that may be

  - directed to another object(s),

  - undirected to any particular object; simply broadcast to any object that registers an interest in it,

  - directed outside the system (for example, as a report).

Team: A number of individuals working together in a coordinated fashion to meet a defined set of objectives.

Team Role: A related set of responsibilities and skills that may be performed by more than one person in a team; also one person may fulfill more than one role.

Transition (State): A change of state triggered by a stimulus. The stimulus may be an operation request, an event, a guard condition(s) or a combination of an event or operation request plus a guard condition(s).

Use Case: A behaviorally related sequence of interactions performed by an actor in a dialogue with the system to provide some measurable value to the actor. A use case represents a collection of scenarios.

Use Case Diagram: A graphic tool for modeling relationships among actors and use cases.

User Object (Class): User objects are highly dependent on the implementation technology used to support the human or device interface of the system. A user object interacts with actors outside the system as well as business objects, data objects, and other user objects. User objects are crucial to providing the front-end of a user service. User objects are typically forms and menus, but do not have to be interactive; for example, a batch report.

User Service: "User services for an application support the activities users will perform. These services also bind together a collection of business services to deliver the business capabilities of the application. User services present information and gather data from the user" (Microsoft, 1996).

Uses: A relationship between use cases in which one use case is said to use the behavior of the other use case (the used use case). The used use case provides reusable behavior across different use cases.

View: A diagram, table, template, or other representation used to highlight an area of concern. Each view shows part of the model and is used to discuss one set of issues.

Wrapper: A component that provides an object-oriented interface to nonobject-oriented software.

Bibliography

Ackley, L. M., & Stringfield, D. (1995, November–December). Keeping the elaborators honest. *Object Magazine*, 36–42.

Allen, C. P. (1991). *Effective structured techniques: From strategy to CASE*. Hemel Hempstead, UK: Prentice Hall International.

Allen, P., & Frost, S. (1996). Component manager. *Select Software Tools White Paper*. Available: www.selectst.com

Allen, P., & Frost, S. (1997a). Legacy system wrapping. *Select Software Tools White Paper*. Available: www.selectst.com

Allen, P., & Frost, S. (1997b). Package wrapping. *Select Software Tools White Paper*. Available: www.selectst.com

Allen, P., & Frost, S. (1997c). Providing data services. *Select Software Tools White Paper*. Available: www.selectst.com

Allen, P., & Frost, S. (1997d). Providing data services. *Select Software Tools White Paper*. Available: www.selectst.com

Allen, P., & Frost, S. (1997e). Service-based architectures: Unlocking the potential of component-based development. *American Programmer*, *10*(7), 18–23.

August, J. H. (1991). *Joint application design*. Englewood Cliffs, NJ: Prentice Hall.

Barnes, B. H., & Bollinger, T. B. (1991). Making reuse cost-effective. *IEEE Software*, *8*(1), 13–24.

Beck, K. (1993). Finding objects the easy way. *Object Magazine, 3*(4), 42–44.

Beck, K., & Cunningham, C. (1989). A laboratory for teaching object-oriented thinking. *OOPSLA 1989 Proceedings (SIGPLAN Notices)*, *24*(10), 1–6.

Benchmarking Partners Inc. (1996). The SAP R/3 business object repository. *Strategic Technologies*, *1*(1).

Berard, E. V. (1993). *Essays on object-oriented software engineering* (Vol. 1).Englewood Cliffs, NJ: Prentice Hall.

Block, R. (1983). *The politics of projects*. Englewood Cliffs, NJ: Yourdon Press.

Boar, B. H. (1984). *Application prototyping*. New York: Wiley.

Boehm, B. W. (1986). A spiral model for software development and enhancement. *ACM Sigsoft Software Engineering Notes*, *11*(4), 14–23.

Booch, G. (1994). *Object oriented analysis and design with applications*(2nd ed.). Menlo Park, CA: Benjamin Cummins.

Booch, G. (1996). *Object solutions: Managing the object-oriented project*. Reading, MA: Addison- Wesley.

Brooks, F. (1975). *The mythical man month*. Reading, MA: Addison-Wesley.

Buschmann, F., Meunier, R., Rohnert, H., Sommerlad, P., Stal, M., et al. (1996). *Pattern-oriented software architecture: A systems of patterns*. New York: Wiley.

CCTA. (1995). *SSADM Version 4+ reference manual*. London: NCC Blackwell.

Chidamber, S., & Kemerer, C. (1991). Towards a metrics suite for object oriented design. *OOPSLA Proceedings*, pp.197–211.

Cleal, D. (1996, March). Optimizing relational database access. *Object Expert*.

Coad, P. (1995). *Object models: Strategies, patterns, and applications*. Englewood Cliffs, NJ: Yourdon Press.

Coad, P., & Yourdon, E. (1991). *Object oriented analysis*. Englewood Cliffs, NJ: Yourdon Press.

Coleman, D., Arnold, P., Bodoff, S., Dollin, C., Gilchrist, H., Hayes, F., & Jeramaes, P. (1994).

Object-oriented development: The FUSION method. Englewood Cliffs, NJ: Prentice Hall.

Connell, J., & Shafer, L. (1995). *Object oriented rapid prototyping*. Englewood Cliffs, NJ: Yourdon Press.

Cox, B. (1986). *Object-oriented programming: An evolutionary approach.* Reading, MA: Addison-Wesley.

CSC. (1995). *Catalyst methodology* (Internal Document).CSC Inc.

Davenport, T. H. (1993). *Process innovation, reengineering work through information technology.* Cambridge, MA :Harvard Business School Press.

DeMarco, T. (1978). *Structured analysis and system specification.* Englewood Cliffs, NJ: Yourdon Press.

DeMarco, T. (1982). *Controlling software projects.* Englewood Cliffs, NJ: Yourdon Press.

DeMarco, T., & Lister, T. (1987). *Peopleware.* New York: Dorset House.

Dewitz, S. D. (1996). *Systems analysis and design and the transition to objects.* New York: McGraw-Hill.

Dijkstra, E .W. (1965). Programming considered as a human activity. In *Proceedings of the 1965 IFIP Congress* (pp. 213–217). Amsterdam: North Holland. (Reprinted in E. N. Yourdon [Ed.], *Classics in software engineering* [pp. 3–9].1979, Englewood Cliffs, NJ: Yourdon Press.)

Dijkstra, E. W. (1969,October). Structured programming. Paper presented at a conference sponsored by the NATO Science Committee, Rome, Italy. (Reprinted in E. N. Yourdon [Ed.],*Classics in software engineering* [pp. 43–48]. 1979, Englewood Cliffs, NJ: Yourdon Press.)

DSDM (1995). DSDM Version 2, DSDM Consortium. Farnham, UK: Tesseract Publishing.

DSDM (1997). DSDM Version 3, DSDM Consortium. Farnham, UK: Tesseract Publishing.

Fenton, N. E. (1991). *Software metrics.* London: Chapman and Hall.

Firesmith, D. (1993). *Object oriented requirements analysis and logical design.* Reading, MA : Addison-Wesley.

Flint, E. S. (1996, September). COBOL legacy programs serve the future. *American Programmer.*

Folkes, S., & Stubenvoll, S.(1992). *Accelerated systems development.* Englewood Cliffs, NJ :Prentice Hall.

Fowler, M. (1997). *Analysis patterns: Reusable object models.* Reading, MA: Addison-Wesley.

Frost, S. (1995, September). The Select Perspective, version 4.0. *Select Software Tools White Paper.*

Frost, S., & Allen, P. (1995, November–December). Object modeling for enterprise systems. *Object Expert.*

Frost, S., & Allen, P. (1996a, January–February). A use-case approach to layering object models. *Report on Object Oriented Analysis and Design.*

Frost , S., & Allen, P. (1996b, March–April). Developing local business objects. *Report on Object Oriented Analysis and Design.*

Frost, S., & Allen, P. (1996c, September–October). Developing user interface objects. *Journal of Object Oriented Programming and Design.*

Gamma, E., Helm, R., Johnson, R., & Vlissides, J. (1995). *Design patterns: Elements of reusable object-oriented software.* Reading, MA: Addison-Wesley.

Gartner Group. (1995, June 7). Rapid application development, part 2: Organizing for success. *Inside Gartner Group This Week.*

Gartner Group. (1996, March 20). Best practices in AD project management, part 2, SPA-650-1293. *ADM Research Note.*

Ghezzi, C., Jazayeri, M., & Mandrioli, D. (1991). *Fundamentals of software engineering.* Englewood Cliffs, NJ: Prentice Hall.

Gilb, T. (1988). *Principles of software engineering management.* Reading, MA: Addison-Wesley.

Gilbert, M. (1996, September). Replace COBOL with objects? Not. *American Programmer.*

Goldberg, A., & Rubin, K.(1995). *Succeeding with objects: Decision frameworks for project management.* Reading, MA: Addison-Wesley.

Graham, I. (1994). *Object-oriented methods.* Reading, MA: Addison-Wesley.

Graham, I. (1995). *Migrating to object technology.* Reading, MA: Addison-Wesley.

Griss, M. (1995, February). Software reuse: Objects and frameworks are not enough. *Object Magazine*, pp.77–79,87.

GUIDE. (1986). *Joint application design* (GUIDE Publication GPP-147). Chicago.

Hammer, M., & Champy, J. (1993). *Reengineering the corporation: A manifesto for business revolution.* St. Leonards, NSW, Australia: Allen and Unwin.

Harel, D. (1987). Statecharts: A visual formalism for complex systems. *Science of Computer Programming, 8.*

Harmon, P. (1995a). Forté and application partitioning. *Object-Oriented Strategies, 5*(4).

Harmon, P. (1995b). Objects and components. *Object-Oriented Strategies, 5*(5).

Harmon, P. (1995c). Objects and components part 2.*Object-Oriented Strategies, 5*(6).

Heinlein, R. (1966). *The moon is a harsh mistress.* New York: Berkeley.

Henderson, C., Rockart , J. F., & Sifonis, J. G. (1984). *A planning methodology for integrating management support systems* (Center for Information Systems Research Working Paper 116).Cambridge, MA: Sloan School of Management, MIT.

Henderson-Sellers, B. (1996). *Object oriented metrics: Measures of complexity.* Englewood Cliffs, NJ: Prentice Hall.

Henderson-Sellers, B., & Edwards, J. (1994). *Book two of object oriented knowledge: The working object.* Sydney, Australia: Prentice Hall.

Hoffman, M., & Killer, B. (1995, September). *Interoperability between and within enterprises* (Technology Marketing Paper).SAP AG.

Horowitz, B. (1993). *Strategic buying for the future.* Washington, DC: Libey Publishing.

Humphrey, W. S. (1990). *Managing the software process.* Reading. MA: Addison-Wesley.

IBM Object Oriented Technology Center. (1997). *Designing object-oriented software: An experience-based approach.* Englewood Cliffs, NJ: Prentice Hall PTR.

Inmon, W. (1996). *Building the data warehouse.* New York: Wiley.

Jackson, M. A., & McCracken, D. D. (1982). Life cycle concept considered harmful. *ACM Software Engineering Notes, 7*(2), 29–32.

Jacobson, I., Christerson, M., Jonsson, P.M., & Overgaard, G. (1992). *Object oriented software engineering: A use case driven approach.* Reading, MA: Addison-Wesley.

Jacobson, I., Ericcson, M., & Jacobson, A. (1994). *The object advantage— Business process reengineering with object technology.* Reading, MA: Addison-Wesley.

Lorenz, M. (1993). *Object oriented software development: A practical guide.* Englewood Cliffs, NJ: Prentice Hall.

Lorenz, M., & Kidd, J. (1994). *Object oriented software metrics.* Englewood Cliffs, NJ: Prentice Hall.

Love, T. (1993). *Object lessons.* New York: SIGS Books.

Martin, J. (1987). *Recommended diagramming standards for analysts and programmers.* Englewood Cliffs, NJ: Prentice Hall.

Martin, J. (1989). *Information engineering* (Vols. 1–3). Englewood Cliffs, NJ: Prentice Hall.

Martin, J. (1991). *Rapid application development.* New York: Macmillan.

Martin, J., & Odell, J. J. (1992). *Object-oriented analysis and design.* Englewood Cliffs, NJ :Prentice Hall.

Mattison, R., & Sipolt, M. J. (1994). *The object-oriented enterprise: Making corporate information systems work.* New York: McGraw-Hill.

McGibbon, B. (1995). *Managing your move to object technology.* New York: SIGS Books.

McMenamin, S., & Palmer, J. (1984). *Essential systems analysis.* Englewood Cliffs, NJ: Yourdon Press.

Meyer, B. (1988). *Object-oriented software construction.* Englewood Cliffs, NJ: Prentice Hall.

Meyer, B. (1990). The new culture of software development. *Journal of Object Oriented Programming, 3*(1), 76–81.

Meyer, B. (1995). *Object success.* Hemel Hempstead, UK: Prentice Hall International.

Mobray, T. J., & Malveau, R. C. (1997). *CORBA design patterns.* New York: Wiley.

Microsoft Corporation. (1996). *Microsoft solutions framework: Reference guide, version 2.0.*

Object Management Group. (1991). *The common object request broker: Architecture and specification* (OMG Document Number 91-12-1). Boulder, CO: OMG Publications.

Object Management Group. (1992). The OMG object model. In *OMG guide* (OMG Document Number 92-9-2). Boulder, CO: OMG Publications.

Object Management Group. (1994). *Common object services specification* (Vol. I, OMG Document Number 94-1-1). New York: Wiley.

Page-Jones, M. (1988). *The practical guide to structured systems design* (2nd ed.).Englewood Cliffs, NJ: Yourdon Press.

Page-Jones, M. (1995). *What every programmer should know about object-oriented design*. New York: Dorset House.

Parnas, D. L. (1972). On the criteria to be used in decomposing systems into modules. *Communications of the ACM, 5,*1053–1058.

Parnas, D. L., & Clements, P. C. (1986). A rational design process: How and why to fake it. *IEEE Transactions on Software Engineering, SE-12*(2), 251–257.

Porter, M. E. (1985). *Competitive advantage*. New York: Free Press.

Pree, W. (1995). *Design patterns for object oriented software engineering*. Reading, MA: Addison-Wesley.

Royce, W. W. (1988). Managing the development of large software systems. In R. Thayer (Ed.), *Software engineering project management* (IEEE Computer Society Tutorial, Catalog Number EH0263, pp. 118–127). (Reprinted from Proceedings of IEEE WESCON, 1-9, 1970.)

Rubin, K., & Goldberg, A. (1992). Object behaviour analysis. *Communications of the ACM, 35*(9).

Rumbaugh, J. (1993,May). Controlling code: How to implement dynamic models. *Journal of Object- Oriented Programming*.

Rumbaugh, J., Blaha, M., Premalani, W., Eddy, F., & Lorensen, W. (1991). *Object oriented modelling and design*. Hemel Hempstead, UK: Prentice Hall International.

Rummler, G. A., & Brache, A. P. (1990). *Improving performance—How to manage the white space on the organisation chart*. San Francisco, CA: Jossey-Bass.

SAP AG. (1996). R/3 system SAP business objects. *SAP White Paper*.

Shlaer, S., & Mellor, S .(1988). *Object oriented systems analysis: Modeling the world in data*. Englewood Cliffs, NJ: Yourdon Press.

Shlaer, S., & Mellor, S. (1992). *Object lifecycles: Modeling the world in states*. Englewood Cliffs, NJ: Yourdon Press.

Sims, O. (1994). *Business objects: Delivering cooperative objects for client-server*. Maidenhead, UK: McGraw-Hill.

Stapleton, J. (1997). *Dynamic systems development method—The method in practice*. Harlow, UK: Addison-Wesley Longman.

Stevenson, R. (1995, November–December). Whatever happened to finite state machines? *Object Magazine*.

Talbot, S. (1996, March). Connectivity: Gateways to success. *Object Expert*.

Taylor, D. A. (1995). *Business engineering with object technology*. New York: Wiley.

Tibbetts, J., & Bernstein, B. (1996, December). Legacy applications on the Web. *American Programmer*.

UML. (1997). *Unified modeling language version 1.1*. Santa Clara, CA: UML Partners. (This is now OMG standard: UML version 1.1.)

Walden, K., & Nerson, J. (1995). *Seamless object-oriented software architecture*. Englewood Cliffs, NJ: Prentice Hall.

Ward P. T., & Mellor, S. J. (1985). *Structured development for real time systems* (Vols. 1–3). Englewood Cliffs, NJ: Yourdon Press.

Wilkinson, N. M. (1995). *Using CRC cards: An informal approach to object oriented development*. New York: SIGS Books.

Wirfs-Brock, R. (1993, November–December). Stereotyping: A technique for characterizing objects and their interactions. *Object Magazine*.

Wirfs-Brock, R., Wilkerson, B., & Wiener, L. (1990). *Designing object oriented software*. Englewood Cliffs, NJ: Prentice Hall.

Yourdon, E. N. (1995). Website and internal Web sites. *Corporate Internet Strategies*, *1*(1).

Yourdon, E. N., & Constantine, L. L. (1979). *Structured design: Fundamentals of a discipline of computer program and systems design*. Englewood Cliffs, NJ: Prentice Hall.

Yourdon, E. N., Whitehead, K., Thomann, J., Oppel, K., & Nevermann, P. (1995). *Mainstream 0bjects: An analysis and design approach for business*. Englewood Cliffs, NJ: Yourdon Press.

Index